New World of Gain

New World of Gain

Europeans, Guaraní, and the
Global Origins of Modern Economy

Brian P. Owensby

Stanford University Press

Stanford, California

STANFORD UNIVERSITY PRESS
Stanford, California

Printed in the United States of America on acid-free, archival-quality paper

Library of Congress Cataloging-in-Publication Data
Names: Owensby, Brian P., author.
Title: New world of gain : Europeans, Guaraní, and the global origins of modern economy / Brian P. Owensby.
Description: Stanford, California : Stanford University Press, 2022. | Includes bibliographical references and index.
Identifiers: LCCN 2021013025 (print) | LCCN 2021013026 (ebook) | ISBN 9781503627512 (cloth) | ISBN 9781503628335 (paperback) | ISBN 9781503628342 (ebook)
Subjects: LCSH: Exchange—Paraguay—History. | Reciprocity (Psychology)—Paraguay—History. | Guarani Indians—Paraguay—History. | Whites—Paraguay—Relations with Indians—History. | Economics—Moral and ethical aspects. | Paraguay—History—To 1811. | Paraguay—Ethnic relations—History.
Classification: LCC F2683 .O94 2021 (print) | LCC F2683 (ebook) | DDC 989.2/01—dc23
LC record available at https://lccn.loc.gov/2021013025
LC ebook record available at https://lccn.loc.gov/2021013026

Cover images: (top) Theodor de Bry, *Avaritia*, 1580–1600, engraving. Source: The Elisha Whittelsey Collection, The Elisha Whittelsey Fund, 1951; (bottom) Bernard Picart, *Daily activities of Native Americans*, 1716, etching and engraving. Source: Rijksmuseum
Cover design: Rob Ehle
Typeset by Motto Publishing Services in 11/13.5 Adobe Garamond Pro

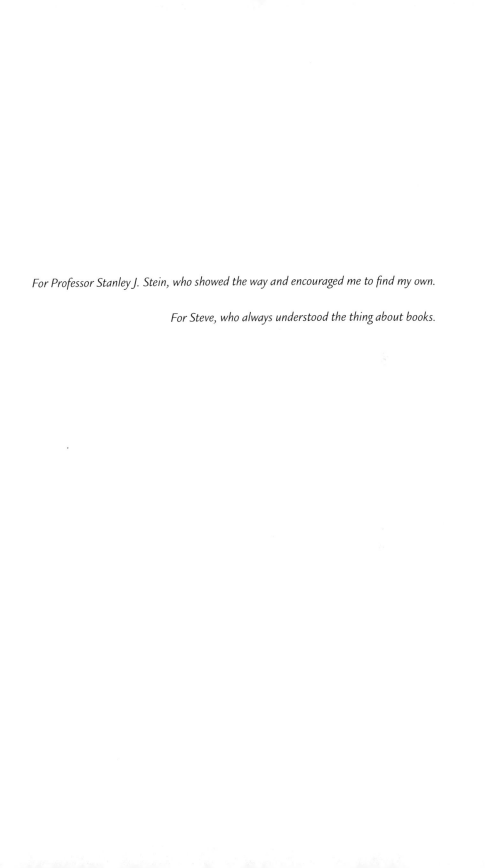

For Professor Stanley J. Stein, who showed the way and encouraged me to find my own.

For Steve, who always understood the thing about books.

"Gain, be my lord, for I will worship thee."

William Shakespeare, *King John* (act 2, scene 1)

"*Oroyopoî,* let us give each other things."

Antonio Ruiz de Montoya, *Tesoro de la lengua guaraní* (1639)

Contents

Maps and Figures

Maps

Figures

With Gratitude

Books like this one are woven of the gifts others make of their time, knowledge, and sympathies. Some can be reciprocated. Others only acknowledged.

I have enjoyed institutional support from the University of Virginia, both in financial resources for research trips and time for writing. I am grateful for the opportunity in 2015 to give a series of papers through the UVa–École des Hautes Études en Sciences Sociales exchange program, which not only allowed me to present emerging ideas to the Séminaire de Recherches sur les Lumières, in Paris, but also enabled me to consult sources in the Bibliothèque Nationale. The invitation to present a keynote address at the summer 2015 Territorio Guaraní International Workshop in Posadas, Argentina, was an honor and could not have come at a better time. A paper at the 2014 Jornada Internacional de Jesuitas in Buenos Aires gave me the chance to encounter the vital scholarly community around the missions and Jesuit studies during an early foray into new material.

Colleagues far afield have given of themselves over the years. I had the gift of some tough questions and sharp observations from linguist and anthropologist Bartomeu Melià, S.J. at the Guaraní workshop in Posadas 2015. His enormous contributions to the field of Guaraní and mission studies are unsurpassed. He will be missed. Professor Guillermo Wilde and Professor Eduardo Neumann were welcoming in Buenos Aires and pushed me to keep going. Professor Tamar Herzog gave me the opportunity to present new ideas to a distinguished group of colleagues at

Harvard in 2015. Lic. Vicente Arrúa Ávalos, director of the Archivo Nacional de Asunción opened the archive to me with a generosity and spirit of collaboration I cannot hope to reciprocate fully. My conversations with Professor Capucine Boidin at Paris III and the Centre de Recherche et de Documentation sur les Amériques have been essential to my understanding and use of Guaraní sources. Her spectacular work, with colleagues involved with the Lenguas Generales de América del Sur project, especially the growing Guaraní corpus, is transformational. I hope to be able to return the gift someday. Professor Shawn Austin, at the University of Arkansas, helped crystallize critical issues regarding interactions between Guaraní and Spaniards in collegial conversations in Spain and Oaxaca. I benefited enormously from a close reading of the manuscript by Professor Julia Sarreal at Arizona State University. Professor John Tutino, at Georgetown, has followed the project for years. Our convergent concern for the histories of capitalism and modern economy have been powerfully generative. His reading of the manuscript and comments have been indispensable in helping me focus the larger argument.

There are as many to thank in Charlottesville. Librarian Miguel Valladares is the wizard of the bibliosphere. His capacity to conjure obscure sources, or just hard-to-get ones, from thin air never ceases to astound. The project would have taken much longer without his help. Fr. Michael Suárez, S.J., director of the Rare Book School at UVa, opened the doors to the Jesuit archives in Rome at an early stage in the research. Friends and colleagues have provided the heartening milieu essential to any sustained scholarly undertaking. Professor Herbert "Tico" Braun has shown that friendship and collaboration are measured in lifetimes. Professor Thomas Klubock generously read parts of the manuscript and offered incisive comments. Professor George Mentore and Professor Richard Handler helped me think about the difficulties and rewards of working at the seams between disciplines. I benefited immensely from a presentation at UVa's vibrant interdisciplinary Movements and Directions in Capitalism (MADCAP) working group. Graduate students Rachael Givens-Johnson and Kimberly Hursh were patient at moments when it must have seemed our discussions had been hijacked by a preoccupation with my own project. Simran Budhwar and Aran Teeling took on the exacting work of helping me put the notes and bibliography into good order. Indexer Kate Mertes captured the spirit of the text. The fine people at Stanford University Press made an intricate process smooth and rewarding:

editors Margo Irvin, Cindy Lim, and Emily Smith; marketing manager Stephanie Adams; copy editor Barbara Armentrout; cartographer Bill Nelson; and art director Rob Ehle. My friends, colleagues, and running crew Professor Paul Halliday, Steve Light, and Professor Christian McMillen listened and offered gentle advice through huffing and puffing.

As he has throughout my scholarly life, my dad listened attentively, and gently asked the what-does-*that*-mean questions that helped me see where I was not making myself clear. My mom always knew it would get done, even when I was unsure. As ever, Bronwyn and Amanda gamely put up with the temporary insanity that accompanies these endeavors. Without their understanding there would be little point.

New World of Gain

INTRODUCTION

Directions

A LAND OF ABUNDANCE that had provided for all became a place of privation and hardship after the arrival of men from beyond the sea. Before this moment in the early sixteenth century, the *Abá* (men or people) had lived in a forest world great for its bounty, if at times unforgiving in the destructive fury of its storms, floods, wars, and hurricanes.[1] Among the Abá, gifts and their return across open-ended time bound people together. The new men, Iberians mostly, seemed interested in the Guaraní (as the Abá later came to be known) only to advance themselves, either through material exchange or by getting the Abá to serve them. This encounter in the interior of South America transformed both groups. Among the Guaraní, contact introduced novel pressures that proved more enduringly threatening to the Abá way of life than anything they had known. The newcomers, motivated by a still inchoate desire for *ganancia* (gain, profit, interest), quickly began to act as though the Guaraní were beyond moral consideration, instruments to personal benefit. Although neither Guaraní nor Europeans were in a position to grasp the larger meaning of the moment, their meeting was part of a global sea change in human relations from the sixteenth century forward.

These pages recount what happened when people without experience of individual gain-seeking as a force in everyday life came face to face with men who aimed to benefit at others' expense. At its most basic, this transformation involved unleashing self-interested material pursuit at the core of human affairs. We tend to take it for granted that human beings behave this way in the sphere of everyday life now known as *the economy*.

Yet, as Karl Polanyi noted in the mid-twentieth century, gain and profit made on exchange had not assumed a dominant role in social life through most of human history.[2] Gain, said Polanyi, had stood as one motivation among others—valor, piety, honor, virtue, status, justice, friendship, gift, reciprocity, subsistence—restrained and regulated by a matrix of moral, political, social, religious, cultural, and legal commitments. Markets had long existed, easing the circulation of goods among human communities. But, argued Polanyi, material gain as a mainspring of action had not been widely acknowledged as valid and certainly never before "raised to the level of a justification of action and behavior in everyday life." Indeed, the ascendance of gain could be compared only to "the most violent outbursts of religious fervor in history."[3] Deep movements began to alter European understandings of social life beginning in the late-medieval period, instituting the buying and selling of labor and land, mediating exchange increasingly through money, and ultimately subjecting livelihood to a general competition among society's members. The slow eruption of gain into everyday affairs gradually overrode the moral, motivational, and institutional bases of social cohesion, and thrust up a new disposition of power and needs that made personal profit and fear of want into dominant features of human conduct. The result was nothing short of a transformation of life in common, one that strained against prevailing understandings of human relations. In the process, all other notions of human economy sank from view, chief among them what I shall refer to as *substantive mutuality*: that cluster of ideas, actions, and commitments anchored in gift, reciprocity, and redistribution binding societies across time.[4]

For Polanyi, gain achieved its apotheosis in human affairs during the late eighteenth and early nineteenth centuries, with the emergence of industrial, market capitalism, first in England, then in continental Europe, and in the twentieth century, "the whole human world."[5] For all its insight, Polanyi's argument reflects a Eurocentric understanding of economic history, one fixated on the Industrial Revolution. I contend that a history of gain extends much earlier, to at least the moment of Europe's expansion beyond the Old World in 1492.

By beginning the story so late, Polanyi could only hint at the profound social and moral transfiguration, the slow-rolling "social catastrophe" that gave rise to the sensibilities, ideas, and institutions we now accept as essential to modern—that is, market—economy. A history that begins with the victory of market society circa 1800 has no way to account for the shock experienced by all those who lived through the moral churn of gain's emergence as the vital force of economic life. Indeed, the late triumph of the new market order expunged all reference to centuries of moral questioning and fears of what would become of social life if men could act as though their desires answered to nothing beyond individual interests. This questioning was not limited to Europeans. Rather, I propose that gain—the desire and capacity to benefit materially at the expense of others, without concern for reciprocity—and the agitation it occasioned, played out everywhere Europeans encountered non-Europeans from the sixteenth century forward.

This was not an early instance of market ideology as we would today understand it. A new world of gain burgeoned in Paraguay (and elsewhere) through the transformation that allowed European men to suppose they could turn whole groups of people to individual advantage, regardless of the harm they might do. This can be seen with special clarity in places like Paraguay, where social, legal, and moral precepts that constrained acquisitive urges in the Old World did not to apply with full force in the New. In the Guaraní, European settlers encountered people toward whom they could act with freedom, even license, compared to how they might treat ordinary folk back home, who were still sheltered by an increasingly tattered set of norms and reciprocities in quotidian life. In Paraguay, settlers were not bound by customary inhibitions that precluded self-interested competition regarding the basic elements of community life—food, shelter, labor, land. Within Europe, according to Polanyi, only traders were able to suspend these constraints, and then only in their dealings with other traders outside given communities. In short, places like Paraguay were central to the process by which gain and its possibilities took root in the European imagination. Of course, Indigenous people had their own norms and customs, their own moral frameworks and ideas of society, grounded in what Polanyi called "the social nature of human agency and the interdependence of our collective existence."[6] The Guaraní referred to *aguĭyeí*—the life of good and healthy interactions among those who lived together. Polanyi argued broadly that economic gain and, ultimately, market relations could come to dominate human affairs only by displacing such ideas as primary axes of life in common, though he never pointed to a concrete historical moment when gain and reciprocity collided.

This book brings such a juncture into focus to consider anew what it has meant for gain to play out at the hub of human collective life. The irony of *gain* is that while its role has been acknowledged as the driving motive in market economies, it has rarely been raised as a topic of historical inquiry unto itself. It is treated, instead, as a background condition requiring no special attention. Within the conceptual frame of Western thinking, the pursuit of gain has been accepted as *the* thing human beings do and are expected to do in situations defined as *economic*—the impulse that is always already present among "modern" humans. In fact, this understanding is the outcome of a historical process, at once practical, intellectual, ideological, and moral. Where European political theories had looked askance at gain through the seventeenth century, and moral discourse had treated it as synonymous with greed and avarice, by the nineteenth century it came to be broadly understood among Europeans as a matter of "irresistible human nature" and even necessity in matters of everyday material life.[7] In consequence, it has been uncommon to consider substantive mutuality on its own terms in historical accounts of the emergence of modern economies, other than to proclaim its demise. By looking to the encounter between Guaraní and Europeans through the prism of differing understandings of exchange, I seek new historical perspectives on the actions, ideas, volitions, and motivations that underlie our social and economic lives. I do so in the hope that we might see unabashed gain-seeking from the viewpoint of those who experienced it as strange and unsettling, so that the familiar and taken-for-granted might come to seem strange and unsettling once again as a matter of broad human concern.

In 1524, when a small band of Europeans first arrived where the rivers Pillkumayu and Ysry Paraguaí joined, encounters with the native Guaraní were tense but not hostile. Relations were mediated chiefly by barter: European goods such as mirrors, beads, knives, and hatchets for food and information. The newcomers professed their interest in finding a kingdom of gold and silver high in the Andes. An alliance of convenience followed in which the clutch of Europeans and thousands of Guaraní trekked west to the foothills of the Incan empire, returning months later, the former with silver and copper trinkets, the latter with captives. By 1525, the Europeans had left and did not reappear for another decade. In 1537, two hundred newcomers paddled upriver, putting in at the site of first contact with the Guaraní over a decade earlier. They founded the city of Asunción that same year. As before, relations were initially conducted through direct exchange. Over time, an unstable mesh of barter, gift, reciprocity, plunder, and currency developed between the Europeans and Indigenous people. Realizing that no great wealth was to be had from these lands, the interlopers turned to the only obvious resource available for exploitation—native people themselves. The Guaraní responded by attempting to draw settlers into a novel interethnic arrangement, offering daughters, sisters, and nieces in the expectation or hope that the outsiders would accept the status and, crucially, the obligations of brothers-in-law. Settlers were more than happy to take women in gift. But they broadly refused to reciprocate or link their fates to native social arrangements, except as convenience or necessity might dictate.

As the number of foreigners grew over the following decades, royal officials began to worry that Indigenous people might be wiped out by overuse. Royal edicts and local ordinances aiming to address this threat were stymied by settlers' insistence that their liberty and material prospects depended on their ability to realize personal benefit from the Guaraní—little enough, many complained. When by the early seventeenth century, law proved incapable of reining in abuses, many Guaraní sought common cause with Jesuit missionaries, who sought to convert them to Christianity. By blending Guaraní ideas of reciprocity and Jesuit notions of the common good, Native people and European priests gave rise to the storied Paraguay missions, places of relative peace and security for hundreds of thousands of Guaraní during a century and a half. In the late eighteenth century, this mission world was laid waste by reforms aiming to force all Indigenous people into a competitive social order at the heart of which lay the pursuit of gain and submission to the goad of want. In a final irony, just as it was collapsing, the mission world became a topic of fascination and a point of anxious moral reflection in European debates over the role of *economy* in social life. In these disputes, champions of transactional commodity exchange succeeded in relegating reciprocity to the silence of permanent "primitive" status in the grand unfolding of commercial civilization.

The challenge in telling this tale is to include Europeans and Guaraní on broadly equal terms. Chronicles of conquest, especially in the New World, have long indulged "myths" that have made it easy to overlook the complexities, ambivalences, and contingencies of such encounters.[8] Two canards have been especially damaging. The first is that Spaniards' actions amounted to little more than pillage and plunder and so do not bear on later economic developments rooted in transactional exchanges. In effect, this has tended to exclude from our histories of the modern, global economic system those Europeans who confronted radical human difference and saw opportunity. The second myth is that Native people, once conquered, had few concerns other than bare survival. This has left us with an untextured sense of Indigenous people and their ideas regarding exchange as they confronted an emergent global political economy at the level of everyday life.

A central argument of this book is that the Guaraní's responses to the novelty of gain in their midst are of a piece with counter-movements among ordinary people who have faced broadly similar pressures elsewhere. With respect to a particular historical moment, E. P. Thompson referred to such movements as manifestations of "moral economy." Writing in the 1970s, he sought an alternative to facile explanations for what were billed as "riots" during early decades of the Industrial Revolution in England. Specifically, he argued that so-called mobs opposing price hikes and food shortages during the late eighteenth century were defending a "delicate tissue of social norms and reciprocities" that regulated how far profit-taking could be pushed at the expense of those most vulnerable in the emerging nexus of cash, prices, and wages. To the notion that English common folk were reacting "spasmodically," Thompson claimed that "crowd action" expressed a "legitimizing notion" regarding a "fair price" in the face of the new market economy.[9]

Moral economy has traveled a tortuous conceptual trajectory. Thompson did not coin the term—it had appeared in late eighteenth- and early nineteenth-century writings among those, especially religious authors, who continued to question still new economic arrangements. Before this time, there had been no reason to refer to a *moral* economy, since *economy* had always been recognized as implicating moral concerns. For Thompson, moral economy was a way of understanding the doings of ordinary folk who resisted the idea that all exchange could be reduced to transactions involving money and commodities.

Since Thompson's time, *moral economy* has expressed a deep sense that something has been missing from conventional *economic* accounts of human motivation and collective life. Anthropologists and political scientists have embraced the concept for precisely this reason—and heatedly contested its usage.[10] I hold with those who recognize in moral economy an effort to reconnect social to economic behavior. The concept invites us to focus on the specific relationships different sorts of exchanges create and what ideas regarding society lie behind them, with the understanding that there is "no unbridgeable chasm" between gift-reciprocity and commodity exchange.[11] This is what makes it possible to bring Guaraní and Europeans into the same analytical frame, without disadvantaging one or the other. When analysis begins from the "real" *economy*—read "market economy"—there is little room for alternative conceptions of how people may relate to each other through exchange. Not surprisingly, Thompson worried about *moral economy*'s plasticity.[12] To avoid conceptual erosion, he rooted its meaning in the particular time and place of his research. Yet Thompson himself recognized that what underlay moral economy might as easily be used to think about Trobriand Islanders as English yeomen, suggesting the concept need not remain trapped in the amber of its specificity.[13] He went no further than this. His doing so at all indicates that the malleability of the idea has been one of its chief selling points—and one of its perils.

Through moral economy, it is possible to see Spanish plunder as part of a larger emerging pattern of human relations. At the same time, it enables us to peer more deeply into what might otherwise be assumed a simple survival instinct among the Guaraní. By distinguishing the supposed peace of transactional exchanges from the violence of pillage, we have avoided close scrutiny of gain and turned away from considering why modern, competitive economic orders seem to be ones of constant strife and social disequilibrium. By the same token, we have dismissed substantive mutuality by assuming it faded from relevance, except among "primitive" peoples—an erasure that is part of the story told here. In consequence, all notions of reciprocity have, in effect, been swept onto the midden of progressive historical development, pertinent only insofar as overcome by gain-seeking in market regimes.

The centuries-long encounter between Europeans and Guaraní reveals an early moment in the emergence of a globalized economic order from the vantage of a confrontation between different notions of exchange. If it is true that a global economy developed in relation to the violent appropriation of labor and land in Africa and America, which has been called "war capitalism," it is also true that there was another clash germane to understanding the crystallization of the modern market world—a forgotten (or repressed) dispute over the terms of human sociability.[14] While struggles over land, labor, and resources have been central to the broader story of capitalism, there have also been struggles regarding how human beings should behave toward one another and how they should arrange their collective lives. We know much less about the latter than we do the former.

Telling this story demands a vigorous treatment of substantive mutuality in historical accounts of modern economy.[15] Its absence has allowed gain to be chalked up to human nature and placed safely beyond inquiry. To correct this omission, gift and reciprocity must be heard to express the intellectual, political, social, cultural, and ethical commitments of concrete historical actors in historical time, in a way that links the intimate to the systemic. There has been some movement on this front. Recent historical scholarship has been more attentive to reciprocity in understanding negotiations between Indigenous people and Europeans in North America.[16] Others have called for a reconsideration of gift-reciprocity in broad historical accounts of capitalism as a step to rethinking human sociability on a global scale.[17] Historians working on widely separated parts of the world have begun to incorporate local understandings more firmly into histories of capitalism, by paying attention to how communities negotiated their own "autonomy," by telling "local histories of global capital," and by showing how "ways of life" long dismissed as "unfit" were viable responses to economic pressures.[18] This scholarship looks to a composite history of modern economic relations as a global phenomenon, a panorama of multiple local histories involving "the whole human world," as Polanyi put it.[19]

While I accept Thompson's baseline regarding moral economy as a "pattern of behavior," I also depart from it in one crucial way: the pattern must be seen to stretch across periods much longer than the convulsive moments Thompson fixed on. This is the only way to regraft gift-reciprocity into our historical accounts of modern economy. Because exchange varies by culture and because regimes of exchange morph as they encounter the duress and temptations of gainful conduct, it is crucial that moral economy encompass deeply considered action over long periods, as well as reactions in the moment. Just as the practice of gain became more firmly entrenched among Europeans over the decades and centuries following initial encounter in the New World, shaped by institutions and politics, substantive mutuality was renewed as an active resource among the Guaraní during nearly three centuries, looking to "relationships and their histories" for judging what might be proper and mutual in social lives upended.[20]

I freely admit that moral economy cannot be pinned down with precision. Thompson gestured toward a "general theory of moral economy" but backed away from providing one. The reality of exchange in human lives is concrete, not abstract. It connects the everyday texture of material life to the shape of obligation among people and within communities. With this in mind, the conceptual role of moral economy is threefold: First, to help us recognize that conventional accounts regarding the rise of economy have left out too much, especially from the perspective of those who have experienced that rise as cataclysmic over shorter or longer periods. Second, to give a name to movements that have often been treated as isolated phenomena—the resistances and uprisings, the accommodations and innovations that are deemed secondary or irrelevant to the supposedly larger story of global economic development. And third, to allow us to rediscover that all exchange is social and all economy moral, disciplinary dithering and ideological niggling notwithstanding. *Moral economy* is therefore a term that makes up in nuance and grain what it lacks in rigor. Ideally, it will fade away as we recall that *economy* is inherently moral, political, and social. To reach such a point, however, we must attend to the rich diversity of particular cases—the one in this book and many others—while looking to a global context.

I have opted for a narrative structure to convey how Guaraní and Europeans confronted each other through different understandings of exchange and its role in human relations. Early modern Paraguay is distinguished by the fact that it was a place where gain, and it louche cousins greed and avarice, were frequently raised in public discourse during the decades after contact. The mission world of the seventeenth and eighteenth centuries represented an experiment in social organization and a sustained challenge to gain as an organizing principle of collective life. Although broadly linear, the account is one of collisions and contestations, of how deep precepts and practices regarding social life unraveled and were rewoven. The arc of the book is broad, spanning three centuries and bridging scales from the personal to the imperial. I have drawn on archival materials and printed primary sources, including dictionaries of Guaraní and Spanish and a growing corpus of Guaraní documents in translation. I have also leaned on the existing literature of colonial Paraguay and the rich historiography of the missions.[21] The conceptual ligatures of the argument are made from the insights of anthropologists, economists, ethnographers, theologians, and philosophers.

Chapter 1 sets a baseline for Guaraní and European social understandings prior to contact in the sixteenth century. For the Guaraní, I draw on the vibrant anthropological and ethnohistorical literature of Amerindian peoples that has emerged in recent decades to ground robust ideas of gift, reciprocity, and conviviality. For Spaniards, I look to the centrality of "friendship" in social life and its concrete manifestation in gift giving and reciprocal practices, even as these norms were beginning to be strained by the pull of transactional conduct. Chapter 2 narrates the meeting of Guaraní and Iberians against the backdrop of early material exchanges, the shock of Spaniards' instrumental and exploitative impulses, especially with regard to women, and Guaraní efforts to respond on their own terms. I contend that this initial period of encounter opened the Guaraní and settlers to the perils and possibilities of a new world of gain. Chapter 3 examines efforts within Spanish officialdom to mobilize royal justice to protect Indigenous people from ongoing devastation. According to Spanish theology and law, human beings were ordained to life together, so Spaniards and Guaraní should form part of a shared social order. And yet by the end of the sixteenth century, law, the instrument for ensuring this outcome, was buckling under the weight of settlers' excesses. Chapter 4 argues that this legal project had foundered by the early seventeenth century. Its failure led many among the Guaraní to cultivate a relationship with Jesuit missionaries seeking to convert them, as a way of escaping settlers' unrelenting demands for Guaraní labor. Chapter 5 contends that the Guaraní entered into a grand pact with the Spanish monarchy, brokered by Jesuit missionaries. Between the mid-seventeenth and the early eighteenth centuries, this alliance gave rise to the mission world as a concrete manifestation of Guaraní substantive mutuality and Jesuit notions of charity and the common good. The idea was that such an alliance might accomplish what the law could not: to insulate the Guaraní from settlers and to rebalance lives disrupted by unchecked gain. Chapter 6 chronicles two events that strained this pact: a settler rebellion in the 1730s and the Guaraní war of the 1750s, which resulted directly from the Spanish monarchy's growing concern with commerce as a tool of sovereignty and inter-imperial competition. Chapter 7 recounts the collapse of the mission world after expulsion of the Jesuits from Paraguay in 1767 and the introduction of reforms aiming to force mission residents into a competitive economy. Chapter 8 considers European debates regarding an emergent market order in which the mission world figured prominently as a point of moral reflection. It was here that substantive mutuality faded in the face of arguments regarding the ineluctability of competitive gain-seeking in human affairs. A concluding chapter amplifies and extends some of the book's key themes.

Because deletion of the Guaraní from historical time is part of the narrative arc of this book, it is crucial to reckon with deep, rarely acknowledged assumptions regarding what it is to *do* history, in the modern, Western sense. Constantin Fasolt has argued that history, as a way of thinking about human time, relies on the strong notion that human beings are "free and independent agents, with the ability to shape their fate" beyond the "thoughtless repetition of custom."[22] By supposing that human actions have made the past, historical practice summons a sense of "control . . . over the world of self and society" in the present, which frees human beings to make the future.[23] This is why historical thinking cannot vigorously acknowledge outcomes purportedly given by tradition (custom), religion (providence), or science (nature). Were it so, humans could not be said to have acted, only to have been acted upon or to have blundered through time. And if this were true in the past, there would be no warrant to assume they can do any differently in the present with respect to the future. Put another way, Western historicizing, as a regime of knowledge, has sought above all to ensure that the future remain open to a specific conception of human agency. Its central purpose is to insist, counterintuitively, that the past does not, finally, fetter the intentional shaping of the future. Historical agency, thus, is a (quite particular) solution to the predicament of how those born into the flow of time to circumstances not of their choosing can nevertheless be said to chart their own paths. There is nothing wrong with this, so long as we are clear about what historians are up to. The problem comes when history assumes an objective stance that subordinates other ways of thinking about human time to this vision.

For the Guaraní, the dilemma is acute. Like Indigenous people across the New World—and enslaved Africans with them, as well as so many others around the globe—the Guaraní were thrust into a historical trajectory premised on the rupture of their world. Whatever may have been their notions of human temporality before the encounter with Europeans in the sixteenth century, nothing could have prepared them for the existential levies they bore afterwards. To see them as historical actors in the conventional sense is to imagine that even after contact with the outsiders, they had some measure of "control over the world of self and society" and were "free and independent agents, with the ability to shape their fate." This does not seem quite right, given the constraints under which they have had to puzzle out their collective existence. Yet, to deny them agency would mean one of two things. Either they would be written out of historical time, where, from the Western perspective, human meaning is made and the future is worked out. Or their entire presence would be reduced to having been acted upon by others. Either way, their historical role would always be diminished compared to European historical actors.

Caution is in order. There is no reason to assume the Guaraní share or shared this conception of human temporal agency. After all, they have mythic and linguistic resources of their own for thinking about their relation to time.[24] They could simply refuse to engage history as a form of knowledge (which arguably makes it presumptuous to insert them into an historical account). Then again, the Guaraní of today might choose not to foreclose options. They might accept a superposition of myth and history, or propose some fusion of the two. A *history* of the epochal change to a novel global social order, with the Guaraní as participants, must face this issue head on.

One avenue for doing so is to think of the *freedom* to which Western historicizing is oriented as an ontological commitment of its own, a horizon in relation to which history can unfold as a human project. It is what redeems history from being a random walk through time and allows humans to contribute to creating their future. Yet freedom, as a guiding orientation, is problematic because it says so little about what people should use freedom to accomplish and for whose benefit. The answer to this riddle has been the Western idea of *progress* which, absent some moving spirit or teleological endpoint, only begs the question of progress toward what. By default, the answer has generally involved some notion of expanded abundance and agency for humanity writ large, even as people across the globe have been denied the historical capacity to "shape their own fates" by the very processes that were supposed to emancipate them. As an idea, in other words, progress remains as philosophically thin as it is emotionally resonant.

Is there any possibility of a parallel and distinct temporal horizon among the Guaraní? If not, the Guaraní, when treated as historical actors in historical accounts risk remaining bound to the freedom-progress axis in ways that would seem to ill fit their experience and might even misrepresent their existential possibilities. Here, perhaps, the notion of *Land Without Evil*, that place of effortless abundance where the joys of mutuality may be had without the burdens of obligation, offers a path.

This idea is one of the most contentious in the scholarship on the Guaraní. Early twentieth-century anthropologists were the first to bring attention to it, linking it to messianic pilgrimages among the Guaraní at times of acute crisis.[25] Debate since that time has been vigorous. The term has been thought to denote a myth growing out of the Guaraní's constant search for new arable lands. Scholars have contested its earlier presence among the Guaraní, claiming that the Land Without Evil was a later cultural invention. Others have argued that it is above all an artifact of Western ethnographic encounters with the Guaraní.[26] What seems beyond dispute is that among contemporary Guaraní, the idea is recognized as a kind of cosmological point of reference, an actual or figurative place of plenty for all and peaceful human interactions.[27]

It is hard to gauge the historical depth of this vision. A seventeenth-century Guaraní-Spanish dictionary by a Jesuit missionary contains the earliest written version of the term. Under the entry for *mârâneỹ*, meaning "good [negation of bad], whole, incorruptible," *ĭbĭ mârâneỹ* is translated as "ground that remains intact, that has not been built on."[28] Given that Guaraní villages moved every few years to open up new clearings in the forest as old fields became exhausted, it has seemed plausible to suppose this could be a point of origin for the mythic meaning of the term. Accounts of two European chroniclers from the late sixteenth and early seventeenth centuries offer the only known historical references to the idea of a mystical land of ease and plenty. These documents refer tantalizingly to a place of "immortality and eternal rest," "a beautiful land where all things would come naturally and abundantly, without any difficulty or labor."[29] It is impossible to know with precision what was being referred to. Translation was rudimentary and chroniclers listened only as hard as necessary to find their way to El Dorado, the fabled city of gold that obsessed European adventurers at that time, or to the land of the silver king high in the Andes.

Between such statements and the scholarship of the twentieth century, there is a gulf. As anthropologist Bartomeu Melià has argued, it is unlikely that the idea of Land Without Evil can be teased out of early history so as to reveal a continuous, traceable thread from pre-contact times to the present day.[30] Yet, it is worth noting that ethnographers and anthropologists have reported that among contemporary Guaraní the idea of *ïbï mârâneÿ* (Land Without Evil) as an actual place has remained intact alongside newer ways of considering it. For purposes of this book, the conceptual problem is that debate over its longevity and meaning among the Guaraní has not been settled.[31] Moreover, the concept presents an evidentiary dilemma, for it does not figure in the few Guaraní texts available to us or indirectly in texts written by Spaniards.

This does not imply that it must be set aside.[32] Despite continuing debate, few would deny that the Land Without Evil encapsulates a metaphysical orientation to a Guaraní way of being in the world, a thing "real and material in their hope."[33] Speaking of present-day Guaraní, Melià has put it succinctly: "The search for the Land-Without-Evil is nothing else than an element, alongside others, of the system of reciprocity, threatened in many ways, but always sought after as an essential point of definition."[34] This is not the only way to conceptualize the Land Without Evil, though it has the advantage of referring to the world of material relationships rather than exclusively to a religious, mythical, or cosmological realm.[35]

Approached this way, the phrase might be said to play a role in Guaraní culture akin to that of freedom in Western historicizing. If freedom may be thought of as the condition for progress along an arrow of time toward material and cultural betterment, the Land Without Evil might be thought of as a temporal horizon that conceptualizes social relations as "a history that must be remade every day."[36] The Land Without Evil would thus stand as "the realistic condition of the economy of reciprocity in this world and in the one beyond," sustained by a collective commitment to "being on the path" toward it.[37] Another way to grasp the comparison is to note of Melià's formulation above that if "freedom" is substituted for "Land-Without-Evil," and "control over the world of self and society" for "the system of reciprocity," the statement could ring unobjectionably true to a Western ear.*

In other words, it is possible to acknowledge the contrast between Western and Guaraní ideas regarding the human passage through time without exaggerating differences to the point of mutual unintelligibility. This, in turn, allows them to be permeable to each other. There is no reason to suppose that the Guaraní lacked or lack temporal consciousness—though it may not mean what Western historians suppose. Reciprocity among the Guaraní might be said to be explicitly temporal. It looks back and forward from the moment, positing its own continual renewal "on the path" that seeks to ensure a coherent relationship among people to and through time and space.[38] The difficulty with this formulation, from the vantage point of Western historical thinking, is that it smacks too much of the "thoughtless repetition of custom" to qualify as genuine human agency. Linear *progress* has generally been paired with *freedom* in Western historicizing for just this reason; without a meaningful idea of advance, human agency can seem almost beside the point. Western historians may nod to past and present efforts to preserve and renew certain ways of being, but these are almost always understood as subordinate to supposedly more assertive forms of action seeking to progress and so create the future. The difference between these two perspectives, thus, is less a matter of the presence or absence of temporality in relation to a horizon of possibility than of distinct orientations regarding an oncoming present. Rather than presume them to be incommensurable, I allow them to commingle without losing their distinctness.

---

*With the indicated substitutions, it would read as follows: "The search for freedom is nothing else than an element, alongside others, of the control over the world of self and society, threatened in many ways, but always sought after as an essential point of definition."

1

Coming to the Encounter

Let us eat together from one plate; let us work together.
Antonio Ruiz de Montoya, *Tesoro de la lengua guaraní* (1639)

They live without love or charity, worshipping only the small idol of their gain.
Cristóbal Suárez de Figueroa (1621)

HISTORY IS MADE from the interactions of people and their ideas about what is worth doing in the world and why. The resulting trajectory is rarely straightforward. Recent scholarship on European global expansion has taught us that encounters across cultural difference and textures of feeling are especially fraught. Nowhere is this more obvious than in encounters between Indigenous people and Europeans in the decades and centuries following 1492.

In *The Great Transformation*, Karl Polanyi noted that "the differences . . . between civilized and 'uncivilized' people have been vastly exaggerated, especially in the economic sphere." So-called primitive economics, he said, had been brushed aside as "irrelevant to the question of the motives and mechanisms of civilized societies."[1] By the nineteenth century, economic "gain" had come to be accepted as the sole form of exchange pertinent to human affairs, the product of an unchanging human nature. At the same time, gift-reciprocity, that other mode of exchange, largely vanished from European reflections on society's arrangements. This book brings both modes of exchange into a single analytical frame by examining the concrete encounter between Guaraní and Europeans from the early sixteenth century to the turn of the nineteenth century. At the moment of contact, Guaraní social life remained firmly rooted in substantive mutuality, though there may have been auguries of change. Among Europeans, reciprocal friendship continued to anchor collective sensibilities but was becoming more individually transactional, a trend widely criticized at the time. Establishing the sight lines of these perspectives is essential to everything that follows.

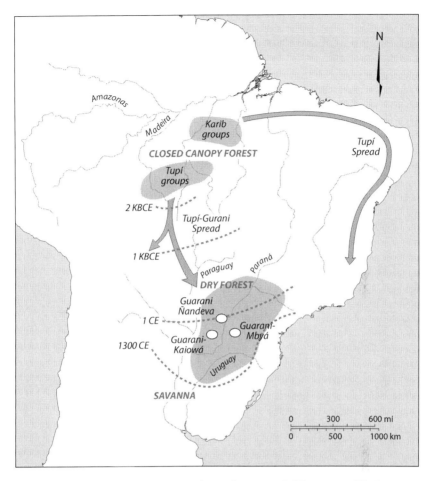

MAP 1.1. Tupí-Guaraní transcontinental spread, ca. 2000 BCE–ca. 1300 CE. *Sources:* Castro e Silva, "Genomic Insight," fig. 1; Iriarte et al., "Out of Amazonia," figs. 1 and 2.

*   *   *

Before the Europeans
Guaraní world

People who knew themselves as *Abá*, "men" or "people," had arrived in the region of the Río de la Plata perhaps two centuries before encountering Europeans in the early decades of the sixteenth century. Best estimates suggest that the Tupí-Guaraní-speaking peoples had spread from southwest Amazonia starting a millennium and a half earlier, reaching southern Brazil around CE 1 (Map 1.1). They had entered the fertile area between the lower Paraguay and Uruguay Rivers, perhaps around the thirteenth or fourteenth century by Western reckoning.[2] They came to be known as *Guaraní*, meaning "warrior" in Tupí, only after meeting Spanish newcomers in the 1520s.

On the eve of European contact, Guaraní communities lined the banks of the Paraná and Uruguay Rivers north to the province of Guairá, fanning out along their tributaries. West lay the Great Chaco, an arid territory dominated by the nomadic Guaycurú. Beyond rose the foothills of the mighty Inca empire. East, toward the great sea, the bellicose Tupí, descended from participants in the generations-long migration out of Amazonia, had stopped short rather than turn inland.[3] At the time, the area of the Paraná-Uruguay Rivers was occupied by other Indigenous groups, chiefly hunter-gatherers. Guaraní peoples mixed with and absorbed smaller bands through kinship, a process one scholar has called social and linguistic "Guaranization." They may even have been undergoing a demographic expansion that was leading them to seek submission of other groups. For instance, around 1522, two years before Aleixo García arrived in the region, two Guaraní groups migrated well northwest of the Paraguay River into an area known as the Charcas and from there had attacked communities at the edge of the Inca Empire, displacing indigenous residents and occupying their lands.[4]

In the early 1520s, the Guaraní population may have reached 1.5 to 2 million, but numbered at least several hundred thousand, spread across a wide forest swath encompassing diverse peoples.[5] Guaraní villagers farmed, but also hunted, fished, and gleaned. Communities ranged from bands of nuclear families to as many as two thousand or more individuals. The smallest grouping was the *teĩi*, or extended family organized around a single lineage group.[6] Each teĩi was bound by kinship and broadly committed to a collective consciousness of autonomy from other groups, rooted in a sense of "us alone."[7] Several teĩi, involving dozens or hundreds of individuals, might share space within a single communal longhouse known as an *oga*.[8] Multiple oga might gather, for reasons of sociability and work or collective defense, to form a village that could consist of several longhouses arrayed around a central open space, embracing hundreds or even thousands of people. These larger groupings might occupy a recognized territory, the shape and edges of which were determined by rivers, forests, and mountains, in relation to other groups, large and small, allies as well as potential enemies. Historical evidence suggests that the consolidation of such territorial areas was still "incipient" around 1500.[9]

Several villages, in turn, might affiliate with one another to form a larger, territory-based tribe, or *gùara*, a loose confederation linked by intercommunal kinship ties allowing cooperation in warfare and festivities on a larger scale. Such gatherings might persist for a period and then splinter, under population pressures or in response to crises associated with weather, food production, or warfare. Members might admit affinities with each other on the basis of a common language, shared patterns of daily life, and recognition of a culture creator.[10] A gùara did not imply a pan-tribal identity so much as a willingness to see and accept a broad commonality, always contingent and balanced against the sense of exclusivity expressed by oré. Variations, especially in quotidian experience, did not preclude acknowledgement of shared linguistic and cultural commonalities or the possibility of novel forms of belonging.

Overall, the many different Guaraní appear to have prized the autonomy, independence, and liberty of extended kinship above other considerations, recognizing nevertheless the need for interaction with others.[11] Before European contact, the single communal dwelling of the aggregated family was the basic level of production, consumption, and sociality. Caciques presided over these oga. These were hardly strongmen. Pierre Clastres has argued that caciques lacked political power as such.[12] A given cacique might be able to call on the labor of multiple wives and their immediate kin. Beyond this, he had no power to accumulate and so could not compel others to serve him, even in war. He exercised prestige rather than authority in two ways: through the generosity of gift giving, made possible by drawing on the extra labor afforded him by polygyny, and through his oratorical prowess, his capacity to voice "society's will and desire," be it a call to war or to a wider generosity and solidarity.[13] Indeed, in practical terms, a cacique's capacity to command obedience was checked by the fact that any man who could gather forty other men, with their kin, was entitled for form a new communal house and become a cacique himself.[14] This often happened when a village had outgrown its immediate territory. Newly formed groups would then decamp to establish communities elsewhere, a move made possible by the vastness, openness, and abundance of the land.

Within the community, caciques helped organize production and maintain consumption through the redistribution of goods and services. Within the longhouse, work was divided by sex. Women sowed, harvested, cooked, and cared for the children, tasks often performed communally. Men hunted, fished, gleaned, raised children, and cleared patches of forest to prepare new fields every four to six years, a laborious, collaborative process accomplished with stone axes. Such activities were generally communal, often within extended families but across them as well. When several such families joined together, complex and fluid reciprocal arrangements emerged between caciques and among individuals, relatives, and friends, both within and between communal houses. One cacique might emerge as *mburubichá*, a first among peers within a broad territory. This might enable a wider circulation of goods through gift and reciprocity, contingent on the ever-present possibility of later splintering. The appearance of a larger tribal identity, however, did not alter the fundamental reality that Guaraní economy was "fragmented in a thousand small existences, organized so that each one could carry on independently from the rest and dedicated to the domestic principle of caring for themselves," though without any necessary implication of hostility or competition between them.[15]

Guaraní society also had a place of honor for shamans (*payes*). They presided over local dances, feasts, and religious rituals and practiced healing and limited sorcery. Mostly they were men, though women who attained knowledge of medicinal plants and proper ritual might also become payes.[16] Other shamans peregrinated among villages within a given territory. Their prestige could rival that of the mburubichás, and like the great caciques they could have multiple wives. They were known for the elegance of their oratory and their ability to summon the numinous in everyday life. This latter faculty is what has led some scholars to refer to them as "prophets" capable of moving whole territories to action, whether war or migration.[17] Their roles remain much debated and appear to have had a less immediate impact on day-to-day production and consumption than was true of caciques.

Substantive mutuality

By all accounts, these arrangements enabled the precontact Guaraní to live well. Ulrich Schmidel, a German soldier and adventurer who chronicled his expedition up the Paraguay River in the mid-1530s, noted that Indigenous people enjoyed an enviable "abundance" of corn, manioc, potatoes, peanuts, honey, fish, fowl, meat, and a native wine.[18] Except in circumstances beyond their control—floods, fires, epidemics—villages and tribes had more than enough food for all. The forest enveloping them and the agriculture carved out from it provided all the resources to fashion what they needed to thrive—robust shelter, weapons, tools, implements, baskets, pottery, clothing, finery. Other than a division of labor between men and women, a broad equality seems to have held within and between kinship groups. Indeed, the Guaraní phrase translated into Spanish as "discord" in Father Ruiz de Montoya's 1639 Guaraní-Spanish dictionary (*Tesoro de la lengua guaraní*) conveyed a sense of lost mutuality and equality.[19]

The Guaraní, in other words, did not live at the ragged edge of survival. Until recently, Western scholarship has tended to dismiss "primitive" societies as condemned to a grinding poverty from which it was supposed everyone could only want to escape. From this perspective, people lacking a clear drive for profit or accumulation could only have lives of unrelenting desperation teetering at the edge of survival, proof, if any were needed, of "primitive economy's intrinsic inferiority."[20]

Recent scholarship paints another picture. The Guaraní appear to have enjoyed what anthropologist Marshall Sahlins called stone-age "affluence"—a plenitude of food and the satisfaction of needs, gotten by devoting "relatively little time to what is called work," leaving ample time for rest, ritual, festivity, and wars of vengeance.[21] This prosperity hinged on the fact that their mode of production did not aim to produce a surplus or promote accumulation, though they may have had the resources to do so. Rather, their chief "economic" goal was to meet individual and collective needs, while reserving an untapped labor potential for unforeseeable crises. Otherwise, they sought to minimize labor in favor of the liberty to pursue other aspects of life (at least among men). More broadly, Guaraní aspired to autonomy understood as a lack of dependence on others.[22] This approach to "economy" implied occasional lean periods—resulting from unanticipated disasters—but the overall abundance and resilience of the forest encouraged confidence that better times would follow.[23] Despite the premium on autonomy, these were not isolated existences. For all the differences among them, diverse Guaraní peoples shared a material culture that eased contact and communication among them, and at times with non-Guaraní. In moving to open up new fields, a village required intelligence about the new area, such as hunting opportunities, medicines, and the territories of nearby villages. Such information would need to be rapidly incorporated into common knowledge, a process that depended fundamentally on an openness to others.[24]

As was true generally of South American Indigenous peoples, Guaraní life was conducted under a dense canopy of substantive mutuality. Reciprocity, gifts, and redistribution were part of a matrix widely shared among South American peoples: even at the height of its power, the Inca empire relied on reciprocity rather than on a trade-based, monetary economy.[25] Reciprocity represented the open-ended commitment to ongoing relationship with others in a context of maintaining peace.[26] In broad terms, the first moment of reciprocity was the *gift*, the object given without expectation of immediate return, but with the reinforced hope and expectation of eventual reciprocation. For anthropologist Marcel Mauss, this "system of ideas" grounded a shared conviction that generosity could guarantee society.[27] Material stuff was not the most important element of the gift. Nor did giving mainly seek reversion of objects as such. Rather, the gift aimed to ensure continued mutual action between parties into the indeterminate future, or until the cycle was disrupted. Gift-countergift reciprocity, in other words, established "bonding value," the worth of "ties and their reinforcement" over time without contemplated end as the essence of social order.[28]

Among the Guaraní, reciprocal gift giving served as a fundamental regulator of interpersonal and intercommunity relations, the "deepest expression of tribal solidarity" and a practice oriented to ensuring the desired relationship with the world at large.[29] This idea found emblematic expression in the obligation of the hunter. The killing of a wild boar, which could provide several families with meat for weeks, was not an occasion for the hunter to hoard the kill for himself—and anyway, most of it would have spoiled before he could eat it all—but an opportunity for him to share with others, to redistribute it and so make a gift of it to the community. To this end, he would refrain from eating it himself, the sign that Guaraní society "did not recognize the individual as an autonomous economic agent" in the context of community life.[30] In this way, he earned the community's honor and respect, while recognizing all the previous times other hunters had given their kills to the community and anticipating all the future times they would do so. "Production" of the meat, therefore, aimed not at individual or even collective accumulation but at an allocation that would project substantive mutuality through time. It was not inconceivable among the Guaraní that a hunter would selfishly kill and eat an animal without sharing, but doing so meant remaining beyond human community.

Though on the eve of contact with Europeans, the Guaraní were as much agriculturalists as they were hunters, a broad sense of reciprocity rested at the core of social life.[31] Illustrative phrases given for the Guaraní word *poî* (*pó* = hand + *oî* = loose/free), listed in Montoya's *Tesoro*, are suggestive. The entry for *poî* clearly signals the connection between *hand* as a metaphor for generosity and specific acts of reciprocity and relationality: "give to eat, and [give] things, share with another," "company in doing a thing," "he works alongside me," "we eat from one plate," "we work together," "let us eat together."[32] The *Tesoro* notes as well that the Guaraní word for "prudence" involved a combination of the root for hand (*pó*) and the word for "understanding, discernment, reason" (*araquaá*), as illustrated by "I distribute things with prudence" (*poaraquaá*).[33] Though glimpsed through the veil of cultural and linguistic translation, these phrases suggest that gift and reciprocity were deeply enfolded into the practice, language, and rationality of everyday Guaraní life.

Similarly, work, as purposive activity oriented to community survival and thriving, also expressed the idea of gift-reciprocity. Sowing and harvesting, fishing and hunting, clearing and cooking all enabled substantive mutuality within what Portuguese Jesuit Fernão Cardim called a "community of all things." As an example, Cardim noted that Indians might make wine and then invite all the neighbors—members of other *oga* or perhaps *teîî*—to help them clear a field for ten hours, after which they would drink together.[34] By linking effort and conviviality, they got done what needed doing, without overt coercion or remuneration. As the Spanish Jesuit Ruiz de Montoya noted, they "have neither buying nor selling because with liberality and without interest, they help each other in their needs."[35]

Certain Guaraní keywords help root the point. Montoya translated *potŷrô* as "to put hands to the task," and *pepî* as meaning "an invitation made to those who help make a house."[36] Work, thus, was not simply bodily labor. It also affirmed communal solidarity. This gave work among the Guaraní (and other Indigenous peoples) a "ludic" and "festive" quality rare (but not unknown) in commercial and industrial societies, a spirit grounded in a mutual imperative of sociality, as in *oroyopoî*, "let us give each other things, let us invite ourselves to eat."[37] Far more than the next meal was at stake. The abundance that impressed Schmidel was most lavishly performed in the grand invitations—*pepîguaçú*—to different *teîî* (kin groups) and even *gùara* (tribes) to join a festivity that might involve hundreds, even thousands of guests from surrounding regions.[38] These gatherings, with music, dancing, games, speeches, drinking, and sometimes ritual cannibalism of a prisoner taken in a war of vengeance, represented the ideal embodiment of peace as envisioned by reciprocity. Just as individual hunters turned over their kill to others, just as women cooked together to feed many, just as people might accept an invitation to help build a house or clear a field, so communities made a gift of conviviality to other communities through these *pepĭ*. Here was reciprocity as a means of scaling relationships to a community of communities.[39] At the same time, as the shared ground for all exchanges, reciprocity defined what it was to be human, enabling the friendship, trust, and conscience that anchored social life.

Hunting, working, and feasting were the Borromean rings of Guaraní sociality. Together, they defined people's relationship to *tecoá*, the particular place representing the "conditions of possibility" for the Guaraní way of being.[40] As a space of living, tecoá itself encompassed three linked realms—forest, farm, and village—that represented the Guaraní relationship to the land practically and cosmologically. Moving among these domains, Guaraní people were able to conduct all meaningful activities expressing their good way of being as sustained by gift-countergift reciprocity in a particular locale. And yet, this was not a land without worry or anxiety. Despite the world's apparent stability, the Guaraní thought of themselves as living under existential menace. Floods, great storms, cosmic fires, and war are bright threads running through Guaraní myth, suggesting that they, like the ancient Aztecs and Maya, may have understood their presence as tenuous and under constant threat.[41]

Gift and reciprocity were broadly enacted through the giving and receipt of women as wives. Precontact marriage patterns remain largely a mystery. Men commonly had a single wife. Girls married young, often to somewhat older, more or less distant cousins, generally with the consent of parents. Jean de Léry's sixteenth-century chronicle of the Tupinambá (kin to the Guaraní) indicates that despite their youth, girls expressed their "will" with respect to potential marriage partners.[42] Except in the case of caciques and shamans, the husband came to live in the oga of his bride and worked for her family as his own. Relationships between men and women appear to have been relatively fluid. Couples could join and, with little fanfare, later part ways, free to take up with other partners. As one Spanish chronicler noted, Guaraní women enjoyed "more liberty" than women in Spain.[43] Unlike ordinary men, caciques generally had multiple wives. Drawing on their labor was the only way a cacique could distribute gifts to the community, the basis of his prestige. Women, especially daughters, sisters, cousins, and nieces, were given in order to cement alliances between caciques, who thereby became brothers-in-law (*tobayas*) to each other, assuming a stance of friendship rooted in gift and reciprocity over time.[44] We know little of how women understood such exchanges, though it is worth noting that even marriage to a cacique or shaman involved no significant change in status or in the work generally expected of Guaraní women.[45]

Vicissitudes of reciprocity

Notwithstanding its cultural depth, gift-countergift reciprocity could fail in ways small and large. If phrases in Guaraní are any indication, idle hands were not unknown. Montoya's *Tesoro* indicates that ordinary people might suffer bouts of laziness: the entry for *ateÿ* contains a phrase meaning "to become slack/lazy in work," implying a fleeting loss of motivation. While this might reflect Jesuit sensibilities, another entry hints that the Guaraní recognized that a gift could "melt" away the capacity to work: "with the gift he becomes slack/inert [*floxo*]."[46] Other definitions suggest that the Guaraní understood there would be shirkers and malingerers who, lacking "calluses," might have to turn their heads in shame or be pressured to help clear a field or raise a house. It seems unlikely that all of these appeared only after contact with the Jesuits, especially given the specific references to Guaraní communal activities. The *Tesoro* also lists phrases pointing to the breakdown of reciprocal sentiment. One of the two entries for *poî*, or "loose/free hand," after giving several positive examples of generosity and sharing, offers a phrase meaning, roughly, "I was given a bad [or small] portion" and another meaning "he is not liberal in giving," making clear that it was not unknown for people to fail in their mutual obligations.[47]

Though we have little direct evidence for the period prior to contact, such failures appear to have been corrected *within* the social order through shame, cajolery, and exclusion rather than through any concentrated power to coerce or punish. Consider the Guaraní sense of bringing someone to understanding or discernment. The idea combines notions of time, clarity, and world, with processes of knowing, deliberating, and judging to achieve something like certainty in correct conduct. One who righted one's own wrong might thus say, "Because I have corrected my-self, I am good."[48] People were said to "come back to themselves" through persuasion and subtle pressure rather than explicit punishment.[49] While a measure of power is implicit here, at both an interpersonal and social scale, there is no hint of direct bodily compulsion as a first resort. By contrast, Montoya's Spanish-Guaraní lexicon for Spanish speakers defines the Guaraní word *amboaraquaa* as "to punish in order to correct," conveying a threat of force.[50] I do not mean to suggest that the Guaraní eschewed physical coercion altogether. Guaraní did not lack terms involving striking. An illustrative phrase indicates that someone might cause another to be beaten (*amboayucá*), hinting at the possibility of a person with authority ordering the physical punishment of a culprit.[51] This is not much to go on and the precise balance between different forms of correction is lost to us. Even so, we should not underestimate the power of communal pressure to uphold social norms, since the alternative for the non-cooperative individual was to leave the social order for the freedom and dangers of the forest, an outcome likely to have been unrealistic, as well as undesirable, for most people.

Reciprocity could also miscarry by becoming its own opposite—*tepí*, or vengeance. If the ultimate goal of reciprocity was to ensure the peace that allowed communities to hunt and fish, sow and harvest, raise children, and hold festivities, vengeance might seem the utter failure of the reciprocal spirit. Yet, it is possible to think of vengeance as "negative reciprocity"—negative because vengeance was never desired for itself, since it temporarily broke the peace substantive mutuality sought to assure.[52] On this understanding, vengeance became a possibility, even an imperative, only when someone or some group took an action that ruptured the cycle of (positive) reciprocity governing sociality generally.

The most spectacular version of vengeance involved war, specifically for the purpose of taking prisoners who might at some point be killed and ritually eaten. If peace was the horizon of meaning for reciprocity, war was the breach of mutuality implicit in the ever-present possibility of misunderstanding and violence between humans. As a taking rather than a giving, the capture and killing of a prisoner might seem the ultimate refusal to recognize the commonality and generosity of the gift and its reciprocation. But there was a subtle logic at work here. War that led to taking a prisoner reflected a previous disruption of reciprocity, perhaps a severed alliance—the "breaking of friendship," as a later

Jesuit missionary put it—an unwarranted intrusion upon territory, or an uncalled-for killing.[53]

But a simple act of tit-for-tat retribution is not what Guaraní vengeance contemplated. A weightier metaphysical question was at stake. In essence, the act of another party's unreciprocal *taking*—a taking without an intention of return—had to be converted back into a gift in order to restore the balance that ensured the continuance of peace. In practice, a prisoner was not simply slaughtered and eaten, as Europeans commonly supposed. A captive might live years within the community before finally giving up his life. During that time, he would have the liberty to hunt and fish unaccompanied, to take a wife, even have children. He would learn Guaraní. He would *become* Guaraní. Children born to others in the village might be named after him.[54] So, when the time came to crack his skull and consume his body, perhaps even as a broth that would allow hundreds to partake, he would be giving the gift of his life and his body to the community (of which he had become a part), much as a hunter might give the boar he had killed.[55] And the moment would be celebrated as part of a festivity enshrining and enacting reciprocity, now repaired by his gift. A small part of him, in the form of ash, might even be sent to other communities as a way to reinforce peace between bands.[56] As a member of the community, he accepted the obligation of making a gift of himself that, by being received and incorporated, could heal the breach of reciprocity that had prompted his capture in the first place. Death, with its finality, could not by itself transmute the unreciprocal into renewed reciprocity—only a valued life given as a gift could do so, which was why the captive had to become Guaraní first.

Did such captives simply accept their fates? Why would they not have fled, given the relative liberty they enjoyed in new communities? There is little specific evidence to answer these questions, but it is possible to speculate. Flight would have violated the premises underlying reciprocity in everyday life. Yet, given that their deaths were foretold, it seems unlikely that captives acted from blind devotion to an abstraction or that their conduct was determined by the mechanical action of culture. To the contrary, there is every reason to suppose that they might at times have been afraid, even tempted by the idea of flight. But where to go? A captive's own people might well have been reluctant to take him in, might even have tried to return him to his captors. Failure to do so would have risked extended warfare. As one taken in the context of *tepĭ*, the captive was part of the weave of reciprocity, even if in its broken or "negative" form; surely his own community would not forgive repatriation of a captive they had taken or might take in the future. Nor could a wayward captive simply join some other group. Lacking kin ties, he would have been an outsider in their lands and likely would not be welcomed, not least because his captors might see harboring him as an affront calling for vengeance and so, for more war. Living alone would have meant dodging all human contact, not so easy a task in forests that were invariably some group's territory.

The alternative was understood and the options clear. This was not simply docility. The captive's life had been forfeit at the moment of capture. In all the ways that mattered among the Guaraní, it was no longer his to keep. Just as his captors commuted his death that he might make a gift of himself to his new community, so he suspended his liberty and, at least ideally, embraced his situation and its outcome as an opportunity to live and die with honor.[57] In doing so, he helped to heal the breach of reciprocity he perhaps had done nothing to cause, but in which he was implicated by being a warrior. That is, he made his death a "productive event."[58] Thus, even at this extreme, vengeance did not cease to express reciprocity. Rather, it restored the cycle of gift-countergift, by reminding everyone how vulnerable the cycle was to being broken.

A caveat is in order. Though the ritual of cannibal consumption aimed to heal a wound to mutuality, it might trigger a cycle of vengeance resulting in perpetual enmity between groups. This was not merely an episodic failure of reciprocity that could be healed by the offer of a gift and its acceptance. Instead, war could in certain circumstances become the very basis of reciprocity, a kind of ontological inversion of reciprocity as peace. According to Pierre Clastres, Amazonian tribes such as the Yanomani had normalized this reversal, engaging in almost endless intertribal violence. They might exchange gifts with other groups, though chiefly to gain allies against tribal enemies with whom they were locked in a circle of vengeance and countervengeance. War in this mode might be understood as a persistent form of "negative" reciprocity in which violence and the taking of captives represented the basis for group identity and in which the eternal fragmentation produced by constant fighting prevented the emergence of an overarching political power.[59] Some among the Tupí-Guaraní also appear to have been quite bellicose before European arrival. For them, intertribal violence affirmed group identity. By incorporating captives into social life before sacrificing them, they enacted vengeance as a form of reciprocity.[60] According to anthropologist Eduardo Viveiros de Castro, among the Tupí "warfare was a method of instituting society."[61] German adventurer Ulrich Schmidel mistook the Tupí's bellicose ways as a means of territorial expansion, though like most Europeans of his time, his imagination was limited by his own experience regarding the purposes of war.[62] French missionary Yves d'Évreux remained baffled by the fact that a son could accept as adoptive parents the people who had captured and eaten his mother after having accepted her as fictive kin.[63]

An inclination to violence appears to have varied among Indigenous groups in Paraguay on the eve of European advent. Guaraní appear to have attacked communities in the foothills of the Andes at the southern extreme of the Inca empire in the late fifteenth and early sixteenth centuries.[64] Guaraní in the area along the Paraná River stood on a war footing vis-à-vis other tribes, especially the Agaces and the Chaco peoples. In the context of enduring animosity between groups, women too may have been taken captive, thereby reinforcing reproductive and labor capacity, though such women were also eligible to marry and integrate into the group.[65] The Tupí, too, remained warlike against other Indigenous groups, one reason perhaps that they later became such staunch allies of the Portuguese. At the same time, before Europeans arrived in the 1520s, other Guaraní in the Paraná region had taken up sedentary agriculture, a fragile social formation easily upset by collective violence.[66]

Warfare aside, the fragility of the gift-countergift cycle is a reminder that there was nothing automatic about (positive) reciprocity among the Guaraní. Its maintenance required constant renewal, demanding individual and collective attentiveness and action. Caciques, ordinary people, and even captives shared an obligation to sustain the mutual relationships across time that ensured the existence and persistence of society itself. They did so by continually reenacting reciprocity within the teíi and beyond, especially in work and redistribution, and with others who entered the sphere of mutual concern. At a wider scale, they did so as well in the great festivities that were the most visible sign of collective commitment to peace among households, villages, and tribes.

Aguïyeí *and its challenges*

Reciprocity is not best understood in terms of the mechanical operations of culture. Linguistic evidence suggests that precepts of virtuous generosity guided collectives and their members. A central Guaraní norm appears to have been *aguĭyeí*, a term Montoya's *Tesoro* defines as "goodness/kindness, health, ease, good, good fortune, vouch for, praise, excuse oneself or explain why one cannot do what is asked of one."[67] As these diverse examples suggest, aguĭyeí could be used in many different ways, all involving a strong sense of right action over time, rooted in a reputation for proper conduct oriented to a sustained state of goodness. Although the last of the principal definitions, given in Spanish as "escusarse" (excuse or explain oneself), might seem an afterthought to otherwise positive terms, it reflects the same qualities as the earlier ones, though in the context of a failed interpersonal obligation: to excuse oneself was a goodness or kindness, because it explained why one could not do what was asked or expected, thus honoring the principle in the breach. A person who provided no such explanation violated the underlying obligation to be forthright with others. The same point could be made ironically, for aguĭyeí could be used in a phrase to describe "someone vile who vouches for himself or calls himself good," announcing the underlying value of reciprocal honesty in interpersonal relations by raising its moral opposite into stark relief.[68] And while words are altogether too easily turned into concepts, it seems significant that the first definition for aguĭyeí is "goodness/kindness" (*bondad*) and that the most prominent counterexample of *poî*—*na chepoî aguĭyeí*— was rendered into Spanish as "he gave me a bad [or small] portion," implying that an open failure of reciprocity negated aguĭyeí.[69] Mutuality, in other words, and the actions to reproduce it were primary to Guaraní sociality, which aimed for every person to live in *tecó aguĭyeí*—a state of goodness, pleasure, and health in relation to others, something that could only be done in the context of robust social relations.[70]

Keeping the spirit of mutuality and honoring aguĭyeí doubtless became more difficult as one moved outward from kin-based teĭí into the realm of intercommunal relationships.[71] Here, caciques' connections were more tenuous, less a matter of self-exploitation and direct reciprocity than within their own teĭí.[72] Gifts, especially of women, played an important role in ensuring alliances. In gifting and accepting women, caciques bound themselves to each other as kin committed to the flourishing of all. Oratory might also bridge the gap to the wider world. The most highly regarded caciques were known for their "eloquence in speech," which allowed them to gather many Indians, as one Jesuit missionary later noted.[73] Their perorations doubtless made many points, but among them phrases renewing and refreshing the spirit of reciprocity as the very basis of social life must have figured prominently. According to Pierre Clastres, this arrangement precluded material accumulation and the direct exercise of power both within communities and between them. Internally, any cacique who violated precepts of mutuality risked losing his following and splintering the community as younger men seeking prestige formed new longhouses (oga). That is, caciques who overreached did not need to be removed. Instead, those to whom they answered withdrew their support and transferred their followership to someone else. A cacique who failed to reciprocate another cacique could lead a community into war, with its threats and uncertainties. In their roles, therefore, caciques—known in Guaraní as *tubichá*—are better thought of as bearers of the prestige to persuade rather than as holders of the political power to command. Those who might become acquisitive were checked by the fact that the power of reciprocity as a norm was widely distributed among all who lived by it rather than concentrated in the hands of a single individual or institution.

These understandings may have been in flux as Europeans entered the Guaraní world. Father Ruiz de Montoya referred to caciques as enjoying a "noble status bequeathed . . . by ancestors," suggesting that the fluidity of influence and prestige may have been hardening into something more like lineage-based authority.[74] Spanish reports from the earliest years of conquest tell of a cacique known as Macaçu, whom Spaniards recognized as "the key to the whole land," in good measure because he was able to unite the Guaraní for war. Macaçu does not appear to have exercised centralized authority and power so much as he projected notability, maintaining alliances through "beautiful speech" and kinship ties with other leaders at varying levels of Guaraní political structure.[75] It is impossible to know with certainty how solid Macaçu's influence was and how recently established. Nor do we know whether he descended from a line of caciques. Nevertheless, glancing references to hereditary nobility hint that the Guaraní cultural aversion to concentrated political power might have begun to weaken just as Europeans were entering the Guaraní world.

Decades ago, Pierre Clastres argued that demographic expansion may have been contributing to the slow emergence of genuine political authority among Guaraní caciques before contact with Europeans, making them "an example of a primitive society . . . that *could have* become the State."[76] And yet, he concluded, a state did not emerge. What had blocked it, he contended, was not the arrival of Westerners. Instead, drawing on Hélène Clastres's work on the Guaraní, he argued that prophets had risen who called the Guaraní away from the path that would have led to a state-like concentration of power, instead offering them a more auspicious quest—to abandon, and so destroy, society by setting off in search of the Land Without Evil, "the earthly paradise" where crops grew themselves, no one died, and people had nothing to do other than dance and feast and enjoy each other's company among the gods.[77]

This emprise, argued Hélène Clastres, took the form of mass movements—what Pierre Clastres called "mad migrations"—beginning in the late fifteenth century and continuing in the sixteenth. The irony of the proposal is clear: to avoid the concentration of political power and thus preserve society, Guaraní prophets mobilized people in a way that required the dissolution of society. To do so, they had to achieve a kind of centralization no cacique or combination of caciques could have produced at that moment. Pierre Clastres's conclusion—a proto-state strangled at birth by a prophetism exercising a power it rejected—remains highly debatable. Even so, a crucial insight remains: Guaraní life had a dynamic of its own before Europeans came along. There is no reason to suppose they were incapable of confronting change or adapting to it in innovative ways that might be in considerable tension with established norms.

Indeed, linguistic traces hint that the Guaraní reflected critically on their social arrangements. Montoya's *Tesoro* defines *tecócatú* as "good life, free." By itself, this characterization is so broad as to be unremarkable. The illustrations that immediately follow it, however, are tantalizing: "*Tecócatú*, they call savages, who live like beasts. *Tecócatú ahe*, this is a savage."[78] The *they* in the first example is surely the Guaraní (since the authorial voice is Montoya's), though the specific words *savage* and *beast* were Montoya's translation. What was being asserted here? On their face, these phrases suggest that life beyond the confines of social convention could be imagined in positive ways, or at least not purely negative ones. Considering that reciprocity and kinship required constant attention, sensitivity to nuance, and forbearance, is it too much to suppose that the Guaraní could devise a metaphysical escape hatch from their constraints? After all, eighteenth-century Europeans did much the same in debating the freedom of noble savages who were unbound by the chains of social conventions Europeans themselves had forged. Why should we conclude that the

Guaraní could not have developed their own philosophical reaction to social life, one involving a kind of idealized individual liberty in contrast to the liberty of being with others in society?

These are complex questions. They are made more so by the fact that the Guaraní may have shared with other people of Amazonian origin what anthropologists have called "perspectivism," an outlook premised on the idea that the "world is inhabited by different sorts of subjects or persons, . . . which apprehend reality from distinct points of view."[79] From this vantage, animals and humans, rather than existing on opposite sides of an ontological divide, share crucial qualities. To say that a "savage" was a man who lived like a beast may thus not have carried the negative connotations for the Guaraní that it may have for Spanish Christians. Quite the contrary. The Guaraní appear to have recognized themselves as just one among many other creatures of the forest—anteaters, birds, monkeys, and jaguars—whose differing perspectives on reality constituted a common world. At least imaginatively, people who lived like animals were simply those who lived beyond the mutuality of people who lived together in society. Such individuals, by leaving the shelter of common life, exposed themselves fully to the freedom and dangers of being predator and prey. To be a "savage" in this sense was to be strong and independent precisely to the extent one stood beyond the reach of social life and exposed to the perils of predation. At a minimum, the fact that so positive a term as *tecócatú* could be connected to the idea of living outside society and beyond reciprocity suggests that the Guaraní could question their own sociality.[80] By describing the savage-who-lives-like-the-beasts as tecócatú, the Guaraní were not announcing their disdain for social life so much as they were noting the burdens society laid on them—hardly a novel problem for philosophizing humans. The fact that they nevertheless chose to live together rather than disperse into the forest indicates that they understood life together, and the mutuality necessary to maintain it, as a trouble worth staying with.[81] This was the world from which the Guaraní stepped as they met unknown Europeans who entered their lands unbidden in the 1520s.

Before the Guaraní
Friendship and society
During the early decades of the sixteenth century, Europeans were just beginning to grapple with the unfathomability of the "New World."

Broad truths—the extent of the globe, the Biblical origins of Creation, the divisions of humanity—had been thrown into question by the new lands and new peoples that had appeared over the horizon. Iberians were the first Old Worlders to visit this faraway place. They bore with them not only established understandings of the world but also changing attitudes and motivations about how to live in it, especially regarding the role of individual gain in the conduct of social life.

Since the mid-thirteenth century, dominant understandings of human society and relations had been rooted in the idea that human beings were social animals. Following Aristotle, Aquinas had stated that men were inclined by nature to live together with other men. This way of being did not have to be explained as an alternative to some imagined unsocial arrangement, for to be fully human was "to live in society."[82] But because there might be better and worse societies, the crucial question was how to bring out the best in people who lived together. For Aristotle, this did not happen automatically. Most men, he acknowledged, sought what was individually "most advantageous" and lived chiefly to satisfy unlimited "appetites." Rulers should therefore stimulate men to the "character and intelligence" that would express justice, courage, reason, and lead them to limit their desires to what was properly due (*phronesis*). That is, society should teach *virtue* so that men might learn to reject lower appetites for higher qualities.

These excellences were to be expressed in social life through *friendship*. For Aristotle, the highest form of friendship was premised on each person wishing only good for the other, according to their virtues and in light of the good of the whole. In this way, the community would be stable and virtuous. This sublime friendship could be distinguished from two other types: friendship of utility, in which one loves a friend for the sake of what is "useful or agreeable" to oneself, and friendship motivated by the pleasure one derives from being in the company of the other. These latter two, noted Aristotle, were far more prevalent than "friendship of the good," and morally inferior to it—not a basis for common life. True friends, by contrast, mutually behaved as it was "just for them to behave," so that they might "delight in the fact" of each other's virtue.[83] Aquinas had absorbed this understanding into Christian theology, seeing charity as Aristotelian "true friendship" extending beyond the virtuous to embrace even sinners, "whom, out of charity, we love for God's sake."[84] For St. Thomas, this love had the "nature of a first gift, through which all gifts are freely given"—thus did charity-as-friendship express God's grace.[85]

This broad idea of friendship as the ground of social life had become firmly fixed in Catholic Europe by the early sixteenth century and remained entrenched, at least in official and theological circles, even after the Protestant rupture. Aquinas had declared that "among all worldly things there is nothing which seems worthy to be preferred to friendship."[86] Spain's medieval legal code, which appeared at the same time as Aquinas's *Summa*, cited Aristotle for the proposition that "friendship" bound men in "mutual obligation" to one another and so promoted concord among those who belonged to the same land.[87] Friendship (*amistad*), declared Franciscan friar Juan Dueñas in 1542, already with more than a hint that the idea needed reinforcing, "is more precious than any other thing in this life" and must orient all human relations.[88] Men must be guided not by interest but by sociable and companionable instincts, concluded Jean Bodin, so that commonwealths "have no surer foundation than friendship and goodwill among men." Without it, republics could not stand and the world itself "could not subsist."[89]

Gift under strain

As a pillar of social order, friendship was made concrete through recognized patterns of gift giving, which functioned as a "mechanism of social bonding." Particularly among elites, gifting served as "an essential relational order, a repertoire of behavior, a register with its own rules, language, etiquette, and gestures."[90] The practice was widespread and deeply significant. It was tied to religious duty and to the idea that the mutual love and charity of true friendship could bind members of society to one another. Almsgiving to the poor, deathbed donations to churches and monasteries, contributions in exchange for prayers and masses—all were forms of social exchange rooted in the charitable spirit of the gift manifested through wider religious structures.

Gifts were hardly limited to the religious realm. They were also the basis of social intercourse in medieval Europe, used to forge and maintain political alliances, to secure marriages, and to ensure family continuity.[91] Even among the poor, gifts of goods and services circulated among neighbors and friends, marked life events, and underwrote community. At the same time, gifts were also a means to competition, rivalry, and influence.[92] Gifts, in short, expressed a pervasive public meaning and were exchanged without "specific, calculated value" in a "gift economy."[93] Worth was realized in the act of giving rather than embodied in what was given.

This system was similar to and different from gift-reciprocity among the Guaraní. As in South America, gifting in Europe was—in principle—not a mere one-off transaction. It contemplated continued relations. Unlike Guaraní gift-countergift reciprocity, however, European gift giving by this time was increasingly oriented to assuring benefits for individuals—intangible ones, such as salvation; social ones, such as prestige or power; or even the manifest value of wealth itself. Donors were often explicitly strategic with respect to these goals, though the "distinct and delicate combination of 'interestedness' and 'disinterestedness'" still checked the crudest manipulations.[94] This points to a crucial quality of the gift economy in Europe at the dawn of the sixteenth century: gift giving helped redress and manage the social tensions of hierarchical difference—between lords and vassals, nobles and common folk, rich and poor. And yet, there is no denying that the widening scope for material accumulation was creating a new form of domination in everyday life, one privileging those who had access to the thickening circuits of transactional exchange. By contrast, Guaraní gift-reciprocity aimed to stymy social inequality and prevent accumulation of any sort, material or otherwise—with the exception of "prestige" as the recognition of openhandedness in redistribution. As Lévi-Strauss said of people like the Guaraní, "Generosity [was] an essential attribute of power," which precluded pursuit of the latter for its own sake.[95]

Spanish law was especially concerned with ensuring justice in the context of a hierarchical social order that recognized accumulation—of prestige, power, or wealth—as legitimate. The fundamental principle for responding to this challenge was the notion that each person should receive that which properly pertained to his place in the social order—*a cada uno lo suyo*. This idea was codified in the opening section of *Las siete partidas*, Spain's medieval legal code. Justice, "by which the world is sustained," would prevail if laws could teach men to obey their superiors and "love one another." For if each man "refuse[d] to do what he would not want done to himself," all could "live in peace, lawfully and with ease, each seeking what accords to him [*a cada uno lo suyo*]," which will "enrich the people."[96] On this precept, each individual had a rightful place in the social order and was entitled to benefits commensurate to that position. Justice consisted of ensuring that benefits corresponded to station. The king might command some redistribution of advantage to rebalance an unjust situation. But in everyday life, gifts and reciprocal obligations aimed to ensure concord and right relations across the hierarchy that separated and connected superiors and inferiors.

This equilibrating mechanism strained during the sixteenth century. Exchanges motivated by an explicit desire for personal enrichment were still widely considered immoral and unjust.[97] Mutual giving continued to be understood not as a quid pro quo but as a grace without expectation of explicit reward, return, or repayment. Social order demanded such a principle, lest unbridled accumulation reveal hierarchy as nothing more than raw power. And yet, the spirit of the gift was dimming. An annotated 1512 edition of *Seneca's Proverbs* hints at how gift and reciprocity were coming to be seen among Spaniards. In elucidating the aphorism "To receive a benefit is to sell liberty," the author ignored the broader context of Seneca's essay *On Benefits* (c. 1st century CE), which sought to lay bare the spirit of the gift and the social and moral rules governing gift exchange and reciprocity.[98] Against Seneca's nuanced and probing treatment of how and when gifts might be offered and accepted, this author explained that all gifts were made pursuant to ulterior and selfish motives. Receipt of a gift under these circumstances, said the author, necessarily implied a loss of liberty. One who got another to receive a gift had the upper hand in a relationship, since the giver thus appeared to love the receiver more than the receiver the giver. In "selling" his liberty by accepting a gift, the receiver bound himself to reciprocate or to be seen as "ungrateful, one of the worst things among us and which can be said of no one." This tortured rationalization bespoke the extent to which gift-reciprocity, which had long ensured social cohesion, was losing ground to a spirit of exchange premised on one-upmanship.[99]

But the idea of the gift did not go quickly. Covarrubias's 1611 Spanish dictionary noted that the "gift" was something given and received with "the hand."[100] Echoing Seneca's original essay, Covarrubias argued that before extending a hand to accept a gift, the recipient should consider whether the giver was motivated by love—that is, by a desire to benefit the recipient rather than by a self-serving intention. A gift properly offered obliged the recipient to accept it, as one might from a friend (or from God—and who would refuse a gift from God?). Even one in dire need could receive a gift given to address the need, if it was extended in the proper spirit of friendship and accepted with the understanding that it should be reciprocated at a later time. Recipients should refuse gifts evincing an intention to bind them, a situation all too common between hierarchical unequals. This was especially a problem, noted Covarrubias, when a poor friend with an ulterior motive sought to give a gift to a rich friend. The reason for this admonition is obvious: if the poor, moved by self-interest, too often succeeded in obliging the rich through gifts, the very basis of hierarchy could be jeopardized. That such a discussion should have appeared in a dictionary entry suggests how central the "gift," with its promise to bind people across time, remained to European life as late as the early seventeenth century—though it also indicates gift-reciprocity's flagging ability to check self-interest.

"There is no one who does not seek his own interest"

By 1500, the mesh of sensibility connecting love and friendship, gift and reciprocity that had shaped moral and social relations in medieval Europe, was wearing thin.[101] Of course, moral prescriptions had often been bent to self-interested concern and strategic calculation, especially by the powerful. Now, however, social forces building for centuries began to impinge more directly on the lives of ordinary people. It was a complex process. For our purposes, three related developments stand out: the effects of monetization in everyday life, the growing practice of bargaining and contracts between people, and the increasingly desperate effort to reinforce morality against the consequences of individual gain.

As to the first of these, the idea and use of money had grown dramatically since the fourteenth century. And yet, a wave of cash and monetary transactions had not broken over Europe all at once. Through most of the medieval period, currency and credit had been limited to the upper precincts of social life and to large cities and market towns, where goods arrived from distant points. Away from such places, money and markets proper were far less common.[102] Local agricultural products were rarely distributed through markets, in part because transportation remained poor but also because localities were not prepared to subject basic needs to price competition. Trade was hardly a novelty, yet most people did not "live by buying and selling," as Marc Bloch noted long ago. Indeed, during the Middle Ages, commerce, even as barter, was simply one way things were exchanged and was not the most important. Goods often followed the circuits of dependency between lords and vassals, reflecting the fact that "wealth and well-being were inseparable from authority."[103] For this reason, the starting point of market transactions as a distinct phenomenon was not local exchange but long-distance trade from the East.[104] This remained the case through the early decades of the sixteenth century, after which it became far more common for goods to be moved among local markets and for them to be brought from afar to local fairs, where they were transacted in money.

Even so, the increase of money in trade did not imply wide use of currency in everyday exchanges. Money as a means of *measure* became far more pervasive in ordinary transactions but without displacing informal and formal credit arrangements, which remained robust throughout the early modern period. Instead, money became increasingly accepted as the gauge of economic exchanges generally. Already in the fourteenth century, gifts, from donations of alms to testamentary bequests, had in some places come to be denominated in "monies of account," essentially a way of relating one thing to another through a measure of relative value.[105] By the early sixteenth century, trade fairs, such as Spain's Medina del Campo, brought together two thousand merchants to buy and sell, and fifteen bankers to clear accounts, trading entirely in bills of account rather than currency.[106] This trend had been building for nearly three centuries and accelerated after 1500.[107] Theologian Tomás de Mercado, writing from New Spain, pointed out in his *Summa on Trade and Contracts* (1568) that the use of money had grown dramatically in recent times, so that now "money is the price and value of all temporal things" and "it is a universal and necessary rule that there be a measure, fixed and permanent."[108]

One effect of this trend was that the accumulation of money was becoming a form of quotidian power. Contemporaries understood the social effects monetization was having, particularly in setting the rich against the poor. So great had the greed for gold and silver become, wrote Antonio Guevara in his *Clock of Princes* (1529), that "rancor and hate" had led the rich to murmur and the poor to blaspheme (and this before the great mineral discoveries in the New World). To the same point, Juan Vives concluded in his treatise *On Assistance to the Poor* (1532) that money, which had once been an instrument for meeting needs and ensuring none starved, had lately become a means of honor, dignity, and power and a device of arrogance, wrath, contempt, and anything money will "reap." Covarrubias's dictionary corroborated the point, noting that the definition of *rich* (*rico*) had transmogrified during the sixteenth century: where *rich* had once simply connoted the status of nobility, "today there has arisen with this noun of *rich*, those who have much money and property, and these are now the nobles, and gentlemen, and Counts and Dukes, *because money subjects all things to itself*." "Life is in money," Vives had already declared, a pursuit at which Spaniards were unsurpassed.[109]

Day-to-day discourse and practice began to reflect the greater centrality of money and transactional exchange in social life. Broad notions of human sociability narrowed as everyday encounters focused more tightly on "bargaining and contract."[110] Covarrubias's *Tesoro* linked *comunicar* (friendly communication) to *tratar* (to treat, or deal with), one definition of which was "to do business, selling goods."[111] Across Spain and Europe, buyers and sellers increasingly haggled over price through the medium of money, even in barter situations, introducing into daily life a kind of routinized duplicity.[112] As Mercado wryly noted, bargains were conducted not between "good Angels, who never lie or fail in their promises" but between men who were disposed to take license in their dealings with each other.[113] Martín Azpilcueta's 1554 manual for confessors warned against misusing words to commit fraud, and Saravia de la Calle's *On the Instruction of Merchants* (1544) noted that those engaged in buying and selling were given to "lying, swearing oaths, perjuring themselves" to mislead each other and bamboozle their customers. And because it was commonly held that "the value of a thing was just what it could be sold for," said Azpilcueta, confessors needed to ensure confessants were clear about their intentions and how they communicated them, lest they fall into mortal sin.[114]

These commentaries were part of a larger moral debate regarding the slow transformation of motivation that had been underway for some time. Italian humanist Poggio Bracciolini published his dialogue *Against Avarice* in 1428. In light of recent developments in a commercializing Italy, Bracciolini took up the problem of greed in human affairs. His argument took the form of a dinner conversation between three fictional churchmen. Antonio Loschi, a pontifical secretary, states bluntly that everything is "done for money" and all men are guided by the desire for "gain." Avarice is a "natural thing" and "necessary" to civic life.[115] Without the goad of greed, there would be neither business nor work, for no one does anything "without hope of it." So, though avarice can lead to excess, those who are moved chiefly by money are the "basis and foundation" of the state.[116] For this reason, concludes Antonio, avarice, once thought a vice, must now be considered a virtue that fosters economy and underwrites charity—an early example of the effort to alchemize greed into good.

Although Antonio accepts this understanding of avarice as a self-evident statement about human motivation, the two other participants in the dialogue insist otherwise, suggesting a widening fault line between moral condemnations of avarice and emergent notions of money and commerce as positive social values. Another pontifical secretary, Bartolomeo de Montepulciano, rails against the "hunger to accumulate wealth" as an "enemy of nature," precisely because it knows no limits. Andrea of Constantinople, a pious churchman recognized for his friendliness and gaiety, agrees, arguing that avarice is unnatural, or else everyone would be born greedy, which clearly is not the case. Rather, avaricious men are few and come to their vice not by birth but "out of distorted opinion." The avaricious person, concludes Bartolomeo, is a "most terrible monster," a "slave" to private interests, opposed to the "obligations of nature itself." Such an attitude, far from promoting social life, is "hostile to everyone." Avarice refuses "friendship," states Andrea, leads men to treat all others as enemies, weakens "social bonds," and destroys "human society," for without friendship, men will fight one another in thrall to an "insatiable greed to accumulate money."[117]

Such fears sharpened in the sixteenth century. In a world of commerce and money, what could check men's worst impulses without strangling prosperity?[118] More and more, gain was coming to be recognized as a spur to economic activity, as Bracciolini's Antonio Loschi insisted. Yet, the widening sphere of commerce continued to provoke profound disquiet in Spain and elsewhere. Cristóbal Villalón, in *Beneficial Treatise on Exchanges* (1546), argued that "greed" and "avarice" were causing "total destruction and loss" of social life.[119] In the same spirit, sixteenth-century English rhetorician Thomas Wilson observed that "if I should wholly minde myne own ease, and followe gain . . . why should not other use the same libertie, and so every man for hymselfe, and the Devill for us all, catch that catch may?"[120] Competition had grown to such an extent, wrote Tomás Mercado from Mexico, that "the whole world is not enough for even one individual, much less for everyone." Citing Aristotle, he warned of dire consequences: "There is no one who does not seek his own interest" at the expense of the "common good," which stood as the moral and political responsibility of all.[121] It was for wise laws and moral rectitude to calm the "furious desire of the seller," while promoting exchange and trade. Merchants should satisfy themselves with "moderate gain," especially in situations where they could bend circumstances to enrich themselves.[122]

The dilemmas of commerce

Commerce, said critics, was reweaving everyday life. Money was becoming an instrument of manipulation, empowering the desire for gain in new ways, turning it into an engine of "economic dynamism and social mobility," as well as of exclusion and inequality.[123] Men's aspirations, once defined by feats of chivalry—mercilessly mocked by Cervantes, who also rued their passing in *Don Quixote*—now were fevered by money. Merchandise, observed Mercado, had inflamed "exorbitant and disordered desires" for acquisition.[124] Indeed, the idea that each man was entitled to seek only that gain commensurate to his merit inverted during the sixteenth century, so that gain, especially as signaled by the accumulation of money and goods, came to be accepted as proof itself of individual merit, with little concern for how it was come by.[125] This was the world of *Don Dinero*—that "Powerful Gentleman" Lord Money.[126] Where once had stood "ancient friendships between each other," lamented the Rooster in Cristóbal Villalón's widely read *El Crotalón* (1552), now everyone sought only "to advance over others . . . through commerce." One advantage of hell, according to a resident there, was that "respect among men" held no sway. So widespread had the "greed of men" and the "thirst for enrichment" become, even among ordinary people, said the Rooster, that Lucifer himself could remark on the shortage of demons to torment the throngs of merchants, money changers, and swindlers that had shown up in recent times.[127]

These writers saw commerce as battering the moral and religious foundations of social life. The Bible had long censured the pursuit of gain. The Old Testament repeatedly warns against "love of money," for it can never be satisfied. The New Testament rails against "abundance of possessions" and condemns "rich people" who seek "luxury and self-indulgence." St. Paul admonished that "love of money is the root of all evil."[128] This was established doctrine. Aquinas had wrestled with such passages. He was of two minds. He feared that men would look after only their own interest, which could shatter social relations because of the boundless acquisitiveness money promoted. In a society of trade, each man would work only for "his own profit," turning him aside from "pursuit of the common good," for commerce introduces "greed . . . into the citizens' hearts," making all things "venal." As a result, honor would fall only to the rich, and civic life would be corrupted. And yet, Aquinas himself inflected these views by admitting that merchants, even when trucking in money, could be useful to the community, for they "brought goods from elsewhere" that were valuable in the city.[129]

This tension over commerce shaped social life in Europe during the sixteenth century. From a theological perspective, society was not just some pragmatic arrangement, a contract struck among men following Creation. The social order represented the essence of human existence as God had intended human beings live it after the Fall. God had made this plain by depriving humans of the means to lead solitary lives—thick skins, claws, horns, speed of foot such as other animals had—and instead endowed them with "reason" and the means to communicate with each other, language. These faculties, while inadequate for individual survival, enabled them to meet their needs—for food, shelter, security— together.[130] Like animals did, humans had to respond to immediate material challenges. Unlike animals, humans depended on a God-given predisposition to and need for sociability. But there was a catch. Since material concerns persisted even within society, men could pursue individual needs or desires at the expense of others, despite the embrace of sociality. Aquinas recognized this difficulty and denied that happiness could consist of wealth and money. Greed would lead each person, especially the merchant, "to work only for his own profit, despising the public good." The greater danger, however, was not simply that a few men might seek their advantage at the expense of others. It was that the unvirtuous and uncharitable few would corrupt the whole of "civic life."[131]

Concerns regarding the morally corrosive effects of commerce were hardly new. Dante had consigned usurers to the seventh circle of hell, along with the violent, blasphemers, and sodomites. He had buried frauds deeper still, in the eighth circle, with those who contributed to the "progressive disintegration of every social relationship, personal and public."[132] Yet, the steady expansion of trade and a continual increase in the use of money slowly softened the condemnation of commercial activity. Even in Aquinas's time, merchants routinely lent money at interest, despite universal theological censure of usury, and civil law effectively condoned the practice.[133] This gap between moral prescription and actual conduct only widened during later centuries, so that not long after 1500, commerce had come to depend so completely on the capacity to borrow, and few were prepared to lend without compensation, that the ban against lending at interest was recognized chiefly in the breach.

In the sixteenth century, moralists despaired as the thousand moral restraints inhibiting self-interested activity were being unraveled by the thousand fingers of the emerging economy's principal mechanism: price. In the 1550s, Azpilcueta argued that gain for gain's sake was immoral; commerce could be justified only if it served the common good rather than private interest.[134] Exactly how remained unclear. Saravia de la Calle worried that if prices were rooted in *costs*, merchants would inflate prices at their whim, defrauding consumers. Domingo de Soto maintained that the price of goods was determined "by the measure in which they serve the needs of mankind . . . for want is the basis for price," though, contrary to Saravia, he believed that costs of production—"labor, trouble, and risk"—had to be taken into account.[135] There are deep complexities here. The main point is that fundamental notions of motivation, desire, value, and morality were being scrambled to the extent price was pervading social life.

This fact became a pivot of social and moral agita. There was a broad consensus that money represented a universal measure of value, or at least a universal means of exchange. And yet, currencies varied from region to region and across time, making it especially easy for merchants to take advantage of the unwary, the less shrewd, or the poorly informed.[136] This was not just a matter of isolated transactions. Reflecting on sixteenth-century society, Mercado noted that while the king sought above all to keep prices low, because the "intent and desire of the republic" was to ensure the "utility and benefit" of all, merchants aimed to buy cheap and sell dear, regardless of the effect on buyers or on the republic. And yet, commercial instincts had advanced so far that Mercado himself concluded that "universal love" could no longer curb excess. At best, the "particular interest" of those who possessed some form of property might allow them to profit while conserving a just "share of goods" within society.[137]

The question of how to achieve this equipoise sparked a theological debate over *just-price* doctrine. Aquinas had held that the price of things should conform to justice along two axes.[138] First, price should reflect a rough equality of knowledge and ability between parties to an exchange—what was known as commutative justice. This principle was anchored in theological norms of charity as friendship. Merchants were understood to be price makers rather than price takers. Every commercial transaction, therefore, and every price represented an exercise in will and intellect—gifts from God—and all such decisions were governed by an ethical obligation to the other party and to society at large.[139] Price setting and commerce, in short, were inherently moral acts and merchants were "morally ruled beings."[140] Manipulating prices to individual advantage was therefore sinful by definition for, in effect, the individual greed of one party subjected the other party. Nevertheless, from the fourteenth century there was growing acceptance, even within the church, that sellers could profit from an exchange so long as their gain was neither excessive nor taken "in order to accumulate more and more."[141] In essence, the demands of commutative justice could be satisfied so long as two conditions held: that the price of a good remain within a range defined by upper and lower bounds reflecting the community's wider sense of the good's worth, and that the consciences of the parties, which could in principle be examined in the confessional, be honest, true, and charitable.[142]

Distributive justice represented the other axis of just-price doctrine. If commutative justice aimed to protect parties in the context of individual transactions, distributive justice was concerned with society as a whole and for all its members. From this perspective, price represented a broad social concern. Municipalities in the Middle Ages had recognized this fact, fixing local prices, especially for staples, such as bread and other foodstuffs upon which the poor depended.[143] The goal of regulation had been to prevent hoarding and profiteering, especially during lean times. With respect to distributive justice, the fundamental purpose of exchange was to allow households to meet "the necessities of life."[144] By the sixteenth century, as ordinary folk increasingly depended on getting fair value for their work or wares or in satisfying basic needs, this issue became urgent. Of course, not all transactions were tainted by fraud or tarnished by uncertainty. But enough were that exchanges generally came under a cloud of suspicion.

Theologically, the reason for wariness was clear. As commerce took on a greater role in social relations generally, price became a crucial mediator of livelihoods among ordinary people. This posed a profound theological and moral challenge: price increasingly dictated the manner and extent to which people gained access to the goods of Creation, which God had explicitly made for all. Merchants who gouged ordinary people were

FIGURE 1.1. Pieter Bruegel and Pieter van der Heyden, *Avaritia* (1558). *Source:* Pieter Bruegel (drawing) and Pieter van der Heyden (engraving), *Avaritia* (1558). Metropolitan Museum of Art. Wikimedia Commons (public domain).

appropriating Creation for their own ends and harming others. Thus, while commercial greed might produce prosperity, it also imperiled social order and God's plan, for it threatened to deprive many, and especially the poor, meaningful participation in Creation.[145] This was why, centuries earlier, Aquinas had argued that social life be organized for the "common good of the many, over and above that which impels toward the particular good of each individual."[146] Price needed to be made to serve society at large rather than just the desires of a few. It was up to merchants to engage each other and their customers according to the principles of commutative justice, a task in which they might be helped by theology, confession, and the law. It was for the king and his subjects, including merchants, to ensure distributive justice in their transactions by embodying and vivifying the *amor affectatio*—the loving disposition and mutual attraction—that grounded life in common.

By the middle of the sixteenth century, despite moral qualms, no one seriously proposed that commerce cease. The question was how a commercial society should be arranged. Theologians sought to frame and limit the motivational upheaval threatened by the individual pursuit of gain as novel economic circumstances gnawed at charity and tempted to sin. Where not so long ago, lust and pride and been the focus of confessor's concerns, in the rapidly commercializing sixteenth century, avarice now ran free. There is no better illustration of this than Pieter van der Heyden's 1558 engraving of Bruegel's *Avarice* (Fig. 1.1). An image of moral chaos before the "small idol of . . . gain" could hardly be clearer.[147]

The sharp-edged literature of the day reflected a profound sense that "the organic web of sympathies," commitments, and norms that had shaped desire and sustained society for centuries was coming undone.[148] The problem was not that notions of friendship, grace, charity, gift, and reciprocity were vanishing. They simply were coming to be seen as negotiable or optional in the face of novel opportunities for gain. Everyday life increasingly seemed an arena of strategic calculation in a field of motivational cues characterized by individual self-regard. Everyone understood this or at least sensed it, though still only a relative few were in a position to benefit from it. This was the world from which Europeans stepped as they met the Guaraní on unfamiliar terrain throughout the sixteenth century and beyond.

*   *   *

To demonstrate a laminar flow, individual drops of different colored dyes are piped into a viscous medium alongside one another. The fluid is slowly revolved in a clockwise direction by a hand crank. What had been single droplets extend, becoming threads and bands that, after several rotations, overlap and intermingle to the point of indistinctness. The direction of rotation is then reversed. After an equal number of revolutions counterclockwise, the apparently undifferentiated color respools, re-forming individually identifiable blots of suspended dye. In other words, even as the initial rotations appear to effect an irreversible mixing and a loss of all coherence, the original droplets are always still present. The purpose of this chapter has been to juxtapose Guaraní and European conceptions regarding the role of exchange in human social life just as they were about to come into contact, so that as they mingle we may nevertheless have a sense of where they began.

2

Of Gain and Gift

Each Christian was forced to take Indian women of the land.
Francisco de Andrada to the Council of the Indies[1] (1545)

. . . because you will not serve us.
Atimonga, Cario-Guaraní tubichá[2] (ca. 1540s)

EUROPEANS ENTERED what came to known as the Río de la Plata region
in 1516. A small group of men led by Juan Díaz de Solís had sailed down
the Brazilian coast to the mouth of the great river flowing from the interior of South America. A landing party was almost immediately attacked
by Indigenous people. The survivors withdrew. In 1524–1526, Aleixo García led another expedition to discover an overland route from the Atlantic coast to a rumored Silver Mountain ruled by a White King. A Portuguese adventurer acting on behalf of the Spanish monarchy, García and
half a dozen followers paddled and trekked from the Brazilian Atlantic coast to the uncharted interior of South America, picking their way
through the jungle, passing Iguazu Falls and crossing the Paraná River.
They struck north along the Paraguay River and stopped at the site where
Asunción would later be founded. There, the tiny band joined a column
of two thousand Guaraní warriors looking to reestablish contact with
Guaraní groups that had migrated to the eastern edge of the Inca empire
decades earlier. After canoeing north along the Paraguay, they trekked
west across the arid Chaco. With the Andes on the horizon, they crossed
into Inca territory. García and the Guaraní immediately secured local allies through gift giving and began to attack Inca outposts. After much
fighting, and fearing Inca troops might be on the way, the newcomers returned via the Pilcomayo River to the Paraguay, bearing silver and copper
artifacts (Map 2.1).[3]

It was several more years before European explorers ventured deeply
into the Plata region, drawn by reports of the Inca's vast wealth.[4] Accounts

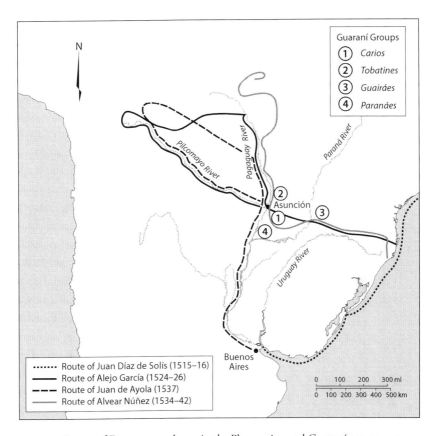

Guaraní Groups
① Carios
② Tobatines
③ Guairáes
④ Paranáes

Pilcomayo River
Paraguay River
Paraná River
Asunción
Uruguay River
Buenos Aires

...... Route of Juan Díaz de Solís (1515–16)
——— Route of Alejo García (1524–26)
– – – Route of Juan de Ayola (1537)
~~~~~ Route of Alvear Núñez (1534–42)

0   100   200   300 mi
0 100 200 300 400 500 km

MAP 2.1. Routes of European explorers in the Plata region and Guaraní groups east of the Paraguay River. *Source:* Kleinpenning, *Paraguay,* 112 (fig. 3.9), 138 (fig. 4.1), 156 (fig. 4.3).

of García's expedition circulated in Spain, arousing promiscuous fantasies of precious metals. Such stories had the power to move men to reward and ruin, even madness, well into the 1540s. Pedro de Mendoza's campaign, jointly funded by the Spanish monarchy and German bankers, sailed up the Plata in 1536. While Pizarro had already invaded the Inca empire from the north by that time and returned to Spain with gold and silver, some hoped that a route east to the Atlantic might still be discovered.[5] Numbering thirteen ships and fifteen hundred men, Mendoza's expedition was charged with settling one thousand colonists to secure a foothold in the area. The fleet founded Buenos Aires on the southern bank of the Plata in 1536. Three months later two-thirds of Mendoza's men had died from hunger.[6] Subsequent expeditions led by Juan de Ayolas, Alvar Núñez Cabeza de Vaca, and Domingo de Irala extended Mendoza's route to the Paraná and Paraguay Rivers. They founded Asunción along the Paraguay River in 1537 at the very place García had joined with the Guaraní a decade earlier.[7]

Other than being an ideal spot from which to seek a route to the Andes, what distinguished the region around Asunción from Buenos Aires was the relative density of human habitation. Nearer the mouth of the Plata, Indigenous presence was thin, consisting chiefly of small bands of hunter-gatherers. Along the Paraguay at Asunción, the Cario-Guaraní were more populous and dense. Their territory boasted large villages, settled agriculture, and clearly identifiable caciques who held sway with larger tribal groups. As many as two hundred thousand Guaraní of various tribes lived east of Asunción in the 1530s and another two hundred thousand north in the Guairá, perhaps five hundred thousand in the wider region—hardly the Central Valley of Mexico with its many millions, but nevertheless a notable concentration of people for early sixteenth-century lowland South America.[8] Moreover, Indigenous groups there appear to have been less hostile than those closer to the coast, perhaps a reflection of their security in greater numbers, their confidence as warriors, and the relative abundance of an economy that combined settled agriculture, hunting, and foraging.

*   *   *

Trade and plunder

When sixty Spaniards disembarked in August 1537 to establish Asunción and build a palisade, the Guaraní seemed prepared to tolerate their presence. Early encounters were mostly peaceful and relatively symmetrical, if marked by mutual caution. The Cario-Guaraní of the immediate area still remembered their alliance of convenience with García in 1524–25. The Europeans' return appears neither to have alarmed them nor particularly to have excited them.[9] According to expedition member Francisco de Villalta, the Guaraní were willing to trade provisions and information for clothing, beads, and metal objects. Fishhooks, needles, knives, and hatchets were of special interest to the Guaraní, objects prized for their usefulness. In forest life, metal knives and machetes, fishhooks and needles had obvious advantages of durability and efficacy over the stone and bone versions fashioned by the Guaraní. These advantages were most obvious with iron hatchets. One of the most laborious aspects of Guaraní material life was the clearing of trees to open new fields as old ones became exhausted. Burning did part of the job. But large trees and stumps had to be removed by hand. Where stone hatchets worked by pulping a tree trunk, metal axes could sever it.[10] A job that might take weeks with stone implements could be done in days with metal ones.[11]

Despite their willingness to trade food for iron tools, the Guaraní pointedly refused to "serve the Christians" with their labor. As a result, and to the frustration of Spaniards, the fort at Asunción took far longer to build than initially anticipated.[12] Villalta's account suggests that tensions between the Indians and the Europeans began to sharpen from that point forward. Occasional bands of Spaniards passing through Guaraní territory had been no strain on local production; as the German explorer Ulrich Schmidel noted, Guaraní agriculture, hunting, and foraging provided abundance. A permanent European settlement was another matter, particularly when its residents seemed to expect the Guaraní to supply provisions and even provide labor.[13] Nevertheless, Asunción's earliest settlers understood the delicacy of their situation. As Schmidel pointed out, thousands—perhaps tens of thousands—of Indian warriors might be called into action on short notice.[14] Even if this was an exaggeration and even if Spanish firearms, steel, and shields were an advantage in battle, European interlopers knew they had to tread carefully in this new land where they were outnumbered by orders of magnitude on a terrain new to them.

A rough balance between Guaraní and Spaniards held until early 1538, when the area around Asunción came under a plague of locusts that devastated Guaraní fields, the ones that also fed European newcomers. The Guaraní went hungry. Many died. Villages turned inward and refused to trade food for Spanish objects, even metal tools. Through the worst of it, Spaniards fended for themselves with great effort. Desperation led Spaniards to raid local villages. "We went about taking food by force and fighting with the natives of that land," Villalta explained in a later letter to the king, "because they would not give it for anything."[15] This plundering enraged the local Guaraní, who had tolerated Spaniards but had never accepted them as permanent residents of the region or acknowledged any obligation to support them. In early 1539, a local cacique planned an all-out assault on the Spanish palisade. The plot, which reportedly involved eight thousand Guaraní warriors, was betrayed by a cacique's daughter, who had been given into Captain Juan de Guzmán's service. Spaniards acted preemptively, hanging and quartering the conspirators and eliminating Native leaders.[16] Guaraní groups responded by decamping for the deep forest, the gravest response to social crisis short of war. The effect on the still fragile Spanish settlement was immediate, for Asunción was utterly dependent on Guaraní agriculture and provisioning for its survival. Settlers feared they might starve. Only by showering the Indians with "gifts and good words" did Spaniards persuade some to stay and others to return to their villages.[17]

The following years were tense. Though there is little to suggest that the Guaraní had made a broad decision to allow the newcomers to remain permanently in their lands, the nature of their relationship began to shift. The pivot toward gifts not only helped keep the peace. It also appears to have led the Guaraní around Asunción to see the Europeans as potentially useful allies in fights against their own rivals. This was not merely a request on the Guaraní's part. One member of the Asunción city council observed that to secure the Cario-Guaraní "in our friendship, it behooves us and is necessary to make war on Indians who are their enemies, and so ours . . . lest they turn their weapons and make war on us . . . and oust us from this land."[18] These campaigns, known as *entradas* (entries), were the occasion for several Spanish-Guaraní victories, which enhanced the military prestige of both and bound them in a novel and highly volatile arrangement.[19] It was not long before Spaniards began to see advantage in fighting against the Cario-Guaraní's enemies. Captain Domingo de Irala noted in 1541 that the alliance had led to the "destruction of many groups of Indians who have shown us no friendship."[20]

These triumphs emboldened Spaniards, for naked force and pillage seemed to be winning the day. Conquistadors could enter enemy villages and plunder as they pleased. These operations must have seemed promising in light of Asunción's growing European population. In late 1541, several hundred Spaniards had abandoned Buenos Aires in order to concentrate their presence in a single settlement. Their arrival in early 1542 boosted Asunción's Spanish population to seven hundred or so (and made it the only European settlement east of the Andes).[21] Although they had brought three hundred Indigenous women with them from the coast to serve in their "homes and fields," it was clear that Asunción would need more labor if the town were not to suffer Buenos Aires's fate.[22] Entradas were a way for Spaniards to acquire goods and especially women. While it was not unknown for Guaraní to take women during wars of vengeance among Indigenous groups, raiding of this sort appears not to have been widely practiced among the Guaraní before European arrival.

In time, success in local entradas turned Spanish sights to more remote areas, especially the lands of the Guaycurú people of the distant Chaco, which promised abundant goods and many captives. Some Guaraní caciques near Asunción allied with Spanish captains and began to take part in joint raids that aimed to accumulate captive women. There were successes. But these forays were not without risks. For instance, a column of nearly one hundred Spaniards and many Guaraní warriors and attendants paddled north on the Paraguay in late 1542, led by Captain Irala.[23] The Spaniards knew they would need local guides to enter the great Chaco desert safely. They quickly discovered, however, that local Guarambarense-Guaraní groups would not show them the way or otherwise aid them. This rebuff appears to have been rooted in the opposition of a prestigious Guarambarense cacique in the region, the mburubichá Acararé. Historian Florencia Roulet has conjectured persuasively that Aracaré, having heard the stories of Spanish raids and the taking of women, called upon local communities to refuse to help the Spaniards.[24] Given the limits of cacical authority in Indigenous society, Aracaré likely said the words that resonated broadly with local people who, despite the newcomers' offers of alliance, may have feared they would be the next targets of European opportunism.

This stance may have been more than just a response to immediate risk. Aracaré may have come to understand that Spanish adventurers posed an existential threat to Guaraní life. Caciques were willing to ally with the Spaniards on equal terms, subject to what Roulet has called "balanced reciprocity." Aracaré may have feared that equality was only an illusion. According to Spanish reports after the fact, Aracaré warned his people that if they did not turn back from the path of serving the Spaniards, they would end up "being their slaves." If instead the Guaraní steadfastly refused them aid, they would leave the land, allowing the Indians to be "free" once again.[25] As Roulet points out, we cannot know what Guaraní words Aracaré used that were rendered as *esclavos* (slaves) and *libres* (free) in Spanish accounts. But it is worth noting that Montoya's Guaraní dictionary gives for *esclavo* a Guaraní word rooted in the act of taking or capturing, as in fishing or hunting as well as in war.[26] A warrior captured during war effectively forfeited his life to his captors, to be killed in an act of ritual cannibalism after a period of acculturation that might last years. In all likelihood, Aracaré was not suggesting that Spaniards proposed to eat Indian captives, though later encounters indicate that some Indigenous groups feared precisely this. What he may have been trying to convey to his listeners was that they risked a broad, permanent captivity and loss of liberty if they acceded to Spanish demands. This would have been an expansion of well-understood ideas regarding captivity, and there is no reason to suppose the cacique was incapable of using a familiar trope in novel ways.

Things did not end well for Aracaré. Irala captured him during a parley and hanged him. To justify Irala's action to the king, Cabeza de Vaca tried to portray the episode as a unified Guaraní rebellion against royal authority, with Aracaré as inciter and leader. This was likely an exaggeration on the governor's part.[27] It is far more likely that local Indigenous groups acted much as they had in response to raids near Asunción in 1538–39, when whole villages fled to the forest, where Spaniards followed at their peril. Aracaré had been in no position to compel a unified response by local villages. He may have enjoyed special prestige among caciques, but this did not give him broad powers of command over disparate groups. If to Spaniards the Indigenous people of this region had seemed to rise up as one, it may say as much about Spanish misunderstandings of Guaraní political arrangements as about Guaraní intentions.

Regardless, Aracaré's murder was not without consequence. He was an ally and kinsman to other local caciques, in particular a "brother" of another regional mburubichá called Tabaré. His ignominious death called for vengeance. But the decision to go to war, or not, remained with the tubichá (cacique or chief) of each local village. Many caciques decided against engaging the Spaniards directly, given the power of European weaponry. Others presented a united front, threatening to kill the interlopers if they did not leave. One Spanish captain tried to mobilize "friendly" Cario-Guaraní against these "rebels," but they refused to join him. Despite the lack of help, a heavily armed Spanish column led by Captain Irala succeeded in breaking through the Indians' entrenched positions, torching several villages in the process. The rebels soon surrendered, promising friendship. The Spaniards responded not by punishing Tabaré and other rebellious leaders but instead by renewing offers of alliance, signaled by gifts—in one instance four hundred bars of iron that could be fashioned into axes and machetes—and good words, a reprise of what had happened after the uprisings around Asunción in 1538–39.[28]

While the uprising sought to redress the imbalance created by Aracaré's death, it also aimed to draw a line in the sand regarding the forcible taking of things and people.[29] One cacique sent a message to Governor Cabeza de Vaca, noting that the Spaniards came into their villages and, "against our will," took things by force.[30] The seizing of Indian women was especially galling. Before the arrival of Spaniards, it had not been unknown for Guaraní to take female captives and integrate them into the community. As Cabeza de Vaca's chronicle of Asunción's early years pointed out, when Guaraní took women captives, they "gave them liberty and did not harm them."[31] The Spaniards were up to something new. By taking Indigenous women en masse, they seemed intent on accumulating them as one might any other resource, thereby removing them from their social and biological role in reproducing Guaraní life, instead turning them to other uses. Some among the Cario-Guaraní appear to have been willing to accept this increasingly instrumental treatment with regard to captive women from other groups. But they deeply resented Spaniards who presumed to take their own women. One cacique complained to the governor that if we have two daughters, you will take one, leaving us one to give to other Indians so that they might serve us, but "you will not serve us."[32] By *serve*, this cacique meant "accept the mutual obligations of brothers-in-law." In other words, the Spaniards' actions not only weakened the Guaraní's capacity to bind themselves to each other through the gifting of women, it also signaled a refusal to engage with the Guaraní reciprocally in pacific and productive ways.

Offering kin, buying women

At this delicate point, both sides seemed to be seeking a way forward. Spaniards appeared to understand that simple trade was not enough to ensure the level of cooperation they required if they were to profit from their situation. And yet, they seemed to sense that violence alone, or the threat of it, might not secure their position in Paraguay. Their presence in the region had depended from the outset on Guaraní forbearance. And even if the tables had been turned somewhat with Spanish victories over the Guaraní in combat, it remained nearly impossible to keep villagers from escaping to the dense forest, where Europeans pursued at great risk. The Cario-Guaraní near Asunción, whatever their ambivalence toward the newcomers, appear to have reconciled themselves to a sobering reality: the outsiders might be there to stay. Caciques and ordinary people had repeatedly witnessed Spaniards' capacity for violence and doubtless understood the dangers of persistent animosity toward them.

Under such circumstances, gifts may have the seemed surest route to some semblance of peace, for friendship mediated by gift-reciprocity was the principal means of securing intercommunal balance. Although we can only speculate on the discussions and decisions within communities, caciques may have judged this approach could be extended to the Spaniards. To do so, they would need to offer the one gift that, in Guaraní experience, could bind groups (even erstwhile enemies) to one another in enduring ways: women. Caciques pioneered the practice of offering female kin to Spaniards. The first known instances came in direct response to Spanish military victories over Cario-Guaraní warriors. On two occasions in 1539, defeated caciques offered "daughters and sisters" to Spanish captains, conveying their desire to "make peace."[33] It was not long before other caciques began to do the same with other Spanish captains, seeking to convert these powerful men into *tobayas* (brothers-in-law). Captain Juan de Salazar forged an alliance with the mburubichá Cupiratí in just this way.[34] In principle, one who accepted a daughter or sister bore a persisting obligation of labor and alliance to the giver. From a Guaraní perspective, this implied peaceful relations among equals looking toward an open-ended future. The shift from the barter of goods to gift, particularly the gift of women, thus represented a broad, uncoordinated effort among Guaraní caciques to bind Spaniards to a dynamic interethnic equilibrium premised on mutual dependence.

Initially, such exchanges appear to have been limited to pacts between caciques and captains. As the practice of offering and accepting women widened, the logic of collective alliance seems to have warped. Spaniards quickly began to proffer goods, especially much-coveted iron bars and tools that had been a staple of trade since the Spaniards' arrival, for Guaraní women. Before long, not only caciques but also ordinary Guaraní men began to offer female kin to common settlers in exchange for goods. According to Schmidel, Guaraní men accepted trifles—"a shirt, a knife for cutting bread, a bar of iron, or any other bauble of the sort"—for their daughters, sisters, and nieces.[35] A scandalized priest noted that young Guaraní men had taken to "trading" their female kin in the "streets and plazas" of Asunción.[36] Such statements smack of exaggerated moral outrage and cultural incomprehension, but they point to the complicated ways transactions in goods, well understood by both sides, were intersecting with underlying Guaraní norms regarding gift, reciprocity, and the role of women in social life.

Indeed, the view that Guaraní were *selling* women and Spanish men *buying* them almost surely misreckoned what was happening at the point of encounter between distinct modes of exchange. Superficially, settlers' reasons for seeking such exchanges seem straightforward enough: the availability of Guaraní women simultaneously solved two vexing problems, one personal, another economic: the paucity of European women in Asunción and a growing need for labor. As to the first, few European women had arrived with settlers during the early years, and not many afterwards. This circumstance had led Spaniards to start taking Guaraní women in raids within a year of coming to the region. The situation changed dramatically once Guaraní men began to offer women in gift. The state of affairs was unprecedented for ordinary Spaniards. Only in fevered imaginings could they have conjured a place where concubines were so easily gotten for tradeable goods. One critic noted in the mid-1540s that the practice of accumulating women had become so widespread in Asunción "that even Mohammed's Koran would not permit such a disgrace."[37] In Spain, religious norms tightly constrained marriage, limiting men to a single wife, with punishments for adultery. In Paraguay, settlers faced a situation in which Guaraní men seemed eager to "trade" their female relatives for trinkets. By 1541, Captain Irala noted that there were 700 "wives" for 250–300 Spaniards.[38] Sex aside, these men also wanted Guaraní women for work. Direct swaps of goods for food had sufficed to sustain a few hundred Spaniards during early settlement. But as their numbers increased, settlers realized they would need an agricultural labor force. They had not come to the New World to be dirt farmers. Their goal was to draft Native people to that work, one way or another. Yet Asunción's residents had discovered something quite unusual compared to other areas of European settlement in the New World. Among the Guaraní, women rather than men labored in the fields. "We find in this land," wrote cleric Francisco de Andrada to the Council of the Indies in Madrid, "the pernicious custom that it is women who plant and collect the provisions, and with the poverty of this land, we would not be able to sustain ourselves, so that each Christian was forced to take Indian women of the land, satisfying their relatives with goods so that [these women] would feed them."[39]

Though this arrangement might seem an uncomplicated transaction—women's labor for goods in trade—the quote hints that the relationships being created as Guaraní women began to pass between Guaraní men and Spanish men were complex, produced by the ill meshing of barter exchange and kinship-oriented reciprocity. The reference to "relatives" suggests that Spaniards could not expect to alienate Guaraní women altogether from their social context. Although it makes no sense to suppose that male kin were negotiating on an even footing—and it is not clear that *negotiation* in a narrowly transactional sense is the right term here—they knew where their daughters, sisters, and nieces were going and they appear to have demanded "satisfaction." This intentionality contrasts sharply with the violent "takings" during raids, which were always characterized as "against our will" by the Guaraní.[40] We cannot know how these women, mostly adolescents, understood what was happening to them. It is possible such exchanges mimicked Guaraní marriage up to a point, which may have been something of a comfort, at least to begin with. Nor does Andrada's account speak chiefly of caciques, captains, and alliances. These exchanges seemed rather more humdrum affairs conducted between common settlers—"from the oldest to the youngest"—and ordinary Guaraní, who were coming to call each other "brothers-in-law" or "fathers-in-law."[41]

Whatever continuities the Guaraní may have discerned between old ways and new practices, norms were being stretched as Guaraní women were drawn or taken into Spanish households. Regardless of status, Spaniards who accepted multiple women acted more like caciques or shamans, accumulating women, than like ordinary Guaraní men, who generally had a single wife. "Christians," said critics, might have twenty to thirty Guaraní women, and those with fewer than five, could be counted as poor.[42] Such numbers may have been true of Asunción's more prominent Spaniards—conquistadors and their retinue. Most settlers made do with fewer, and some with none (an even distribution would have meant roughly three per man in 1541). Nor did these men abide strictly by what Guaraní men expected of brothers-in-law. No Spaniard expected to join one woman's oga and work for their new families, as Guaraní tobayas would. Instead, settlers removed women to their own homes (likely with little thought to the gift-giving generosity expected of a cacique or sha-man). And while Guaraní women under Spanish control labored much as they long had—farming, cooking, weaving—now they did so away from their communities of origin to support men who were social, cul-tural, and physical aliens. Such women also continued to perform one other task critical to Guaraní social life: raising children. Regardless of how it had happened, most Guaraní women probably understood that service to settlers also implied bearing their children. Up to a point, this may have been in keeping with Guaraní understandings regarding the gifting of women, though off-kilter because Spaniards were still recent ar-rivals and their status and role remained ill defined. The mestizo infants born of these unions, therefore, were something new—they came to be called "youth of the land"—creatures of an unstable cultural frontier me-diated by violence, turpitude, practicality, gain, and at times, perhaps, even a degree of affection. Whether they thought of it precisely this way or not, settlers who impregnated Indian women were taking a stake in Native bodies and thereby making a claim on the Guaraní future. At the same time, inadvertently or not, they may have contributed to the sense among the Guaraní that kinship could be stretched to include the new-comers. For from a Guaraní point of view, the child born to one of these women was kin to their kin—if strangely—so that a settler's home with many Guaraní children might have been seen as something like a rela-tive's house.[43]

Although these were still early times, the barter, violence, alliance, kinship, reciprocity, and labor that mediated the exchange of women be-tween Guaraní men and Spanish men became the basis for all that fol-lowed. When women passed from tubichás (caciques) to Spanish captains, the relationship spoke to alliances in the context of political, economic, and military relations between the two sides. But when the exchange was between settlers who lacked the authority of captains and Guaraní who did not share the prestige of caciques, emphasis seemed to be on more mundane concerns.

As currency in these realms

Very quickly, Spanish demand for Guaraní women outstripped available supply, making Asunción a deeply divided place. Governor Cabeza de Vaca and the captains, such as Domingo de Irala, might have scores of In-digenous women; their closest friends and allies, thirty or more. Some of these women were gifts from local caciques seeking alliances. Others were the result of raids to more distant regions. At the same time, as the governor observed in 1542, many settlers lacked weapons and even clothes.[44] Would-be conquistadors were known to melt down their swords so that they might have metal to trade for women. Some did not even have a single Indian woman to their name, an accepted definition of destitution at the time.[45] The Guaraní, by all accounts, could drive a hard "bargain" in goods for women and for Indian labor in general. Theirs could be an "expensive friendship."[46] As a consequence, many settlers had limited chances to improve their situation, snared as they were in a Catch-22: they could neither acquire the iron bars necessary to receive women in gift nor could they directly pay for Indian labor.[47]

Poorer Asunceños (Spanish residents of Asunción) were often forced into debt to those with assets or position. These often went unpaid, creating unwanted dependencies. In 1545, one man wrote to his aunt in Spain asking her to cover a substantial debt he owed to a wealthier settler. He had joined a raiding campaign to acquire Indians but had come away empty-handed. With the borrowed money, he had bought an Indian "slave girl" for twenty-five iron bars, along with two parcels of land for an additional sixty-five, which he acknowledged was far more than he should have paid. He hoped his aunt would "unburden [his] conscience" by paying ten or fifteen *ducados* against the debt. Although it was technically illegal to "sell" Indians by this time—by royal edict in 1542—he pledged to resell the girl and the land for "more than the just price, or twenty just prices." If all went to plan, he implied, there would be plenty with which to repay his dear aunt.[48] We have no report of whether she requited his rather calculated affection.

Men such as these had not left Spain to live in misery and dependence in the New World. For the most part, they were moved by the same impulses that drove emigrants to other parts of America. Adventure, certainly, but more crucially a sense that they might make something of themselves, acquiring wealth, or at least setting themselves up for a life of relative ease and independence. Everyone knew the story of how the Inca had ransomed himself from Pizarro by filling three rooms with gold and silver.[49] But fever dreams of mineral wealth may have been cooling in Asunción by 1540, since no mines had been found in the area. Absent any other exploitable resource at this edge of empire, they had turned to the one thing on offer: Indigenous women.

The desire to acquire Guaraní women had fueled the entradas, such as the one that resulted in Aracaré's murder and sparked the subsequent uprising. But the dangers, expense, and scant rewards of these campaigns led many Spaniards to look closer to home. Ordinary settlers began unsanctioned raids (*rancheadas*) of Guaraní communities around Asunción. Rather than the more formal and expensive affairs of the Chaco, these were little more than an entrepreneurialism of rapine. Effects on Native communities were devastating. Raiders would enter an Indian hamlet and demand food, weapons, hammocks, and especially women. If they met resistance, they might strip the village bare, kill the men, and burn the buildings.[50] Once in hand, captive women were distributed to individual settlers, generally through the patronage of captains. Many were left out of these distributions. Hangers-on benefited from raids only by indebting themselves to others to gain the services of a single Indian woman, as with the loving nephew above.

This acquisitive violence was generated by slippage between gift and gain on both sides of the ethnic divide. Spaniards self-consciously sought to become tobayas when able to do so—that is, when they could give the iron bars or tools Guaraní men demanded—though they did not intend to work for their brothers-in-law, as Guaraní custom required. Guaraní men continued to offer female kin in gift, hoping for stable relations with the newcomers, even as settlers demanded more women than could be supplied without resort to force. At the same time, caciques appear to have become newly transactional in "contracting" with their Spanish brothers-in-law to exchange women taken from enemy groups.[51] Although this suggests that Guaraní men were learning to traffic in women—so long as doing so involved someone else's women—we must recognize that villages near Asunción were under constant pressure to give more. So while the taking and exchanging of captive women ran against their understandings of female roles in the maintenance and reproduction of society, the Cario-Guaraní may have seen this new practice at least partly as a means of keeping their own communities from being raided—the Spaniards' pursuit of gain refracted as violent self-preservation among the Guaraní.

Through all of this, Asunción's Spaniards increasingly treated Indigenous women who served them in decidedly instrumental, even commercial fashion. Complaints to the king and to ecclesiastical authorities regarding the "vice in women" mounted during the 1540s.[52] Settlers, said Francisco de Andrada, had adopted the "bad custom" of "selling these Indian women amongst themselves for goods," trading them for dogs, horses, and weapons.[53] This was not merely a crude extension of direct, unaccountable barter. Captain Domingo de Irala, for instance, "sold" a "free" Cario-Guaraní woman to a friend to pay for a red cape and a velvet tunic, making sure to properly notarize the transaction. The son of a prominent Spaniard likewise "sold" two Indians, a man and a woman captured from the Agaces, for a velvet cape and a mattress.[54] Indian women might be bartered for branded slaves from Africa or given in trade to Portuguese slavers in exchange for cloth and iron, both of which served as currency. Indian women could be used to satisfy debts upon the death of a settler, though documents might declare their service to new masters to be "without prejudice to their liberty," lest the parties violate the prohibition against enslaving Indians.[55] One incensed priest wrote to the king that "Christians of this province" sell Indian women at "excessive prices" amongst themselves, "as if they were slaves, even though they are your Majesty's vassals." Such matters, he noted, were "deeply felt" by their fathers, who may have considered themselves betrayed by a tobaya who treated their daughters as little more than commodities.[56] Guaraní women were routinely referred to as *piezas* (pieces), as African slaves were and as one might refer to coins or items for sale.[57]

Indian women could even be gambled away. A horrified priest told King Carlos V of an incident in which a player had put an Indigenous woman in the pot and lost. As the winner was leading her away, the loser insisted she be stripped bare, because her clothes had not been part of the wager. (We do not know what the winner did with this woman, and we can only imagine what went through her mind as she was led away, though it is worth recalling that before the arrival of Europeans, Guaraní women likely voiced their "will" in regard to marriage partners.) Such wagering was common, lamented this friar, for women had become "as currency [*moneda*] in these realms."[58] In a place where iron bars and tools were the closest thing to a consensus currency, subject to a table of monetary equivalencies, and where these items were so often used in exchange for women, this priest's characterization does not seem unwarranted.[59]

Settlers knew their conduct was illegal. And so they dissembled when explaining their treatment of Indigenous women, arguing that they were not trading people but only their services, as they passed women's bodies from one settler to another (a quite modern idea that abstracted work from the biologically and socially embedded quality of corporeal activity).[60] Others argued that in taking Indian women, they were "rescuing" or "redeeming" captives who might otherwise have been eaten by their captors.[61] In effect, such disingenuous statements used women's captivity by Indigenous groups to justify subjection by their Spanish redeemers or rescuers. This indicates that among settlers, possession and control of Indigenous women's bodies were the order of the day, a fact that conditioned whatever obligation they may have felt toward their Native brothers-in-law and the women they had received through them.

It is tempting to describe these women's situation as tantamount to enslavement. Their experience, certainly, is part of slavery's broader story as a framework of domination during Europe's early modern expansion.[62] Defaulting to this characterization, however, elides nuances of Indigenous experience, meaning, and agency.[63] Although Guaraní had a word (*tembiaihú*) that Montoya's *Tesoro* translated as *esclavo* (slave), the term more properly designated a captive taken in the hunt (if an animal) or in war (if a person).[64] Pointedly, where the Spanish *esclavo* was one who lacked the capacity for a free act, in Guaraní the word conveys the sense of "a thing taken that is loved," suggesting that captives were those who had been torn from their social relations.[65] Women given in gift would almost surely not have likened themselves to captives in this sense. Because they had been given, they would have expected to maintain contact with their home communities, even if under very different circumstances than they had known. Indeed, encomenderos depended on those links to recruit other kin to labor in Asunción, though it seems likely those ties could strain when Spaniards mistreated women. To this point, Montoya's *Tesoro* refers to an intriguing Guaraní phrase for a "bought slave," *tembiaihúbó*.[66] This was almost surely a later coinage (the *Tesoro* was first published in 1639), since the idea of "buying" a captive would have made no sense prior to European arrival. The fact that such a term arose at all strongly hints at the powerful dynamic to which Guaraní women were exposed as Europeans settled in the New World.

Liberty! Liberty!

The treatment of Indigenous women and the devastation of Native communities provoked an official reaction to the free-for-all Spanish-Guaraní relations had become by 1544. During the earliest years after Asunción's founding in 1537, Domingo de Irala had governed the tiny colony with little oversight. Ordinary settlers admired him, mostly for his ruthlessness in sacking Indigenous communities for valuable resources.[67] When Cabeza de Vaca became governor in 1540, he initially continued Irala's policies of allowing settlers to raid villages with impunity.[68] He soon changed course. Acknowledging the rancheadas' effects on surrounding communities and anticipating the king's edict of November 1542 barring the enslavement of Indians across the New World, Cabeza de Vaca had ordered all raids on Indigenous villages to stop, whether by Spaniards or Indians themselves.[69] Settlers ignored his order. Some Guaraní may have as well. The governor saw this as an invitation to chaos. From talking to Indians, "who come every day to complain that the Christians caused them great harm in their homes, taking their goods by force," he feared "great harm, unrest, and disturbance in this land."[70] He proclaimed that the Indians should be treated well, as vassals of the king that they were. Spaniards were not to enter their homes, a prohibition he backed up by posting guards on the roads leading toward the villages, so that "free Indian women" not be sold or contracted for or be traded for slaves or be enslaved. He also commanded that the Guaraní be given gifts and be paid for their work.[71]

This did not endear the governor to Asunción's settlers, who preferred Irala's free-wheeling approach to pursing gain. One anonymous writer noted that Cabeza de Vaca treated settlers like "slaves," where Irala had allowed them to be "free."[72] Such men resisted new policies, pillaging Indian villages despite prohibitions.[73] By early 1544, Asunción's "entire commons, nobles and plebeians" alike, had begun to grumble that they were lost at the hands of Governor Cabeza de Vaca and his small circle of familiars, essentially treated as "slaves without the liberty to go see their king."[74] One opponent stated baldly that the governor should "not expect that people will reform themselves" and adapt to new rules.[75] Inequality of condition had sowed seeds of discord among settlers, so that "we could not come together, we fought with each other day and night," as one observer later recalled.[76]

This was not just a naked struggle over resources. Resentments ran deeper than simply whether Spaniards would be able to continue raiding Indian villages. Even if great wealth was not in the cards for most Asunceños, all would have hoped for a "stable occasion and opportunity for profit." [77] Equally important, they would have banked on some measure of personal liberty and individual independence, for the New World was a place where men of middling and even lower rank might escape the customary dependencies to which they had been subject at home. Spanish literature in the first half of the sixteenth century hints at how powerful this desire for *libertad* (liberty) had become among Iberian common folk, especially men of the lower ranks. "We would rather die with liberty than live in subjection," states a fictitious peasant to the Roman Senate in Antonio Guevara's *Clock of Princes* (1529).[78] To be subject to another person meant not being able to act according to one's own will. The free man is "he who does nothing against his will, nor has anyone who makes him do it by force."[79] To be at a master's beck and call, asserts Villalón's Rooster in *El crotalón* (1552), is to sacrifice a "free and generous heart." Far better to be "a poor cobbler . . . who wants nothing more than his own natural liberty," for happiness is to be found in the "huts and houses of those who though poor in treasure are rich in liberty."[80] At its core, this liberty was not conceived of as political freedom from the obligations of subjecthood to the monarch. Vassalage remained the condition of liberty, as all vassals were free and equal in the eyes of the king. To writers such as Guevara and Villalón, and others like them throughout the sixteenth century, *libertad* implied a broad, popular aspiration to individual autonomy, to not being bound to "another's will," a sensibility increasingly identified with money and trade.[81]

Cabeza de Vaca's ordinances wounded this sentiment. In April 1544, matters came to a head. According to a report written by Cabeza de Vaca's secretary in 1545, several men—a barber, a weaver, a cobbler, and two members of city council—entered the governor's chambers, yelling "Liberty! Liberty!" over and over, and placed the governor under arrest.[82] Accusing him of treason, they chained him to a bed, saying, "Now you will see, Cabeza de Vaca, how you have treated gentlemen"—a puffing up of their actual status, given their vocations. The secretary's report stated that they then addressed the crowd that had gathered. "We have done this to free you, because he wanted to take what's yours and have you for slaves." Another man stood up to lead the crowd in a chant, "Gentlemen, everyone in one voice say liberty, liberty," and so they did. And when some began to murmur that the king's governor should be freed, the conspirators threatened to kill him. Cabeza de Vaca's own version of events is substantially similar, though he notes that the mob in front of Domingo de Irala's house, the governor's one-time friend and now nemesis, called Cabeza de

Vaca a "tyrant who wants to kill us and destroy us."[83] Shortly afterward, the deposed ex-governor was sent to Buenos Aires and on to Spain. Domingo de Irala was elected in his place until the king could appoint someone else.[84]

According to the secretary's report, it could hardly have been clearer what motivated those who rose up in the name of liberty. No sooner had the governor been taken prisoner than "free" Indian women began to be sold through the subterfuge of folding them into transactions for houses or parcels of land, with no mention of the women in the contract of sale and only a gentleman's agreement regarding their value in the deal.[85] At the same time, Irala, as the new governor, immediately granted "licenses to enter the [Indians'] lands."[86] Armed men went into Indian villages and "against their will" took "their women and daughters and hammocks and other things, by force, and without paying for them."[87] Subsequent reports estimated that tens of thousands of Indian men were killed or went missing during these operations, which lasted years, and thousands of Indian women were brought back to Asunción for service.[88] These may have been exaggerations to gain the king's attention, but the elevated figures speak to the magnitude of what happened. Irala himself was accused of selling Indians to Brazilian traders for iron tools immediately after the governor had been exiled. Once in Brazil, they were "registered" and branded as slaves. Some may even have been sold into service in Portugal, a tendril of connection to the emerging Atlantic traffic in enslaved bodies.[89] Knowing such reports would reach the king's desk, Irala and his followers dispatched two Franciscan friars to Brazil to carry a letter to Spain informing the king of recent events, from the rebels' perspective, of course. To fund the trip, the friars were given fifty Guaraní girls, whom they sold to buy male slaves to accompany them on the journey.[90]

As before, village raids provoked resistance. Some Guaraní went to the new governor to complain, expressing their despair, noting that they too enjoyed "liberty" as vassals of the king. Because of bad treatment, they warned, many were fleeing to the forest.[91] These pleas fell on deaf Spanish ears. Guaraní around Asunción began to mobilize for a direct confrontation with settlers, as had happened after Aracaré's murder two years earlier. During 1545, caciques around the region, including traditional and recent enemies, such as the Agaces, consummate canoeists, joined the uprising, with kinship relations and reciprocity the glue holding the coalition together.[92] It was likely the largest and most cohesive response yet among the Guaraní. The Spaniards, meanwhile, allied with the Guaraní's enemies, the Guaycurú of the Chaco, who just years earlier had been attacked in the entrada that led to Aracaré's death and the subsequent uprising.[93]

Hostilities lasted for a year and a half before the various Indigenous groups sought peace, after devastating losses. Aware that frontal battles against Spanish weaponry were a losing proposition, the Guaraní resorted to guerilla tactics, a novel development from the perspective of their war culture. Spaniards responded by adopting a scorched-earth policy. The outcome of the rebellion was not a foregone conclusion. "The Indians had risen up and everything was on the verge of being lost," one witness noted.[94] Another, writing a decade after the fact, observed that "the whole land had risen up . . . in fact or in secret."[95] But as fighting continued, as the Spaniards' Chaqueño allies became involved, and as settler tactics took their toll, the resisters were ground down. Everyday survival became harder and harder as villages were gutted and their people scattered. Guaraní attacks on Asunción came to little. Caciques began to lose the capacity to mobilize warriors and villages to support them. The heat of death and destruction evaporated the rebels' resolve. Group by group, village by village, cacique by cacique, they sued for peace. By late 1546, the fighting had died down. A decade had not yet passed since the foundation of Asunción.

*   *   *

A report describing conditions at Asunción following the ouster of Cabeza de Vaca recounted an incident in which an unnamed Guaraní man sought to recover his wife from settler Andrés Hernández. This unnamed woman had earlier been taken by force from her village by Garcí Venegas, Governor Irala's lieutenant and one of the main conspirators against Cabeza de Vaca. Venegas had given her to Hernández.[96] Her husband had gone to Venegas to plead for her return. Speaking through interpreters and weeping, he had offered his twelve-year-old daughter in his wife's stead. Venegas refused because, he said, the man had complained to others about the situation. Venegas then called on the man's cacique, Lorenzo Moquirara, a tobaya to Venegas, to have the man beaten to death. He was never heard from again.

While we cannot know what was in this man's mind—though his weeping hints at a heavy burden—there was a clear logic to his request. By asking for his wife in exchange for his daughter, he was framing the

issue in familiar Guaraní terms, perhaps hoping that a proper relationship could be restored: his wife would return to his side to work the fields,
cook, raise children; having accepted his daughter, perhaps Hernández
would become his tobaya, bound by some semblance of kinship obligation. Could this have been an effort to repair the harm done by Venegas's
having forcibly taken his wife? As a captive, she could not stand for the
gift that might bind men to one another as tobayas. That neither Hernández nor Venegas was willing to consider the request and that Venegas had
asked Moquirara to kill his own Guaraní kinsman, suggests the unstable blend of instrumentality, reciprocity, and violence that had developed
since Spanish arrival.

The lesson of this incident seems clear. At this early stage, Spaniards
might abide by Guaraní expectations of alliance and reciprocity, but only
up to a point. They were willing to be called tobaya, but no Spaniard
would put himself in the position of working for an Indian brother-in-
law (the husband may have understood this, given experiences of recent
years). Any settler who did so would have undercut the Spanish idea of
liberty as autonomy from the will of others. By asking a Guaraní cacique to kill a member of his own community, Venegas signaled how messy
and unhinged personal and social relations had become relative to Guaraní expectations: what he asked of his nominal tobaya would have been
unthinkable from the perspective of Guaraní reciprocity just a few years
before. Although we have no evidence one way or another, it seems im-
probable that Moquirara followed through on so preposterous a demand,
which could only have undermined his prestige among the Guaraní. He
more likely encouraged or allowed the man to flee (doubtless without his
wife). We can only imagine what this unnamed man must have thought
of the harsh new reality he inhabited.

Spaniards like Venegas did not misunderstand what the Guaraní
wanted. Nor did they simply reject it. They seem, rather, to have grasped
that they would need to accommodate themselves to Guaraní norms,
up to a point, in order to subject Indigenous people to their own survival, gain, and liberty. Venegas made this clear in rejecting the husband's
request and ordering his death. In effect, during this initial phase after contact, Spaniards in Asunción recognized Guaraní notions of gift-
reciprocity and kinship, but chiefly as constraints in relation to other
goals. At the same time, broadly speaking, the Guaraní were trying to
adapt those very ideas to bind the newcomers within a novel interethnic

arrangement. The tension in this situation had produced moments of sharp resistance and violence, suggesting just how hard it was going to be to find a point of balance.

Each side in this encounter was seeking to establish the terms to which the other would be held. Guaraní confronted this challenge through their understanding of what it was to live according to a principle of substantive mutuality that could include all, so long as the newcomers would accept the obligations of reciprocity. Asunción's settlers had arrived in Paraguay with still inchoate ideas regarding what it was to make one's way in the world. These were men who had left everything they knew, families, friends, and communities, for the opportunity make something of themselves, or at least improve their lot. They had fantasized about mineral wealth but had ended up with nothing more than the bodies of other humans to exploit and soon came to see the Guaraní as destined to "serving others."[97] Their desire to gain something in this situation quickly became intertwined with a raw passion for individual liberty that saw any dependence on another as tantamount to slavery This, in turn, had led them to rise up against a governor who sought to enforce royal decrees against abuses of Indigenous people.

Put another way, settlers' acquisitiveness and dreams of liberty, their identity and subjectivity, came to be identified with the freedom to subject Guaraní women to the fiction of being commodity and currency. It was a fiction because, from a Spanish perspective, while women might be exchanged for other objects and put to use, they were ultimately not like either because, from the Guaraní perspective, they were implicated in the fabric of biological and social life itself—through childbirth, the reproduction of social order, and the maintenance of peace. Claims that women were not being enslaved but only their services traded, raiders' insistence that they were redeeming or rescuing Indigenous women from captivity, settlers' instrumental acceptance of the tobaya label—all indicate that Spaniards knew their conduct was, at a minimum, disorienting for the Guaraní and at odds with their own legal and moral precepts. The fact that they claimed not to be doing what they so manifestly were suggests that from early on gain would be a self-denying attitude toward human relations.

For their part, the Guaraní hardly seem to have been oblivious to what was happening. The cycle of friendship with and resistance to the newcomers hints that they too were struggling to find their footing in a changing world where a novel desire to use people as means to individual ends was becoming a baseline of conduct among European invaders. They faced new pressures. By participating in raids alongside settlers, some Guaraní men learned they could treat women captured from enemies in newly instrumental ways. This ran against their own understandings of the role women played in the maintenance and reproduction of society and eroded the principles that sustained their own way of being.[98] They sensed that the newcomers would always seek to "receive without giving" or at least give no more than absolutely necessary.[99] This was the great paradox that began to unfold during these early years. The exchange of women as a way of extending kin relationships and establishing a framework for peace flowed into increasingly expedient and transactional Spanish understandings that were eroding and warping substantive mutuality as the Guaraní understood it.

The non-negotiability of Spaniards' use of Indigenous women, now implicated in the very idea of settler liberty, thus posed for the Guaraní a stark choice. They could capitulate, with the risk to collective survival and mutilation of mutuality this implied. Or they could undertake a fight they sensed they could not win and that would lock them into a cycle of vengeance and warfare, reciprocity only in its negative, unsustainable form. At this stage, it was unlikely they could have predicted where either of these would leave them, or whether there was another path.

3

Limits of Law, Love, and Conscience

Only . . . the service of their own persons.
Encomienda Ordinances of 1556

They treat us with much love and goodwill.
Spokesman of San Blas de Ytá, 1613

AFTER THE HOSTILITIES of 1545–46 had been quelled, Asunceños faced a pressing question: how to ensure the permanent survival and prosperity of European settlement. Early hopes of great wealth were giving way to a struggle for subsistence that at times may have made some nostalgic for the old country. With few alternatives, settlers had turned to Indigenous women as a chief source of exchange value and labor.[1] Having absorbed the lessons of violent confrontation, the Guaraní had looked to gift-reciprocity and kinship to reestablish the equilibrium broken by the aliens' intrusion. Settlers, willing to embrace the label of tobaya though not its spirit, seemed intent on converting Indigenous women into coin, commodity, and labor. If this was an incipient social order, plunder and opportunism seemed poised to strangle it at birth. In essence, settlers' desire for accumulation at the expense of the Guaraní had produced a self-demolishing logic that put the project of creating a shared social order at risk.

The problem was hardly unique to Paraguay. Across the New World, worries were growing that Spaniards were annihilating the Indigenous population. By the early 1540s, the treatment of Indians had become a matter of intense debate in officialdom's highest circles. Among the most vocal critics, Father Bartolomé de Las Casas railed against Spaniards who had set out to "swell themselves with wealth" in the New World and assume a status above that of their birth.[2] For thirty years Las Casas had defended the New World's Natives. He was finally heard in 1542, when Emperor Carlos V promulgated legislation aiming to ensure "the good treatment and conservation of the Indians." Las Casas had been instrumental in writing these New Laws, which forbade the enslavement of Indigenous people, as the "free people and royal vassals that they are." They were not to be taken in war, even in the case of rebellion, or pursuant to any exchange of any sort with other Indigenous people. No one was to "serve themselves of the Indians . . . against their will." Royal officers were charged with their "conservation and good government" across the New World as a matter of "our [royal] service and in unburdening our conscience."[3]

References to conservation bespoke a deep concern for the destructive potential of the Spaniards' presence among Native peoples. As the New Laws were being issued, Las Casas presented the Council of the Indies with a story of atrocities against Indians by Spaniards whose "insatiable greed for money" would be the "ruin" of the kingdom. The document told of conquistadors who had set upon the natives as "cruel tigers" might "gentle lambs" in their search for gold and silver and whatever other profit might be got. Father Las Casas embellished for effect. But his point was clear. Without royal action, he warned, the Natives will be "finished off in short order . . . and there will be no Indians to sustain the land."[4] Just since Columbus's arrival, he wrote, fifteen million Indians had died in the New World (a tally he would raise to forty million two decades later).[5] Put another way, the entire project of Spanish settlement and the continued existence of Indigenous people themselves was at stake. Of course, Las Casas was conflating a variety of factors contributing to the decline of the Indian population, among them war, work, abuse, and especially epidemic disease. (Regardless of the reason, upward of 90 percent of all Indigenous people had died across the hemisphere by the early seventeenth century.[6]) His concern, however, was that in this new land, Spaniards might end a whole people and destroy a society (and an empire) in the making. The call to conserve the Indians, therefore, appealed to the king's role as "heart and soul of the people," allowing "all to be united with him," so that in their "accord" the kingdom would be "protected, kept and made right."[7] To conserve the Indians, therefore, was to rein in the "greed and ambition" that had produced a "disorder" so great that Lucifer himself could not have done better, as Las Casas noted.[8]

*   *   *

Moral hazard of the New World

The disorder to which Las Casas referred, far from being a simple policy failure, was rooted in the fundamental paradox of all efforts to legislate the relationship between the New World's Indigenous people and the Spaniards who decided to make their lives there: the protection and conservation of the Indians had been entrusted to the very people who were drawn to the New World by the chance to pursue gain at Natives' expense. In a place where moral and legal rules were thinly drawn or nonexistent and where accepted mores were seen as optional, at least vis-à-vis Indigenous people, this was a devastating dilemma.

As a matter of legal principle, the king's New Laws settled the issue of the Indians' status by acknowledging them as "our vassals." Broadly speaking, vassalage in the Iberian context was rooted in notions of reciprocity between hierarchical unequals. As a political relationship, it expressed the grace of the gift running from lord to subject and vice versa. Reciprocity was thus the main font of the king's legitimacy; he had to uphold his end of a reciprocal relationship or risk being seen as unable to administer distributive justice.[9] As such, vassalage contemplated an ongoing mutual "liberality" between parties—a "giving without regard for reward in order to do good and grace to the needy"—rather than of contractual quid pro quos.[10] This is what Covarrubias meant in the early seventeenth century when he characterized the word *vassal* as "correlative" with "lord," such that, according to Saavedra Fajardo, king and subject were united by "reciprocal ties of benevolence and love."[11] In the New World, this reciprocity contemplated that Indians would pay tribute, initially in service and later in kind or in currency, in exchange for the king's protection from the Spaniards who had been set over them. This might seem a fairly straightforward arrangement. In fact, the relationship between the king and his Indigenous vassals was being mediated by settlers' rough desire for gain and accumulation.

In New Spain and Peru, the Spanish monarch faced the challenge of administering vast populations of Indigenous people who shared little cultural, social, or political common ground with Spaniards. At the time, the easiest solution was to privatize the task, awarding conquistadors legally binding *encomiendas*. Dating to the Spanish Reconquista, these grants bound their holders, known as *encomenderos*, to a "trusteeship over people" rather than entitling them to own land.[12] They were allowed to benefit from the labor of Indigenous people in their charge, but only if doing so would serve the common good and not unduly burden Natives themselves. In principle, though the day-to-day management of the king's new vassals was given into private hands, this was not a charter for profit taking. By law, encomenderos were obliged to act pursuant to the king's own conscience, protecting the Indians and preparing them for Christian life. In fact, as Las Casas's *Brief Account* made plain, by 1542 the abuses by encomenderos as they pursued material benefit at the expense of Native people were legion and legendary across the New World.

By referring to *conscience*, and specifically to unburdening the royal conscience, the New Laws were pointing to another broad concern. In the mid-sixteenth century, conscience was the faculty that enabled humans to know good from the bad. To lack conscience was to be "without a soul."[13] All Christians were responsible for the state of their souls in the "forum of conscience," which was why confession was a sacrament: it was where human beings could discern whether their actions in the world were in keeping with divine and human laws and correct themselves as necessary.[14] Humans, after all, were fallen and would naturally sin. To confess was to "unburden" (*descargar*) one's conscience and to set oneself on the path of right. Everyman, thus, was morally bound to seek virtue—synonymous with justice—a quality no less natural to humans than sin itself, if harder to achieve.[15] Society's fundamental role, and government's, was to orient individuals to virtue, a collective moral project to ensure the common good, to align and harmonize the many diverse things of the world—"people as well as various affairs."[16] In early modern Spain, the king accomplished this by legislating and applying law to govern social life (lest people become "idiots"—that is, private persons who "do not communicate with others, who do not have judges, nor enter into community").[17] Subjects were responsible in conscience to the king's just laws (though it was for the church, not the king, to judge them).[18] Of course, the king was no less prone to sin than anyone else, which was why he always had a confessor. He was not just any mortal because, as king, he shouldered the moral weight of the republic: he could sin as a private person, like all of his subjects, but also as the prince.

This was not just a matter of the monarch's own frame of mind. Even when not directly responsible for malfeasance, he was obliged to correct misconduct among his subordinates. Failure to do so put him under a moral cloud. That is, the king could sin by failing to correct misdeeds among those acting in his name.[19] In this way, conscience was the keystone of the moral edifice of Christian government: "Conscience, beginning with the king's, was the premise and preoccupation of that public order in which Christian government was considered the only legitimate order and had to be on display at all times."[20] The New World, with its novelty and distance, presented a particular challenge to right rule and good governance. By appealing to "our [royal] conscience," the New Laws sought to impress upon all the king's ministers, officers, and justices the gravity of their charge: if they did not take the measures needed to rectify excesses in the New World, not only might the Indians perish, the king's immortal soul would be in peril.

The monarch's moral hazard was rooted in the notion that God had allowed Spain to discover this new continent (rather than permitting some other nation to do so) for one reason alone: to ensure the Indians' eternal salvation. In theological terms, material riches were incidental to this larger mission, God's gift to Christendom to help bring the spiritual project to fruition. In principle, the king bore the responsibility of carrying out this spiritual enterprise. As theologian and jurist Domingo de Soto framed the matter in 1556, if Spain had acquired the New World only for its riches and exclusively "for our benefit," the "decorum of justice and equity would have been broken."[21] Yet, even as De Soto was writing, Spain's economy was being transformed. Money, commodity exchange, and profit were overtopping the levees of quotidian conscience, especially among those who went to the New World not to save Indians' souls but to prosper. The New Laws sought to balance these competing demands. They were the point of intersection between established moral and theological imperatives and emergent economic behaviors poorly understood and little theorized.

While Las Casas famously argued that it might have been better had Spaniards never set foot in the New World, he remained chiefly concerned for the society that was taking shape and that might fail if the Spaniards' rapine was not curbed. Put another way, material ambition threatened to exterminate Native peoples before something like true Christian society could take root. In the dominant understanding of the day, at least in Spain, this would have been a political and theological disaster. Society was not only natural to humankind, it was a gift from God that could not be refused. To have failed to address the ongoing destruction of the Indians—these newly discovered children of God—would have been to reject God's grace, something no proper Christian ruler could do— certainly not a Catholic monarch.

The fact that society was still to be made from the encounter of opposed perspectives on exchange and social life distinguished the New World from the Old. Writers in Spain and more broadly in Europe feared

that avarice and greed would so weaken existing structures and norms as
to make them incapable of buttressing the new commercial economy being built atop them. The New World during the sixteenth century lacked
the legal and normative matrix that in the Old World still limited gain
at others' expense. In Europe, feudal lords might take advantage of their
vassals, but they were in principle bound by reciprocal obligations to
them. Peasants expected lords to abide by their devoirs, at times demanding they do so. Ordinary men, not bound to lords but lacking land or
family power, faced limited prospects in recruiting others to their material aims. In the New World, by contrast, even common settlers could
project their desires for betterment and liberty upon a whole class of vulnerable others whose legal and theological status remained enablingly uncertain. Because they had no clearly defined place in the web of relations
that organized society—indeed, because a New World social order was
still unformed—the Indians were acutely exposed to economic self-love
among Spaniards.

The New Laws sought to protect Indigenous people from abuse by
the king's other vassals, the Spaniards themselves. Up to a point, legislation acknowledged the New World's complex reality. Broadly speaking, encomenderos often collected far greater tributes than they should
have. They demanded personal service from the Indians, denying the liberty due them as the king's vassals.[22] To curb this undue power, the New
Laws ordered that encomiendas be limited to two lives—that of the original recipient and that of one generation of heirs—after which they would
escheat to the monarchy.[23] Meanwhile, tributary and service obligations
were to be "moderate" and always with an eye to the Indians' "conservation." In fact, passage of the New Laws provoked resistance. Encomenderos in Lima killed the viceroy in 1546 to protest the new restrictions. Mexican encomenderos opted for noncompliance, and royal officials did not
push the matter, fearing a Peruvian-style rebellion.

For their good and conservation

The broad concerns and tensions underlying the New Laws soon began
to reverberate in Asunción. In early 1542, Governor Cabeza de Vaca, anticipating new measures, ordered an end to village raids, explicitly stating that the Guaraní were "free" and not subject to any sort of purchase
or contract.[24] A few years on, Governor Domingo de Irala, who had opposed these provisions, reluctantly acquiesced to royal will, barring any

Spaniard from entering an Indian's house—or even approaching within fifty paces—without a license and prohibiting Indians over the age of thirteen from serving in Spaniards' homes.[25] Although violators were to be fined ten iron bars, Irala's orders regarding enforcement were perfunctory, with none of the grave language of *conservation*, *good government*, *disorder*, and *conscience* solemnized in the New Laws.

Nevertheless, Asunción's residents opposed the ordinances as an undue infringement on their liberty. In 1546, for instance, Asunción resident Martín de Orué petitioned King Carlos V directly, requesting that he be allowed to enter the forests to treat and exchange with the Indians, "without any impediment," as had been the practice before the governor had forbidden it. The king saw no merit in the claim and denied relief.[26] This appears to have been an isolated ruling; Orué's mistake had been to ask permission. Those who simply acted fared better, leading to unsanctioned raids that wreaked havoc on Native communities.

The violence of appropriation may have created paradoxical and unsettling incentives for Indian women. Women taken in raids might prefer their children be fathered by Spaniards, perhaps thinking their offspring would escape indentured servitude.[27] Some appear to have sought alternatives to the dangers and random sorting of rancheadas by giving themselves into settlers' service, thus exercising a measure of control over their fate.[28] Others may have hoped for better treatment in exchange for encomenderos' "goodwill" that might enable them to persuade brothers or nephews to come to Asunción to work. In this way, they may have shifted some of the burden of labor from themselves to male kin. Such connections may also have made certain villages less vulnerable to raids by other settlers, who might think twice before cutting in on a fellow Spaniard. These possibilities must remain speculative, but they do point to a crucial insight: women's roles in Guaraní life were morphing in unexpected ways.

The number of Guaraní men in service to Spaniards increased after the 1550s, most recruited via the hyphae of women's kinship reaching back to home villages. Decades later, a Jesuit observer would claim that during this early period, male kin of women accepted in gift by Spaniards had rushed with alacrity to serve their new tobayas/*cuñados* (Spanish for brother-in-law) as a point of honor.[29] While Guaraní men doubtless felt the tug of kinship, this characterization, which suggests an unproblematic, voluntary submission, deflects attention from the ways motivational cues were being scrambled by novel circumstances. Reality was far more textured. Some came to serve Spanish tobayas, hopeful for a glimmer of reciprocity, perhaps food or, less likely, some tradeable goods.[30] A man might agree to serve a settler who held his female kin, thinking that they might be better treated if he stayed or, alternatively, fearing they might be further mistreated if he refused, as one royal official suggested in 1553.[31] Either way, imperatives of individual and family survival were undercutting substantive mutuality with respect to broader communities. This exacerbated the splintering tendencies characteristic of Guaraní economy, now in ways that served Spaniards at the expense of wider kin-group autonomy.[32]

At the same time, settlers' understanding that women represented *value* was upending the Guaraní's relational world. Women's actions and fates, not just men's, were forging unprecedented relationships with the newcomers. In broad strokes, from the vantage of all they had known, Guaraní at mid-century lived a muddled reality in which kinship and friendship were smeared together with coercion and self-preservation in day-to-day life.

By 1553, inequalities among settlers and the stresses on Guaraní communities had led to a bitter debate regarding Asunción's future. Pedro Dorantes, the king's agent in Paraguay, proposed that Paraguay belatedly establish the encomienda, which had been in place elsewhere in the New World for two decades. On the basis of his long experience in New Spain, Dorantes envisioned a system in which Indian men would travel from their home villages to Asunción to work for settlers several months a year. Encomienda grantees would have Indigenous labor without resorting to rancheadas, on condition that they convert the Indians to Christianity, collect tribute from them on behalf of the monarchy, and treat them as the vassals royal law insisted they were. The matter was urgent, Dorantes argued, because despite the king's repeated calls for the "good and conservation" of the Natives, settlers' conduct vis-à-vis Indian women had become "prejudicial to our consciences and to the population of the land." Indian women taken into Spanish homes, he noted, had stopped having children with Indian men.[33] The Native custom of "selling" female relatives and the Christians' willingness to "buy" them portended "total destruction." To avoid this calamity, concluded Dorantes, the Indians should be gathered into "Christian villages"—*reducciones*—so they could "serve the Christians with less work." Raids, he pointed out, were already illegal and had only ever distracted settlers from the more important task of seeking gold and silver mines. Only if the Guaraní were parceled out into encomiendas could the existential threat to the Indigenous population be confronted.[34]

Governor Irala took Dorantes's statement as a rebuke. Discovering gold and silver, he insisted, had always been his primary concern.[35] He had not pushed the encomienda, because the land was poor and the Natives "few and scattered." Since the Guaraní had no principal leader, collecting tribute from them was difficult. Instead, insisted Irala, caciques and Guaraní men preferred to give their daughters and sisters to Spaniards to forge kinship relations. If Dorantes proposed a plan that did not harm settlers or the Guaraní and benefited God and the king, declared Irala, he would take the necessary steps. If doing so sparked a new rebellion, Dorantes and his followers would be to blame, and their property, not his, would be forfeit.

The king's agent shot back that Irala's invocation of the "old custom" of exchanging women failed to mention the violent raids on Guaraní villages and ignored the fact that those taken against their will were not paid for the services they performed.[36] This was a "great prejudice," because settlers had no alternative to "buying" Natives. Only the encomienda would right things, insisted Dorantes, allowing the Indians to work less and for just one person rather than being "vexed by all." Evangelized and "conserved," they would " multiply" for "the good of all." Spaniards would be able to get back to searching for gold and silver. No settler would be favored over another and each would have "what is his due," the fundamental tenet of Spanish justice. Failure to institute the encomienda would result in a "loss as certain as gain was doubtful," warned Dorantes and, as His Majesty had repeatedly noted, it is far better to "conserve than to profit." The governor does not want settlers to serve the king. Nor does he want the Indians to enjoy the king's protection.[37]

In conventional economic terms, this was a debate over access to capital, or at least to a valuable, though wasting resource. Dorantes, in effect, was arguing that Irala's tactics—especially the rancheadas and the wholesale truck in Guaraní women—were depleting the Indians, putting the very basis for Paraguay's economic activity at risk. In short, he was pointing to one of the wider social consequences of unrestrained gain, what economists today refer to as a tragedy of the commons. In essence, Dorantes was arguing that Indigenous women themselves were being used up as a common resource by Spaniards acting purely out of individual self-interest.[38] Meanwhile, Irala spoke the language of kinship in relation to the Indians, though he was concerned above all for their role as laborers. The pivot of this dispute was that the "uses" of indigenous women were overdetermined: they figured simultaneously as objects of gain, a commodity, a source of labor, a form of capital, a source of rents, a currency, a binder of alliances and reciprocities, and as sexual partners or victims. Any one settler's actions did not a crisis make. But when aggregated, settlers' behavior jeopardized the "resource" in question: Guaraní women and with them, the Guaraní as a source of value to Spaniards in the long run.

Dorantes was not oblivious to moral concerns. But on the matter of conserving the Guaraní, higher obligations converged with practical and material ones. Each settler pursuing his own gain had every incentive to take as many Indians as he could and use them as he saw fit. Though we lack the numbers to judge the accuracy of Dorantes's statement regarding "total destruction," the cumulative effects of disease, overwork, violence, displacement, and the decline of Native women of childbearing age boded ill for the future.[39] Of course, Dorantes was also making a moral and political point regarding the king's conscience: it simply could not be that a just king would preside over the annihilation of a people, especially his own vassals, if it was in his power to prevent it.

The Guaraní had never faced such pressures before. A tragedy of the commons, as describing a particular resource-use challenge, depends upon the idea that some aspect of the world be thought of in terms of individual calculations of advantage or gain, without regard for collective effects. Barring the utter breakdown of the norms and structures governing their social lives, it had been unthinkable for the precontact Guaraní that women could be used and depleted to dangerously low levels. After all, they were responsible for the reproduction of collective life, by giving birth, by farming, by child-rearing. Exchanges of female kin between Guaraní groups were a means to that reproduction on a broader scale. From this perspective, economic *value* between and among individuals simply did not capture the importance of women's roles.

Dorantes did not oppose the governor lightly. Irala was the most successful conquistador/settler (early entrepreneur) in Asunción. He had found a way to exploit the only readily available resource in the region—the Indigenous people, and women specifically—through a mixture of political cleverness, a highly instrumental cultural sensitivity, and ruthless violence. Though the New Laws were still contested in Mexico and Peru, Dorantes saw an opening in the king's insistence that the Indians be "conserved." He knew how to use this word, setting the imperative of conservation against settlers' more immediate concern for profit/gain, rhetorically elevating the preservation of the Guaraní, and hence the kingdom, above the interest of any one person or group—a precise definition of the king's obligation. Of course, Dorantes's own self-interest was implicit; he doubtless hoped to receive an encomienda, and ultimately he did. He was also the king's agent, responsible for keeping an eye on things and reporting back issues that might burden the royal conscience. And so, he called for the encomienda by invoking the king's duty to protect his Indian vassals "for the good of all."

Once in place, the encomienda would serve vital social, religious, and economic ends. Each encomendero granted the exclusive right to exploit the labor of a certain number of Guaraní would be responsible for converting his charges to Christianity. In short, the encomienda would serve not profit but a rough reciprocity: evangelization and proper care in exchange for allowing the king's Indigenous vassals to supply labor. These terms were formalized in contracts recognized by Spanish courts, enabling the encomienda to accomplish three intertwined economic goals: organize the mobilization of Guaraní labor to sustain the settler population and, ideally, generate a surplus; ensure timely payment of royal tribute by their encomenderos (in effect, a tax-farming scheme); and make sure the laboring population sustained itself.[40] Finally, in principle, encomenderos agreed to defend the settlement and the region from internal and external threats, whatever they might be—Indigenous uprisings, Portuguese incursions—thus saving the monarchy the expense of a standing army it could neither afford nor hope to muster.

After much dispute, Irala finally bowed to the inevitable and granted encomiendas in late 1555, interposing the law between settlers and the Guaraní. He had opposed formalizing a relationship that had been governed by unofficial mechanisms, from raids to the gifting of women. But the king had ordered him to proceed, so he parceled out 20,000 Indians, mostly Cario-Guaraní around Asunción, among 320 settlers. He did so self-interestedly, awarding himself 300 and his protégés 200 each. He spread the remainder thinly, leaving many settlers with a handful and roughly half of Asunción's male citizens with none at all. (The average

distribution ended up at 30–40 per grantee; an even allotment would
have been about 62).[41] To all intents and purposes, Irala allocated Asunción's available capital—Guaraní bodies—in a way that instantly created
classes of haves and have-nots among Europeans.

Many settlers were incensed. "He took the whole country," complained
Bartolomé García (a commoner, to judge by his name) to the Council of
the Indies in Madrid.[42] The governor had given encomiendas to new arrivals, passing over many who had been in the city much longer. García was
not among these, but he received only sixteen Indians. Moreover, "his" *encomendados* would have to travel so far from their home village to Asunción (eighty leagues, or nearly four hundred kilometers) that García declined to accept them, figuring that managing their conversion, collecting
tribute from them, and coordinating their comings and goings would be
more trouble than it was worth. For such men, Irala's self-serving actions
represented a local failure of reciprocity between the king and his Spanish
vassals, who had given much and netted nothing.

Nor had Irala said anything about how the encomienda would be regulated, if at all. In an April 1556 letter to the king, Asunción's treasurer
and two other local officials close to Dorantes argued that the new encomenderos needed to be reminded of their obligations. Distributing the
Indians, they agreed, was "convenient" to their "conservation."[43] But only
if they worked less and were paid, as the king's decrees demanded. "If this
is not done they will be lost," stated the letter. At this stage, the concern
that the Indians be paid was a reflection of how encomenderos "collected"
tribute from their charges—by receiving goods (food or cloth) of a certain value from each male tributary or by accepting the Indians' "personal service" and then transmitting a small part of its value to the royal
treasury. Official documents later referred to "extortions" to describe encomenderos' practice of overcharging their encomendados and underpay-
ing what they owed the monarchy. It would have been better, insisted
the letter, to limit the number of encomiendas, contrary to what Irala
had done. At a minimum, the governor should be required to issue ordinances assuring the "good treatment of the natives." If all was carefully
done, insisted these officers, Spaniards would be free to settle new areas
and subject new Indian groups to the encomienda. In time, this would allow more settlers to begin trading in cotton, hides, and sugar. In short,
according to these royal officials, the encomienda, if properly and con-
scientiously rolled out, was the key to conserving the Indians, promoting

Paraguay's economic development, increasing the monarchy's revenues, and discharging the king's conscience.

Governor Irala responded by issuing ordinances in May 1556. The irony is that they came into effect well after the 1542 New Laws had sought to abolish the encomienda in Peru and Mexico in favor of direct tribute contributions by Indigenous people to the treasury.[44] Though Irala parroted the language of the New Laws regarding conservation of the Indians and their importance to "the Republic," his main priority was to ensure the natives' availability to settlers. Indigenous communities would provide encomenderos a certain amount of work through the labor rotation (known as the *mita*) that cycled people in and out of Asunción for up to three months a year. This "service" was taken to satisfy the Indians' tribute obligations to the king. According to Irala's ordinances, this labor could involve construction, field work, hunting and fishing, and other tasks set by encomenderos. In addition to the labor they owed encomenderos, village Indians were also subject to the *mandamiento*, a contract system that "rented" laborers on a temporary basis to settlers who could pay. In principle, those who performed this work earned a wage (in cloth or, less commonly, iron), though half of their earnings went to the Asunción treasury. Indian men could also be drafted into corvée labor to build roads, bridges, and forts.[45] When not tasked in these way, Indian men were to farm in their home villages, however distant they might be, to sustain themselves and their families.

While the ordinances stated that Indians should enjoy "good treatment," Irala was more concerned that they obey their encomenderos and that they not create "confusion" by leaving their villages to visit kin elsewhere.[46] The law's preamble acknowledged that many Indians had died from "exhaustion and toil" in the past. For this reason, their labor should be "moderate . . . as far as possible," as His Majesty intended. As this phrasing suggests, Irala's law was riddled with exceptions that undercut firm enforcement of measures to protect the Indians from abuse. Thus, while no more than one-quarter of men assigned to an encomendero were to be away from their villages at any given time—so that an average stay would be three months of the year—up to half could be drafted for "demonstrated necessity." And while Indians were not to be overworked, the law offered no specific provision capping work hours or limiting how long they could stay in Asunción. Similarly, encomenderos were forbidden to lend or rent their charges to anyone else, though Indians might work for someone else if certain conditions were met: they "expressly agreed" to it, the task was "honest and bearable," they were paid for their labor, and the encomendero did not profit from the arrangement. Such ambiguities opened the door to abuses. It also enabled mitayos to make individual accommodations. In short, in many of its most crucial provisions, Irala's ordinances nodded to royal will and to the rhetoric of conservation, but kept settlers' options open in a unpromising economy. After all, as the law stated, the Guaraní had no gold or silver to offer, no cattle or crops, or anything of profit that might be bought and sold—they had "only . . . the service of their own persons."[47]

Although the treatment of women had been one of the motivating factors for this legislation, women were not often mentioned in it. On paper, only men were subject to the labor rotation, so the law focused on them. But the ordinances did make clear that female kin of an encomendado were not to be rented out or contracted for work. Nor were wives whose husbands died to be taken by anyone, whether their husband's encomendero, other settlers, or Indian men, upon severe penalties of fines and imprisonment.[48] We might speculate that the prohibition against widows being taken by settlers aimed to prevent an unseemly competition to secure women who after the death of their husbands had no one to defend them. As to barring other Indians from "taking" such women, the law explained what was really going on: widows were leaving their villages to live with kin elsewhere. This "ancient custom," said the law, needed to cease, probably because such moves risked disrupting the collective livelihood of villages, and indirectly of encomiendas, that depended on women's domestic labor.

Despite official protestations of concern for Indian women, legal niceties tended to bow to local exceptions, as illustrated by women's spinning. In the face of prohibitions against forcing Indian women to work, Guaraní women close to Asunción came under enormous pressure to spin thread. This operation was generally overseen by encomenderos' wives, who went to Indian villages to supervise what amounted to an early putting-out system. Indigenous women were given an amount of raw cotton and expected to spin it into thread within four days, turn over the thread, and take more cotton, on the same deadline. There was more to this than making the material to fashion clothing: bolts of cloth also served as a medium of exchange in Asunción, so that, in effect Indigenous women were producing the raw material for minting money. Although the precise value of their work is unknown, great effort was put into keeping them spinning, often with little if any compensation. Father Martín González, one of Irala's harshest critics, wrote to the king after the ordinances were enacted, noting that it was common for young Guaraní women to spin cotton shackled and punished so harshly that many chose to starve themselves to death. He reported them as weeping in confession that "they would rather die . . . than live with so much work."[49] Pregnant mothers would kill their own babies in the womb, he claimed, fearing encomenderos who saw pregnancy and motherhood as a loss of service. Some mothers killed their own daughters, he said, to spare them such lives. While Father Martín may have exaggerated, the despair he evokes speaks to the cramped possibilities of Paraguay's transactional economy, to the law's limits in regulating abuse of Indigenous people, and to the particular stresses imposed on Guaraní women.

Much, in other words, continued as before the encomienda. Encomenderos played fast and loose with the labor rotation and sought ways to "rent" *their* Indians out to others. The rancheadas ground on and may even have accelerated, as those without an encomienda or with only a few Indians in service returned to raiding. Indeed, enthusiasm for such forays remained high in Asunción. The bishop himself had called from the pulpit for expeditions to distant Amazonia to take more Indians. His Excellency falsely attributed this idea to the king, noted one critic, even though he knew that royal edicts had forbidden razzias.[50] Two years later, a royal decree explicitly reprimanded Irala for pursuing "unjust war" against northern Indian groups to take Indian women by force and by barter, which had led to an uprising against their "bad treatment." The king commanded those who had any of these people in their possession to free them immediately and allow them to return to their villages.[51] The order was ignored. Nor did circumstances improve for many Guaraní. Irala's ordinances had failed to mention the thousands of people who no longer lived in villages of their own but served permanently on the estates and in the houses of encomenderos. These were Guaraní who had been reduced to "personal service" during the initial years of raiding. Grandfathered into the encomienda after 1556, these people—known as *originarios* or *yanaconas*—hunted, fished, worked the fields, spun cotton, and raised children (often mixed-race children born of Guaraní women and settlers). By law, they were not slaves and so should not be sold, abused, or overworked.[52] In practice, persistent complaints made clear that they had few genuine protections.

Tensions of growth

The encomienda regime began to show positive economic results from roughly 1560. A ruinous 1553 expedition to seek gold in the Chaco—the last of many such disappointments—had extinguished hopes of mineral wealth in Paraguay. Financial and human losses of this and other failed ventures turned settlers' energies toward a local economy that seemed "rich in provisions" compared to a few years before.[53] Routinized Guaraní labor was producing more goods more consistently than earlier. During the 1560s, Asunción's encomiendas offered sugar, wine, preserves, honey, leather, pork, wax, and palm wood, in addition to abundant staples, including corn, beans, squash, melons, figs, and cotton.[54] One observer noted that fishing and hunting remained robust and that the number of sheep and cattle was growing after the introduction of stock animals in 1555 and 1568.[55] Wood for boats and ships and cotton for sailcloth were abundant, and Guaraní laborers, who worked in the shipyards alongside mestizos, supplied the pitch, cordage, and lumber required.[56] A regional trade began to take shape, jump-starting an increasingly reliable circulation of commodities. New towns were founded—Ontiveros, Ciudad Real, Villa Rica—conveniently located in areas where tens of thousands of Guaraní lived, many of whom had only just come under the encomienda.[57] Well-off settlers began to exchange local products for luxury goods imported from Spain, including finer clothes, weapons, and household products—though Asunción remained a highly unequal place. This city at the "edge of empire" began to experience a churn of goods, ideas, debts, and people from other points within the Iberian world—Mexico, Lima, the Caribbean, Saõ Tomé, Lisbon, Cádiz, and Madrid.[58] Work rhythms intensified as managers sought new ways to boost production. Encomenderos no longer expected Guaraní laborers simply to sustain them. They increasingly called on them to produce a surplus for trade. By all indications, the Guaraní were working harder ever.

By 1570, Asunción faced a chronic labor shortage, a function of economic growth and also of demographic squeeze. Just as the economy was beginning to expand, Paraguay's first smallpox outbreak scythed through Guaraní communities, two years after encomendados started shuttling back and forth from their home villages to Asunción for labor rotations.[59] It is not known how many died, though effects on communities were devastating. A more immediate concern among Asunceños was the flow of people into and out of the town. Broadly, Guaraní laborers were supposed to come and go every few months. But some men were finding reasons to stay. New occupations—weavers, carpenters, blacksmiths, and the rafters and canoeists, porters and carters essential to moving goods over longer distances—demanded greater permanence. Some Guaraní, especially from Asunción's immediate area, began to pursue novel options. Transportation work was attractive to young men, requiring little training and enabling them to visit kin in other communities. In some cases they struck out on their own.[60] As the demand for work increased, encomenderos began to push back against their responsibilities, or outright flout them. Irala's ordinances had been enablingly vague as to how long Guaraní could be made to stay during work rotations. Encomenderos took full advantage of such imprecisions, keeping men in service for as long as possible. Larger encomenderos began to employ *pobleros* (administrators) to manage labor flows and maximize output.[61] Abuses followed. It was not uncommon for Indian men to serve their encomenderos for a year or two at a stretch—well beyond the legal limit—without returning to their villages during the entire period. As Father Martín told the king, their absence put a tremendous strain on wives and children who stayed behind; many were "dying of hunger."[62]

The tension between the encomienda's legal framework calling for the "good treatment" of the Indians and encomenderos' incentives and motivations became sharper as the economy grew. Against their own economic interests, encomenderos were expected to "compel and urge" the Indians to limit their labor rotations to three months a year.[63] But this had become a fraught matter. Encomienda *pobleros* had every incentive to keep people working. Part of this burden fell on local Guaraní leaders, who came under pressure to ensure the continual flow of laborers to Asunción, with the menace of violence for failure to comply.[64] The threat was credible because of the patchwork way encomienda grants overlay Guaraní village life. An encomienda might include a whole village, or one village might be divided among various encomiendas, or a single encomendero's workers might come from several different villages. The ordinances had said nothing about how all this was to be coordinated. Guaraní leaders faced a complex task that could easily break down and lead to internal dissension. Persistent failure of the labor rotation to Asunción risked punitive enforcement by encomenderos, the effects of which might fall indiscriminately on one or more villages. Women and children who stayed behind were especially vulnerable to collective punishment, as Guaraní men knew. To the extent they sought to stay together, in other words, villages had little choice but to comply with growing labor demands, though individual accommodations—which could include wives and children accompanying husbands—pushed many communities to the edge of survival. This is what Father Martín meant in complaining to the king that women and children were suffering: the encomienda had disrupted the Guaraní economy, pitting a newly institutionalized labor arrangement against villages that were being forced to fend for themselves just as broader intercommunal connections were beginning to weaken.

The matter may have been even more complex than Father Martín realized. Encomenderos had quickly formalized processes to "rent" Guaraní out among themselves and to settlers who had not received an encomienda—a practical response to labor shortage and inequality among Spaniards. They did so by taking advantage of the loophole in Irala's ordinances that allowed encomendados to be "rented" or "lent" to others if the Indians consented.[65] Some Guaraní men appear to have participated in this subterfuge for reasons of their own. As the ordinances themselves suggest, it was not uncommon for men to overstay their labor rotations. One reason they did so was distance. For those whose villages were far away—two to four weeks of arduous, dangerous travel—remaining near Asunción may have been appealing and safer. By remaining in Asunción after their rotation had finished, they could exchange their services for goods. It matters, of course, whether they were being coerced to stay or chose to seek *conchabos* (day contracts) on their own. Both happened. The former suggests that the ordinances were ineffective in restraining encomenderos, who might pay lip service to the need to "conserve" the Indians. The latter hints that Indigenous men were operating in a new arena of personal agency, even as the line between coercion, consent, and the pressure of survival had blurred. In this context, encomenderos were in a position to serve as brokers during times of labor shortfalls.

Indigenous men who came to Asunción, even if only for a time, joined a broadening provincial economy and labor pool that included a surging population of mestizos born of Indian mothers—mostly women who lived in or around Asunción rather than in distant villages. By the

1560s, there may have been as many as ten thousand of these mixed-race progeny in Asunción alone, just as the number of "true" Spaniards was beginning to tail off.[66] Not subject to the encomienda, these "youth of the land" connected Europeans and Guaraní across a cultural gulf. Some men served as *lenguas* (interpreters), work that allowed them to accumulate women, much as better-placed Europeans did. For the most part, however, mestizos anchored the emergent day-labor market around the city. We do not know the going rate other than that it was paid in foodstuffs, cloth, and perhaps iron. Guaraní men often found themselves working alongside mestizos who, like everyone else, including Spaniards, spoke Guaraní. From them, Guaraní men learned the rudiments of Spanish farming—wheat, sugar, the plow, the care of pigs—and how to navigate the incipient labor market.[67] Some younger Guaraní men were attracted to the possibility of making their own way by earning wages of cloth and food. Such work promised a certain ease of movement and perhaps freedom from communal obligations in their home villages.

Under pressure from settler gain-seeking and the deeply constrained agency of Indigenous workers, Guaraní collective life warped. Villages faced new challenges as married men began to overstay their labor rotations to seek *conchabo* work. Without this labor, women and children who remained in home villages were forced to rely more heavily on communal labor in order to survive.[68] However, it is crucial not to overstate this point. Husbands surely understood that their wives and children experienced hardship while they were gone, and available evidence indicates that most men worked and returned to their villages, more or less as the ordinances contemplated. Nor should we suppose too readily that Guaraní men were so naturally attracted to wage options that they simply turned their backs on their families and communities. Such suppositions would do little more than indulge individualist assumptions regarding human nature (precisely what is at stake in this book). Still, Guaraní men's expanded participation in Asunción's emerging labor market may have aligned Guaraní women ever more closely with village life, emphasizing the importance of communal work as a guarantee against starvation and as an expression of collective identity.

With economic growth, tensions between Spaniards and natives flared. New rancheadas near Asunción, as well as in more distant areas still being "pacified," led Indigenous groups to push back. In 1559, Asunción suffered a general revolt from villages in the near south, where there had been much settler raiding before and after introduction of the enco-mienda.[69] The reach and vehemence of resistance prompted one royal official to comment that "there was great rebellion in the land," requiring three campaigns to tamp it down.[70] By the 1570s, Spanish officials were reporting that those who rose up were "rebelling against the service of God and His Majesty" and against "their encomenderos."[71] Settlers saw a root-and-branch rejection of Spanish rule. In fact, the uprisings coincided with the intensification of efforts to alleviate Asunción's persistent labor shortfall.

Resistance by the Guaraní and small adjustments by Spanish authorities were symptoms of a larger problem: the encomienda was straining to keep pace with an expanding economy, leading many settlers to abandon even the pretense of ensuring the good treatment and conservation of the Guaraní. This was not a concern limited to Paraguay. In 1581, the Council of the Indies submitted a consultation to the king, with "admonitions regarding things of the Indians that require a remedy."[72] The document noted that in the New World there was a great shortage of "knowledge-able people of conscience who try to unburden your Majesty's conscience, in whose name they govern." These royal officers, said the council, think that service to your Majesty consists only in "conveying much money, without consideration for the means or whether they are licit." Although the consultation focused on the moral "state of ruin" in Peru, several points broadly paralleled conditions in Paraguay, especially those regarding the use of women and the taking of lands.

A year later, in 1582, the king issued a royal edict addressing conditions in the Río de la Plata and Paraguay.[73] "We are informed," began the order, "that in that province the Indians are being destroyed by ill treatment done them by their encomenderos and that the said Indians are so diminished in number that in some places more than a third of them are missing." According to Father Martín González in a letter to the king in 1575, Spaniards had taken one hundred thousand Guaraní women since 1544, of which sixty thousand had perished.[74] In another missive, he had named over one hundred and fifty individual Asunce-ños, mostly Spanish *lenguas* (and the occasional mestizo son), each of whom had brought anywhere from "a few" to over two thousand Indian women to Asunción from further afield.[75] The higher figures were likely inflated, because González was trying to make the king understand what was at stake. At a rhetorical level, Father Martín appears to have succeeded. Employing what had become tropes of Indigenous extremity, the royal order noted that Indians were often treated "worse than slaves . . . many being bought and sold" among encomenderos. Women die and are "broken" by the "heavy burdens" put on them—field work, housework, cotton spinning—chiefly because there were no limits to what could be asked of them. Echoing Father Martín's earlier accusations, the decree noted that women committed suicide and even killed their own children at birth, "saying that they want to liberate them from the work they suffer." They were "being put an end to so quickly . . . that something must be done." The Indians had conceived a "great hate for the name of Christians and have Spaniards for liars," noted the edict. None of his commands had availed, wrote the king, because "my ministers" refuse to execute the laws. The decree enjoined the governor to enforce all provisions relevant to ending "the calamities and work that these wretched people suffer by means so contrary to reason and justice."

By this time, royal officials in Asunción had begun to explore alternatives to so fully committing the Indians' lives to four hundred or so encomenderos.[76] In 1580, Franciscan missionaries were allowed to establish their first reduction at Los Altos, forty kilometers from Asunción. The idea was to gather several smaller villages into a larger town of between 1,000 and 1,300 people to make it easier to coordinate and regulate labor rotations to and from Asunción. This was crucial, since encomenderos seemed incapable of restraining themselves from destroying the Indians, even though by all accounts profits were dropping as the number of Natives declined.[77] What was new in Los Altos was that two Franciscan friars were put in charge of the town. Their job was to ensure Guaraní subsistence and to take responsibility for evangelizing the Indians. In effect, the king seemed to accept that encomenderos might never live up to their obligations under the law. Over the next couple of decades, Franciscans founded nine other reductions north along the Paraguay River and east toward the frontier with Brazil, each congregating six or seven existing villages overseen by a pair of friars.[78] In general, local resistance diminished immediately after establishment of a reduction.[79]

What distinguished Franciscan oversight of Indian towns (*pueblos de indios*) was that the friars did not seek commercial profit or gain. They were oriented first to Christian charity, which, at least at the level of interpersonal relations, lent them a disinterestedness more in keeping with

Guaraní understandings of gift-reciprocity. Like settlers before them and Jesuits after, Franciscans made gifts of material goods—especially hatchets and other metal tools—in order to connect with Indigenous people. Unlike settlers, they did not accept women, even when offered in gift. They embraced personal poverty and made a point of magnanimity. According to historian Louis Necker, this allowed them to occupy a position analogous to that of Guaraní caciques, whose prestige was rooted in generosity toward others rather than in accumulation or command.[80] Crucially, however, they did not set themselves against the encomienda, as the Jesuits later did. As a result, though they were not personally driven by self-interest, or at least not a material self-interest, the broad labor regime oriented to maintenance of the encomienda continued as before, if now in a somewhat gentler register. They saw themselves as "tireless vigilantes for the Royal Conscience," accepting the encomienda as a given, seeking to balance the work demanded of the Indians against the protection owed them under the king's law.[81] In short, they sought to tame the encomenderos to behave within the moral and behavioral limits laid down by royal decrees and religious demands on conscience, without challenging underlying arrangements.

Available evidence suggests this was a Sisyphean task. Through the latter decades of the sixteenth century, encomenderos were keenly sensitive to Asunción's labor woes. Although the number of cases is small, court fights between encomenderos over individual tributaries, women more often than men, hint that even the labor of a single person could be worth the expense of a lawsuit.[82] One encomendero might sue another for injury to an encomienda Indian.[83] Other disputes arose at the seams between kinship networks and the legal categories of the encomienda.[84] The most common case of this sort involved the question of who could claim an Indigenous person whose kinship was unclear.[85] The "fluidity" of Guaraní kinship, which had long hinged on the movement of women within or between villages, did not mesh well with the logic of Spanish paternal descent.[86] Thus, the wife of a man or the child of a woman could end up being claimed by more than one encomendero. Some encomenderos sought to manipulate Guaraní marriages. By pairing a male tributary from one village with a non-tributary, "foreign" woman from a different village, an encomendero might gain added tributaries with the birth of offspring, an arrangement typically upheld by Spanish courts. Of course, Guaraní caciques might or might not abet these machinations, for they could influence how and whether women moved, in effect determining which of two encomenderos a particular person might serve.

Encomenderos were not alone in going to court. By law, Guaraní were entitled to seek legal redress. Successes appear to have been relatively infrequent and rarely unequivocal. In 1590, Hernando and Mariana filed a petition against the heirs of Pedro Orué to be freed from servitude. In a document now pocked and hard to decipher, they claimed to have served Orué for forty years as "indios yanaconas," bound "by force and against our right to liberty."[87] More than once they had sought their freedom but Orué, "as a powerful person," had made it impossible for them to "reach justice." Upon his death, they had approached a legal advocate to plead for their liberty. They began by reminding King Felipe II that they were his "vassals." As such, they were naturally free, like other men, and entitled to the salary they had lost over many years of service. Mariana further stated that her daughter, Estefanilla, had been kidnapped to serve in Orué's house, "as if she were his slave, in prejudice of the liberty" His Majesty had promised. They wanted to go live with Mariana's mestizo son, Juan de Cuenca, "not subject to tribute nor under the dominion of caciques"—a statement recognizing the role local leaders played in organizing labor for the encomienda.[88] Orué's heirs opposed the petition, asserting that Hernando and Mariana were "customary servants" (*yanaconas de costumbre*) and that the king had granted their service and that of their descendants to Pedro de Orué and his heirs decades earlier. They reminded the judge that they too were royal vassals, entitled to the king's protection. Pedro's brother also intervened, insisting that the estate owed him money and that granting Mariana and Hernando's petition would prejudice his claim to the debt by denying him the value of their labor.[89]

The judge's ruling was a bittersweet victory for Mariana. For though she was "put into liberty" and allowed to go live with her son, Juan, neither her husband nor her daughter were freed. The ruling is hard to compass. Mariana alleged that she had been taken "by force." But so had her husband, Hernando, and their daughter, Estefanilla. The judge said that Mariana should be granted liberty because, as the mother of Juan de Cuenca, she had had a child with a Spaniard. Nothing in Spanish law recognized this assertion, because it would have led to a flood of similar claims by other Guaraní yanaconas who had borne children to Spanish fathers. So what justified the outcome? We can only guess. One possibility is that Juan de Cuenca, who was acknowledged as a *vecino*, or voting member of a Spanish community, enjoyed sufficient status, despite being a mestizo, that it would not do for his mother to be bound in servitude or used to settle the debts of another encomendero.

Amid such contests, Paraguay's economy continued on a slow upward trajectory. By the 1580s, locally grown sugar was finding its way to Chile and Peru, though not to Europe because Brazilian sugar, produced by hard-driven African slave labor and better technology, was cheaper. Production and export of Paraguay's famed stimulant, yerba mate, usually drunk in tea form, began to pick up in the 1590s. Harvested and processed at the northern town of Mbaracayú, *yerba*—a varietal of wild-growing holly—had found markets in Santiago, Potosí, and Lima by 1600. Production of cotton fabrics also saw an upswing. Their quality was good enough that outside merchants selling imported goods began to accept payment and settle debts in locally produced cloth, sparking a demand for competent weavers. Iron, mined near the frontier with Brazil and ground and smelted painstakingly by Guaraní hands, was transported to Asunción, where it continued to serve as a currency and underwrite the transactional *amistad* (friendship) at the point of contact between Spanish commerce and Guaraní gift exchange.[90]

Overall, conditions were sufficiently hopeful that a few Asunceños began to dream of genuine wealth. High in the Andes, Potosí's silver-mining boom was powering an emergent ocean-going trade economy of truly global reach, linking Madrid, Mexico City, Lima, Potosí, and Manila.[91] By 1600, Spanish silver mined by Indigenous people and cast in the form of bullion and coin had become the world's first global currency. Cerro Rico (rich mountain), as Potosí was also known, accounted for 60 percent of all silver mined in the world. A place with no population in 1545, when silver was discovered, it had become a city of 160,000 by 1600. Most food had to be imported and with such a population, it had become a maw that "devoured" cattle by the tens of thousands. Against this background, Asunción's cattle ranchers, mostly Spaniards, fantasized that they might export cattle on the hoof to the highlands for enormous profits. Despite such longings, the distance and rigors of travel to Potosí were too great, limiting the trade in cattle to the Plata region, though some found an outlet in Brazil, where prices for hides and tallow remained high.[92]

If Asunceños were heartened by these developments, Guaraní were on edge. The mid-1580s to the mid-1590s saw at least five instances of Guaraní resistance, which one Spanish captain referred to as wars of "fire and blood."[93] These took place at Franciscan reductions, as well as in areas only recently subject to the encomienda. In a process sharing the spirit of English "enclosure," new encomenderos often occupied fertile lands that had either belonged to Guaraní villages—now emptied out by disease or raids—or served as a commons for networks of villages. Most Spaniards could acquire rural property, though often without anyone to work it but themselves. For men who had not come to the New World to work with their hands, ranching seemed a way of getting by. By the late 1570s, cattle herds had expanded to the point that they were beginning to encroach on Indigenous lands. Ranchers, unwilling to build corrals and pay shepherds, allowed their animals to graze freely. According to a 1578 complaint, it had become common for cattle to enter Indian villages, where they trampled family gardens. The resulting "great need and hunger" was leading whole communities to decamp to "remote parts" of the forest, said an ordinance passed that same year. Ultimately, ranchers were ordered to build corrals and tend their herds. We do not know if this was an intentional strategy by ranchers to expand grazing land. At a minimum it suggests that a growing economy could threaten communities' access to the fields that ensured day-to-day survival and buttressed their relationship to the land.[94]

"There will be no goodwill between parties"

By century's end, the plight and future of the Guaraní became a matter of deep concern within Spanish officialdom. A string of decrees and ordinances from the late 1590s to 1612 indicate that the monarchy understood the challenge in terms of trying to resolve the problem of the encomienda once and for all. Governor Juan Ramírez de Velasco's 1597 ordinances cited the "great disorder" characterizing encomenderos' use and abuse of the Natives in Paraguay, which had led to their "notable harm and diminution," and proclaimed that it was necessary to "unburden the Royal Conscience."[95] Encomenderos were well served by "the great lack of regulation," noted Ramírez. They routinely kept Guaraní workers beyond the three-month limit, some even staying all year, with grave consequences for "things concerning human life" in their home villages. In the pueblos overseen by encomenderos, there were many widows and orphans who had no gardens from which to feed themselves. People were leaving for the forest, reverting to the old ways. Encomenderos acted "without fear of God and in scorn of Royal Justice." In flagrant "disrespect" for the king, they referred to the Indians as "theirs," even though they were the king's vassals. To compound matters, settlers had violated earlier prohibitions against taking Indian lands. In the context of rancheadas, free-range cattle grazing, and depopulation, encomenderos and others had occupied Indigenous farmlands, forests, fishing areas, and hunting grounds, which had led many villagers to work for settlers and mestizos just to survive. Indigenous groups themselves had at times contributed to the problem by retreating to oft-flooded marshlands to avoid contact with settlers and mestizos. In doing so, they had exposed themselves to diseases that spiked during the flooding season.

These concerns must be understood against the backdrop of economic developments that were driving new forms of rent seeking and profit taking in Asunción. By the 1590s, it had become common for merchants and local authorities to "bet" on the outcome of harvests—effectively futures contracts—which, according to Ramírez, had increased pressure to lengthen work hours and had begun to distort the prices of basic staples. At the same time, merchants increasingly sold goods on credit, inflating prices, locking others out of the market, and indebting many with scant means.[96] This only increased pressure on the Guaraní, who were being squeezed as workers and as consumers by an economic system that seemed incapable of limiting their exploitation, even to unburden the king's conscience.

As rhetorically powerful an indictment of the encomienda as it was, Ramírez's statute had little practical effect in Asunción, for in 1603 a new governor promulgated another set of ordinances regarding "treatment of the Indians." King Felipe III had passed a decree in 1601 abolishing the "personal service" of Indians across the New World, decrying the "injustices and abuses" inflicted on them by Spaniards of all stripes.[97] Echoing that law, Governor Hernandarias de Saavedra's new ordinances noted the "carelessness" of the encomenderos vis-à-vis the Guaraní, who were being "consumed and finished."[98] Fault lay with Irala's 1556 ordinances, stated Hernandarias, which had sought the "utility of the encomenderos more than the good conservation" of the Guaraní. This had led the encomenderos to an "unbridled" and "disordered greed." Rather than urging them to good behavior—an approach that had failed for decades—Hernandarias took another tack. His ordinances required encomenderos to build churches, appoint them lavishly, and make sure the Guaraní attended Mass.[99] In exchange, the Guaraní would be gathered into Christian villages, thus making them available for labor while ensuring their conversion. This gambit was telling, for it suggested that neither appeals to conscience, royal or otherwise, nor to encomenderos' own broader interests were working. Instead, encomenderos were being exhorted to deploy the visible traces of religion as a public sign of compliance with public obligations that seemed to be honored almost exclusively in the breach. This proposal betrayed the law's helplessness in the face of the "greed" it so roundly condemned. The notion that encomenderos who sloughed off royal calls to proper behavior might build churches, adorn them, and ensure attendance at services smacked of desperation. Despite threats of stiff fines and punishments, including loss of encomienda privileges, there had never been effective, sustained enforcement of provisions protecting the Guaraní. This legislation was no different.

The last self-conscious effort to conserve the Guarani through law spanned the period between 1606 and 1620. Francisco de Alfaro, a prominent royal official, wrote to the king in 1606 asking for a "universal rule" to govern the encomiendas and limit abuse of the Indians once and for all.[100] Every royal effort to address the "misery of these poor people," he said, had been converted into harm by "the greed of the Spaniards." Royal officials, from the viceroy to *audiencia* (royal court) members, to governors, even churchmen, sought to help only themselves, without any "color of justice," for it was much easier to "wrong" the Indians than to "redress their wrongs." The king agreed that a "general law" was necessary, for Alfaro's letter bears a marginal notation commanding the audiencia to verify and remedy such cases immediately. Felipe III then appointed Alfaro as inspector general, charging him to put Paraguay's encomiendas in order.

Modeled on similar laws in Peru, Alfaro's 1611 ordinances aimed to align Paraguay with the rest of the New World.[101] As royal law had long demanded, the Indians were finally to be recognized as "wholly free" vassals of the king. In lieu of in-kind contributions or personal service to encomenderos, individuals would pay tribute directly to the royal treasury in Asunción in what was known as "coin of the land"—cloth, foodstuffs, yerba—in effect substituting a head tax for the messier and venal mediation of encomenderos. Otherwise, the Indians would be free to seek wages from anyone who would hire them, dramatically expanding the wage-labor pool then dominated by mestizos. They were not to be burdened like beasts or sent to the yerba groves, "even if they wanted to" (a nod to the entanglement of coercion and consent). They were to have weekly rest days to attend church. Women were not to serve in encomenderos' homes. New pueblos de indios would consolidate existing villages (an old idea that had only ever been partially implemented). In time, these would be governed not by Franciscan friars or secular administrators but by councils (*cabildos*) of Indigenous officers chosen by village elites, as was the case elsewhere in the New World. These native cabildos would manage the labor draft, so long as it persisted, and ensure tribute was paid on time. Broadly speaking, the ordinances sought to reorient Paraguay's labor relations, ending Indigenous dependency on and subjection to encomenderos by allowing individual Indians to enter an emerging wage market. This was thought to be the only way to ensure the Guaraní's conservation—a mordant irony, given that the encomienda had been hailed in 1556 as the only solution to Spaniards' abuses.

But much had changed over the preceding fifty years. As happened throughout the New World during the sixteenth century, the indigenous population had collapsed. An accurate count is impossible for Paraguay, given the lack of sixteenth-century censuses. Epidemic disease accounted for much of the decline; Asunción suffered three smallpox outbreaks up to 1612.[102] Official descriptions emphasized deaths due to raids and war, suicides and low birth rates, sheer overwork and flight to explain why the Indians "were ending." One conservative estimate puts the total number of Indigenous people in Asunción's orbit at roughly 50,000 by 1630, half what it had been half a century earlier. North toward the Guairá and Villa Rica, the decline may have been more precipitous still, from 160,000–200,000 at contact to 60,000 by 1630.[103] Not surprisingly, the size and number of encomiendas declined steadily over the period. The original 320 established in 1556 had averaged 63 people. By 1650, the number had dropped to 26.[104] In 1611, Alfaro commented that many encomiendas were "not worth consideration," numbering fewer than 10 encomendados.[105]

Alfaro's law was widely opposed. In Asunción and other Spanish towns, encomenderos and ordinary vecinos (voting members of the city council), as well as clergy, railed against the change. By eliminating personal service and the labor draft (in effect, abolishing the encomienda), Alfaro's law threatened to upend settler society. At the core of the reform was the idea that Indians possessed liberty just as Spaniards did, as royal law had long held. Settlers worried that the Guaraní might take their freedom altogether too seriously. Here was the fundamental contradiction of all efforts to incorporate Indigenous people as royal vassals into a New World social order that needed to exploit them. The Mercedarian friar Francisco Luxan de Medina noted in 1612 that once released from their obligations to their encomenderos, the Indians would refuse to "rent" themselves out (work for a wage). They would instead flee to the forest, where they would surrender to their natural indolence and drunkenness.[106]

A contemporary report noted that something like this had in fact already happened just outside Asunción. "With a false voice of liberty," some Indians had started to "wander from one place to another," thieving and telling other Indians that they should stop serving their encomenderos and refuse to "serve by wages or in any other way." Another group of people seem to have done just that. Claiming not to know where they were from or where they belonged, the band had occupied a small territory upriver from Asunción. Blessed with water, wood, good fishing, and land for small fields, these people wandered "idly" about, according to an official report, recognizing no encomendero and showing no inclination to seek wages.[107] And as Friar Luxan had noted, if the Indians refused to work, each Spaniard would have no choice but to cultivate their own food just avoid starving to death. Harvests would collapse and there would be no money for churches, monasteries, or the clergy, no trade in merchandise, no alms.

Given decades of complaint against encomenderos and repeated efforts by royal officials to rein in abuses, it is tempting to suppose that the Guaraní would have welcomed a law abolishing personal service and ending their dependence on the encomiendas. The situation appears to have been more complicated. Although evidence is limited, a fact-finding mission in 1613–1614 strongly suggests that many Guaraní also opposed Alfaro's law. A judge commissioned by the audiencia convened a meeting of local leaders and townspeople in each of four Guaraní towns near Asunción—Tobatí, Ytá, Yaguarón, and Altos. Together, they amounted to between three thousand and four thousand people subject to the encomienda.[108] Through an interpreter, the judge proclaimed the king's authority and read out Alfaro's law, urging residents to accept the idea of working for wages and paying tribute individually from what they earned. It might be hard at first to break with their customary ways, he conceded, but with time "it will become gentler and easier . . . and it matters to your conservation to have this way of living."[109]

All four communities opposed the new regime, insisting that they preferred to serve their encomenderos as they long had.[110] Given their proximity to each other and their near unison language of complaint, it seems likely this was a coordinated response. The communities' spokesmen gave several reasons for their position. The new law would take away the "liberty" they enjoyed in serving their encomenderos, they said. As things stood, their encomenderos treated them well, did not abuse them, and did not give them too much work, which enabled them to serve them out of "goodwill, love, and kinship."[111] And, they said, the encomenderos loved them in return, making them good Christians and providing medicines when they were ill. To force them to adopt the new law would be to take away their "liberty . . . to choose what is best," which they had been told they could do. Laboring for wages and paying tribute directly would mean more work for all, which they felt would cause them great harm, for the proposed wage rate (one real per day) would not be enough to sustain them, even if doubled. Moreover, their encomenderos would suffer, they argued, because in their poverty they would be unable to pay the wage. In the new way of doing things, there would be no more "goodwill" between parties. Those who rented (employed) day laborers would demand too much work and not pay enough. Those who opted only for wages and contracts would not last, becoming thieves and highwaymen, endangering the Republic. The Guaraní caciques pointed out that villages had begun to empty out as people returned to the forest to avoid that fate. They had no power to stop the villagers, nor could they force them to accept the arrangement, they asserted.

The contrast between these claims and Alfaro's charge of "great and intolerable . . . abuses" against the Natives that "continued and were growing," could hardly have been starker.[112] Indeed, Alfaro dismissed the Natives' testimony as the product of "inducements and trickery." And there is no denying that their statements tracked the settlers' stance against the law almost to the letter, from invoking liberty, love, and kinship to asserting encomenderos' good treatment of the Indians, to citing the danger to the Republic in accepting the new arrangement.[113] Encomenderos almost surely knew what their encomendados would say, at least in broad strokes. But to conclude that these Guaraní were reading from a script likely overstates encomenderos' capacity for coordination among themselves; it also would give little room for a Guaraní viewpoint.

To figure a Guaraní stance in this matter, it is necessary to reflect on the nature of Guaraní economic and social entanglement with settlers during the sixteenth century. Decades of experience had taught the Guaraní, first and foremost, that Spaniards sought personal benefit from the Indians, whether in terms of wealth, status, survival, or liberty from dependence on others. And yet there is barely a hint of this in the towns' declarations. Indeed, the four cabildos presented a nearly unbroken façade of adamantine satisfaction with the status quo. "Nearly," for there is one small crack in the plaster of their otherwise smooth wall of opposition to the proposed law. As did the other towns, Ytá observed that townspeople wanted to serve their encomenderos "gently and with goodwill," as their ancestors had done. Yet Ytá qualified this point in a way the other towns did not. They could serve their encomenderos now, said Ytá's spokesman, because encomenderos for many years "abstained" from inflicting the "abuses that anciently and without consideration" they once did. He said that they "treat us with much love and goodwill," allowing the people of Ytá to enjoy "liberty" and ensuring the "conservation of our wives and children."[114] We cannot know how much time had passed since encomenderos began to "abstain" from abuses, but this remark at least hints at encomenderos' long history of violence against the Guaraní—the only such glimmer in the entire bill of particulars against Alfaro's law.

Though interpretive caution is in order, this statement suggests the possibility that by the early seventeenth century, in the face of law's broad failure to protect them from mistreatment, these four villages had worked out arrangements with their encomenderos that both sides had come to talk about in terms of kinship and love, which is to say reciprocity. While settlers had never intended to labor on behalf of their tobayas as native practice dictated, these Guaraní appear to have cast their relationship with encomenderos in broadly mutual terms. The language and practice of *cuñadazgo* (brother-in-law-ship) had permeated such relationships since shortly after contact, and with them notions of gift and reciprocity, as historian Shawn Austin has shown.[115] Though cabildo spokesmen did not offer details, the reference to "gifts in our illnesses" hints at the sort of reciprocity that may have been uppermost in the minds of people who had lived through repeated smallpox epidemics across the sixteenth century—a more self-consciously transactional reciprocity expressed through the language of substantive mutuality.[116] At the same time, Guaraní references to "love" resonated with Spanish political theory that lords and vassals were bound by "true affection."[117] This connection is what cabildos may have been signaling by insisting that they had not been "imposed upon, cajoled, coerced, or threatened by any person"—a distinctly legalistic formulation—for any hint of compulsion rooted in power and "interest" would have negated the claim to true, disinterested "love." In other words, the cabildos were able to ground their rejection of the new law in terms that satisfied both Guaraní and Spanish understandings regarding social life, within certain limits.

There is no reason to assume that this affection was entirely instrumental or merely rhetorical. Displays of genuine care could run in both directions. The report of Guaraní opposition to Alfaro's law noted, perhaps with some exaggeration, that no encomendero went to his grave without ensuring some Masses were said for "his Indian women who had died."[118] More concretely, encomenderos' wills not uncommonly remembered individual encomendados, if in small ways. For their part, Indigenous servants might give some of their earnings to a poor encomendera, even though she "does not ask them for anything."[119] One Spanish opponent of the new laws observed that encomenderos and encomendados often grew up side by side in extended communities linked by kinship as well as by circumstance.[120] As Alfaro and even critics noted, many encomiendas were small, their encomenderos poor. In such situations, as cabildo statements hint, fates were shared, up to a point.

Alongside this politics of emotion, the cabildos pressed one hard-edged point: they did not wish to become day laborers compensated in wages and individually responsible for paying tribute as a head tax. All four villages declared that Alfaro's arrangement could only mean more toil for them, which would tear their communities apart. Wage earners were expected to do "excessive" work, stressed the spokesmen. One village member had traveled to Peru to see how labor was organized there. The report was not encouraging: "Natives who enter into contracts and provide service for pay do not endure the difficult work and *slavery* in which they find themselves without the liberty they enjoy with their encomenderos."[121] If Alfaro's reform takes hold, stated one cabildo, they would "come to be known as journeymen" and there would be no more "goodwill between parties." They would rather be satisfied with "gifts" and other things that the encomenderos give them, said the cabildo from Altos, than be "forced" into the liberty of working for wages.[122] This point was later echoed by Asunción's general counsel, who in 1618 traveled to Madrid to argue against further efforts to implement Alfaro's law. Adding detail to the cabildos' statement, he noted that encomenderos supplied the Indians with tools, oxen, and clothes to do their work. If Natives had to be paid for their labor, encomenderos would have no reason to "help them, cure them, or hide their thefts" nor allow them to "use the encomendero's estate as if it were their own."[123]

This depiction of encomenderos as suffering but good-hearted masters who freely provided the means of production to their charges, tolerated thefts, and gave over their land to those who worked it was likely no less overblown than the insistence that the Indians served entirely out of "love and goodwill." But it does point to a pivotal fact: encomenderos, not Guaraní, controlled access to capital goods (tools, oxen, land) that were critical to producing the surplus on which Asunción's economy and Guaraní survival depended. As Jesuit Marciel de Lorenzana commented, encomenderos exerted "great dominion" over their charges, employing legal subterfuges regarding marriage arrangements to pass them among themselves.[124] They did so "without the Indians daring to say a word," because the Indians had neither land, nor horses, nor chickens, nor even clothes that did not come from their "masters," which they gave and withheld "by whim." Nothing in the record suggests this was going to change. What can be said is that by blending appeals to liberty and love with the spirit of barter, gift-giving, and kinship, the Guaraní of these four towns may have found a way to temper their subjection somewhat and face the profound strangeness of having been converted into someone else's exploitable asset.

One way to understand Guaraní opposition to Alfaro's reforms, thus, is as an effort to defend a hard-won response to settler overexploitation of the Guaraní as a common-pool resource. Efforts to conserve the Guaraní through law speak to this point, especially with regard to the early mistreatment of women. The encomienda had originally been established to address the danger that the Guaraní would be "finished off," in Las Casas's words. As a matter of policy, the idea had been to assign a certain number of Natives to a single encomendero—a kind of privatizing of the resource—and regulate their treatment so that they would not be "vexed by all."[125] But in a context of persistent labor shortfalls, it was not long before encomenderos were renting out "their" Indians to those who had none, multiplying their work unsustainably. Endless royal decrees ordering the good treatment and conservation of the natives had had little effect. In response, the Guaraní tried to mobilize reciprocity and kinship to secure a measure of control over their circumstances. In a sense, they created what might be called a gainful reciprocity, a "locally evolved rules system" to bind encomenderos into a tenuous community of interest that could constrain their exploitation to tolerable, or at least survivable, limits.[126] As the cabildos claimed, before the ordinances they had been able to ensure the "conservation of [our] wives and children."[127] The nuances of this arrangement and how stable it had been remain elusive and may never be perfectly clear. Certainly, the threat to flee to the forest—which figured prominently in the towns' own arguments against the new ordinances—as well as the ligatures of reciprocal and communal "goodwill" may have subtly limited what encomenderos could ask of them, compared to the rigors of the wage system. But against the devastation they had faced since contact, they may have found in the language of kinship, love, and reciprocity a fragile means of negotiating the terms of their enclosure. That fragility may have made Alfaro's vision for their lives seem especially risky.

The final chapter in the official debate over Alfaro's reforms—and of legal efforts to regulate the use of indigenous people in Paraguay—opened in early 1618 when Bartolomé Fernández, Asunción's general counsel, went to Madrid to persuade the Council of the Indies and the king to void the reforms. He echoed opponents of Alfaro's law, Natives as well as encomenderos, insisting that the Guaraní had been brought into Christian polity to serve Spaniards only "through friendship and kinship, as those Indians call it." (This final clause does hint that the sentiment may have run more strongly in one direction than the other.) They lacked the drive to earn wages, said Fernández, and so could not satisfy their tribute obligation any other way than by continuing to serve their encomenderos. Left to themselves, they would become lazy and return to eating roots. The land would be destroyed, warned the procurator, because neither Indians nor Spaniards would work for wages and there were no black slaves to take their place. Alfaro had not understood the situation on the ground and had imposed a solution drawn up for Peru that was ill-suited to Paraguay. The best approach, said Fernández, was to restore the status quo as it had stood before Alfaro's mistake: admittedly, the encomienda "was a form of subjection, but it is very free and gentle because of the good relationship and treatment the encomenderos give."[128] The king was having none of it. Fernández's arguments were not new and Alfaro's reforms had never been only about Paraguay. They were part of a broader effort to end the encomienda across the New World in favor of more reliable mechanisms for managing labor and securing tribute. To this extent, Fernández was not wrong about the bad fit between Alfaro's solution and Paraguayan realities. Nevertheless, in late 1618 Felipe III issued a curt decree reaffirming the 1611 ordinances.[129]

By the early 1620s, the relationship between settlers and Guaraní represented a broad zone of misorder—legal prescription did not match lived reality and lived reality itself was muddled. One thing is clear: between Aracaré's warning in the 1530s that the Guaraní might end up "captive" to Spaniards and the four towns' early-seventeenth century statements of contented service much turbulent water had flowed. Through it all, law had largely failed to check the imposed dependence and exploitation of the encomienda. The Guaraní, or some among them, had adapted as best they could, marshaling reciprocity to assure a margin of survival, a situation that may have seemed tenable compared to the alternative. The testimony of Ytá, Yaguarón, Altos, and Tobatí, thus, is a window onto lives that had been turned upside down since contact. Yet, their representations did not convey the full complexity of the situation (and more research is needed): these communities were all close to Asunción and in aggregate their numbers accounted for only a third of those subject to the encomienda in the wider region, and not more than half of those near Asunción.[130] Other communities may not have found the modus vivendi these four did with their encomenderos. The two groups characterized in the 1613 report as refusing to serve any encomendero suggest as much. To this point, Jesuit missionary Marciel de Lorenzana noted in a 1621 letter to the king that while Guaraní in the vicinity of Asunción admitted the Spaniards to their lands "via cuñadazgo and kinship," they had seen that Spaniards did not treat them as "brothers-in-law and relatives but as servants." And so, they had begun to "withdraw and not serve the Spaniard." Indeed, when they heard the word *Spaniard*, they thought "pirate, thief, fornicator, adulterer, and liar." As to Asunción's Spanish residents, Lorenzana observed caustically that despite their claims to poverty, many had recently begun to sport expensive silks and fine fabrics, peddled by the many merchants who frequently came to town, going into debt with each other to afford these luxuries.[131] Of course, there is good reason to be skeptical of this missionary's depictions of relations between Guaraní and Spaniards. At the time, he and other Jesuits were actively evangelizing, and the supposed evils of the encomienda were a convenient target. Nevertheless, his description, vague though it was, hints that Guaraní were capable of quite different responses to the challenges they faced.

They should repair their consciences

One way to think of the Spanish monarchy's legislation on behalf of the New World's Indigenous people, from the New Laws in 1542 to Alfaro's 1611 ordinances, is as an early exercise in macro-scale social protection, law as a counterforce to the self-destructive tendencies of gain left to itself. The language of conservation in response to the consumption, finishing, ending, or diminution of the Guaraní under the pressure of Spaniards' disordered greed made this clear. This was one of Polanyi's central points: the unleashing of economic self-interest within the social order creates a dynamic which, if not controlled, endangers the very "substance of society" over the long term. Of course, Polanyi was talking about gain expressed through self-regulating markets in early nineteenth century England. In sixteenth-century Paraguay, this peril took a rawer form, making the situation there sharper and perhaps more urgent than in the Old World at the same moment. For in Paraguay, as in the New World generally, society remained an unrealized project just as ordinary settlers were learning to navigate a world in which legal and moral regulation was lax, at best.

This is why the monarchy's persistent call for *conservation* is so critical to understanding the fortunes of the New World's Indigenous people. The pursuit of gain, or even just survival at the expense of others, not only threatened the mistreatment of specific individuals or communities—it put at risk the very possibility of a social order shared by Indigenous people and Europeans. Herein lay the great irony of Spanish political theory and action vis-à-vis Indigenous people: whereas the king was, in principle, obliged to protect the weak from the powerful, in the New World the Spanish monarchy found itself having to defend its Indian vassals as a group from its Spanish vassals. At this moment when the full measure of economic self-interest was yet to be taken, conservation of Indigenous people represented the monarchy's ideological commitment to shared social life as humankind's natural condition, with Christian polity its highest expression. Ensuring the conditions for that sociality was the king's paramount job, a responsibility effectuated through law guided by royal conscience in service to justice.

But law was not the king's responsibility alone. Conscience was the animating principle of a moral and legal order that aimed to restrain human beings from their worst instincts by orienting them to the common good.[132] Every person was liable in conscience to society at large, so that ideas regarding good and bad would suffuse social life—justice by another name. This precept was thought to be especially urgent in the New World, given abundant temptations to economic self-love at the expense of others and recognizing the king's limited capacity to guide conscience with the rigors of judicial correction. Thus, in his *Admonitions and Rules for Confessors of Spaniards in the Indies* (1552), Las Casas had denounced those who enslaved Indians or otherwise profited from their use. He enjoined confessors to an unbending moral rigor with the "great ambition and insatiable greed" of their encomendero penitents. Confessors should be unsparing with these wayward souls, charging them with restitution of all the harms they had done—a kind of restorative reciprocity in which those who had become rich off the sweat of Indians would give up all their wealth as the only way to merit forgiveness. Otherwise they should not be absolved. Nor was this just a matter of personal salvation: no one was blameless, insisted Las Casas, for they were all individually and "*in solidum*"—collectively—responsible for the cataclysm they had inflicted on the New World's indigenous people.[133] While some confessors may have found this severity morally satisfying, it is hard to imagine that many actually sought to apply it across the confessional's grille. After all, Las Casas had effectively placed the entire Spanish population of the New World, or at least its most advantaged, into mortal sin redeemable only by surrendering all they had gained.

Still, conscience's critical role in animating the tissue of love and charity binding society together remained central to legal and social thought throughout the sixteenth century. The dedication to Manuel Rodrigues's *Summary of Cases of Conscience with Beneficial Admonitions for Confessors and a Treatise on the Judicial Order at the End* (1596) made the point concisely: "What benefits conscience will aid the republic."[134] In a similar spirit, Father Diego de Torres, the first Jesuit provincial of Paraguay, penned "Instruction for the Consciences of the Encomenderos" in 1609. Just as the Jesuits were lobbying for the law that became Alfaro's ordinances, Father Torres took a position echoing Las Casas's, calling on encomenderos to "repair their consciences" by freeing the Guaraní to whom they had denied liberty, lessening their work, stopping their abuse, and paying them fairly.[135] And yet, he noted, Asunción was not Potosí. So while he agreed they were morally bound to offer restitution for the harm they had caused the Indians, Father Torres concluded that it should be "moderate, in view of the encomenderos' poverty." Above all, conscience required that they agree to the abolition of personal service, the only way to preserve the Indians. A few years later, the king echoed Father Torres's appeal enjoining confessors to exhort "any persons" who had ever held Indians to "repair their consciences with great care, for everything will be necessary and they should pray to God that they succeed."[136]

By this time, however, legal (and theological) exhortations aiming to check Spanish abuses of the Guaraní rang hollow. *Pobleros* (encomienda administrators) were likened to "demons" who, lacking all "virtue," should be thrown into the ocean depths with a millstone about their necks, for the good of the Indians.[137] A hand-wringing royal decree noted pointedly in 1608 that despite "my many letters, provisions, and ordinances," encomenderos still often treated the Indians "worse than slaves," many of them being "bought and sold from one encomendero to another," with ensuing "calamities."[138] Some of this was recycled language from the many earlier orders. Still, it reveals that imperial officialdom widely acknowledged that encomenderos and other Spaniards tended to act mainly out of self-interest and that their doing so undermined royal authority. In a place so far from the throne, where the decision whether and how to punish was often up to an official with deep personal connections and where the legally enforced good treatment of the Indians threatened settlers'—not only encomenderos'—economic livelihoods, the call to conscience as the basis for legal and moral regulation was fading.

With this, the Spanish monarchy's decades-long active project to protect the Indians from mistreatment through law reached its limit in Paraguay. Partly this was a matter of Paraguay's circumstances. In central Mexico, with its larger Indigenous population and robust legal processes, the possibilities for law (if not precisely for conscience) were in some ways greater.[139] But early Paraguay also reflected the shifting registers of morality, self-interest, and law among Europeans who left the Old World for America in the sixteenth century. As Las Casas had noted decades earlier, the specter of the Indians' "ruin" had hung over Spain's New World undertaking from the outset. In response, Spanish kings had employed the tools they had to hand, dating to the late medieval period—law reinforced by conscience. If the "external forum" (*fuero exterior*, the dictates of law backed by the promise of just punishment) aligned with the "internal forum" (*fuero interior*, individual conscience in light of long-accepted principles of justice enforced in the confessional), men would moderate their gain-oriented behavior.

From the vantage of modern notions of law and contemporary sensibilities, this reaction may seem quaint, even hypocritical. In the heat of the times, they were neither. Rather, the endless stream of decrees from Madrid demonstrates how seriously the Spanish monarchy approached its obligation to protect the Indians while simultaneously ensuring they could be exploited, within certain limits. It bespeaks, as well, the growing futility of that task, at least in terms of older understandings. Broadly, the problem was that the emerging motive of gain was eroding the bonds linking conscience to law, just as Paraguay's distance and local circumstances made it next to impossible to enforce legal precepts reliably. That the Spanish monarchy was unable to strike a balance between these competing goals in Paraguay suggests what could happen in a place where even ordinary men might imagine profiting at the expense of others, where powers of enforcement were weak, and where the vulnerable lacked effective means to defend themselves. In this faraway place, conscience could not bear the moral weight being thrust upon it. In the process, the Spanish monarchy's capacity to uphold its obligation of reciprocity to its Guaraní vassals reached its limit.

*   *   *

As the seventeenth century dawned, calls to *conserve* the Indians, dulled by repetition, and anxious appeals to *conscience* were little more than symptoms of a creeping realization—that the empire of gain was vanquishing moral obligation in Paraguay no less than in Europe itself, if with distinctive inflections. Moral imagination and material desire, long intertwined in the European ethos, were uncoiling from one another to occupy distinct spheres in the minds of settlers. In this new world, where even evangelization was learning to genuflect before self-interest, Paraguay's lack of riches appears not to have dampened settler gain so much as twisted it into an avarice of desperation. If the Guaraní at times found a way to enlist kinship, *goodwill*, and *love* in response to ongoing calamity, we should not suppose they were under any illusion about their situation, so much as they sought to bend its terms not only toward survival but also toward their understanding of human sociality.

4

Beyond Predation

A life as far removed as possible from the contagion of avarice.

Formula the Institute (1540)

To see with my own eyes if . . . you are not men but monsters
who . . . cannot be spoken with.

Emissary from Mburubichá Tayaoba,
in Montoya, *Spiritual Conquest*

IN LATE 1609, two Italian Jesuits and an Asunceño priest struck northeast
along the Paraná River from Asunción toward a territory known as the
Guairá. Still thinly populated by Europeans, the area was home to tens of
thousands of Guaraní—two hundred thousand by a contemporary estimate.[1] About the same time, two other Jesuit missionaries headed southeast to the region between the rivers Paraná and Uruguay. Communities in both areas faced growing pressures. In the Guairá, Spaniards from
smaller settlements, such as Ontiveros, Ciudad Real del Guairá, and Villa
Rica, were looking to expand encomiendas. At the same time, Brazilian
slaving parties out of São Paulo had targeted the region. In the southeast,
unreduced Guaraní villages had resisted evangelization for decades and
fought efforts from Asunción to subject them to the encomienda. Both
Jesuit groups went with the permission and support of Governor Hernandarias de Saavedra.

These small expeditions took place against the backdrop of ongoing
debates over the treatment of Paraguay's Indigenous population. Encomenderos were looking to less-explored areas for new sources of labor.
Governor Hernandarias aimed to get ahead of these moves by allowing
Jesuits to establish missions that could shield the Indians from encomenderos and insulate them from the newer threat of Brazilian slaving raids
operating across a porous frontier. He envisioned these villages as a string
of strategic hamlets along an eventual land route to the Atlantic, which
would allow Asunción to connect directly with coastal trade without having to detour south to Buenos Aires.

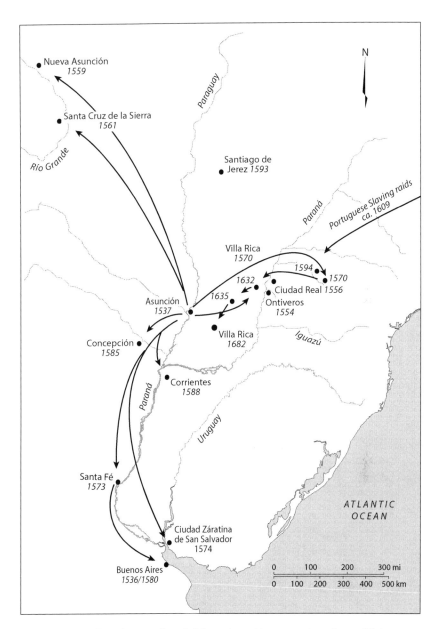

MAP 4.1. Spanish settlements founded from Asunción, 1540–1600. *Source:* Kleinpenning, *Paraguay*, 180 (fig. 5.1).

The broad question was whether these areas would be subject to the economic and institutional arrangements that had gelled in Asunción, or perhaps become something else. Asunción's shrinking encomiendas were no longer the active force they had been, though they remained the foundation of local production and ordinary settlers still thought of encomienda grants as the baseline for social status. An emergent class of merchants was beginning to look beyond the encomienda, seeking more Indigenous workers who might join the growing population of mestizo wage earners. These groups were opposed to, or at least constrained by, the governor, royal officials, and Jesuits who agreed that the Indians needed to be protected but lacked a clear vision of how best to do so, given the law's limited capacity to stem abuse. Many Guaraní, from a place of bitter experience, appeared to be seeking new alignments.

*   *   *

"We all know how the Spaniards have treated the Guaraní"

Jesuit missionary Father Marciel de Lorenzana had set out southeast from Asunción in late 1609. Governor Hernandarias had ordered him to proceed cautiously, not with violence but "only with doctrine and preaching." Though opposed by many local caciques—who the father described as "bellicose"—Lorenzana had encountered small groups of receptive Guaraní along the way and had established the mission town of San Ignacio fifteen leagues short of the Paraná. Emboldened by his success, he soon crossed the river to open contacts among new groups, taking advantage of the fact that a few of those who had "become Christians" were kin to villagers there. Though Father Lorenzana had begun by offering and receiving gifts, initial reactions had been of "displeasure." Whenever people come talking about salvation, said the gathered residents of one village, "it was in order to turn [us] over to the Spaniards, who make slaves of [us]." Where once upon a time they served Spaniards as "friends, and kin of [Guaraní] women," he reported others as saying, now they face "excessive work." As these words indicate, some communities had already fallen under the encomienda. They appear to have been looking for some alternative to the "miserable servitude" so many had already suffered. Lorenzana did his best to allay their concerns. He told the caciques that the Spanish king, "for the love he has for [you]," had signed a law to protect them from mistreatment and was sending an emissary to enforce it.[2]

Hearing this, caciques of the two rivers convened a council to discuss how to proceed, deliberating for many days. They invited the great cacique Tabacambí to convey the council's conclusion in the name of all the peoples of the region. According to Pedro de Lozano's later account, Tabacambí spoke to Lorenzana, saying that if the Jesuit's words were true, his people were prepared to become "sons of God."[3] But, he cautioned, they all knew "how the Caraí [Spaniards] . . . have treated the Guaraní" and they were "gripped by a great fear." Except for that "heavy yoke," they would already have "given [their] ears" to his preaching. The Guaraní, said Tabacambí, would allow the king's envoy into their territories, provided he declared unequivocally that they were "*mboyas* or vassals of the *great king* of Spain, and that we have no obligation to serve any Caraí, but instead that . . . we be his vassals, free like the Caraí, without service or labor draft . . . and that we will be able to live in our lands always, giving his Majesty some tribute in recognition of our vassalage." On these conditions, we will "very gladly be vassals or *mboyas* of the *great king*" and "make ourselves Christians." Apparently, Lorenzana had thought this pronouncement a bit cheeky but he promised to pass the message on.

In many ways, just being heard represented an achievement. Guaraní in the region of the Paraná had resisted settlers' incursions since 1556. They had killed many Spaniards and had harassed travel along the river continuously. They had refused evangelization, saying that God's law sought only to force them "into the service of Spaniards." Although the immediate question was whether Lorenzana and other Jesuits would be allowed to proselytize in the area, an underlying concern, as Guaraní villages and Tabacambí himself made clear, was whether they could mitigate encomienda service, or avoid it altogether. Lorenzana understood this. Though he refused to commit to anything, he noted that the king had sent his officer Francisco de Alfaro to put things right.

We cannot know with certainty whether or to what extent the words attributed to other Guaraní and to Tabacambí were their own. Like all Jesuits of the period, Lorenzana deeply opposed the encomienda as a stumbling block to conversion. Tabacambí's clear denunciation certainly obliged this view. And yet, there are reasons to accept the account of Tabacambí's discourse as broadly representative of a still-inchoate position of Indigenous groups. First, the whole area was coming under renewed pressure from Asunción, for the labor situation there had not improved. Caciques likely feared what would come next and may have been looking

for some way to head off disaster. Second, the concerns attributed to Tabacambí and imputed generally to the Guaraní ring of concrete historical
experience; the suspicion that evangelization might be a stalking horse for
more material ambitions could have referred to earlier encounters, perhaps with Franciscan missionaries, that had not panned out as hoped.
Third, the claim that Indians had once served Spaniards as kin hints that
these Guaraní may have understood that *cuñadazgo* had reached its limit
as a means of mitigating encomendero abuses.[4]

As to substance, Tabacambí and other Guaraní would have known
what they were asking. The idea of being the king's vassals was hardly
novel. The New Laws of 1542 had declared them so, and subsequent legislation, despite its failures, had reinforced the idea as a horizon of possibility. Tabacambí's speech grasped vassalage precisely, making clear that
he and other caciques were not merely accepting terms. They were proposing a political and economic relationship with settlers and the king
distinct from the one Guaraní had known to this point. They recognized the Spanish monarch as a *mburubichabeté* (a cacique among caciques), and his emissary, Francisco de Alfaro, as *mbaequaapara* (one
who knows or understands much and who promises certainty).[5] They demanded not merely spoken words, but *quatiá*—that is, formal writings,
pictures, drawings, or papers with the same gravitas as Christian sacred
texts, providing guarantees, such as a cacique good to his word would
give.[6] In offering to become mboyas of the king, Tabacambí made clear
that they would not be reduced to personal service or accept the encomienda's labor rotation. They were to be free (*libres*) like Spaniards, entitled to law directly under the king himself rather than indirectly through
the encomienda. They wanted to be safe in their lands and were willing
to pay some tribute as a sign of their status, though Tabacambí refused
to say how much. Nor did he indicate what the Guaraní would do with
their liberty, if granted it.

Tabacambí's position appears not to have represented a stable consensus either within Spanish officialdom or among Indigenous people.
Although Governor Hernandarias had admonished the missionaries to
proceed peacefully, he soon pushed for a military expedition east of the
Uruguay River to subject the people there directly, perhaps to accelerate
the push toward the Atlantic coast (or perhaps he was "concerned to acquire glory and gilding his interest with public utility," as a seventeenth-
century Jesuit critic put it).[7] He was persuaded to abandon the plan, mainly

because it would have violated the king's order not to evangelize by arms. Similarly, among the Indians, nothing was firm in relation to Jesuit pretensions. Father Lorenzana had trekked to the Paraná region in the company of the cacique Arapizandú. The cacique had traveled to Asunción to petition the governor to establish a mission in his territory. Lorenzana had obliged, founding San Ignacio in an area that had already been claimed by encomenderos. Arapizandú's tactic of approaching the governor suggests that some among the Guaraní were actively hoping an alliance with the Jesuits might give them some leverage vis-à-vis other Spaniards. And yet, it was not long before Arapizandú fell out with the Jesuit fathers and joined with Tabaca, another cacique, to stand against further evangelization. Perhaps he had lost prestige among caciques who had resisted such incursions for so long. Perhaps, like caciques and shamans before and after him, he chafed at the idea of monogamous marriage, which could only undercut his prestige among his own mboyas (followers). According to Lozano's account, he was ultimately persuaded to abandon this path and return to San Ignacio, where many residents had refused to follow him into the forest. As with Hernandarias, in this still unbalanced reality, the possibility of violence touched all decisions over how to proceed, despite royal condemnation of it. The question for the Guaraní was whether there was any other way.

Necessary things

To parse the encounter between Jesuits and Guaraní, it is crucial to understand what the missionaries thought they were up to in going to largely uncharted Indigenous territory unarmed and only in pairs. Anyone entering the theater of evangelization carried detailed instructions from the Jesuit provincial Father Diego de Torres explaining how they were to approach their work.[8] While many points stress religious matters—how to teach the Indians prayer, ritual, and catechism, when and how to speak to them about salvation—Father Torres's directives had just as much to say about the physical, material, and social aspects of new communities and their economic organization. Sites should be chosen carefully, seeking fertile land above the flood plain, ensuring access to fishing, and finding respite from mosquitoes, so that converts might thrive. Father Torres specified the layout of the communities in order to concentrate people. He charged his missionaries to teach the Natives how to raise pigs and chickens and to help them "with all charity" in planting corn, manioc, and cotton. He instructed that the poor and travelers be fed and the sick cared for. The fathers should accept nothing from the Guaraní beyond what was strictly necessary, so as not to "burden" the residents, and they should give everything they had as "gifts." Above all, the priests should bar Spaniards from the communities once they had been established. If some did enter, the fathers should ensure residents were not mistreated or "in any way" removed as *piezas* to work on encomiendas. Father Torres clearly had the struggles of previous decades in mind.

These injunctions revealed a Jesuit commitment to the material realities of those they proposed to evangelize. For Jesuits, conversion was not simply a matter of interior change. It depended on mediating between the material world, especially the human bodies that lived in it, and the soul's disposition to accept the grace of God. Theologically, this position reflected the Jesuits' close alignment with Aquinas's understanding of human personhood. On Aquinas's view, there was a fundamental "union of body and soul." A person was the unique combination of a specific soul and a specific body that allowed that "particular man" to *be* in the world. This distinctness was a function of how human beings interacted with the rest of the material world through bodily senses.[9] Materiality was no mere sidelight to human life, but integral to it. Echoing a point Aquinas had made, Jesuit theologian Juan de Mariana wrote in 1598 that human beings, in the postlapsarian world, were born "naked and frail" and therefore required the help of others to survive and thrive.[10] This implied an irreducible ethical and humanistic dimension to action in the world, one dependent on material realities. Theologian Denys Turner has glossed this idea by arguing that for Aquinas "human beings are *essentially* world-dependent." Among other things, this means that being human is intrinsically relational, for the world consists, in part, of other beings. As Turner puts it, for Aquinas "human beings are a form of life requiring the existence not only of other persons . . . but also forms of life other than their own." As such, human lives play out within "systems of natural reciprocity" that are the pivot of the world as God's creation.[11]

Any Jesuit granted permission to evangelize in Paraguay would have been familiar with these ideas through three basic sources—the *Formula the Institute* (1540) and the *Spiritual Exercises* (1548), both composed by the Jesuits' founder, St. Ignatius of Loyola, and the broad principles summarized in the *Ratio Studiorum* (1599). The *Formula* represented the mission statement of the newly established Society of Jesus. Expressing deep moral concerns regarding self-interest, it stated that those who would join the Society should seek a life "as far removed from all contagion of avarice" as possible and instead focus on "necessary things."[12]

The *Formula*'s spare statements were given body in Loyola's *Spiritual Exercises*, which also established the animating practice of what became Jesuit worldly spirituality by 1600. Through a program of prayer and meditation, the *Exercises* cultivated a sensibility grounded in the idea that "caring for the body was vitally connected to caring for the soul."[13] Over a month-long retreat, priests undertook an examination of conscience in which corporeal awareness provoked spiritual opening. Those who embarked on the exercises—and Torres instructed the Paraguay missionaries to do so at least once a year—were to recognize the "great diversity" of human activity and to visualize God's people, "some white, some black, some in peace, others at war, some crying and others laughing, some well, others infirm, some aborning, others dying." Exercitants were to imagine themselves in Christ's presence. While eating, they should see in their mind's eye how he eats, drinks, looks, and speaks. They should smell the sulfur of hell and hear the screams of the tormented. They should then carry these images and sensations to all of their labors, particularly their interaction with others, so as to "redeem the human species." In this way, they would learn indifference between wealth and poverty, honor and dishonor, life and death and be able to look upon total strangers and desire only their perfection—Aristotle's friendship of the good in Christian vestments and for all people.[14] If done rigorously and in good conscience, the *Exercises* could reshape desire and create new habits of body and soul aligned with what God wished for *all* human beings, allowing the practitioner to choose freely that which God desired and to act in the world through the charity demanded by God's grace.

The *Ratio Studiorum* standardized the principles to which all Jesuits were held in their worldly activity. As a course of study, it sought to ensure that postulants were "as well disposed toward [the writings of St. Thomas Aquinas] as possible."[15] Would-be Jesuits learned that body and soul were unified and that "human nature cannot be without sensible matter." The essential virtue for engaging the world was charity—the "free, self-giving, generous love" that could surpass even "the power of the will," as Aquinas noted.[16] No mere injunction to right thinking, charity was a rigorous demand to love one's neighbor more than one's own body, a tenet not a few Jesuit missionaries followed to martyrdom. It was only through one's own body "as organ of the soul's power" that one could express charity by providing others with the "necessaries of the body" that would enable them to choose salvation. Like individual gain, Jesuit charity addressed itself to the material world and the bodies in it. Unlike gain, charity recognized all bodies as being in mutual dependence in relation to God's larger creation.[17]

These ideas turned Jesuits away from monastic quietism. Aquinas had said that the "active life" in which a man delivers the "fruits of his contemplation" to others is "more perfect than the life that stops at contemplation."[18] Jesuits agreed and embarked on a mission that sought to match the scale of Europe's post-Columbian expansion. "We are not monks!" proclaimed Jerónimo Nadal, an early Jesuit commentator. "The world is our house."[19] In the spirit of this "worldly asceticism," Jesuits fanned out from Europe, reaching Mexico, Peru, Brazil, India, the Philippines, China, and Japan by the late sixteenth century.[20] In some places, their ministrations provoked backlash. In 1588, they had been cast out from the territories of a preeminent military lord in Japan who claimed they were "destroy[ing] the root of the Japanese kingdom." Shogun Hidetada issued an edict in 1614 barring them altogether.[21] Their presence in Paraguay, which ramped up just as the failure in Japan was sinking in, was therefore part of a truly global salvific enterprise. If medieval monasticism had fled inward from the world, the Jesuit ideal called for flight toward the world, in all its materiality. This is why Torres, Montoya, Lorenzana, and other missionaries in Paraguay maintained an abiding concern for the physical well-being of the Guaraní.[22] As Montoya later explained, the goal was to secure "the calm essential for Christian living" in order to "advance the people in virtue."[23] In other words, the material conditions of everyday life were intrinsic to preaching the gospel itself. José Cardiel summarized this understanding in the eighteenth century, showing how rooted this idea became over the one hundred and fifty years of mission work: "When all that is necessary for sustenance is well, all that is spiritual increases and flourishes."[24]

Watching with great care

Jesuits who went to the forests had to figure out how to put these ideas into practice. Their commitment to materiality was apparent from early on. Like Spanish explorers before them, they relied on gift giving to mediate first encounters, just as Father Torres had instructed them. Belgian

Jesuit Justo Van Suerck, after a year in Paraguay trying to convert the Guaraní, offered this description of how to approach potential converts:

> When one comes upon them the first time one should not speak to them of God, or the faith, or of the other life; all efforts must be made to persuade them to . . . come to a single place to live together. . . . [Little] is accomplished by even the best arguments of apostles, or any orator, compared with the far more powerful attraction exerted upon the Indians by all manner of baubles; such as needles, pins, knives, scissors, mirrors, combs, pieces of glass . . . and other objects of value in Europe, which are here the price of souls. Offering only a single knife, a few rings of glass, or any bagatelle of this sort, it would be easy for me to convince a cacique to move where I indicate with his entire family, in other words, 100, 200 or 300 individuals.[25]

Much is revealed and much obscured in this quote. In 1629, when he wrote these words, Van Suerck was still new to mission work.[26] We might suppose that this young missionary, twenty-nine at the time, remained troubled and ambivalent about the instrumentality of such an approach, as he revealed by referring to "the price of souls," perhaps unconsciously betraying a deepening European reflex to think of all exchanges as fundamentally transactional, even in supposedly transcendent matters. Still, his training was clear, and his own limited experience, as well as that of more seasoned missionaries, told him that appealing to material goods over talk of God, doctrine, or salvation made good sense. Though the Jesuits had begun learning Indigenous languages, communication remained difficult during these early years of evangelization.

Spanish culture had long recognized the value of gift giving as an opening to others. Covarrubias noted that the Spanish definition for "one who gives" (*regalador*) was "a friend who seeks to impart kindness to others" (a meaning not yet reflecting more cynical understandings of gift giving).[27] Jesuits took it for granted that gifts could signal goodwill. They also knew that settlers had exchanged goods with Indigenous people for decades, often with undesirable outcomes. Perhaps this was why Van Suerck and other Jesuits were often agape at the Natives' eagerness for "baubles." Caciques might come out of the forest with their followers and "brazenly ask" for axes, knives, and fishhooks. Echoing Van Suerck, Father Ruiz de Montoya spoke of "purchasing" the Indians' "goodwill" for the price of an ax.[28] For Jesuits, this was part of God's plan, which could only be discerned in action. Father Pedro de Oñate noted that it was a matter of "providence" that the gift of a hatchet could bind Indians to a new village as though by "shackles and chains" (a glimmer of recognition for the subtle coercions of material desire).[29]

Of course, such statements oversimplified what was happening and exaggerated the efficacy of bare material exchange. Jesuits knew they were entering into arenas of Indigenous alliances and enmities that had been upended by European presence. Showering one group with gifts might alienate another, for these gifts could shift balances in a region. Indeed, there was a "deadly politics of giving" that could end with a "martyr's halo" for missionaries who misread the signs.[30] As José de Acosta pointed out in 1600, it was essential for Jesuit missionaries to know how to give and receive gifts, so that potential converts would be drawn by "liberality" rather than "submission"[31]—and so that priests could avoid a good death long enough to accomplish something.

The distinction between liberality and submission, while strategic, also represented a fundamental theological commitment. Gifts were a material reflection of the idea of grace, the notion that the uncynical acceptance of that which is freely given could ground a lasting relationship—between missionaries and Indigenous people, and ultimately between Indigenous people and God. This relationship could come about only through an uncoerced interior assent, since God's grace could be accepted only through an act of free will.[32] This deep point was advanced chiefly by Jesuit theologians Luis de Molina and Francisco Suárez, both of whom wrote during the sixteenth century.[33] Though the details are intricate, the essence of their position was that God's gift of grace—that is, the invitation to salvation—could be completed only by a free human choice to accept it. The job of the missionary was to create the conditions that could lead to this choice. For Jesuits, this meant addressing the Guaraní through the most elemental point of contact available under the circumstances: bodily needs for sustenance and security.

Theological notions of grace and free will may not have meant much to the Guaraní at the time. Nor need they have. Regardless of how Jesuits understood Guaraní volition, Guaraní language was rich in vocabulary for willing, wanting, and desiring, as well as for actions appropriate to them.[34] Conversely, there may have been something bitter in the idea of being subject to the will of another who treated one badly, which Montoya's *Tesoro* linked to the Guaraní word for sickness, pain or bad feeling, difficulty or vehemence.[35] Whether they had any inkling of this Guaraní sensibility at the time, missionaries took it for granted that it was in the Guaraní's hands to decide whether to accept God's grace, that "habitual gift" that enabled men to move through the world by free will.[36] A gift, by its nature, could not be forced (at times a frustrating proposition for missionaries). Strong-arm tactics could only negate any apparent acceptance of Christian faith. As Aquinas had held, "It is contrary to the nature of the will's own act, that it should be subject to compulsion and violence."[37] And so, the Jesuits of Paraguay refused to carry weapons when approaching Indigenous groups, relying instead on the unencumbered gift in lieu of the violence and trickery Native people had come to expect of Europeans generally.

In other words, the Guaraní did not have to understand the intricacies of Jesuit theology to interpret these signals more or less as they were intended, or at least to have acted on them in ways Jesuits could accept as an opening to proselytization. By the early seventeenth century, Indigenous groups had had longer experience with intercultural gifting than Jesuits did. They could receive metal tools and accept seeds from missionaries during times of extreme necessity without having to consider that the Jesuits thought of themselves as ministering to Indigenous bodies *and* souls.[38] In some instances, they may even have approached the missionaries with a calculated shrewdness. Brazilian anthropologist Eduardo Viveiros de Castro once quipped that there is no reason to suppose that the Guaraní were incapable of seeing missionaries as idiots savants who could be counted on to give valuable goods in exchange for empty gestures.[39]

For both sides, the most important implication may have been the obvious one—gifts bespoke peaceful relations. During the sixteenth century, this had been the basis for exchanges of Spanish material goods and Guaraní women. But the dynamics of gifting between Guaraní and Jesuits differed crucially from this relationship, for the Jesuits were bound by vows of celibacy. From the perspective of Guaraní gift-reciprocity, this may have presented something of a puzzlement. If missionaries would not accept women, they could not become tobayas. And yet, the Guaraní understood that Jesuit gifts were an invitation to establish a long-term relationship with the priests.

If not kinship, what could be the basis for enduring relationship with these strange men? The dilemma was acute. The logic of reciprocity demanded the Guaraní requite the Jesuits' gifts, yet the fathers could not accept what Guaraní men were most keen to offer. On the other hand, compared to the treatment they had come to expect from ordinary Spaniards, the Guaraní of the early seventeenth century may have seen the Jesuits as relatively harmless; they asked that the Guaraní tolerate their presence and listen to what they had to say, without overt compulsion. This is not to deny Guaraní resistance, especially to missionary efforts to promote monogamy over polygamy—what missionaries called "carnal liberty"—among shamans and caciques.[40] One shaman (*paye*) sparked a short-lived rebellion in the early 1620s, promising his followers, ordinary Guaraní men mostly, that they, like the caciques, would be able to have multiple wives.[41] This would have been a profound change, for a cacique's prestige was rooted in the fact that most men had one wife (it would also have been unsustainable for the obvious reason that all men could not have multiple wives). The shaman's promise, in other words, represented a form of political opposition. Other Native groups sought to connect with the missionaries. Some offered to build houses and churches so that the priests would stay or pled with them to establish a village and "raise a cross."[42] In these communities, the alternative to trying to convert the missionaries into brothers-in-law appears to have been to accept their presence and give gifts of labor that could secure a community. The Jesuits reciprocated these overtures. Montoya reported that missionaries during these early years spent as much time in the fields, tilling and teaching the Guaraní use of the plow and ministering to those who fell ill during frequent epidemics, as preaching to them.[43]

Of course, Native communities had reason to be wary of Spaniards bearing gifts, since gifting so often served ulterior motives. Montoya recounted the story of a Spanish layman in the Guairá who claimed to preach to the Indians through "deeds," giving away his clothes much as the Jesuits themselves gave gifts to caciques, for "if I can win them over the rest will do what I want," explained the man.[44] Overlooking this self-interested claim and embarrassed that they themselves did not have anything to give to the Indians, the fathers sent the man on his way. Shortly the Guaraní revealed what had gone on. The man had been "auctioning" off his clothing, "purchasing" with each garment an Indian woman or child. They thought he was acting for the priests, presumably to take people to the missions. When they learned otherwise, they were incensed. The missionaries regained their trust only when the fathers set the record straight that Jesuits did not truck in Indian bodies, as so many other Europeans did.

Distrust could run deep. Guaraní had to learn how to distinguish those who might help them from those who would harm or subject them. In the Paraná, Father Lorenzana observed that during initial entrées to new territories, Indians often assumed the Jesuits were "spies" for the Spaniards.[45] One time, when Lorenzana met a large a large group of Indigenous people and their leaders, the caciques accused the missionary of being a "deceiver" who, under cloak of evangelization, sought war so that he could turn them over to Spaniards as "slaves."[46] They declared that they would not give anyone up or trade away captives they had taken in a recent war against a rival tribe. They promised to kill the priest if he continued to preach. "Christian Indians" accompanying Lorenzana then spoke to the caciques. These go-betweens noted that they continued to enjoy "the liberty that we have." "We are not [the Jesuits'] slaves," they said, perhaps using the Guaraní word for *captive*. To date, the missionaries have "asked us for nothing, nor have they taken anything. Instead, they have given us everything they have." Moreover, "with their eyes they will not even look at our women," which "filled us with amazement, as a thing never seen." Of course, Lorenzana could have put words in the intermediaries' mouths. But assuming they did speak as reported, their reassurances did not have the desired effect, for the caciques rejected Lorenzana's request (though their statements appear to have delayed action long enough for the father to escape and for his Guaraní allies to liberate the captives).

No less often, Indigenous people acted as though they credited the missionaries' intentions. The *Annual Letter* of 1612 notes that caciques might seek out roaming Jesuits to let them know where their villages were and to ask the fathers to come as soon as they could.[47] It is hard to imagine they would have done so without prior intelligence that the missionaries behaved differently from settlers and could be counted on not to use the information for ill. According to reports, caciques might leave their children with the missionaries to be catechized, likely with the idea that the Jesuits would bring them to the village—a powerful gesture of trust. This may even have been a ploy to force the Jesuits' hand. Since there were few missionaries and many Guaraní communities who hoped to welcome them, leaving the children could at least impose an obligation on the missionaries to return them to their parents. Such were the risks and choices Guaraní faced in circumstances requiring that the very meaning of exchange be constantly calibrated.

Thus, caciques might investigate the Jesuits before making a decision about whether to engage. Father Montoya told of being evaluated by the emissary of a prestigious local cacique. "Father, do not be upset that I am watching you with such great care," Montoya reported him as saying. He had come to see with his own eyes whether the Jesuits were "monsters," whose "cruelty is such that your everyday food is human flesh, as the shamans claim," rather than "men" who could be "spoken with."[48] This inversion of European tales of cannibalistic Amerindians suggests that Spaniards' behavior had begun to be understood, and feared, as a new kind of predation, a possibility calling for great caution. Satisfied, he told Montoya that he would bring the cacique Tayaoba to him forthwith. He was good to his word.

One clear point in these vignettes is that Indigenous people were capable of a wide range of responses in their encounters with Europeans. There were, of course, good reasons for Guaraní to worry that the Jesuits might be just one more group of grasping Spaniards. Yet, there were equally good reasons for Indigenous communities to treat these missionaries differently from other Spaniards. Residents of the village of Ñanduabuçu noted that they trusted the Jesuits because they came with crosses in the hands rather than cords with which to beat them.[49] And as the speech of the Jesuits' allies to the bellicose caciques suggests, it was critical that the Jesuits came only in pairs, offered gifts, took nothing, and would not accept women in exchange—the precise opposite of so many Spaniards. The claim that their conduct was "a thing never seen" hints at how unusual the Jesuits may have seemed compared to settlers and even other clerics (excepting the Franciscans). In other words, some Indigenous groups were able to persuade themselves that they might benefit by admitting the Jesuits into their midst. Could it be that the Guaraní saw a glimmer of something new in this relationship? Here were men who could not be tobayas, because they would not accept women, but who nevertheless were willing to work alongside the Guaraní, a tantalizing opportunity for lives of peace long ago denied by the narrow instrumentalism of settlers. In short, perhaps those Guaraní who took up with

Jesuits did so as a social innovation that promised materially better circumstances than they had known to that point under Spanish domination. And while many Indigenous groups never accepted the missionaries, evidence indicates that the Jesuits received more requests to found villages than they had manpower to meet.

Two decades on from the Jesuits' first forays into the Paraná and the Guairá, a notable alignment was forming as Jesuit commitments to the material well-being of potential converts intersected with Guaraní concerns to find an alternative to the exploitative dynamic that had come to dominate across Paraguay. In the Guairá, tens of thousands agreed to be baptized during these years many, perhaps with an understanding similar to the one Tabacambí had proposed to Lorenzana in 1610. By 1628, fifteen mission towns (reductions) had been founded there. At a time when the three Spanish communities in the area numbered no more than one thousand each, these towns were home to upwards of forty thousand Guayarense-Guaraní, with Cario and even Tupí who had fled areas that had come under attack by Portuguese slavers and other Indian groups.[50] In the Paraná, the first reduction was San Ignacio Guazú, founded by Father Lorenzana. Residents there were already subject to the encomienda, so initially their status differed little from what it had been, though the Jesuits took greater care to hold encomenderos strictly to what the law allowed. This became somewhat easier after 1618, when the king ordered that Alfaro's ordinances be obeyed to the letter. Which is not to say that the law began to work as intended—in fact, it was widely skirted. Nevertheless, by referring to royal decrees, the Jesuits were able to set some limits to encomenderos' capacity for abuse, at least with respect to Indians who had thrown in their lot with the fathers. By 1628, after the establishment and consolidation of many reductions, there were nine mission towns in the middle Paraná region, home to thousands of Guaraní, many of whom had avoided the encomienda.

"Like animals that are hunted"

By the 1620s, the Guaraní world had been turned inside out during the century since first contact with Europeans. If the forest had provided abundance and villages had ensured security, in the changed world of European presence Guaraní lives were raw and exposed. Growing numbers lived in officially designated *pueblos de indios* (Indian towns) that had congregated smaller villages to make their residents more readily available to encomenderos and to an emergent *conchabo* (wage contract) system. These communities, often cut off from earlier intercommunal networks, met their own material needs with difficulty. By the early seventeenth century, day-to-day existence among Asunción's Native communities was a jumble of mandated labor rotations, personal service, communal obligations to their villages, and a patchwork labor market in which individuals might be rented out to others or, with whatever free time they might manage, hire themselves out for pay. Some, perhaps especially those serving poorer encomenderos, appear to have found ways to live in the "love and goodwill" of a kind of shared penury with low settlers who were kept from destitution by only a few Indian bodies.

Even better off Spaniards pled poverty, noting that because there was no money in Asunción, Europeans were lazy, leaving them no choice but to exploit the Indians.[51] And while Spanish *vecinos* (citizens) had largely ignored Alfaro's law between 1611 and 1620, even as some Guaraní did accede to wage arrangements, it simply was not enough to sustain the city. Many settlers sought other ways to turn a profit from Indian labor.[52] Sugar, produced in Paraguay and traded to Santa Fé and Buenos Aires for goods imported from Spain, had been undercut by Brazilian sugar, powered by enslaved African labor. Meanwhile, Asunción's wine was losing out to new producers closer to Buenos Aires, and cattle, notwithstanding vivid dreams of export to Potosí, had not panned out.

In this context, the systematic production of yerba mate seemed an answer to economic woes. The tea-like stimulant was ubiquitous in Asunción and its hinterlands and was prized as far away as Buenos Aires, Peru, and Chile. Guaraní had long used it for ceremonial and medicinal purposes before the arrival of Europeans (much as other Indigenous cultures used tobacco). Over the decades after 1537, it had become a means to ward off hunger and to keep sharp in the forest. Settlers had incorporated it into their daily lives, drinking it "without moderation or restraint," according to one caustic observer.[53] Because of its connection to Indian ritual (and therefore deviltry) and because it was tarred as a moral vice among Asunción's men, women, and children alike during the sixteenth century, yerba only belatedly came to be seen as having economic potential.[54] Despite ecclesiastical condemnation, Spaniards by the early seventeenth century saw opportunity in its systematic production and widespread consumption. According to one calculation, twelve Indians produced tribute—economic rent—of 135 pesos a year. By contrast, a dozen Indians "rented" out to work in the yerba groves (*yerbales*) during the legal limit of two months a year could earn ten times as much, netting a substantial profit beyond tribute (and many were kept far longer).[55] This had allowed processsed yerba to become the chief means of exchange and a substitute for silver.[56]

By the late 1620s, yerba had produced a gold-rush mentality among Spaniards. The yerbales came to be referred to as "mines" during these years, a designation that allowed king Felipe IV to keep the groves out of Portuguese hands and enabled collection of the royal *quinto* (tax).[57] Activity was especially intense around three towns: Mbaracayú, Villa Rica, and Ciudad Real de Guairá. Mbaracayú, a village predating Spanish arrival, had attracted hundreds of Europeans hoping for a big score. Encomenderos saw a far more profitable use for Indigenous labor than mere field work. Merchants began to imagine a product that might be profitably exported not only to Potosí, Lima, or Santiago but perhaps even Europe (as had already happened with tobacco and chocolate). Poor Asunceños who scraped along by borrowing or "renting" Indians from encomenderos saw a chance to provide vital services to boom towns like Mbaracayú.

The result was a free-for-all. Effects could be fateful for the Guaraní. A young Guaraní man from Asunción pled "for the love of God" not to be taken to Mbaracayú. His encomendero had rented all seventeen Indians of his household to the yerba mines. All of them had perished. Upon hearing this, their cacique had "died of shame." If it came to that, said this lad, he would abscond to avoid going.[58] Other Spaniards deceived Natives, saying that they were taking them to build houses and to clear fields, deeply familiar tasks for the Guaraní and ones that generally involved collective labor on behalf of a community. For all the high hopes among ordinary settlers, some of whom came out well, the principal beneficiaries of the yerba trade appear to have been middlemen and brokers in Asunción and other Spanish towns.

It was in this "veritable far west," as historian Carlos Garavaglia called it, that early Paraguay's most identifiable product had its origins, a place where life had taken on value as individual labor, and the law, far from being merely a dead letter, had been tortured into defending gain by the very authorities who were supposed to enforce limits on Native exploitation.[59]

A document from 1630 reveals the broad implications of this development and suggests the deep worries that led so many Guaraní to seek out mission life. In August of that year, the Jesuit missionaries in residence at the reduction of San Ignacio del Ypaumbucu along the Paraná River read two royal provisions out loud to the town's council and residents. These Guaraní had already been subjected to the encomienda when Jesuit missionaries had established the reduction. As such, they were still bound to serve their encomenderos, who were keen on sending them to gather and process yerba in Mbaracayú. One of the decrees reminded the assembly that labor rotations were limited to two months, as spelled out in Alfaro's ordinances two decades earlier. A second declared that the Indians were under no obligation to go to the yerba mines at Mbaracayú during times of illness (the rainy season, when many in the village tended to be sick) and that at all other times they might do so only if they chose to. The clear purport behind this public reading was to remind the gathered residents of San Ignacio what limits the law had set with regard to their labor in the yerba "mines."

When the priests were done reading, the town council responded by addressing themselves directly to the king on behalf of all the residents.[60] They spoke from harsh experience in Spanish yerbales. Production of the leaf demanded hellacious work in remote places. The process involved finding and harvesting the yerba in the forest, compressing and firing the raw plant, hauling the mash to camp in 100-kilo loads, toasting it over a slow fire for three or four days, followed by arduously beating and grinding the leaves to powder.[61] Jesuit accounts indicate that the jungle was dangerous, the smoke thick, the work relentless, and food scarce. The finished mate was then bound up in large leather sacks and carried on Indian backs to the river so it could be shipped downstream.[62] The Guaraní had long made their own yerba, of course, but their process bore little resemblance in intensity and scale to these stygian sylvan mills of seventeenth-century lowland South America.

The document registering San Ignacio's reaction was spoken first in Guaraní, taken down by a local scribe, and then translated into Spanish by Jesuit priests. In considering it, we have the advantage not only of the original Guaraní and Spanish texts but of a modern Spanish retranslation of the original Guaraní text, which allows for a more nuanced analysis.[63] As though standing before the throne, San Ignacio called for "our King" to "see us" and to "know us." Things are not now as they once were, said the cabildo, when "we saw ourselves as poor and were beset by Spaniards." By repeating the phrase "our King," the council may have intended to identify themselves directly with the royal person and his authority, making him figuratively present.[64] They reminded him that Spaniards had not "believed" or "obeyed" his order forbidding Indians from going to Mbaracayú during times of sickness. In fact, said the cabildo, people are constantly being forced to go, and they are dying there. The place is filled with the bones of "our vassals" and our "beloved ones," so many that our communities are being "made poor." Young people are fewer and fewer because "we no longer have children," and the women cannot stop crying for their dead husbands and sons—a powerful way of saying that biological reproduction itself was being threatened, as were other crucial aspects of community life. "We no longer make houses, we no longer make fields," declared the council (according to the retranslation). This phrasing is worth pausing over. The original Spanish translation describes the residents as "not able to have houses or fields." This distinction is revealing. To *have* no houses or fields was narrowly a matter of possession. But to be unable to *make* houses and fields implied not only a lack of shelter and food, but also a deeper loss of the collective experience and reciprocal labor that made houses and fields possible: among the Guaraní, raising communal ogas (longhouses) and clearing fields was always done collaboratively, part of how communities reaffirmed themselves through gift and reciprocity. This distinction suggests that Spanish officials, perhaps even the Jesuits, did not fully understand what was at stake for the Guaraní.[65]

We bring back nothing from there, the council continued, other than *câneõ*, or "fatigue/fatiguing work," a phrase that appears in the Spanish original simply as *trabajo* (work), without the Guaraní sense of drudgery, exhaustion, and lack of meaning.[66] They deceive us and beat us. They pursue us "like animals (that are hunted)," charged the cabildo, implying that Spaniards were making the Guaraní into prey, the very essence of unsocial, unreciprocal behavior (as Tayaoba's emissary had suggested to Father Montoya decades earlier in deciding to investigate whether the Spaniards were "monsters" who could not be spoken to). They also treat us like "domestic animals," observed the council, effectively denoting the Guaraní as inferiors. The original Spanish version of the document drew no distinction between these two phrases. In both cases, the reference to animals was rendered in the Spanish as "animals without reason," conveying only a sense of hierarchical debasement with no acknowledgement of predatory behavior. We ask that the king be "kind and respect us"—"merciful, one who does not let the fire go out," rather than "one who is inhuman, does not know how to treat others" in Guaraní.[67] "We do not want to go to Mbaracayú," insisted the council, for the Spaniards "are our enemies." This was a heavy charge to level against the king's other vassals. But in Guaraní, it was full with meaning—likely lost on its Spanish readers, including the Jesuits. The Guaraní word translated as "enemy" denotes a person who does not habitually "love well/is well disposed toward others."[68] This is a telling usage that might be glossed as one who appears to have no interest in sharing life in common. That this word was preceded by the exclusive *our* pronoun, meaning "us but not them, we alone, not being kin," conveys the profound alienation residents felt from those who were preying on them.[69]

The crucial point for San Ignacio was to persuade "our King" to forbid them from going to Mbaracayú. Alfaro's ordinances had stated they could go if it was their "will" to do so.[70] The problem, as the council noted, was that if the king said "go if you want to go," the Spaniards would force them to and claim that they had done so of "our own accord," even though it is "false and a lie." And so, if "our King" tells us, "Don't go to Mbaracayú, even if you want to," the Spaniards could not take them. Experience had taught these Guaraní a hard lesson: in a raw economy of gain, the appeal to free will could be just another way of cloaking exploitation and abuse.

San Ignacio's subtle and knowing plea was backed by missionaries who were present during the discussion. They vouched in writing for the truth of the account and agreed that, under these circumstances, "free will" (*voluntad*) was a trap that sought only to provide bodies for the yerbales, like the galleys or mines where condemned men were sent to die. They insisted that town residents should "in no way, at any time, or under any circumstance" go to Mbaracacyú, that "graveyard of Indians."[71] Of course, Jesuits had every reason to oppose a policy that subtracted people from the missions at a delicate moment in their evangelization.

While this entreaty was made by and on behalf of a single village, it bespeaks a deep insight regarding the horizon of possibility Indigenous people faced three decades into the seventeenth century. From the perspective of those most vulnerable to exploitation, anyone who remained within the Spanish economy confronted coercion as a pervasive condition of everyday existence—whether compliance with encomenderos' orders, the predatory appropriation of bodies, a duplicitous appeal to free will, or perhaps most insidiously, individual freedom as a kind of self-inflicted compulsion.

But more was at issue than just material circumstances, what the San Ignacio council called "our repeated and habitual suffering" at the hands of Spaniards who ignore "our King's" laws. In pointing out that they were being treated as prey, that they earned only *fatigue* at the yerba mines, that they were no longer having children, that they were unable to *make* houses and fields, San Ignacio was arguing that their conception of the good life was in danger of becoming unlivable. They were posing the question of whether there was a path forward for them beyond bare material and bodily survival. And if so, how they might find it. To a greater or lesser degree, this was a question for all Indigenous people whose lives were now unavoidably entangled with Europeans and their ravening ways.

In this regard, a striking feature of the document reporting San Ignacio's application to the king is the lack of religious reference. If God was invoked or a prayer offered during the reading of the documents, the fact did not find its way into the record. Missionaries intoned the legal texts in question and the council responded immediately, referring to the king, and later to the governor, without once mentioning God or Jesuit evangelism. The cabildo stressed the conditions at the Mbaracayú mines, the attitudes of settlers who mistreated them, and the king's words read out by the Jesuits. Save for passing references to baptism and the Gospel, the Jesuit postscripts are entirely consistent with this tight focus on the material experience of the yerba mines, the pursuit of gain that drove it, and the way Spaniards set the king's laws aside for their own benefit.

This emphasis is revealing. On the face of the document, it could seem that the Jesuits had set everything into motion by reading the legal texts in question. Yet the deliberate theatricality of the moment and the material concerns behind the words strongly hint that the council was at least a coequal partner with the Jesuits and perhaps the prime mover behind the event. Capucine Boidin has argued persuasively on linguistic grounds that the cabildo's statement was originally composed in Guaraní. Though it was presented as a spontaneous speech, and may well have been delivered as such, the marks of Guaraní oratory indicate that it had been prepared in advance, implying that the council called the gathering to stand before the governor and the king to raise their own voice.[72] This

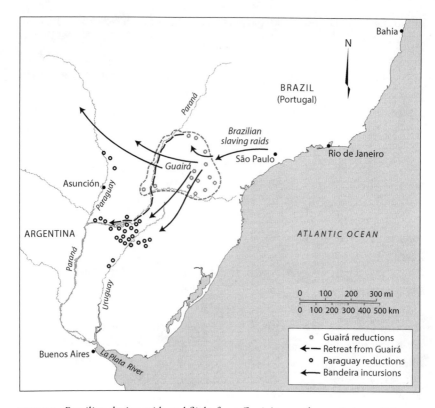

MAP 4.2. Brazilian slaving raids and flight from Guairá to southern missions, 1628–1632. *Source:* Atlas Histórico do Brasil. FGV-CPDOC, https://atlas.fgv.br/marcos/igreja-catolica-e-colonizacao/mapas/missoes-jesuitas-na-bacia-do-paraguai.

was what they meant by noting that in the past it had "seemed our King did not know us" but that "henceforth he will see us . . . since there is no one else to care for us."[73]

In theory, all Indigenous people could make such a claim. The New Laws of 1542 and subsequent legislation had enshrined the idea, at least in principle. In practice, through most of the sixteenth century and into the seventeenth, Indigenous people in Paraguay had difficulty reaching the king's justice. San Ignacio's stand was a calculated attempt to do so. They enjoyed two clear advantages. The community spoke with a single voice and they were able to offer Jesuit testimonials to back their claims. By addressing their words directly to the king rather than relying on Je-suits to plead for them, they were challenging the monarchy to recognize them as the vassals the law had declared them to be. That they did not use that word to describe themselves, as mission residents later did routinely, hints that they wanted to gauge the king's response before offering the gift of their reciprocal allegiance, as Tabacambí had proposed twenty years earlier.

Whether or not the residents of San Ignacio understood it precisely this way, the logic of their argument amounted to a brief on behalf of society itself and made perfect sense from a Spanish theological and political perspective. Spain's civilizing project in the New World was premised on establishing a shared Christian republic with a place for Spaniards and Amerindians. God had ordained men to social life so that all might thrive in God's sight.[74] To this end, people owed each other charity above all else. By complaining that they were being dragged to Mbaracayú against their will for the private benefit of others—the free will granted them by God's grace and assured them by royal law—they were reminding the king that the fate of a Christian order was being threatened by indiscriminate gain-seeking. In essence, they were telling the king that if steps were not taken, settlers who were learning to "live for oneself" and call it liberty, heedless of the common good, might strangle a shared society in the cradle.[75] At the same time, they were affirming their own understanding of social life as a guarantee against the predatory disembodying of their labor.

"We must flee"

While facing the yerba rush, the Indigenous people of the Guairá had to contend with another challenge: the infamous slave raids out of Brazil known as *bandeiras*. Through the sixteenth century, Paulistas had relied on native populations north of São Paulo for labor. By 1600, plunder, overwork, disease, and dislocation had ravaged Indigenous communities in Brazil, turning the Paulistas' gaze westward to the Guairá, then under Spanish jurisdiction. Early-seventeenth-century bandeiras were ragtag affairs, blending coercion, kinship, and small-scale razzias across the notional border separating Portuguese and Spanish realms. The first raid of note set out from São Paulo in 1602–1604 and took seven hundred or so Spanish encomienda Indians. Other raids followed sporadically through the 1610s and into the 1620s, generally taking hundreds of Native captives at a time. During this earlier period, women and children appear to have been the main targets, representing 70 percent of one inventory from a

1615 bandeira. Some columns were led by Portuguese captains acting on orders from São Paulo's governor. Others were headed by privateers, supported by Indigenous Tupí allies, enemies of the Guaraní, or mixed-race *mamelucos*. Toward 1620, Spaniards began to feel the pinch of these incursions. In 1619, vecinos in Asunción complained that up to seven thousand Indians had been rounded up and sent to Brazil to be sold off as slaves, a technical violation of the law against the enslavement of Native people and, more crucially from their perspective, a loss of labor at a time of acute shortfall in Paraguay.[76]

Through much of this period, Brazil's own labor challenges were kept in check by the importation of slaves from West Africa. Most enslaved people who arrived at the Bay of All Saints (Salvador da Bahia) stayed to work the northeastern plantations that were making sugar into the world's first industrial export product.[77] A relative few were shipped down the coast to São Paulo to labor on expanding wheat farms and homesteads. The number of slaves imported to Salvador, rising since the late sixteenth century, spiked between 1616 and 1625, reaching fifty thousand, five times the number a quarter century earlier.[78] In 1624–1625, however, this flow was interrupted when the Dutch West India Company attacked Salvador, only to lose it the following year. Nevertheless, Dutch corsairs began to harass Portuguese slaving ships, doubling the price of slaves. Unable to afford them, Paulistas turned to the Guairá, where they had operated with relative impunity for decades.[79]

Demand for cheaper labor resulting from disruption of the Atlantic slave trade sparked a rapid increase in the scale of bandeiras. Amid a labor shortage attributable partly to disease, Paulistas claimed that Spanish encomenderos of Villa Rica were intruding on Portuguese territory to take Indians for their own personal service. This was probably true, though at the time there was no hard border between Spanish and Portuguese territories. To remedy the crisis, a massive expedition of over two thousand Paulistas and Tupí allies, led by Antonio Raposo Tavares, set out for the Guairá in 1628 into a situation of "instability and uncertainty."[80] Disease and interethnic rivalries, the latter intensified by Spanish presence, had deranged the human and physical landscape, even as Jesuits had baptized tens of thousands and established fifteen reductions. Within a year, Tavares's bandeira had captured thousands of Guaraní and returned them to the auction block in São Paulo.[81]

Raids quickly became highly commercialized, militarized trafficking operations. Violence exploded. Paulistas adopted scorched earth tactics to drive villagers into the open and deny them safe haven. But slavers also offered gifts of iron implements and promises of reciprocity, much as Spaniards and missionaries long had, to draw people out. In twisted impersonations of Jesuit missionaries, Paulistas and Tupí allies might engage shamans to bear crosses and other Catholic paraphernalia to dupe and confuse unreduced groups. The goal was to extract as many people as possible. Tavares's bandeira also attacked recently founded missions. Montoya described the trade in his account of an assault on the mission of Jesús María.[82] The Indigenous Tupí served as "bankers or brokers" for buyers in São Paulo, he noted. These "contractors," or *mû*—which in Guaraní could refer simultaneously to "friendship" and "contract," though it may also have played on the word for "spit, or expel a thing from the mouth"—had divided the land into districts, setting up exchange tables where Indian men, women, and children were sold, "as one might a flock of sheep or a herd of cows," for axes, cutlasses, knives, and hats brought from the coast.[83]

Once a large enough group of captives had been assembled, they would be sent nearly four hundred miles to São Paulo in canoes, "at considerable profit." Coffles were marched back through the forest for months, manacled and hobbled, with many deaths along the way—a verdant Middle Passage (Figure 4.1). Costing two or three pesos in tradeable goods in the Guairá, branded *piezas* (pieces) fetched fifteen or twenty in smaller Brazilian towns and up to fifty in São Paulo or Rio de Janeiro. Between 1628 and 1632 (when Brazil was still under the Spanish monarchy), as many as sixty thousand Guaraní were taken in this way and sold at auction in São Paulo, "as though they were slaves," in clear violation of royal law, wrote the governor of Buenos Aires to the king.[84]

For the Guaraní, consequences were calamitous. Desperation to avoid such a fate turned people against one another. In one case, a Guaraní man was able to "buy" his own freedom by seizing another and binding him over to the *mû*—the instrumentalism of competitive survival. Individuals were known to snare others to obtain the "going price" for an ax or a cutlass. At a broader scale, the Portuguese incited Indians to wage war against each other so they could bring captives for "appraisal and sale."[85] Violence among Indigenous villages had not been unknown before the Europeans had come. Insults or failures of reciprocity could trigger wars of revenge.[86] By treating people as a resource to be gained, Europeans introduced novel incentives that mingled with established social understandings in unanticipated ways. Meanwhile, São Paulo came to be known as a place where "Castilians, Portuguese, Italians, and people of other nationalities" could make money by enslaving and so "live as they like in freedom, without the constraints of law."[87]

For many Native groups, the missions of the Guairá and elsewhere may have seemed a way to protect themselves from the "insatiable ferocity" of the "wolves" of São Paulo and the acquisitive violence of the Tupí.[88] Caciques might approach the missionaries to seek protection against both.[89] Whatever it was the Jesuits wanted, it did not seem to involve forcible taking. To the contrary. Under the circumstances, the missionaries' overall behavior may have seemed something like a gift and an invitation to open-ended reciprocity across time in the interest of peace, plenty, and bodily security, now in a new register. This is not to suggest that the Jesuits asked nothing of the Guaraní, but at this early point in the history of the missions, the fact that they offered refuge from Portuguese and Tupí raiders as well as Spanish encomenderos may have distinguished them in the minds of many.

The Jesuits appear to have shared this understanding. Montoya argued that the missionaries' principal goal was to protect the Indians and secure "the calm essential for Christian living." As things stood, the Guaraní were too exposed to "displacement, hunger, turmoil" to make a truly free choice to become Christians.[90] It was for the fathers to secure conditions that would enable the Guaraní, in time, to abandon their "savage and barbarous customs and live with order and political custom," as the Third Council of Lima had charged all missionaries in 1583.[91]

While it is clear that the Jesuits saw themselves as being involved in a civilizing mission, it would be a mistake to suppose this impetus alone explains their conduct during this formative period of missionary activity.[92] Obituaries of priests who served in the missions indicate a far more mundane resolution to preserve the Guaraní from want and harm. Of course, these were eulogies for friends and colleagues, charged with hagiographic energy. Still, they bespeak the Jesuits' best sense of themselves. Thus, one priest was remembered for doing anything to "secure [the Guaraní's] material well-being," including building houses, tending fields, and distributing food and clothing to residents, "so that they would not escape to the forests, to live only from hunting." Others were praised for "providing everything necessary for life, such as clothes and food," for preaching the truths of the Gospel but also for discovering and applying medicines with which to "save their lives and bring them back to health," so

FIGURE 4.1. Jean Baptiste Debret. *Indian Soldiers from the Coritiba Province Escorting Native Prisoners* (ca. 1830). *Source:* Wikimedia Commons (public domain).

that they might then remedy the ills of the soul. One missionary was so attentive to the poverty of his flock that he came to be known as the "father of the poor."[93]

Such efforts met with some success. A 1629 letter reporting on conditions in eight mission towns noted that the missionaries had "improved temporal matters" by keeping the residents from being sent to the yerba mines, notably expanding cattle herds, and helping ensure fields were productive. Still, some opposed the changes Jesuits were proposing, which many ordinary Guaraní were in the process of accepting. One cacique, angry that so many of his followers had allowed themselves to be baptized, said that he would never become a Christian, proclaiming that instead of going to Sunday Mass, he would go to the forest to hunt with a few others.[94] This tension seems to have been the result of a widening gap between certain caciques and many common people who, in the growing uncertainty of forest life, found advantage in the material security of larger communities.

The tragedy of the early Guairá missions was that by the late 1620s they had become irresistible targets for the bandeirantes.[95] For raiders like Tavares, it was a simple matter of efficiency. By concentrating scattered

Indigenous groups in larger, denser towns, as Father Torres had instructed, the Jesuits had inadvertently made it easier for the Portuguese and their allies. Rather than track small groups or individuals through the forest, they could plunder settled communities. Missions were attacked and thousands captured. The matter quickly became a political and existential crisis for the residents of the Guairá. New mission communities had to consider their options and decide how best to respond.

Their deliberations were complicated by the fact that Spanish encomenderos from Villa Rica and Ciudad Real saw opportunity in the Indians' plight. The Jesuits had chosen sites well away from Spanish towns precisely because distance would help buffer residents from the importunities of settlers. For villagers, the distance meant long trips for labor rotations. But it also meant that settlers had limited opportunities to force them into extra work or personal service. Faced with stepped up attacks by Paulistas, Guaraní communities and Jesuit missionaries asked Spanish towns to send troops to protect them. It was their duty, claimed one missionary, reiterating the point that encomenderos were under royal obligation to keep their charges from harm.[96] Spanish captains and encomenderos rebuffed such requests, arguing instead that the Indians should move closer to the cities, where they could be more easily defended. One captain noted in early 1630 that several reducciones had already been razed by the Portuguese, and two more faced the same fate. It would be better if they moved "closer to this city, where they will be safe and favored by their encomenderos," because at a distance of eighty leagues, "we cannot arrive in time."[97] Ciudad Real even sent an emissary, with a notary, demanding caciques move their villages for their own safety. According to the notary, Father Juan Agustín de Contreras responded that the caciques of the two communities had met on their own initiative, "without saying anything to us," and discussed what to do. They had decided they would not leave their pueblos, even if the Portuguese came, "giving as a reason that moving would amount to subtle destruction," since a new place could not easily be found and because the king himself had ordered them not to move. They are resolute, said Father Juan, even though we have begged them to move to avoid the danger.[98]

This explanation and the reference to the king's commands likely cloaked a deeper concern. What the caciques seemed to understand was that settlers were using the threat of the bandeiras to pressure Native groups to resettle around Spanish towns. Their concern was likely genuine, to the extent that they feared Paulista raids would deny them desperately needed labor. As it was, the Paulistas also targeted settler communities, creating a constant bleed of workers. Of course, encomenderos also wanted tighter control over their labor force. For their part, Indigenous communities that had taken up with Jesuit missionaries found themselves between a rock and a hard place. If they stayed put, they were vulnerable to Portuguese raids with no one to defend them, a fact that worried Spaniards and upon which they were willing to play. If they moved nearer Spanish towns, they would face intensified labor demands from settlers. They were willing to make tribute in the form of labor rotations, as Alfaro's law permitted, but the fact that settlers could not easily raid distant villages rendered personal service impractical. It is telling, therefore, that even in the face of the Portuguese threat, these Guaraní communities refused to live any closer to their encomenderos.[99]

There is no reason to assume that the missionaries drove Guaraní decisions in this affair. True, we know of this incident only because a Jesuit spoke to a Spanish notary. Moreover, the Jesuits had made enemies of the encomenderos in Villa Rica and Ciudad Real by purposely locating newer missions so far away. So, attributing the towns' refusal to move to the caciques was, at a minimum, politically convenient for the missionaries. And yet, because the caciques and their followers were best placed to evaluate the risks and judge how to proceed, because Father Juan was in no position to force them to do anything, and because they had been acknowledged as free vassals of the king, there is a strong argument that the caciques acted on their own counsel.

Their decision-making was necessarily contingent, for conditions were mutable. As Brazilian raids to the Guairá escalated through the 1620s, and as people were hunted down in the forests, banding together in the missions had made sense. Now the mission towns had become traps. And so, communities began to consider a more radical alternative. There were other missions to the south in the Paraná, further from the Portuguese frontier. Discussions began about whether to flee in that direction. The Jesuits were of two minds. They had put much work into the Guairá missions and did not want to abandon them. On the other hand, these communities were "threatened by imminent destruction," as one report noted.[100] By 1631, the signs were clear and "fear of the Portuguese had taken hold."[101] At Santa María del Iguazú, community leaders went to the priest and told him that the moment had come. "There is no time to lose," they said. Portuguese spies were everywhere. The people were about to scatter to the forests. If they stayed, they would be lost. "We must flee, father. What are we waiting for?"

A gift-giving spirit

The situation was dire indeed. Since Tavares's 1628 bandeira, independent Guaraní villages had been ravaged and many recently established Jesuit reductions had been emptied out. Tens of thousands had been hauled away to São Paulo. The remaining mission communities found themselves with few good options.

Flight involved a perilous journey of hundreds of leagues, a Trail of Tears marked by pursuit, slaughter, starvation, disease, and drowning (Map 4.2).[102] Logistics were daunting. The idea was to float downriver along the Paraná, go overland around the great Guairá Falls, and then return to the river to complete the trip. Residents of the missions at Loreto and San Ignacio (a different one from the one in Paraná) hastily built seven hundred rafts and uncounted canoes—an "amazing sight," said Montoya. Missionaries bought as many head of cattle as they could find, a crucial contribution to the ultimate success of the exodus. As many as twelve thousand people set off, barely ahead of an advancing bandeira and chased by troops from Spanish cities hoping to take as many people as they could before they were gone, a final opportunity to secure valuable capital. The refugees reached the falls dogged by the Portuguese. They detoured on foot, managing to avoid a trap laid by Spaniards, and made it back to the river, though without the rafts and canoes that had brought them to that point.

As news of the hegira reached missions further south, communities there responded with an outpouring of what the Jesuits called "charity."[103] These communities in the Paraná and Uruguay region had been founded during the same period that Jesuits had moved into the Guairá. They were far enough from both Asunción and the Brazilian frontier that they had enjoyed relative peace up to 1630. Some had even become "prosperous."[104] Towns hastened to help those still on the march. According to Jesuit reports, the residents of Encarnación de Itapuá sent porters upriver half a dozen times with provisions for those descending. The fathers had collected food as alms, but Indians had also "taken food from their own mouths to help their afflicted brothers from the Guairá," reported the Jesuits' Annual Letter for that year. Others in the community filled canoes with corn, paddled them up to the falls, and returned in makeshift rafts so that some among the refugees might finish the trip more comfortably in the canoes.[105]

As the "pilgrims" began to arrive in the south, towns welcomed them. According to the Jesuit *Annual Letter* of 1632–1634, Acaray, Corpus, and Itapuá along the river received hundreds, even thousands at a time, and "it was a huge spectacle to see the contest over hosting them," wrote a Jesuit witness.[106] With "great affability," many residents opened their homes to the guests and went to live in rough huts instead. Communities "laid waste" to their own fields "down to the roots" to feed the new arrivals and slaughtered their own herds of cattle, remaining "wretched with hunger" themselves. At the mission of La Limpia Concepción del Uruay, described as a "metropolis" comprising distinct Indigenous "nations," the residents extended a "gift-giving spirit and shelter" to the "great troops" of people in "extreme necessity," treating them like "brothers" and hosting them for over a year. Another mission, itself just off a drought, opened up new fields and "filled the land with extraordinary abundance . . . and with remarkable generosity share[d] with the needy in other towns." San Ignacio gave up two-thirds of its own provisions to feed the pilgrims. The town of San Cosme y San Damián sent huge quantities of food to new settlements. In San Miguel, missionaries professed amazement at how much food was collected and carried to those who needed it. Mission after mission offered the newcomers land and shelter in the territory between 1630 and 1633, material gestures of extraordinary importance. For all that, this was a period of hardship. Many died of privation and disease. Montoya wrote, "The memory of the great abundance they had enjoyed in their own lands made vivid the miserable state in which they found themselves," though they seemed to agree that it was better than being dragged off to São Paulo.[107]

Amid this tragedy, the Jesuits heralded the "fervent charity" of these "new Christians" as evidence of evangelical success.[108] In their more self-congratulatory moments, they explained it in terms of the risks they themselves had assumed; the rigors, at times martyrdom, they had embraced; and the alms they had raised. They did not neglect to mention their roles, as when they persuaded a local Spaniard in Corrientes to sell cattle on the hoof to feed the refugees and those who received them.[109] Still, most missionaries knew not to exaggerate their part since, theologically, the Guaraní's charity required an exercise of free will pursuant to

God's grace. And so, the Jesuits expressed gratitude for God's providence, deflected credit from themselves, and otherwise marveled at the generosity and compassion shown by mission residents who went above and beyond in receiving the Guairá refugees. Many southern residents, said the missionaries, worked so hard that they sickened and became "martyrs to fraternal charity."[110]

Such effusive praise for the Guaraní could be read as a virtuous understatement by the fathers regarding their role in the migration's success (though in other instances they were more explicit in touting their accomplishments). So, while missionary descriptions acknowledge but do not dwell on priests' efforts, the Jesuits' internal organization and their capacity to purchase cattle and other animals—at a time when the Society was strapped for resources—were crucial to refugees' survival on the march and for communities that received them. And yet, it seems clear that disaster would have ensued if residents of the southern missions had turned their backs, dragged their feet, or worried only for their own survival. The missionaries simply were in no position to command the outpouring of "charity" they described. They might appeal to residents' better angels or cajole them. If anything, however, their language rings more of men who found even their own efforts surpassed. Montoya, after describing measures that missionaries had taken, noted that even as their villages were recovering from a period of want, the residents of the southern missions demonstrated a "remarkable generosity with the needy in other towns."[111] In other words, whatever the Jesuits' part in all this, the strong implication is that decisions among Guaraní community leaders and ordinary folk drove what appeared to missionaries to be a supererogatory response.

It makes little sense to suppose that the refugees' reception was a result of a deep and explicitly "Christian" spirit newly ensconced in the Guaraní soul. Given the recency of missionary activity, there had been no time for that. Jesuits themselves understood conversion to be a process that unfolded over time, not something that happened from one day, or even one year, to the next. Some, perhaps many Guaraní had adopted elements of Christian practice and outlook.[112] But to rely too heavily on something like "true conversion" to explain the southern missions' charity diminishes Indigenous ideas regarding the treatment of others and underplays what must be thought of as a process of change by which time-tested norms shaped responses to unprecedented challenges.[113]

Another approach is to consider that southern residents reacted from a spirit of generous sociality, one rooted in Indigenous understandings that allowed the Guaraní to meet a human tragedy in ways the Jesuits could recognize as charity. Certainly, there is no reason to suppose that Indigenous people were unmoved by the specter of mass human suffering. Calamity had always loomed over forest peoples in the form of storms, floods, droughts, fires, locusts, and famine. In Guaraní myth, the world was a fragile thing that at any moment could tremble and succumb to its ultimate fate—total destruction and the annihilation of people.[114] During disasters, communities might fracture, dispersing into the forest to survive.[115] In flight, they might come across people not from the same *guàra*, or kinship group. Under the logic prevailing prior to European advent, those who did not belong to a guàra or to groups of related guàra would have to pass through a territory without stopping. They might be helped on the way, but they should not stay. And yet, during the exodus from the Guairá, thousands of people, many of whom likely had no immediate clan or kinship ties to those in the southern missions, were given comfort and aid and allowed to remain.

Part of an explanation may be that the decades-long process of subjecting Indigenous communities to encomiendas had so jumbled the relationship between land and people that new ways of thinking had become both possible and necessary. Among the Guaraní, the principal idea of territory implied lands occupied by related kin groups. To communities that lived through the disruptions of the sixteenth and early seventeenth centuries, it simply may not have meant the same thing to share space with non-kinsman as it had before.[116] As in the mission town of La Limpia Concepción, "various Indian nations which speak different languages" now lived cheek by jowl, headed by different caciques who may once have held each other at arm's length or even been rivals.[117] After the immediate emergency of flight, many groups, both hosts and new arrivals, may have adopted a wait-and-see attitude regarding their novel situation, a sign of how much pressure they faced from the broader economy and from Brazilian slave raiders.

While such an account would be consistent with basic survivalism and minimal mutual toleration, it is not entirely satisfying as an explanation for the exuberant quality of the southern missions' reaction, at least as characterized by the Jesuits. Here, we must be a bit more adventurous.

One piece of the puzzle may be to acknowledge a fundamental tension within Amerindian societies—that between a sense of autonomy rooted in a deep attachment to "our" particular way of doing things in a particular place on one hand and, on the other, a profound commitment to the capacity to be social, not only within the group but with others. In this latter regard, anthropologist Eduardo Viveiros de Castro has argued that Amerindian thought was (and is) characterized by a "fundamental . . . 'opening to the Other.'"[118] I take him be describing a philosophical or ontological attitude grounded in the idea that no human person or community is complete unto itself, however fond of its own way of being in the world. For Amerindians, he argues, the encounter with the other, for better and for worse, is (and was) necessary, for without it, the world remains fundamentally closed. In this vein, anthropologists Joana Overing and Alan Passes have argued that South American Indigenous communities, especially Amazonian groups and their offshoots, have maintained a fundamental commitment to a "convivial sociality" that allows them to prize their own way of being and to project a code of caring, loving, and friendship to others beyond the confines of kinship exclusivity.[119]

This aligns with the views of anthropologist Bartomeu Melià, who asserts that reciprocity is the deep root and mycelium of Guaraní life and cosmology, a value and principle enacted by gift exchange, feasts, and alliances seeking the peace and tranquility that allow communities to thrive and to establish intercommunal relations.[120] Before and after European contact, feasts among the Guaraní were triggered by *pepĭ*, or invitations from one community to others. Hundreds, even thousands, of people from surrounding villages and territories might gather to sing, dance, and eat.[121] These celebrations performed abundance, reciprocity, and gift and expressed a shared commitment to sociable values—enactments, perhaps, pointing to the social and cosmological horizon where lay the Land Without Evil.

The Guaraní appear to have understood these values as easily disrupted by violence. Montoya's *Tesoro* gives for the Guaraní word *maramôna* the Spanish word *guerrear*, "to make war." According to the entry, *maramôna* was rooted in a word (*mara*) rendered in Spanish as "sickness, villainy, ruin, affliction, crime, delinquency, adversity, . . . calumny."[122] The antisocial quality of these words is clear, suggesting that the Guaraní saw the act of making war as negating tecó aguĭyeí, or that normative state of health and pleasure that brings many friends and allows people to be protected.[123] By comparison, Covarrubias's dictionary of Spanish defined *war* and *violence* by reference to conflict and force, with no reference to ruptured sociality.[124] (Here it is worth noting that one of Montoya's example phrases for *maramôna* is "all the life of man on earth is war," almost surely an unattributed reference to Job 7:1 from the Vulgate, "Militia est vita hominis super terram."[125])

Of course, Indigenous understandings of sociality as the ground of being in the world cannot be bracketed from violence. For Viveiros de Castro, violence among Amerindians is ontologically primary, taking the form of vengeful war and cannibalism that expressed how ritual death of the enemy could serve the "long life of the social body" by repairing the breach of reciprocity.[126] His point is that even in violence, the Tupi-Guaraní maintained a focus on reciprocal sociality. Overing and Passes as well as Melià deny the primacy of violence. Melià sees war as what happens when "positive" reciprocity fails. Overing and Passes conclude that violence cannot be, and among Indigenous people never was, accepted as socially generative. Rather, violence "lurks at the heart of the social to disrupt the sociality so precariously wrenched from the universe," a view perfectly consistent with the idea from Montoya's *Tesoro* that violence and war represented the breakdown of tecó aguïyeí as a sustained state of social goodness.[127] From this perspective, society and its members must be especially attentive to maintaining sociality through "persistent or constant virtue" and the "customs" of life together, in the words Montoya's *Tesoro* used to render *tecó* as "state of life, condition, being [in a place]."[128] This is not inconsistent with the fact that precontact Guaraní feasts might involve not only singing, drinking, dancing, and eating but also the sharing of a captive's body.[129] While cannibalism faded after the arrival of Europeans, invitations and feasting did not. If anything, they may have become especially important as a relatively stable platform for fostering the sociality that could accommodate the autonomy of doing things "our" way and the desire to be social, now under novel conditions.

The sociable opening to the other was not without danger for Indigenous people, as is clear from the story Montoya told about one of his forays into new territory. The envoy from the powerful local cacique Tayaoba had explained his scrutiny of the Jesuits as an effort to ensure that the missionaries were men who could be "spoken with," rather than predatory "monsters" who devour other men.[130] We cannot know precisely what Guaraní word or phrase this man used that Montoya translated as *monstruo* (monster). Clear references in Montoya's *Tesoro* and his Spanish-Guaraní *Lexicon* hint that in Guaraní a monster may have been thought of as a creature that was "twisted," "fierce," "corrupted," "misbegotten," "terrible," "cruel," "abominable." Against the idea that *men* are those with whom one can speak (and not be eaten by), these words convey a vivid sense of unsociable behavior. Such a beast might be likened to one who has "exchanged the being of man for that of beasts," who no longer lives in the "enjoyment, contentedness, abundance" of community but alone, like the jaguar, who must live "where there are no men."[131]

According to Viveiros de Castro, the crucial distinction between people and animals, among Amazonians, is not that the former have souls and the latter do not, for "the original common condition of both humans and animals is not animality but rather humanity" (the inverse of the Western idea).[132] All creatures, animals and people, had souls and thus appeared to themselves as human persons, while appearing differently human to the other. A jaguar, for instance, would relate to other jaguars through the jaguar version of culture—mating, hunting, and kinship practices. To a jaguar, blood was the manioc beer so central to the social lives of the Guaraní. And to a jaguar, a person (a human, in the Western sense) would be prey.

The riddle posed by strangers, therefore, was not their humanity as such or whether they had souls, but what kinds of humans they were. What had to be determined was whether they were the sorts of creatures people would recognize as other people rather than monsters, predators, spirits, or the dead. An abiding concern for Amerindians was that things were not always as they might seem, for what appeared to be a person might actually be a jaguar, fierce monster, or spirit, seeking to transform people into prey or ghost. The only way to decide was to attend carefully to how the creatures in question behaved, how they hunted and fished, what they ate, how they drank, how they communicated—in short, what kinds of bodies they had, what they did with them, and whether they were sociable. This is exactly what the emissary from Tayaoba had noted in explaining his close attention to Father Montoya's conduct.

Of course, even people might be or become unsociable. In Guaraní, individuals who left the kinship group or clan to live on their own in the forest were called *tecócatú*, those "who live like beasts"—that is, men who abandoned good customs and so gave up "the way of men for that of beasts."[133] Whole clans might behave unsociably, refusing to accept invitations to feasts or failing to reciprocate them, or act as enemies, killing and taking captives not in vengeance for ruptured sociability but as a matter of course.

This suggests another reason the Guaraní of the southern missions might have opened themselves to the people from the north, at least provisionally. Like Tayaoba's emissary who observed Montoya and the Jesuits "with such great care," the Guaraní of the southern missions may have thought it imperative to determine what kinds of humans the refugees were. Since they did not know them as kin (though distant kin relations were possible), giving the guests food and shelter provided an opportunity to observe them, to see whether they were what they appeared to be or something else. Even if the hosts were convinced early on that their guests were not jaguars, spirits, or monsters—or had never really considered that they might be—in a reality where Spaniards acted as predators by treating the Guaraní as "animals that are hunted" and even some Indigenous people, like the Tupí, had done the same, the question of what strangers were was more urgent than ever.

I tread carefully here. If the southern Guaraní had been reticent about the newcomers, they could simply have refused them hospitality out of an abundance of caution if nothing else. Missionaries might have balked. But since missionaries' own testimonies suggest that communities deliberated over their actions, it strains credulity to suppose the Jesuits could simply have ordered residents to outdo themselves. On the other hand, the hosts may not have assumed the refugees were other than they appeared, only that they might be, a possibility that demanded investigation, given risks. After all, so much had changed in recent times. If they were men who could be spoken with and if they were not predatory or bellicose, to withhold welcome and aid would have been to deny them a chance at sociality, with the genuine prospect that this would be understood as an insult or even an invitation to vengeance. Thus, there were practical reasons for figuring out what the refugees were. The guests were numerous and even if they did not take up residence within established communities, many would likely live nearby, making contact with them unavoidable. Since established southern communities already occupied the best sites near rivers, a situation that could have been disrupted by tensions, perhaps it was better to know than to remain uncertain.[134] Moreover, and despite a desire for autonomy, there may have been a deep recognition among both refugees and hosts that survival and thriving required contact and communication with each other. Before the arrival of Europeans, groups that decamped to another part of the forest to open up new fields had depended on information gotten from surrounding villages to settle quickly and learn of the risks and uncertainties of new surroundings.[135] In this case, given demographic pressures, this deep obligation of material culture may have weighed more heavily than ever before.

As both hosts and refugees came to understand the other as being committed to reciprocal human sociality, it was possible to formulate a strategy of conviviality and alliance that had the best chance of integrating everyone into the territory, a new *tecoá*—a place of Guaraní being— unlike any they had previously known. Gifts of welcome, food, and shelter would have signaled a desire to live alongside one another in peace. The sources say little about those who received these gifts, except to suggest that they were very glad to be alive and taken in. Yet we do know that by accepting these gifts, they were committing themselves to their reciprocity in the fullness of time.

As a coda to this account, it is crucial to recognize that many in the Guairá did not join the exodus south. Despite the dangers, as many appear to have stayed as fled. We have little direct evidence of their reasoning. Some may have been less concentrated, closer to the edge of the forests where they could disperse, not without hardship but with what they may have thought of as a lesser risk than a several-hundred-mile trip through trackless jungle. Some may have chosen to throw in with Spaniards and rely on *cuñadazgo* relationships with encomenderos to protect them. Others may simply have been unable to leave, stricken with diseases that had flared as people returned home from the yerba mines. Nor can we dismiss the possibility that some who remained had simply lost confidence in the Jesuits and were unwilling to follow them on what may have seemed a mad trek. Missionaries eager to gather and evangelize may have overpromised the protection they could provide. Perhaps future research will shed more light on such issues. Broadly, the fact that groups were divided this way speaks above all to the confusion of circumstances Indigenous communities faced in this roiled land.[136]

*   *   *

Philosopher Jonathan Lear has argued that Crow people in the United States during the late nineteenth and early twentieth centuries faced what he calls the problem of "reasoning at the abyss."[137] Ordinarily, claims Lear, practical reason—that is, the reasoning of everyday life—is oriented to what is useful, proper, or pleasant within a particular cultural frame. As the Crow were forced by the U.S. government to abandon nomadic life for reservations after 1900, it had become unclear to them whether their conceptions of the good life could continue to make sense. The problem for a Crow leader like Chief Plenty Coups, argues Lear, was how to lead his tribe when the "larger context for the significance of one's acts" was no longer unproblematically available in reflecting on what to do. Lear's metaphor is a sharp one. We see Chief Plenty Coups standing at an abyss, with his back to all that had made a way of being possible. What was to be done at this place where "a way of life becomes anxious about its own ability to endure" and no obvious way forward presents itself? How might Chief Plenty Coups fashion a "livable conception of the good life" from the wreckage of a way of being? I pose these questions because the challenge for the Guaraní, as for the Crow, and not just caciques but everyone, was not merely what to do, as though answers were more or less to hand. Every decision about what to do was in some way vertiginous, an exercise in reasoning near the abyss. Any interpretation of their actions must accept this fact as the horizon of possibility defining the Guaraní ability to adapt to the reality they had come to inhabit—and to the world some of them subsequently created.

With this in mind, we might ask whether the idea of the Land Without Evil can speak to the flight from the Guairá. No documents I have found mention it. So the question is not whether the exodus can be understood in terms of a migration bearing the cosmological significance of searching for the Land Without Evil. The Guaraní were fleeing death and destruction, seeking survival, perhaps daring to hope for something better. The question, rather, is whether the Land Without Evil as a touchstone for Guaraní mutuality can help us think about those on the receiving end of the crisis, those who went above and beyond, even putting themselves at risk to help the refugees. If, as Melià has proposed, the Land Without Evil may be understood as the name for a state of virtue manifested individually and collectively through a broad commitment to substantive mutuality, then perhaps the response of the southern communities can be seen as expressing that spirit of responsibility for sustaining a world rooted in tecó aguïyeí, the life of mutuality and sociability.[138] Could it be that these Guaraní confronted crisis by reaffirming and even expanding fundamental moral and behavioral precepts in the face of uncanny circumstances?

In light of this question, my point regarding the flight from the Guairá and the reception refugees received in the south is to propose an explanation that does not credit the Jesuits for what happened at the expense of Guaraní agency, attribute the Guaraní's reaction to their having become rational, charitable Christians in very short order, or reduce their response to a simple survival imperative. Their conduct may certainly be understood as charity, precisely as the Jesuits did, or in terms of a survivalist reason, as a strict utilitarian might. But as explanations, these refuse to acknowledge a Guaraní frame for reasoning on their own terms. True, much had changed. My gist is that a century after contact with Europeans, the Guaraní still had cultural resources from which to respond to the human tragedy they experienced and witnessed. Not merely old ideas, but deep commitments reimagined for a reality in which some men now commonly acted as predators toward other men and in which reciprocity as a way of being seemed at risk. While Guaraní lives continued to change as they became more embedded in mission life during subsequent decades, gift-reciprocity as a fundamental principle proved powerfully adaptive, even generative of new possibilities for sociality as a counterweight to the wanton demand for Indigenous bodies.

Through this prism, the flight from the Guairá and its dénouement may be seen as the symbolic founding of what became the Guaraní mission world, the first moment of birth when those Guaraní who had decided to admit the fathers into their midst began to see a larger community as one way to a future that looked beyond the encomienda, beyond the bandeiras, beyond the instrumentalism that seemed to drive Europeans. For the Jesuits, it was proof of charity's power. For the Guaraní, I have argued, it may have been a practical realization and at the same time a glimpsed insight that they could confront change in constructive ways on terms at least partly their own, terms supple enough to fit new circumstances. From this perspective, the missions represented an emergent mutual commitment between Guaraní and Jesuits to the solidarity of avoiding predation and responding to bodily needs of sustenance and security, grounded in distinct but resonant ideas regarding human sociality.

5

The Guaraní Mission World

A civilized, human way of life.

Antonio Ruiz de Montoya, 1639

With our hands alone we have put straight and healed this land.

Nicolás de Ñeenguyrú, 1753

IN 1637, Father Antonio Ruiz de Montoya traveled to Madrid to ask King Felipe IV to protect the Indigenous people he and his fellow Jesuits had been ministering to for nearly three decades. He argued that the "right of charity" and "the common good" demanded "peace between Spaniards and Indians, a thing so difficult that in more than a hundred years since discovery of the Western Indies, to this day it has been impossible to reach."[1] Montoya's plea, published in 1639, appealed to the monarch's responsibility to arrange the relations among men so as to secure "peace, which is the principal social good," as Aquinas had put it long ago.[2] In reminding Felipe that the role and place of the "Indians" had never been satisfactorily worked out in the New World, Montoya sought to rescue the Indigenous people of Paraguay from the "disordered greed" they had suffered at the hands of Europeans for over a century.[3] He advanced two concrete propositions: to free the Guaraní from service to encomenderos and to keep them from being taken by the Paulistas. They should not be idle, he hastened to add, but they should be able to pay His Majesty's tribute unharried and provide for their families. Montoya declared that his motive in approaching the royal "font of justice" was to ensure the Guaraní be able to enjoy "the meadows allotted them by nature (I mean, their own lands) and exercise the liberty that is common to all . . . protected by the powerful arm with which His Majesty . . . defends his own vassals."[4]

As these statements show, the Jesuits saw the missions as sheltering the Guaraní from the bodily burdens of the encomienda, the yerba mines,

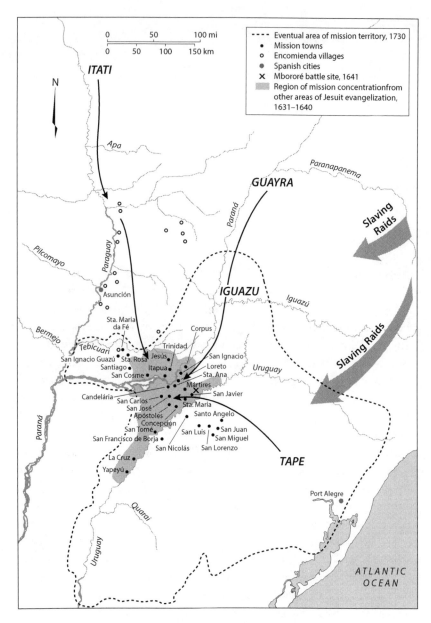

MAP 5.1. Guaraní-Jesuit missions. Concentration from other areas of evangelization (1631–1640). *Source:* Kleinpenning, *Paraguay*, 272 (fig. 6.4), 1616 (fig. 13.1).

and the bandeiras, the key to conversion efforts. But it was also the case that Guaraní mission residents decided to face material threats by allying with the missionaries, while continuing to rely on their own understandings regarding human relations. This chapter tells the story of how these concerns entwined to create a novel structure of feeling in response to the world of gain that lay beyond.

*   *   *

Sealing a pact

The years immediately following Guaraní migration from the Guairá were hard ones for the communities of the Paraná-Uruguay Mesopotamia. Between 1631 and 1640, Guaraní from Itatí, Iguazú, and Tape also converged on the area (Map 5.1). Everyone faced the challenges of living alongside unfamiliar people. Disease broke out as previously separated populations mingled for the first time. By Jesuit accounts, five thousand died in epidemics between 1634 and 1636. Simultaneously, Paulistas and their Tupí allies shifted their operations and began to raid along the Uruguay River, crossing west into Spanish territory to attack new missions. Such incursions claimed thousands. Panic ensued among residents. Many fled disease and violence, surely wondering if they would ever have peace.[5] By the mid-1630s, twenty-six newly founded missions had been snuffed out by bandeiras—more than half of all the mission communities in the region.[6]

In the face of what looked increasingly like an existential threat, Jesuits and Guaraní decided to make a stand. By 1639, Guaraní troops were training, crafting guns, and making gunpowder under Jesuit direction, though the king had not yet granted permission for an Indigenous militia armed with arquebuses.[7] Mission sorties against Paulista fortifications east of the Uruguay prompted counterattacks. To meet them, Nicolás Ñeenguyrú and other Guaraní caciques mustered an army of 4,000 Guaraní warriors to meet 400 Paulistas and 2,700 Tupí at the peak of Mboboré, on the western bank of the Uruguay (Map 5.1). Led by Jesuits who had fought in Flanders before taking vows and armed with European and Indigenous weapons, including canoes outfitted with small cannons, the mission force thumped the Brazilians in March 1641. A royal decree approving a permanent Guaraní militia came in 1642, ending the long season of harassment from the bandeiras. The victory at Mboboré and the

autonomy and safety afforded by a permanent fighting force bearing firearms thus amounted to a second moment in the birth of the Guaraní
mission world.

In 1647, Governor Jacinto de Lariz marked this moment by tour-
ing the twenty existing missions in the Paraná-Uruguay region, with
their thirty thousand residents. Each community consisted of Guaraní
thatched longhouses and a new church built in similar fashion, organized
around a central open space. The notary accompanying Lariz dutifully
reported what happened at each stop. Everyone in a given village—"the
caciques, principals, and the whole common"—gathered in the central
space to hear the governor declare, through an interpreter, that he had
come in the name of King Felipe IV, "so that you will know that you are
his vassals . . . and to make amends for those who have offended you and
given you bad treatment, and so that you will be paid and satisfied for
the work you have done"—language deeply familiar to the Guaraní from
Alfaro's ordinances.[8] Guaraní translations of this speech have not come
down to us, though the idea of making amends could have been rendered as *tepĭ*, or the act of relieving an affront. Since *tepĭ* also implied vengeance, Lariz's promise may well have allowed the Guaraní to conclude
that the king would take their side against those who had done them
harm.[9] Caciques, principals, and townspeople then proclaimed their vassalage. Guaraní men agreed that they would take up arms for the king,
particularly against the Portuguese who, with the Tupí, had killed and
captured so many Guaraní. Municipal council (*cabildo*) members were
then chosen, as royal law required, as well as captains of the militia. Caciques declared that they and their mboyas (followers) had come together
to cultivate their fields in peace. They noted that they had not yet paid
tribute. The governor thanked them for their fealty and charged them
with maintaining "peace and calm" and always "hearing the voice of His
Majesty, as loyal vassals who come to his service." The residents vowed
they would always do so. The governor concluded by pledging to protect
and favor them in the king's name, as often as necessary, against encomenderos and "any other persons who might cause you injury and harm."

The idea of vassalage was no mystery to the Guaraní as Governor Lariz
made his way from mission to mission in the middle of 1647. But the contrast between this ritual and the way Guaraní had long been treated by
settlers, vecinos, and local officials must have seemed striking, even hopeful. The call-and-response structure of the encounter strongly hints at the

reciprocal qualities of the relationship being forged. Basic principles of Spanish governance recognized that king and vassal enjoyed a "tacit company, in loss or in gain, in which harm or reward is common to all."[10] Lariz's solemn ceremony performed this "tacit company," suggesting that the monarchy and mission residents were agreeing not merely to a quid pro quo but to an enduring commitment in which the Guaraní would answer the king's call, fight for him, and otherwise live in peace, and the king would protect them and ensure their just treatment. In effect, the missions represented a concrete response to the failure of law to protect the king's Guaraní vassals from his Spanish vassals. Among the Guaraní, Governor Lariz's declarations may have resonated with the oratory expected of an *mburubichabetè*, a great chief, whose grave words could bring people together and bind them to each other. As a legal matter, this mutual pledging brought the mission Guaraní into the Spanish imperial realm, while allowing them to stand apart from settlers and local authorities motivated by self-interest—the Guaraní mission world's third moment of birth.

The gestation had been long, nearly three decades of effort by the Jesuits, in Paraguay and in Spain, and conversations among the Guaraní about how to face their circumstances. The idea of an alliance can be traced back at least to 1610, when the great cacique Tabacambí had proposed the lineaments of such an arrangement to Father Lorenzana. From that point forward, Guaraní groups seemed intent on avoiding "odious" service to Spaniards, escaping the yerba mines, and protecting themselves against the Paulista dragnet that snared so many over decades.[11] Jesuits reported that Guaraní were prepared to flee to the forests if something was not done. Understanding that flight would imperil conversion efforts, Father Montoya had traveled to Madrid to lay his case before the king and to bargain the Guaraní's political relationship to the monarchy.

His timing had been propitious. Portugal and Spain had been jointly ruled by the Spanish monarchy since 1580. During these decades, imperial boundaries remained ill-defined and unmonitored, allowing Brazilian raiders to operate with impunity in Spanish territory. In 1640, a new king assumed the Portuguese throne, separating the kingdoms once again. What had been an unregulated zone now became a focus of geopolitical testiness and commercial competition. In the victory at Mbororé, the mission Guaraní had proven their worth to the Spanish king, who reciprocated in 1642 by permitting mission militias to bear firearms.

Montoya had parleyed the moment into a "pact" under which the Guaraní would be recognized as vassals *cabeza del Rey* (head of the king)—that is, directly under royal jurisdiction rather than indirectly through the encomienda.[12] This was not simply a matter of behind-the-scenes maneuvers by Jesuits. Historical linguist Capucine Boidin has argued that it is unlikely the Jesuits would have conceived of a "monarchical pact" if they had not been "constrained" to act in certain ways by Indigenous caciques like Tabacambí or by arguments like the one advanced by the council and caciques of San Ignacio in 1630 to avoid service at Mbaracayú.[13] These leaders knew to expect no help from local Spanish power holders. They also understood how to draw on the language and spirit of past laws, however unevenly they might be enforced in practice, to negotiate an outcome at least partially on their own terms, within the flexible constraints of Spanish rule. By subscribing to the pact, mission residents were choosing to enter an unfamiliar and uncertain arrangement. The importance of the king's promise of protection was undeniable. But their decision was almost surely not dictated solely by a survival reflex. They were also making a statement about the kind of world they wanted to live in.

"Content, free, and trusting in your shelter"

The social and moral stakes of the decision to join the missions can be heard in the words of a cacique who strongly resisted incorporation. In 1645, just before Governor Lariz visited the twenty missions, a cacique named Mborosení, who had been captured by the Paulistas but had later escaped, railed against the fathers. According to a Jesuit account, Mborosení addressed a crowd of Indians who had welcomed Father Pedro Romero into their midst. He accused the fathers of rounding people up, imbuing them with a thousand superstitions, and herding them into reductions. They prohibit multiple wives "even for caciques," forbid drunkenness, and condemn "venereal pleasures" (a Jesuit translation, surely), he warned. "Compare this misery to the liberty that we and our ancestors enjoyed, who were able to do whatever they wanted." He urged the Guaraní to be wary, for once "caught in the net," they would be trapped. "Wherever the new religion imprisons souls, bodies remain subject to a harsh slavery," he concluded, offering a decidedly material cast to the perils of Jesuit evangelism.[14] He exhorted his listeners to rise up and grant martyrdom to Father Romero. Shortly afterwards they obliged.

We can imagine the passion with which Mborosení delivered these words. He was, after all, a tubichá, expected to speak eloquently. He seemed to want his listeners to consider that taking up mission life was not solely a matter of survival but also a question of the lives they wanted to lead. On its face, his bill of particulars was unremarkable—quite possibly old news for his listeners and certainly Father Romero had heard it all before; caciques like Mborosení had been inveighing against monogamy for decades. For the missionaries, Mborosení's "liberty" amounted to little more than libertinage, a freedom to do whatever they wanted—drink and fornicate—without responsibility or purpose.

So flattened a sense of what liberty might mean in a Guaraní context leaves us with no way to think about what Mborosení's audience might have heard, beyond a call to polygamy and inebriation. Perhaps the most straightforward Guaraní equivalent of the Spanish *libertad* (liberty) was *yepé*, which Montoya's *Tesoro* gives as "liberty, escape," either from captivity or from a status of service.[15] This may have been part of what Mborosení was trying to get at, as suggested by his image of being "caught in a net." But his more powerful idea, at least as far as his listeners were concerned, may have been to link the liberty of a lost precontact world to the idea of multiple wives. This amounted to an invented nostalgia, for he seemed to suggest that ordinary Guaraní men, like ancient caciques, could enjoy a privilege most had likely never enjoyed—typically, Guaraní men had just one wife—if only they would follow him.

We can only speculate about what depths of meaning Mborosení drew on by invoking liberty in this way. According to Montoya's *Tesoro*, the Guaraní word *tecócatú* meant "good life, free [*libre*]," a definition glossed by reference to "savages who live like beasts."[16] Jesuits would have understood this latter phrase negatively (and there is no guarantee that Montoya got the full meaning of so important a term). For Jesuits, to live like a "beast" was to reject a human life of rationality, sociality, and civitas.[17] For the Guaraní, however, "savages who live like beasts" were not less human than people, since people and animals alike were humans endowed with souls. Rather, they were people who had chosen to live apart from the society of other people, fully exposed to the opportunities and risks of being predator and prey. *Tecócatú* hints that the Guaraní might have seen in this choice a kind of freedom unavailable within society. Mborosení's invocation of liberty, though rendered by Jesuits in terms of doing whatever they wanted, may have resonated among his male Guaraní listeners precisely because it referred to the imagined good life enjoyed by "savages" who turned their backs on the safety of society and embraced the at-times terrifying liberty of the forest.

Yet, the Guaraní could also think about the fundamental conditions for the good life and liberty in terms of the protection from predation collective life offered. The San Ignacio council in 1630, in the closing lines of its petition to be free of the yerba mines at Mbaracayú, had noted in Guaraní that they had no one but the king to "look out for us," employing a word meaning "mercy, care." One who refused to extend such care could be characterized as not knowing "how to treat others," in contrast to someone who treated others well and was "kind."[18] If the king did not look out for them, stated the council, they would surely continue to be "worn down" and "made anxious" by those who would "hunt" them. They asked His Majesty that those others no longer be allowed to "pursue" them as predators do prey.[19]

An alternative to living with the dread of being pursued by other men may have involved the idea of *robiâ*, which Montoya's *Tesoro* translated as meaning "credit, obedience, honor, esteem, trust, firmness, tenacity, content [with]."[20] This definition suggests another way the Guaraní may have conceived of a good life. Rooted in a sense of "finding oneself well, being accommodated," one gloss in the *Tesoro*'s long entry for *robiâ* was a Guaraní phrase given in Spanish as "I am content, free [*libre*], and trusting [*confiado*] here in your protection/shelter."[21] Although caution is in order, given possible Christian overlays (or outright misunderstanding), this hints that life-in-common could represent freedom from the risks and dangers of predation. And since the forest, where predators lurked, figured as a male space, we might consider that this understanding of *liberty* was at least partly gendered, since women far less commonly exposed themselves to the perils of predation. From this perspective, society need not have figured as a site of non-liberty but could instead be imagined as a place of freedom *not* to live like beasts, who could never escape the threat and anxiety of becoming prey. Thus understood, *liberty* and its associated *contentedness* depended fundamentally on trusting in the shelter that social life offered from being hunted, a register for *liberty* rooted in the very sociality rejected by those who might choose to live like forest creatures. While this point must remain conjecture, perhaps those who refused Mborosení's call, instead daring to take up life in the missions as vassals of the Spanish king, were opting for a particular vision of how they wanted to live, emphasizing the liberty and contentedness of trusting in the idea of life together in peace and safety over the liberty of being able to do whatever they wanted.

In the still roiling environment of seventeenth-century Paraguay, such a choice could have made sense within an expanded framework of Guaraní understanding. Village life had long been structured by the demands and comforts of gift and reciprocity expressed through the conviviality of shared labor, meals, and feasts. The importance of asserting this as a kind of freedom could have made perfect sense, especially given the pressures Indigenous people were under. This may have been particularly true of women (though Jesuit sources shed little light in this direction). Given complaints through the sixteenth and early seventeenth centuries about women who chose not to give birth or who killed their own children or resided with polyamorous encomenderos, it is entirely plausible that Guaraní women might see advantages in monogamous marriage to an Indian man (which was the general Guaraní pattern in any event) and the relative stability of daily life. As Mboroseni's words indicate, polygamy became a rallying cry against the Jesuits by hinting that ordinary Guaraní men might enjoy a privilege long associated with cacical prestige. This could put women into delicate situations. Montoya noted that a cacique who opposed monogamy had fled to the forest, taking a number of children in tow and their mothers with them.[22] We cannot know what led these women to decamp nor what the cacique and his followers intended for them, though explicit mention of the children hints at the possibility that the mothers in question had little choice.

Contrasting Guaraní visions of liberty require no resolution. In Western political thought, society and liberty have long been in tension, a product of the opposition between liberty conceived as the utter lack of restraint on individuals—being able to do as one wants—and a view rooted in the Hobbesian idea that society is the name for the individual's surrender of liberty to the State. Whatever sense this might make in a Western register, it bears recalling that among the Guaraní, as among Amazonian peoples generally before European contact, there appears to have been no state as such, as Pierre Clastres and others have argued. Nor had there been any sense that individuals who lived together were ontologically prior to society. To live *in* society was to be *of* society. The virtuous life of aguïyeí obliged each person to reciprocity. And while a Guaraní man might choose to leave society and live like a beast, one who did was necessarily alone and at risk of becoming prey. For precontact Guaraní, in other words, there had been neither state nor sovereign individual (terms whose opposition evince a Western understanding of political order). There is, therefore, no reason to assume that liberty and society were opposed concepts among the Guaraní. In this view, society was not to be feared and liberty did not contemplate freedom from all restraint. If anything, the point was to strike a balance between the danger of being prey and the danger of being ruled too closely.

Perhaps this helps explain Guaraní openness to an alliance with the Jesuits and their willingness to become vassals of the Spanish king.[23] Such an arrangement offered the possibility of defending and reconstituting a certain understanding of life together rather than facing men who hunted other men. Before the arrival of Europeans, jaguars had been the apex predators of the forest world, and everyone knew that outside the village, people risked being attacked. But jaguars represented an utterly different sort of threat if they came into a village, perhaps to snatch and eat a child, as was known to happen.[24] In such circumstances, predation became an existential, even ontological threat, for it intruded upon the peace of collective human life. The *Tesoro* entry for the Guaraní word conveying "enjoyment, contentment, abundance" stated that "jaguars are found where there are no men," implying that the places where men gathered—society by another name—were conceived of as havens from the jaguar's claws.[25] By the early seventeenth century, the Guaraní no longer feared only jaguars and other forest killers. Now they were pursued by settlers, Brazilian slavers, and even hostile tribes intent on trading Indian bodies for other goods, predators who regularly disturbed village life.

This amounted to a new form of predation, requiring a conceptual adjustment. Men had long fought each other in vengeance. Some, like the Tupinambá, had organized social life around violent conflict as such. But this had not been acknowledged as a universal condition, for men were also naturally inclined to sociality. To the extent Guaraní now thought of themselves as being hunted like animals by other men, they were having to acknowledge that fundamental categories of experience regarding social life had been upended. Against this backdrop, the liberty of the trusted protection promised by mission life and vassalage may have seemed worth a try to salvage the possibility of sheltered contentedness.

At the moment of his speech, Mborosení appears to have won the day; his listeners killed Romero and another missionary. But this was not the only option—as tens of thousands of Guaraní made clear over coming decades. To these many, life in the missions may have seemed an opportunity to heal sociality from the deep wounds inflicted by decades of European predation on the Guaraní. Jesuit and Guaraní ideas regarding the value of social life converged on this point. For the Jesuits, through Aquinas, God had ordained society so that human beings might perfect themselves in each other's company and with each other's help. (After all, men had been born without the claws that enabled other creatures to live alone.) Those who undertook "good works" benefiting their fellows thereby advanced their own virtue by contributing to the common good through charitable acts—the grounding principle for all Jesuit action. Similarly, aguïyeí as an enduring state of goodness or right action, could be realized only collectively and only if individuals acted from the spirit of reciprocity rooting all social relations. Neither of these views was possible if individuals pursued private interests at the expense of the good works and reciprocal openness that made sociality possible. Together these distinct though not incommensurable principles were the basis for a collective, cross-cultural alternative to the settler economy of gain.

Reseeding life together

During the decades following flight from the Guairá, the Paraná-Uruguay region became a gathering place for Guaraní and others from areas near and far (Map 5.1). Jesuit counts indicate that during the fifty years after Governor Lariz's visit in 1647, the population of the missions tripled, from 28,000 to nearly 90,000 people (22,000 families) across twenty-eight towns, mostly the result of in-migration—people were voting with their feet. Sixty priests and five lay brothers lived there in 1700.[26]

This growth was partly the result of a wrenching spatial reorganization spanning Guaraní territory. By 1620, royal officials recognized that two hundred or so Spanish vecinos (voting citizens) already occupied the best lands around Asunción. Wealthier encomenderos had leveraged their power to take control of native territory opened up by disease, overwork, and violent displacement. As settlers reached out to more distant zones for labor, Indigenous communities in Itatí, Iguazú, and Tape, where Jesuits had evangelized, felt a strain on the village-fields-forest complex that had buffered them from the settler economy. In the 1620s, encomenderos renewed their push to relocate Indigenous populations into pueblos de indios (native or Indian towns) closer to Spanish settlements to make it easier to mobilize their labor. Such was the fate of two previously established Franciscan reductions in Itatí. Jesuit villages too were forced to move either because they were threatened by bandeiras or under pressure from encomenderos. The situation was exacerbated by the fact that even Spanish communities were not always fixed in space. The town of Villa Rica, for instance, relocated five times between its founding in 1570 and 1636 (and three more times after that; Map 4.1), drawing new Guaraní villages into its orbit with each move. This process was not complete until the 1660s.[27]

The denial of living space (tecoá) interfered with the movement so crucial to Guaraní communal dynamics—occupying new lands, founding new longhouses, responding to internal pressures, and coordinating relations among villages. Larger groups often broke down, fragmenting into the smallest units capable of survival, scrambling the circuits of everyday life. As networks of reciprocal and solidary exchange stretched, these diminished groups found it increasingly difficult to resist incorporation into the settler economy.[28] Some communities melted away as individuals leaked out to encomiendas or into the general labor pool. A few might still claim that their encomenderos treated them "like kings."[29] But most who lived in or near Asunción and other Spanish towns continued to serve as indentured yanaconas to encomenderos, offered their labor for food and clothing, or sustained themselves by fishing and hunting.[30] In desperation, some gave themselves up to the yerba trade, paying their tribute obligations by toiling in the yerbales, often under the supervision of African slaves. If they were lucky, they might earn a surplus to gamble or drink away in Mbaracayú. The more fortunate might earn wages (in cloth, iron, or yerba) as carters or bargemen crucial to moving yerba from forest to market. Although this might seem an essentially individualizing process of seeking a personal fate or dodging communal obligations, and there was surely some of this, men might also earn tradeable goods to support families overburdened by labor demands and debt. People were making decisions, but they were doing so in the gray zone where coercion, necessity, and choice blurred.

Legal disputes from this period hint at the stresses of this highly fluid situation. In 1666, two non-mission villages opposed a Spaniard's petition for three hundred men to work in the yerbales near Villa Rica.[31] Alfaro's law, they noted, forbade "renting" Indians' out for such purposes.

In their filing, they recounted a familiar story of the inhuman conditions of yerba work, arguing that removal of so many men would destroy community life. Mbaracayú, they pointed out, had been a village of two thousand souls thirty-five years earlier. Now only five hundred lived there, because so many had died or fled violence and mistreatment, they said. Some claimed that the "common good" was served by the "exchange and commerce" of yerba, noted the petition. But such a policy "should not be called the common good," since it was only for a short time and would devastate the province for the "exorbitant profits" of merchants. Surely, argued the petitioners, there were other ways than yerba for Spaniards to earn profit—wine, tobacco, cotton. The record contains no decision on this matter. Other cases during these decades indicate that wage work by Indians invited fraud and abuse by employers. Indian employees might be bilked of yerba promised them in payment for transporting shipments down river. Others who contracted for ten months work might be paid for only two months, the legal limit for a labor rotation, a clear ruse to bamboozle the vulnerable. In other cases, Indigenous people might sue encomenderos for liberty or salaries or to stop mistreatment and overwork. Few of these plaintiffs found sympathy from judges.[32] Meanwhile, discord and litigation among Spaniards over Indigenous wageworkers had reached such a pitch in the 1690s that the governor himself called for an end to wage contracts, which seemed to benefit everyone but workers.[33] Nothing came of it.

Against a gain-driven external economy, seventeenth-century Jesuits promoted a vision of social life that aimed to align individual virtue with the common good through charity. From the missionaries' perspective, this meant bringing the Indians into "a civilized, human way of life," converting them from "rustics [country-dwellers] into Christian citizens."[34] By learning to raise cotton with which to clothe their nakedness, the Indians would overcome their "laziness" and turn away from the forest altogether. Where the forest, a broad commons of abundance and liberty but also risks and uncertainties, had always enveloped the Guaraní, the Jesuits saw only an untamed space, the antithesis of a proper human life. Under Jesuit tutelage, men rather than women would learn to "labor and sow." By mastering the ox-drawn plow and cattle husbandry, they would have neither reason nor desire to "roam the forest in search of sustenance."[35] Though convinced of this conceit, early missionaries took the long view and did not impose their design with unbending rigor, opting instead for an adaptive flexibility that allowed much of Guaraní life to continue as it had been.

As mission communities grew after the mid-seventeenth century and new quotidian arrangements took form, residents adapted to a novel environment. The biggest change, certainly, was that mission communities were largely spared the unremitting pressure of encomenderos and Paulistas. In this more peaceful and secure setting, the familiar and the untried mingled. Men still hunted and fished. Women continued to work family plots, though increasingly men did as well. Some men learned trades, carpentry, ironwork, weaving, and cobbling. Mass was becoming a daily affair, though it was still new enough that many, especially older folk, quietly resisted attending. Mission communities were hybrids of Spanish and Guaraní spatial and organizational ideas. Alfaro's ordinances had specified that new Indian towns be laid out in a gridded Spanish style—a plaza and radiating streets encircled by farm lands (Fig. 5.1). This much was not so unfamiliar. Guaraní villages before Europeans had also been organized around a central open space surrounded by a semicircle of longhouses, beyond which lay farm lands. Within the longhouses, on the other hand, change was afoot. Large, undivided interiors were gradually partitioned, with the idea that each nuclear family have its own space, in keeping with Jesuit efforts to promote monogamous marriage.[36]

Community dynamics also began to shift in the face of demands for *convivencia* (coexistence) among different groups. At first, Jesuits and Guaraní seemed to agree that inhabitants of a given mission town should hail from the same guàra (tribe). Over time, as new groups joined existing missions, residents learned to live in larger, more diverse settlements. *Cacicazgos* (cacical groups) generally remained intact, but now jostled one another in ways they would not have before. People from different guàras might now reside in what amounted to the same customary living space (tecoá). Between mission villages, new relationships took hold. Varying circumstances produced diverse outcomes, so that no two mission towns were the same.[37] Centrally located towns straddling the Paraná and Uruguay region developed close ties. Edge communities looked to the center but also remained connected to surrounding areas and to the "unreduced" people who lived there. For instance, Yapeyú, founded in 1627 south along the Uruguay River, maintained relations with nearby "nomadic" neighbors who did not join the missions (Map 5.1). Residents of

Yapeyú hunted and fished on the same grounds as these "unbelievers," a relationship lubricated by the exchange of women, which produced kinship ties between the groups who occupied a cross-hatched region.[38]

From mid-century forward, the mission cluster forming in the Paraná-Uruguay region represented a haven from the chaos of the outside economy. For many, as for those who had come from Itatí, Iguazú, and Tape, the irony was that a measure of tranquility could be had only by leaving their home regions—their tecoá—and migrating long distances, a process of decades that stabilized only around 1670. During these years, the immediate challenge for mission communities was to work out the principles of interaction in everyday life between Jesuits and Guaraní and among Indigenous residents themselves—and to figure out what it could all mean.

At this early stage, the missionaries' commitment to personal poverty played a key role in promoting mutual trust. Official precepts were clear: the fathers should minimize burdens on residents, keep nothing for themselves, and instead give "gifts" as liberally as possible.[39] This stance was strongly reinforced. Father Torres's 1609 instructions had directed all priests to read Alonso Rodríguez's treatise on spiritual perfection and virtue, which enjoined Jesuits to embrace "poverty" and avoid any sense of "mine and thine" to prevent "self-love" from taking root.[40] Obituaries, with their hagiographic sheen, suggest that missionaries embraced this austerity, allowing them to depart this life as "lover[s] of poverty," who engaged in a kind of competitive self-abnegation, tearing up their own blankets to clothe the naked and dressing so poorly that "poverty itself would have been ashamed."[41]

The ideology and practice of non-accumulation resonated powerfully with Guaraní tenets of social life. Trust could not be rooted in kinship, since the fathers could not accept the gift of women. Nor, in principle, could missionaries receive material goods for themselves. The challenge from the Guaraní perspective was to bind the Jesuits to proper social conduct nevertheless. Here again, Guaraní ideas of gift-reciprocity mortised flexibly with Christian charity. One missionary reported that the Indians of a new mission village brought vegetables, fish, fruit, honey, and other things to him every day, allowing him to pass these items on to the needy and the sick.[42] From his vantage, these donations might have seemed straightforward acts of charity from the Indians to him and from him to other Indians. Yet this gifting may also have been a chance for Indigenous people to gauge his behavior and bind him to certain norms. By watching what he did with the goods, givers were able to determine whether he redistributed them for the good of the community as a whole, as a cacique might—equally an expression of the common good and of aguïyeí—rather than keep them for himself. By repeating their action, they were signaling how he should behave, suggesting that new mission residents were quite consciously helping the fathers understand what was expected of them.

Among residents, reciprocity mediated interpersonal and intercommunal relations as the mission world took shape. The Jesuits' *Annual Letters*, with all their limitations as sources for registering Guaraní points of view, bolster the sense that substantive mutuality permeated everyday life within mission communities during the mid-seventeenth century. Montoya had noted that the Guaraní "very cooperatively assist each other" in tending their plots, neither buying nor selling, instead "freely and unselfishly help[ing] others in their needs, and show[ing] great generosity to people passing through."[43] As this unembellished description suggests, the first wave of missionaries understood Guaraní reciprocal openness largely without a Christian filter. While missionaries quickly came to think of Guaraní generosity as charity, perhaps especially after the Guairá exodus, they were clearly describing reciprocal behavior rooted in premission, even precontact times.

Later reports indicate that mutuality spread quickly within and among newly formed mission towns. *Annual Letters* from the 1640s, when memories of the flight from the Guairá were still fresh, remarked on the Guaraní's readiness to help others, whether by mounting a daring mission to rescue people who had hidden in the forest to avoid capture by Paulistas or by caring for the sick during times of disease. From roughly 1650, the missionaries remarked on how "generous" the Guaraní were, acting out of a desire to serve others, even strangers. They comported themselves with such composure, reported one priest, that it was remarkable how, "from being barbarians, they have acquired such refined customs" that they "treat one another with benevolence and are helpful to each other." During epidemics, their "work of charity" was notable and could even extend to Spanish towns suffering a contagion, a kindness toward the very people who otherwise would have exploited them if possible (though this could simply have been good propaganda in the Jesuits' ongoing conflict with settlers).[44]

By the 1660s, Jesuit reports were extolling the "mutual charity" mission towns generally had with each other. What Montoya had described in 1639 as caciques' "extraordinary liberality" in sharing their "abundance" with the "needy" in other towns became an anchor of intercommunal relations.[45] Thus, in 1666, the priest of Nuestra Señora de Fe noted with pride that the residents had "shown their charity" in coming to the aid of other Indians who had been "cruelly attacked" by the fierce Guaycurúes, expending a great deal of "sweat and labor" to help them rebuild. The priest at San Ignacio de Itatí observed that villagers' "mutual charity is not confined to the walls of their houses, but extends to surrounding villages," some of which were overseen by secular clergy rather than Jesuits.[46] Several mission towns contributed corn, garbanzos, and beans for planting, as well as oxen and horses to help found the new town of San Juan in 1698. Other communities sent people to help San Juan residents build the church and houses for all.[47]

These reports are striking in two ways. First, they leave a strong impression that a sense of mutuality extended beyond kin- and guàra-related affiliations, a social innovation under unfamiliar circumstances. Second, they emphasize residents' initiative, rather than priestly prodding. For instance, a 1660 report from La Candelaria, one of the missions' larger towns, noted that residents had aided a nearby community when it had decided to relocate.[48] So great was the "disinterest and love" of La Candelaria's residents, said the letter, that the fathers had been obliged to "put an end to their charity," for they had become so "distracted by helping raise new buildings" that they were neglecting their own fields. They had allowed themselves to be carried away by charity, implied the writer, a sign of their Christian virtue, but also of their improvidence.

The people of La Candelaria likely understood their actions differently. Raising houses had long mobilized whole communities around communal work and conviviality. Neighboring towns had typically been connected by kinship ties, which always gave a more heartfelt urgency to lending a helping hand. We know nothing more of this particular instance, but the missionary's concern that the residents of La Candelaria were neglecting their own crops bespeaks not so much forgetfulness or an overbrimming charity on residents' part as it attests to the continuing power of Guaraní sociality to shape everyday life. In the logic of reciprocity, such help implied future reciprocation—a kind of insurance against uncertainty, as well as a baseline understanding of mutual commitment through time. It was also the right thing to do. And while the priest took it for granted that he had called residents of La Candelaria back to their senses and to their own fields, the fact that he had to be so emphatic hints that the missionaries may have had less influence than they supposed and may not have fully grasped the role Guaraní mutuality played in binding the mission world together.

For instance, the Jesuit *Annual Letter* of 1644 noted that the villagers of San Ignacio Yaberirí had found a curious way of "exacting vengeance" from another village, which had offended them grievously. "Their vengeance consisted of inviting them to a certain feast and offering them a great banquet, without mentioning what had happened." Afterward, noted the writer, the other village behaved like good neighbors and even turned out to help repair the church that had burnt down.[49] The irony of vengeance as a "work of charity" is only apparent. In using the word *vengeance (venganza)*, this Spanish account was almost surely translating from the Guaraní. A baffled missionary may have asked how village leaders had decided to act as they did. Someone must have told him that it was a matter of *tepĭ*, which according to Montoya's *Tesoro* could mean "vengeance" or "free from" (*venganza* or *librar*), but also "payment" or "price" (*paga* or *precio*).[50] This word, rendered in Spanish simply as *venganza*, hints at a deeper Guaraní strategy for facing the problem at hand. Thus, one prominent usage example in the *Tesoro*'s entry for *tepĭ* was the Guaraní phrase, "I free myself from the affront that they would do me." Depending on the offense, such a thing might once have led to war, with the prospect of vengeance through prisoner capture and ritual cannibalism.

But violence risked upsetting a delicate balance, which could lead to instability and uncertainty, precisely what people had joined the missions to escape. And cannibalism, even for ritual purposes, had largely petered out by the seventeenth century, as Indigenous groups found less space for movement, contended with economic pressures, and came into closer contact with Christianity.[51] (In the missions, certainly, the only real hint of anthropophagy was the Eucharist.) The relevant question was how to act in the face of intercommunal tensions. *Tepĭ*, for the Guaraní, did not imply the individualized tit-for-tat adjustment of accounts that *venganza* did for Spaniards.[52] It looked, instead, to reestablish a relationship that had been broken in time. And it was generally performed in the context of a *pepĭ*, or invitation to a feast, as typically accompanied the raising of a longhouse.[53] By welcoming the other village to a banquet, the offended town was offering to repair the breach caused by the offense—to free them from an affront—but was also exacting *tepĩ* by making a gift that imposed an obligation to reciprocate in the future. Which is what happened. The residents of the offending village became good neighbors, demonstrating their commitment through the collective labor of rebuilding the church. All in all, this was a vindictive generosity finely calibrated to preserve peace and promote sociality in challenging times. A similar case twenty years later hints that this was a recognized strategy among the mission Guaraní for dealing with sticky intercommunal situations. An *Annual Letter* from the mid-1660s reported that the residents of a mission town responded to the insults of certain "barbarians" (perhaps a group outside the mission world) by "paying bad conduct with generous benefits" in lieu of "bloody vengeance."[54] In this way, wrote the father, they exacted their "revenge," which consisted of bringing the barbarians to Christianity, or at least to peace, by "charitable services"—that is, by the generosity of material gestures.

It is notable that Jesuit writers described these situations without taking credit for them. The clear implication is that the Guaraní were conducting this diplomacy and that the fathers were, at best, told what caciques and the cabildo had already decided or done. While the missionaries might understand such cases as peacemaking through charity, their thinly penciled portrayals indicate that they never quite recognized what they were seeing.

Although mutuality remained central to the emerging mission world, residents also experimented with more transactional exchanges. A case in point involved the Guaraní men who traveled from missions towns to collect and process yerba leaf in distant groves, under the supervision of caciques. Many hundreds went each year. The Guaraní had long harvested and processed the leaf for their own use. In new mission communities, yerba could serve individual and collective ends simultaneously. Men returning from the groves might hold back some yerba for themselves and sell a portion of it in Spanish towns along the route home. According to missionaries' reports, they might also "sell" small quantities within mission communities, acting as "absolute owners" of their personal stash.[55] While these men may well have been using yerba as a form of internal currency in limited ways, there is no reason to suppose residents understood such transactions as being incompatible with exchanges made to strengthen mutual ties. Montoya noted that when referring to the act of buying (*comprar*), the Guaraní generally resorted to a word meaning simply exchange, where the underlying concern seems not to have been profit but whether any given encounter promoted a general equality or leveling between parties.[56] In this spirit, exchanges involving yerba appear to have been conceived across a fluid range of meanings. Thus, having returned from the yerbales, these men might also give yerba to kin or to others who could not make the trip. And they typically presented a small amount of yerba to the resident missionary, an act Jesuits described as "alms." Beyond such limited exchanges, most of the yerba these men produced ended up in a common fund, stored in a room where "yerba of the community was kept," as an officer who had accompanied Governor Lariz observed in 1647. This was a continuation of earlier practices. Montoya had noted that the Guaraní had long produced yerba to help "remedy certain needs of their villages," such as buying horses to help them tend cattle herds or purchasing cotton with which to clothe themselves. Jesuit reports from the mid-1650s indicate that producing and storing yerba "for the common good of the villages" and to answer "cries for help" from other villages persisted and even strengthened in mission towns.[57]

While Guaraní and Jesuit visions of social life never aligned perfectly, securing the material bases of community life remained a broad point of agreement through the seventeenth century. Reporting on the state of the Paraná-Uruguay reductions after decades of evangelical effort, the *Annual Letter* of 1700 insisted that the faith simply would not have "taken root" but for the fathers' "solicitude and care that everyone have food and dress, but also houses to live in, lands to pasture and preserve their cattle and finally everything necessary for human and political life."[58] This view appears to have been shared by Indigenous people who joined the missions, though they may have had a different understanding from the Jesuits of who was primarily responsible for the satisfaction of basic needs. Two encounters circa 1690 indicate that mission residents stressed such concerns over explicit religious proselytization, especially in encounters with unbelievers.

In one instance, missionaries accompanied by a Guaraní militia officer came across a group of unconverted Indigenous people. According to the *Annual Letter*, the officer, with gifts in hand, told the strangers that they could save their souls by joining the missions and that doing so would "free them from the dangers Spaniards, Tobas, and Chiriguanos [hostile Indigenous groups] put them in every day." In the missions, he said, they would be able to live without "fear and surprises."[59] The caciques announced that they would be pleased to bring their people to the designated spot. What is striking about this dialogue is that even in a Jesuit telling, mission residents pointedly emphasized protection from opportunists, whether Europeans or other Indigenous people, and a certain tranquility over explicitly religious tonalities.

Another encounter from the same period reinforces the impression that the missions had come to be known as refuges from danger and uncertainty, places of relative abundance, and nodes of intercommunal connection. According to a Jesuit account, an expedition of missionaries and mission residents operating between the Pilcomayo and Bermejo rivers south of Asunción were approached by caciques from thirteen villages who wanted to hear about the missions.[60] Through an interpreter, mission residents spoke to groups of "unreduced" Indians regarding "the order and good manner" of their treatment by the missionaries (a Jesuit-sounding phrasing, it has to be said). The fathers, said the residents, provided "a thousand goods" and there were no Spaniards to "bother" anyone. Yes, "these are the fathers we have been looking for," responded the caciques, noting that a plague of locusts had recently "taken over their lands and stripped them." The caciques immediately proposed a site where cattle could be brought and a new town established that would convene all thirteen villages. Once that was done, they hoped a trail could be opened between the new community and the missions. The report closed by observing that there was "no doubt that if the cows come, they would gather all the villages in short order." Here again, the accent on both sides of this encounter, those who aspired to join the missions and those who already lived there, stressed the material abundance and relative tranquility of mission life. But by asking that a trail be opened, the newcomers were also signaling a yen to reconnect with a wider, mutually supportive community.

And, in fact, mission residents during the middle and late decades of the seventeenth century knew a freedom of movement they had lost during the period of intensive Paulista and encomendero raiding through the 1630s. Townsfolk crisscrossed mission territory, visiting kin and friends, delivering messages, carrying goods, celebrating weddings, participating in feasts. Men traveling to the yerbales or to cattle roundups in the eastern plains might stop in neighboring towns along their routes. Spouses

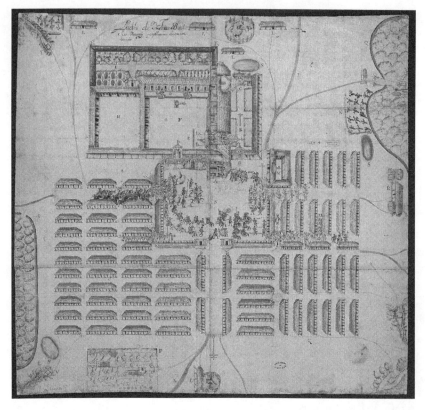

FIGURE 5.1. Plan of Mission San Juan Bautista, 1753. *Source:* España. Ministerio de Cultura y Deporte. Archivo General de Simancas, MPD,02,014.

might live in different towns and travel regularly between them, though missionaries tended to frown on such arrangements. During the earliest years of mission communities, the fathers seemed relatively unconcerned with this sort of movement. In 1685, however, the provincial Thomás Donvidas wrote a letter to the fathers warning them against "excesses . . . in the name of charity."[61] Hospitality toward guests from other towns, he said, had gotten out of control, to the point that it had become common for people to travel among towns, where visitors were welcomed with music, "too much food," nighttime festivities, and a general relaxation of religious observance. He advised the missionaries to curb this cordiality, which seemed to advance no obvious purpose. Provincial Juan Paulo Oliva made similar noises in 1690, ordering priests to stop residents from overdoing the invitations to other towns. Taken together, these documents suggest that as a new century approached, the fathers had begun to cool toward the reciprocal and solidary practices that had animated the mission world through much of the seventeenth century.[62] And yet, this was precisely the sort of connection the thirteen Pilcomayo villages had heard about and seemed so keen to take part in.

"For the common, for themselves, and for everyone else"

The decades straddling 1700 were a period of remarkable energy within the mission world. Protected by their status as vassals *cabeza del Rey*, with each village chartered by royal decree, mission communities thrived as villages outside the mission orbit did not. Up to the 1670s, stress had been on ensuring multiethnic *convivencia* amid an influx of recent arrivals and on working out the relationship among residents and missionaries. The 1680s to 1730 were years of active consolidation. The carved stone churches that astonished travelers to the region in the mid-eighteenth century were built during these decades. The church at San Miguel, for instance, took ten years to complete and involved a thousand Indians working with Jesuit architects and engineers. By one report, it was worth a million pesos.[63] These houses of worship were adorned with polychrome sculptures of Jesus, Mary, and the saints, executed by Guaraní artisans trained by Jesuits, working in mission workshops.[64] The architecture and execution of these temples represented a "complex cultural interaction," combining Jesuit and Guaraní ideas of structure, material, and space.[65] The amount of labor and resources that went into them bespoke a considerable communal surplus.[66] Each temple, thus, was a gift of the community to itself, an insistence on the "general point of view" over the narrowness of the "particular point of view."[67]

During these years, mission towns that had been loosely connected were integrated into a network of communication, reciprocal exchange, mutual support, and obligation. At a time when isolated towns outside the missions might still be assailed by Paulistas, as happened to four pueblos de indios near Villa Rica in 1676, this broadened sense of security and robust connection was deeply reassuring to mission residents.[68] Communities of several thousand people were linked at a distance of two to at most ten leagues (roughly six to thirty miles), via a network of regularly maintained trails, bridges, and rivers, with a chapel every five leagues, inns with beds along the way, and guardhouses.[69] With rare exception, every mission was within a day or two on foot of one or more others, enabling the movement of goods and people along circuits of kinship, reciprocity, and religious festivities. Even a critic could marvel that a letter marked "Urgent" could transit one extreme of the territory to the other in a couple of days.[70]

Material conditions within the mission world reflected a hard-won stability and plenty. One Jesuit historian, with a swell of pride he might later have had to confess, noted the "extraordinary prosperity and grandeur" of the missions in the early 1700s.[71] As a rule, communities were well provisioned. Every household had a field on which to grow its own food. Families received weekly meat rations taken from communal cattle herds, a dietary novelty now fully integrated into Guaraní life. Want was rare, though epidemics could spark an exodus (as during the 1740s). Orphans, widows, the elderly, the sick and even wayward women were supplied from community stores. Birth rates were high, despite epidemics and locust plagues in the early eighteenth century. The missionaries made a point of this, giving every incentive for people to marry young, girls by fifteen, boys by sixteen. The community generally helped new couples set up their households. Child-rearing was considered an obligation shared within the community at large.[72] Around 1700, the total number of Indigenous inhabitants of the mission world reached 100,000. By the early 1730s, 141,000 people lived in thirty towns ranging in size from 2,500 to 6,000, the result of a boom in births beginning circa 1690, a sign of collective well-being.[73] This number represented something on the order of four of every five Indigenous people in eastern Paraguay, hinting at the extent to which the encomienda regime was in retreat.[74]

By the early eighteenth century, new work routines began to reflect the increased scale of the mission world. Ordinary residents tended their individual plots four days a week, growing corn, manioc, sweet potatoes, beans, and other crops to feed their families. They worked communal fields—by 1707 known as *tûpâmbaé*, or God's land (though the root meaning of the Guaraní word denoted something to be admired, such as a gift of alms)—twice weekly during half the year, producing tobacco, sugarcane, wine, and cotton, all tradeable in the outside economy.[75] After 1700, yerba *caámini*, the highest grade and most expensive varietal of the plant, began to be cultivated in mission groves. This innovation saved travel time, reduced the risks and expense of seeking the plant in the wild, and gave the missions a dominant position in the production and trade of the default currency for the entire region (to the chagrin of local grandees and merchants).[76] Goods produced in the towns were then exchanged in the external economy for the few items not fashioned in mission workshops.[77] Cotton grown in communal fields was spun into thread by Indigenous women spinners and woven into garments by male weavers, keeping all mission residents clothed year round. Guaraní fabricators who apprenticed with missionaries cast cannons and bells, built striking clocks, polished lenses, printed books, and made musical instruments, including organs, turning their skills to collective displays of defense, organization, and aesthetics.[78] Guaraní cowboys traveled to distant grazing grounds to bring back free-range cattle for community distribution. Mission towns met annual tribute by paying one peso in yerba for each adult male up to the age of fifty, delivered directly to royal authorities in Buenos Aires. In effect, tribute became an obligation satisfied collectively by the entire mission populace, relieving individuals and small groups of the burdens of paying it on their own.

For the most part, pueblos de indios faced greater pressures. In those communities, whatever surplus could be squeezed out of residents generally went to encomenderos, or those who could pay wages. In Asunción, Spaniards and Guaraní might live side by side, but the economy benefited the former, however poor they might be. Direct competition among settlers for labor produced cross-cutting incentives that strained the bonds of Indigenous communities. Merchants often hired any who presented themselves for work, even if they were ducking communal labor somewhere else. A desperate encomendero might poach someone else's workers in this way, though he would rail against fellow encomenderos who did the same and punish *his* Indians who evaded communal obligations. This was the reality of competitive gain-seeking and individual survival that made collective subsistence outside the mission world so dicey for Indigenous people.[79] Pueblos de indios also struggled to meet tribute demands. According to an official government report in 1701, two-thirds of male Indigenous tributaries were unavailable to do the work needed to satisfy tribute, because so many were absent on labor rotations to encomenderos, had been drafted for unpaid corvée (*mandamiento*) labor on roads, bridges, and buildings, or had fled their villages to avoid communal labor in favor of seeking a *conchabo* (paid labor agreement). And while those who worked for wages elsewhere contributed to communities upon their return, they often remained away for months at a time or longer, leaving children, the elderly, and especially women to do the (unpaid) work necessary to sustain themselves *and* make tribute payments.[80]

By contrast, the mission world during the first three decades of the eighteenth century became a vast redistributive ecosystem, linking communities and connecting the mission world as a whole to commercial circuits in the outside economy in carefully regulated ways—a fully realized "economic system without profit."[81] Warehouses, larger versions of the rooms where Guaraní villages had stored yerba during the seventeenth century, now stockpiled goods produced communally on common lands. Food stored there might be doled out during emergencies—such as a locust plague, epidemic, or drought—or used to aid other mission communities running short of supplies. These storehouses also held yerba, tobacco, and cotton destined for external trade. Guaraní boatmen took these products to the Jesuit *oficio* (business office) in Buenos Aires or Santa Fé, where they were traded for other goods that were transported back to the missions. Return shipments included the knives and axes distributed to Guaraní men each year, and the needles, scissors, and beads given to women, as well as firearms for the militia.[82] The warehouses also served a crucial quotidian function within the missions, as disbursement points for communal goods, especially beef from community cattle herds.

Warehouses thus played a crucial symbolic role in everyday life. At the most basic level, they represented the baseline of material security that had attracted so many to the mission world over decades, where it was matter of principle that the Indians "lack for nothing in what they need for dress and food."[83] But the warehouses also signaled a changed relationship between reciprocity and redistribution. Among the Guaraní, the two had always been connected in the person of the cacique, whose prestige hinged on his ability to perform generosity by redistributing goods to community members. The emergence of the storehouse and regular distributions from communal supplies shifted some of this redistributive work away from caciques to larger institutional arrangements that reflected reciprocity, but now at a new scale of collective life.

The Jesuits' broad commitment to the common good underpinned missionaries' activities. Aquinas had said that "the common good is the end of each individual member of a community, just as the good of the whole is the end of each part."[84] Yet, Jesuits recognized that in the contemporary world, Europeans were learning "to live for oneself" and call it liberty.[85] Through the seventeenth century and into the early decades of the eighteenth, the fathers' stated goal had been to spare the Guaraní this fate. Like tecó aguïyeí, the common good was a supple principle that could bend to meet circumstances. In effect, the two understandings coexisted in a creative tension that allowed them to adapt to one another, up to a point, without sacrificing core convictions. This is perhaps most easily seen in the relationship between family fields (abámbaé, or thing of man) and communal fields (thing of God, or tûpámbaé) in everyday mission life.

Missionaries initially drew this distinction shortly after the turn of the eighteenth century, part of their civilizing effort to encourage Guaraní to leave the forest and fully adopt agriculture. For Jesuits, realizing this goal hinged on the disposition and use of property in the world. As a theological matter, property was a consequence of human nature after the Fall. In the beginning, argued Jesuit theologian Luis de Molina in the sixteenth century, God had made the world in common. All of God's children had an equal right to participate in Creation.[86] But because original sin had fated men to self-love, a universal regime of common property would lead to shirking and thus to scarcity. In the ensuing struggle over limited goods, the weak would be subjected by the strong. The common goods of the world therefore needed to be divided so as to ensure everyone would benefit from God's gift of the world to all. This had led to the idea that each person should have his own piece of common creation for, in the context of human fallenness, individual ownership would lead men to work, thereby securing the tranquility necessary for social life. Common property could be beneficial, allowed Molina, so long as men would work. But, as a matter of distributive justice, a deeper principle was in play. Regardless of its precise form, property, as Jesuits understood it, answered to the common good, especially in its concern for the vulnerable. If in recent times private property had seemed to thwart God's original design by becoming the object of accumulation and an instrument of avarice, the problem was one for theology and law, not a call to ratify an unjust distribution of Creation's goods.

Before encountering Europeans, Guaraní had no conception of property, private or common, nor need for one. Land had been abundant and their social ideas precluded a few from accumulating it to the exclusion of others. Rather than property, land was space within which groups of people lived together according to a particular *way of being*.[87] From a European perspective, land worked communally by the Guaraní looked like common property because the Guaraní had drawn no distinction the Jesuits could recognize as private or individual. In fact, what Jesuits were seeing was simply a different relationship to land and labor, and their role in human affairs. The Guaraní were of the view that living in the world entailed certain activities—farming, hunting, cooking, child rearing, house raising, field clearing, moving, feasting—that defined the very essence of what it was to live together in the land and that these activities required no motivation beyond the fact of their necessity, worthiness, and general benefits.

With Molina, early modern Europeans generally assumed that men would evade work if they could and that only a division of goods and the spur of necessity would persuade them otherwise. Jesuits agreed, with the proviso that property, whatever form it took, must ultimately serve the common good. By institutionalizing two forms of land use—one individual, one collective—the Jesuits were trying to have the best of both worlds. Through the abámbaé's usufruct, they aimed to persuade the Guaraní to adopt a more individual and private approach to matters of household economy, while guarding against the avarice private property encouraged and the inequality it produced (at least among early modern Europeans). But by creating the tûpámbaé, they were acknowledging what they understood to be a Guaraní preference for cooperative work, while looking back to a prelapsarian arrangement of Creation. It was a delicate balancing act, and not all missionaries believed the distinction worth keeping. At least a few imagined they might establish a perfect regime of individual property and that the Indians might be better for it. Provincial Lauro Núñez noted in 1694 that "some" fathers, out of a desire to "defend their Indians," aimed to create "Ideal Republics" in which "everyone would be [their own] lords, and none would need to serve another, nor work for another," for each person would have "his own property" and not require anything from anyone else.[88] (Ironically, many settlers might have shared this view, at least for themselves.) Núñez warned against this trend, concerned that such independence might erode residents' willingness to undertake collective work outside mission territory on behalf of the Jesuits or the monarchy.

Despite differences, Guaraní and Jesuit understandings regarding land were not incompatible. Though abámbaé and tûpámbaé were both neologisms, concepts the Jesuits needed to frame their own aspirations and understandings in terms of the common good, neither represented a stark novelty for mission residents. The notion of the abámbaé as a life-time usufruct was new. But use of the land referred back to the domestic plots extended-kin families had always worked cooperatively. So, even as the fathers pushed the Guaraní to think in more private ways about their abámbaé, mission residents continued to help each other in tending them (though they might at times neglect them, missionaries complained). *Tûpámbaé* as a word for communal land was an unfamiliar usage to the Guaraní, but the idea of putting hands to the task on behalf of the whole community was not. As Guillermo Wilde has argued, the tûpámbaé, for all that it was a Jesuit coinage, shared the spirit of gift, reciprocity, and re-distribution that lay at the heart of Guaraní sociality before contact with Europeans.[89] Nor was this so very different from land use and land tenure in Spain itself. Though private property was well understood in Iberia, communal land use and collective ownership of pastures, woodlands, and fields remained part of the broader matrix of sympathies and dependencies that defined late medieval and early modern social relations.[90] For the missionaries, in other words, the distinction between abámbaé and tûpámbaé did not represent anything radically new. The Guaraní, meanwhile, seem to have thought less in terms of property than in relation to a mesh of labor, land, reciprocity, redistribution, and solidarity oriented to community thriving.

In everyday life, this web could bind communities in ways that made sense both to Guaraní and to Jesuits. According to missionary Jaime Oliver, mission residents in the eighteenth century celebrated their local patron saints by attending mass, following which the cabildo and caciques of the town issued an "invitation" (*pepî*) to a *curúguaçú*, a great banquet reminiscent of the intercommunal feasts of precontact times.[91] Residents and caciques would gather and the missionaries would offer "fat cow[s]" from community herds, along with bread, honey, salt, yerba, and tobacco from the warehouse. Men added game birds, and women chickens raised in their households. After a proper blessing, each cacique would retreat to his own longhouse and distribute the bounty to kin and followers, who then ate in the festive company of others. This one public act was replete with meaning. It efficiently reminded the community of its labor in the communal tûpámbaé (yerba, tobacco), its investment in public goods and their redistribution (cattle), its dependence on the domestic work of women (bread, chickens), and its relationship to the forest as a domain of abundance and freedom (honey, game birds).

From the perspective of this ceremony, any sharp distinction between common land and individual plots would seem to reflect more a Western fixation on the idea of property than a Guaraní understanding. Nearly a century after Father Montoya had noted that Guaraní families possessed fields of their own but typically preferred "to help each other with great concert," missionary Luis de la Roca observed that caciques still commonly gathered their mboyas during sowing and harvest seasons to work together on each other's domestic plots until all of them were done.[92] By making collaborative work out of what the missionaries intended as individual labor, the Guaraní were vivifying their continued commitment to common endeavor as an anchor of reciprocity. This obligation might also be scaled to match the new realities of the mission world. One missionary noted that when some residents had to travel for trade or to more distant work sites, they were not paid, "because they do it for the common, for themselves and for everyone else." Those who stayed behind covered for those who traveled on mission business while they were gone, repairing their houses, working their domestic fields, and taking their turn on common fields.[93]

New things and old

Despite such statements, the Jesuits recognized that one of their greatest challenges lay in mobilizing the labor that made the mission world's relative security and prosperity possible. By the eighteenth century, Jesuits were of the view that men were naturally disinclined to work (the same assumption that grounded the need for private property). While missionaries had long commented on Guaraní sloth, through most of the seventeenth century they had seemed more broadly admiring of residents' charity than disparaging of their supposed idleness.[94] As the mission world reached its zenith in the 1720s–1730s, the fathers pushed residents to become more productive and adherent to work schedules. Official precepts and provincials' letters indicate that the missionaries sought to choreograph the day through the alternation of churchly and work-related functions. Mass in the early morning. Work through the afternoon. Vespers at dusk. Bells marking changes during a six-hour workday. The idea was to give residents time only for what the fathers thought was necessary or important—"work" or worship. (One critic noted that there were even bells to prompt residents to conjugal duties.) From available descriptions, there is no doubt that missionaries were guided by a broad desire for greater control over residents' labor.

They were often disappointed.[95] With Austrian asperity, Father Antonio Sepp complained at the end of the eighteenth century that Indian men frequently neglected their family plots, preferring, as he put it, to swing in their hammocks all day, working only if hounded and lashed.[96] Provincials during the 1720s raised similar concerns regarding the abámbaé, but offered few concrete suggestions to remedy what was, essentially, a structural issue: priests simply could not directly supervise residents when outnumbered thousands to one.[97] Instead, they relied on caciques and "captains" to oversee workers and bring "the lazy" in for a "light" lashing, as might be meted out to a lad who had misbehaved. But, as Father Cardiel noted acerbically, Indian supervisors rarely brought people in for punishment, being kin and kith to those they oversaw.[98] And while zealous priests might make a point of checking up on the caciques and work "captains" to ensure they were keeping people at their tasks, their efforts availed little because of what Cardiel described as "the childish carelessness and laxness of the Indian."[99] The perception of Guaraní lethargy persisted right up the Jesuits' expulsion in 1767. Father Jaime Oliver, for instance, alleged that residents would go hungry to avoid working, instead wandering about aimlessly and working only when a priest was present.[100]

To accept such characterizations at face value is to elevate Jesuit concerns and their underlying biases over the perspective of mission residents. When Oliver said that residents would rather go hungry than work, he failed to account for three critical facts of mission life in the eighteenth century. First, though well settled by this time, the mission world remained enveloped by forest. During the four days a week they were supposed to be working on their domestic plots, men could easily leave their villages to hunt and fish, as they had done since earliest mission times. The forest was always inviting—and abundant. Second, Oliver did not account for the fact that the Guaraní had radically modified their diet during the seventeenth century: they had acquired a taste for beef and enjoyed the means to consume it regularly. Enormous cattle herds ranged in mission grazing lands southeast of the main cluster of towns. Distributed weekly from central warehouses, meat made it possible for people to feed themselves without the work of cultivating labor-intensive crops—such

as European wheat, rather than native manioc, which took much less effort—as Father Sepp observed in 1696.[101] Third, Jesuit complaints about
Guaraní work habits may have been as much about the way residents
worked as about their failure to work. Provincial de la Roca noted in 1714
that domestic plots were attended to when caciques gathered their followers to work domestic lands cooperatively until all were finished.[102] This
suggests that the Jesuits' complaint may have been rooted in the fact that a
preference for collective labor ran contrary to efforts to persuade Guaraní
commoners to think in more explicitly individual terms. In other words,
the missionaries feared their "civilizing" project might miscarry.

So, if men were swinging in their hammocks or wandering about, it
may have been because the missions' success in banishing want made it
possible for Guaraní to enjoy a relative liberty that the fathers could only
see as a failure to behave more like European yeomen. Indeed, it might be
said that the Jesuits contributed to the very problem they decried, for as a
matter of principle, they rejected the most powerful tool they might have
used to discipline work: hunger. There was no ambivalence on this. Provincial Luis de la Roca stated clearly in his Precepts of 1724 that no Indian
could be denied food as a punishment for failure to work.[103] Of course,
it is reasonable to suppose that relative security from want, in stark contrast to the external economy, was one of the main reasons residents did
not desert the missions, barring extraordinary pressures (as we shall see).

Jesuit condemnation of Guaraní laziness may thus have reflected the
fathers' tacit recognition (and mounting frustration) that their capacity to motivate through intimidation and coercion was limited. An early
eighteenth-century document, written in Guaraní and meant for priests
as well as Guaraní caciques and officers, hints that persuasion and appeals
to the common good and to Guaraní notions of good work may have
played a role in ensuring the missions' relative abundance. Chapter 27 of
the Luján Manuscript, a work "catechism" regarding artisanal labor, takes
the form of a dialogue in Guaraní between Pedro and Miguel, two mission residents.[104] Pedro is the supervisor, charged with keeping Miguel,
a weaver, on task. In the document, Pedro urges Miguel, asking him to
hurry, because people need the cloth he is making. Miguel responds that
he is almost done with his work, which in Guaraní is given as *embiapó*, a
word meaning "activity that seeks a worthy end," rather than work that
produces only the exhaustion of *câneó* and is to no greater purpose. No
one else can do this, Pedro says. Miguel responds, "Let's go. I'm at it."

Pedro insists: "Will others do your work for you if you are not diligent? Will men come from other villages to do it? No, I don't think so." "No," says Miguel, "we will make the effort to finish."

There is much to be said about this tantalizing text, which was likely produced at the instance of missionaries but with Guaraní input.[105] The salient point is that Pedro never does more than hie Miguel on. He neither threatens him with physical harm nor suggests he will go hungry if he fails. Instead, Pedro refers to Miguel's work as worthwhile and important, reminding him of his obligation to the community at large. At one point, Pedro implores Miguel to be diligent, using a Guaraní word connoting the tenderness involved in grooming another (rather than a more strident word of urgency).[106] Melià has argued that this attitude, associated as well with women's cooking and the fashioning of useful objects, was at the root of Guaraní attitudes toward work as mutual, reciprocal, and gift-oriented.[107] Yet, by noting that people from other villages would not be coming to help—hinting that Miguel might hope they would—Pedro seemed at pains to shift Miguel's thinking away from an underlying expectation of mutuality toward a more individualized work ethic, a point doubtless insisted on by a missionary. Pedro stops just short of shaming Miguel, though the chastening of collective disapproval is implicit. For his part, Miguel always responds to Pedro's urgings with alacrity, saying he is on task and will finish the work. Now, this fictional Miguel was a weaver rather than a field worker and perhaps higher in some as yet poorly understood social hierarchy in Guaraní mission society, so interpretive caution is in order. Nevertheless, the fact that even under a cajoling pressure, work continued to be framed in communal terms suggests that mission residents in the eighteenth century might still approach day-to-day life in broadly non-utilitarian, non-competitive ways, even as missionaries were pushing them to adopt a more self-directed attitude toward labor and economic prospects generally.

This possibility must be understood in relation to the missions' broad success in meeting societal needs. From at least the late seventeenth century there was enough labor enough of the time to have made the mission world prosperous and safe, the pride of residents and the envy of outsiders. Jesuits saw the opportunity for more and complained that the Guaraní were too lazy to take up the challenge. From the fathers' vantage, the Guaraní were declining the chance to become more civilized by becoming more productive. But mission residents, including *indios del común* (commoners, of the community), may well have seen this collective abundance in a different light. I can only speculate on this point, but if physical punishment for failure to work was unreliably reported and administered, as Cardiel alleged, and if there was no general fear of hunger, as Luis de la Roca's Precept made clear there should not be, ordinary Guaraní may have been able to think about work in ways that did not require abstracting it wholly from the broader weave of everyday life.

Two missionary accounts speak to this idea. In 1719, Father Antonio Betschon told of the "nocturnal feast" common among field workers.[108] Returning from the day's labors, farmhands would slaughter the ox they had just been plowing with, rather than return it to a community corral. They would build a fire, tossing the wooden plow in if they lacked other kindling, and pass the night eating rare meat, sleeping, and generally carrying on. The waste of time and tools clearly offended Betschon, for he saw only "negligence and improvidence" in their actions. In describing the event, he may have exaggerated. He may also have misunderstood. One way to see the action of killing and eating the ox would be as exacting revenge or a price (*tepî*). As I have argued, the Guaraní could be quite canny in mobilizing reciprocal revenge as a way to defuse social tensions. Such an explanation, which echoes modern notions of resistance translated into a Guaraní cultural frame, assumes that these men were seeking revenge for something. Overwork, perhaps, or having to work at all, or a general dissatisfaction with being told what to do? An alternative gloss is that by killing both the beast and time in this way, these men were re-enacting gatherings of old when a boar had been brought from the forest for everyone's enjoyment. In this instance, it bears noting that the Guaraní word for meat also meant "invite to a meal/invite to work (together)."[109] A second episode suggests that, in certain instances, work itself could be the occasion for asserting quotidian freedom. Father Sepp griped in a 1732 account that it was not uncommon for men to rise before sunup to take the cattle out to pasture rather than attend Mass. Maybe these shepherds were Indigenous Stakhanovites, only too eager to do their bit. Or, since tending the herds was light enough duty and allowed them to be with others in an unsupervised environment, it was a way to combine work with a convivial evasion of religious obligation. What these incidents suggest is the possibility that in a context of reliable abundance, new patterns of everyday being might be borne so long as the conviviality that nourished life in common remained robust.

Though we must read through the veil of Jesuit misperceptions, substantive mutuality appears to have suffused everyday mission life during the first half of the eighteenth century, imbuing attitudes toward work, enlivening quotidian encounters among mission residents, and conditioning relations between communities. At the level of daily interactions, we can see the first of these in Father Cardiel's crusty comment that residents too often "wasted" much of what they grew in their domestic fields, "giving it away for free, or selling for a bagatelle, giving a thing worth ten for a thing worth one."[110] Cardiel's complaint, from the vantage of emerging notions of economic rationalism, seemed to be that the Guaraní failed to grasp the relative value of things in relation to labor. The idea of exchange parity was probably not a mystery among mission residents. Currency may not have circulated, but equivalency tables were used in exchanges between towns. Guaraní who traveled to Spanish towns to trade yerba, tobacco, and cotton for other goods destined for community use knew that items were being exchanged commercially and that such exchanges implied equivalency of value. In seeing only a defective version of buying and selling, Cardiel may have missed what was going on. His statement assumed that work could be treated as interchangeable with its product: to give away the fruits of one's labor or undercharge for it amounted to a failure to appreciate the *value* of work in the context of commercial exchange and the centrality of work as a distinct activity in social life. For those involved in giving away for free or "selling for a bagatelle," this may not have been the point. What Cardiel saw as a witless waste could just as easily have been a series of reciprocal exchanges unconcerned with relative value or the opportunity for gain, but deeply interested in reaffirming reciprocal relation with others (though the fact that a price might be charged at all points to a changed reality).

At times, Cardiel seemed to recognize this possibility. "So great was the sincerity" of the Guaraní tradesmen who plied their craft in the open-air patios around the central plaza—cobblers, weavers, blacksmiths, and others—that they did work for others without charging, since they were compensated from common stores. And yet, he noted, some of these artisans ended up with more than others from the warehouse because "they worked more than others." This might hint at a reward system in some incipient hierarchy of labor. But it is crucial to note that artisans, while plying their trade, generally did not plow their own fields, such was the demand for their products within the towns.[111] In this regard, it is worth noting that the pool of common goods supporting artisanal work also fed orphans, the sick, and widows who could not fend for themselves—in fact, anyone who, for whatever reason, did not have enough to eat or clothe themselves at any given time. By giving the fruits of their labor without charging, artisans recognized that they were being provided for by the common, while reenacting the generous redistribution that had long grounded the prestige of caciques.

At the same time, mission residents, even indios del común may have been involved in transactional exchanges with outsiders. From the seventeenth century forward, the missionaries had sought to exclude Spaniards and others from trading within mission territory, fearing that greed would grip residents and lead them to abandon the missions for the external economy. And yet, as vassals of the king and as a matter of natural law, the Guaraní were entitled to own property and engage in commerce. This could help account for the delicate advisement given by provincial Antonio Machoni in 1742 that it would be "more convenient" if outsiders did not bring their wares to sell in mission towns in exchange for yerba *caámini*. He could simply having been issuing a general warning against the practice, as previous provincials had done.[112] But the explicit mention of caámini suggests another possibility. Beginning in the eighteenth century, yerba came to be cultivated within mission territory (Figure 5.1). Yerba workers had traditionally been allowed to keep a small amount of yerba for themselves. With 140,000 residents in the 1720s, the mission world was by far the largest "market" for goods in the region, dwarfing Asunción by a factor of ten. Adventurous peddlers would certainly have been drawn by the opportunity to obtain caámini, the currency of the wider economy. Transactions would likely have been small and fleeting, perhaps featuring personal adornments not made available from common stores. This point must remain speculation. To raise it is to caution against assuming the mission world was hermetically sealed from the commercial world beyond. Conversely, if such encounters were indeed taking place, as with yerba exchanges described earlier, there is no cause to conclude that residents would have seen them as abrading the thick cord of interpersonal mutuality running through everyday life.

A strong sense of reciprocity also seems to have held *between* mission towns. A community might send cattle to a neighbor short of meat, even as Jesuits feared doing so might deplete the town's herd.[113] Cotton might be lacking here, while corn or vegetables might be short there. As

Cardiel put it, there was much "buying and selling" between towns. No cash was involved in these exchanges, as "surpluses" in one place went to meet "what is needed" in another. Flows of goods were registered in an account book according to a table of equivalencies. Cabildos and missionaries oversaw these exchanges, though they appear to have understood them differently.[114] Cardiel saw them as straightforward intercommunity trade. But again, in referring to buying and selling, he was employing a commercial metaphor to describe exchanges that blended immediate transactional qualities, or at least the meeting of needs, with the longer-term imperatives of intercommunal, substantive mutuality. As Cardiel himself observed, not without a tone of disapproval, towns maintained large debts with each other "at all times," which might rise or fall according to situation.

Crucially, there seems to have been no explicit concern for equivalency of value at the moment of transfer other than the (likely unstated) expectation that at some future moment the gesture would be reciprocated. The mission town of Yapeyú, for instance, was known to "trade" thousands of head of cattle to other towns for yerba and cotton, though not in amounts reflecting the value of the cattle given.[115] This asymmetrical practice continued through the 1730s and 1740s, even though decades earlier the Jesuit provincial had ordered missionaries to clear debts between towns promptly.[116] That these arrears remained unsettled points to a deliberate policy by Guaraní town councils not to close accounts.

This indebtedness speaks as well to the negotiated quality of the Jesuits' influence over the day-to-day economies of mission communities. Guaraní *mayordomos* (stewards) tracked the flow of goods into and out of the warehouses. They answered to the cabildo and, ultimately, to the missionaries, who could remove them. Yet mayordomos were not simply the missionaries' accountants.[117] If anything, their intimate knowledge of daily affairs and keen attention to relative value could strain relations between the Guaraní and the fathers. In one instance in the early 1740s, for example, mayordomos in Loreto, undoubtedly with support from the cabildo, complained to the Jesuit provincial that the town's priest had shortchanged a routine shipment to Buenos Aires, returning goods of much lesser value than the ones they had sent.[118] The provincial curtly responded that the town had been in such deep debt to the business office from prior shipments that what they had conveyed was barely enough to cover it.

We lack further details of this incident. But the friction itself speaks volumes. Clearly, the missionary had taken it upon himself to clear a deficit without alerting the cabildo or the mayordomos to what he was doing. When the mayordomos later found the discrepancy, they registered their concern. It seems unlikely they miscalculated, given that they drew attention to the gap in the first place. In this connection, it is telling that the business office in Buenos Aires had transferred part of its own arrears to the missions in 1737, imposing a cost mission communities should not have borne.[119] Whether the shorted goods went to settle some part of that debt is unknown. But the cabildo would surely have been aware of the possibility. Beyond such practical considerations, there may also have been a deeper point of principle at stake in this disagreement. Unlike Jesuits, who treated outstanding debts as a problem requiring a settling of accounts, the Guaraní saw advantage in them, an expression of substantive mutuality over time at intercommunal scale. Although in this case the debt was with the Jesuit business office rather than some other mission community, the cabildo may have responded as they did to confirm their view that not all debts demanded closure and certainly not without their consent. Cardiel himself grudgingly acknowledged the benefit of mutual indebtedness. In 1747, a moment when plague in the mission world had strained towns' ability to provide food and clothing for all, he remarked that but for this "frequent charity" there would be "much more penury" within the communities.[120] Pueblos de indios in the external economy, under constant pressure to produce for others and unable to generate surpluses for themselves, mostly lacked this sort of robust capacity to rely on help from others.

The complex and tensile matrix of land, work, abundance, transaction, and mutuality that bound the mission world together contained one other element that conditioned social relations during the decades up through the 1730s: the phenomenon of office holding, or what Wilde has called "native bureaucracy."[121] As vassals of the Spanish king, mission residents were entitled to select their own local councils on a yearly basis and govern themselves, subject to royal law. This arrangement dated back to Alfaro's ordinances and Governor Lariz's visit to mission territory in 1647. Indigenous leaders chose council members, a dozen or more, in consultation with the missionaries. The *corregidor*, a primus inter pares among cabildo members, who held the position for up to five years, was similarly selected, though technically his appointment was subject to confirmation by the governor in Buenos Aires (largely a formality, when bothered with at all). By the eighteenth century, cabildo elections played an important role in assuring broad representation among different groups within communities. Caciques, as traditional leadership figures in Guaraní politics, often served as cabildo members. But others might as well. An effect of this was that office holding layered forms of authority and status rooted in Spanish law and royal policy—external sources of political meaning— over the traditional kin-based role of caciques. Recent scholarship suggests that office holding may have contributed to emerging hierarchical distinctions among Native elites, perhaps even to familial "lineages."[122] Missionaries in the eighteenth century encouraged the process. Cardiel noted that cabildo members and corregidores were "esteemed like nobility" and their children learned to read and write.

To an extent, the reference to nobility reflected Jesuit efforts to shoehorn Guaraní political arrangements into European categories. In this spirit, provincials ordered that Indigenous officers be allowed to dress in ways that marked their status. But this was not merely a Jesuit projection. Cabildo members were notoriously keen to bear the staff of office that signified their authority.[123] A growing sense that position was a means to status may have been spurring a broad desire for official roles in mission communities. An estimated one in ten residents exercised an official function: beyond the cabildo were militia captains, artisans, and numerous church functions, such as sacristans and musicians.[124]

This might seem a recipe for the empowerment of an incipient political class. Certainly, office tended to rigidify status and create asymmetries, especially between officeholders and Indian commoners. Guaraní political culture had long opposed the concentration of command in leaders by denying them the capacity to accumulate. But where traditional caciques had performed prestige through generosity, officer holders exercised authority in relation to the larger structures of mission life—from the relationship to the missionaries to supervision of the warehouses, to mobilization of labor. There are hints that some officers may have sought to leverage position to material ends. Cardiel noted three examples of officeholders who made arrangements with mission purchasing agents to buy goods in Buenos Aires. One corregidor planted yerba on his family plot and arranged to have it traded for cloth, knives, glass beads, and baize "for his home."[125] While it would be easy to suppose that the corregidor in this instance was accumulating wealth, we might ask how many knives and beads and how much cloth and baize he could have used personally. Could it be that he purchased these goods to distribute them as gifts to followers, employing transactional means to accomplish reciprocal ends that could further boost his standing as corregidor? Regardless, such instances were the exception, admitted Cardiel. Few "emulated" them, lacking "acumen" for such behavior because of their "limited nature."

Despite such developments, the system did have checks. Most officers served one year before rotating off the council, little enough time for great personal mischief. Nor, for the most part, was office holding completely separate from the warp and weft of social relations more generally. Caciques often served on the cabildo, but they also remained responsible to their "partialities" (their kin-based groups) throughout their tenure and after leaving the council. Corregidores were at greater risk of accumulating power, in good measure because their tenure was so long. This was why official Precepts pointed to unspecified "grave inconveniences" of allowing them to serve more than five years at a stretch.[126] The fathers were admonished to look out for "distributive justice" with respect to all officeholders to ensure that those who had been "bettered" by position not get carried away.[127] Here it is worth recalling that missionaries themselves were forbidden to have "any sort of property" and were supposed to treat "things of the community" strictly communally. Which is to say that the fathers would have had every reason to lend a sympathetic ear to complaints of misconduct or excessive accumulation by officeholders.[128]

The final check on the mission political system as it had taken shape by the 1730s may have been the indios del común themselves, who continued to exert a subtle but weighty pressure on leaders through time-tested expectations regarding power and its purpose. In 1742, for example, provincial Antonio Machoni remarked in a worried tone that caciques' "vassals" often did not "venerate" them sufficiently.[129] The problem, as he saw it, was that caciques lacked the capacity to display status and assert hierarchy. To correct this, he ordered that more caciques be allowed to serve on the cabildo and that they be given the means to dress in ways that would raise their standing among their mboyas (followers). Machoni did not explain further. Given that one of the caciques' main responsibilities was to help keep workers on task—the thankless and vulnerable position of lower middle management, in modern parlance—we might suspect that the vassals' lack of "respect" and "veneration" bespoke some discontent regarding caciques' roles in arranging social life. As a matter of long tradition, caciques had motivated broad kin groups by performing generosity and persuading people to work together. If they did not live up to the prestige conferred on them, their followers might stray.

Something similar, if not quite as literal, may have been happening here. By the eighteenth century, caciques had become responsible for organizing labor on both communal land and domestic plots. With respect to the tûpâmbaé (communal land), they were joined by new work captains in meeting the schedules and forming the crews necessary for particular jobs.[130] But the task of ensuring that family gardens were tended fell largely to them, with all the challenges that entailed, as we have seen. Thus, caciques blended kin-based roles and new institutional functions. The withdrawal of respect by their mboyas could have reflected this fact. Caciques no longer acted only from the dictates of generosity. Now they had to coax their followers to adhere to a work regime ordained by wider imperatives and structures, even as they may have been seeking to enhance their own status within the community. By withholding their veneration, mboyas may have been setting limits to what could be demanded of them, drawing on deeper understandings of power in social life. Caciques cannot have been entirely oblivious to their dilemma. As Cardiel pointed out, these same men were also known for refusing to report their vassals for dereliction, bespeaking the delicacy of their position and some awareness of constraint. Machoni assumed that projecting hierarchy and authority would solve the problem of respect and veneration. It did not occur to him that commoners might be exercising a check on just how far caciques, as well as Jesuits, could push them.

*   *   *

Writing after the Jesuits' expulsion in 1767, Father Oliver explained the missions' success this way: having accepted "the faith of Christ," the Guaraní had been given "all the temporal goods . . . they could have desired," as they "had been promised."[131] In good Jesuit fashion, this statement affirmed the deep connection between the temporal and the spiritual in the making of mission life. But this was revisionist history. In Oliver's characterization, the Indians had accepted Christianity and then been rewarded materially. In fact, early evangelizers had led with gifts of material goods and only later preached, and throughout the life of the missions they had been as attentive to mundane as to higher concerns. Perhaps Oliver's inversion can be put down to the fact that as evangelization had given way to institutionalization, latter-day missionaries no longer remembered so clearly how the mission world had got to where it was.

It would be a mistake to suppose that the Guaraní saw things just as the Jesuits did after more than a century of living together. The mission world had insulated many tens of thousands of people from the exploitation of the external economy. It had nurtured a recovery of the Indigenous population, decimated during the sixteenth century. Without diminishing the role of Christianity in residents' lives, which Oliver was so eager to elevate, I suggest that the Guaraní mission world be thought of as a place where elements of primitive abundance were reclaimed in everyday life and underlying values of reciprocity, mutuality, redistribution, and gift were renewed—not unchanged. Residents had accepted deep novelties—unfamiliar religious practices, greater work discipline, exposure to transactional relations in material and social life, the advancing shadow of individual incentives, the routinization of office, hints of social hierarchy—with all their tensions. But they had found ways to absorb these without losing themselves. They did so, in good measure, by refusing to abandon their own well-established understandings of how human beings were to relate to one another.

From this perspective, the mission world stood as a collective endeavor made concrete. At a moment of high tension in 1753, the mburubichá (great cacique) and corregidor Nicolás Ñeenguyrú wrote a letter from the town of Concepción to the governor in Buenos Aires. He expressed immense pride in what had been achieved in the mission world, proclaiming that "with our hands alone we have put straight and healed this land."[132] The implication is clear. The mission world had not simply been erected. Rather, the Guaraní had collectively put hands to the task (potirõ) to remake the world from the havoc of the sixteenth century. In doing so, they had found a way to recover what Ñeenguyrú's letter referred to as ore recó aguïyeí, "our good way of being," that sustained the state of goodness, pleasure, and health that befits human life properly understood—now in a new and precarious register. The Guaraní hand imagery in this epistle speaks for itself. Missionaries could also have caught an echo from Paul's first letter to the Corinthians—"And we labor, working with our own hands."[133] They too had labored, as Oliver seemed at pains to point out.

This is a reminder that the mission world represented an entente between Jesuits, the Guaraní, and the Spanish monarchy. Within the missions, the pact owed as much to Guaraní principles regarding social life as to any special novelty introduced by the Jesuits, whether ideological, managerial, technological, or disciplinary. Individual interest was present, but only to the extent it did not undermine "collective interest" and substantive mutuality as fundamental tenets of mission political—and moral—economy.[134] The crucial insight is that a shared concern for the physical and moral perils of the economy of gain and convergent notions of the common good and tecó aguïyeí made it possible for residents to escape European predation by reaffirming life in common, now in full awareness of that other world that could not be ignored.

For the missions were not completely cut off from the outside economy. Few residents could have been entirely unaware of that other life. People came and went from mission communities continually. There were ample opportunities for people to glimpse, or even mingle in, the transactional arena. Some residents, mostly men as best can be told, departed mission towns for Spanish ones. Except during times of crisis, the outward flow appears to have been more a trickle than a cascade. In the 1750s (a period with its own challenges), Cardiel put the number at one in a hundred. This may be an underestimate. But even if it was fivefold, it would have paled alongside absentee rates ranging to 20 percent in Asunción and Villa Rica, as well as other pueblos de indios.[135] People lit out because they had been censured for failing to tend their family plots or because they had been accused of being "killers of oxen and calves." Some decamped because they had committed "sins of lust," knowing that "over there" (outside the missions) they could do such things with near impunity. Regardless of why they left, things rarely went well for them, said Cardiel, perhaps with a moralist's schadenfreude. Men would hire themselves out as day laborers but quickly lose everything in gaming or drink. Having seen the other life, some returned. Often, alleged Cardiel, they were rebuffed by their communities, who feared their influence. Most did not come back, traipsing from one town to the next in search of a few pesos, poorer and more exposed than they had been in the missions.

Ironically, if the external economy had held greater attraction to residents of the mission world, tensions with the Spaniards might not have become so sharp. As it was, by 1730, Asunceños and local officialdom deeply resented what they thought of as the Jesuits' illegitimate control over the province's crucial resources: Indigenous labor and land. In one rambunctious meeting of the Asunción municipal council in 1732, the Jesuits were accused of having "subjected, laid low, and ruined" the entire province of Paraguay. They had committed "fraud" against royal tributes and kept many Indians locked up. Worse, they had violated "natural and divine law" by enriching themselves from the wealth of others. By comparison, council members averred, there were many Indians in Spanish estates who were well treated, as the king's law demanded. One member of the council declared that the missions had taken all the best lands and forced good Spaniards to pay tribute to them, thus offending their liberty and inverting the proper order of things.[136] The Jesuits responded by reiterating that the monarchy had authorized the missions as a way to protect the Guaraní from the tyranny of the "ravenous wolves" who would invade the missions if they could and subject their residents to gain's regime.[137] Battle lines were being drawn.

6

Good Economy of the State

> They have this miserable province subjugated and ruined. . . . They
> have taken its meager riches.
>
> Cabildo of Asunción, 1724

> How can it be that our King . . . wants to lose us and to put an
> end to us?
>
> Letter from the town of San Luis, 1753

DURING THE DECADES following Governor Lariz's visit to the missions in 1647, the mission world had flourished under the Guaraní pact with the Jesuits and the Spanish monarchy. Reciprocity at a scale greater than any the Guaraní had experienced was broadly respected, or at least acknowledged, by all parties. Mission communities had lived up to their collective obligation to pay tribute in a timely fashion and mission citizen-soldiers had answered the king's call scores of times to defend Spanish territory, serving with distinction and generally without compensation.[1] The Spanish monarchy had made good its end of the bargain, allowing mission residents to stand apart from a regional economy oriented to profit for Spaniards and service or wage work for Indigenous people. Throughout these decades, settlers had resented what they saw as the Jesuits' control of a vast labor pool and enormous swaths of land. But rail though they might against a perceived injustice, these farmers, encomenderos, merchants, and officials had understood that there was little to be done so long as the monarchy favored the missions.

Circumstances began to unsettle this equilibrium in the early eighteenth century. The Bourbons had triumphed in the War of the Spanish Succession between 1701 and 1714, unseating the Hapsburg dynasty that had ruled the Spanish empire since 1516. On one side, England, Holland, and Austria had backed the Hapsburg heir to the Spanish throne in hopes of gaining access to American markets. Portugal had sided with England, worried that it might be reabsorbed into Spanish domains. On the other side, France, Spain's traditional rival, had supported the Bourbon

Felipe V, also with the idea of benefiting from Spain's New World commerce. This bloody affair had played out in dozens of theaters small and large in Europe, the Mediterranean, North America, the Caribbean, and South America. Mission militias had played a pivotal role in securing the border between Spanish and Portuguese territories. In 1705, nearly four thousand Guaraní troops, on orders from the governor in Buenos Aires, had besieged Colonia del Sacramento (on the north bank of the Plata) and decisively expelled Portuguese colonists there.

Hoping to restore a measure of control over American affairs and eager to shore up Spanish transatlantic commerce and revenue collection, Felipe V became more vigilant of the Spanish frontier with Brazil after new boundaries were drawn in the Treaty of Utrecht (1713), which ended the war. Despite being on the losing side, Portugal ended up with more territory in South America, at Spanish expense. Inter-imperial tensions flared in the region. Mission militias continued to meet incursions by the Portuguese and their Indigenous allies. By the mid-1720s, settlers, encomenderos, and pueblos de indios too were being asked to contribute men and resources to secure frontier zones, exacerbating the chronic labor shortage in Asunción, Villa Rica, Corrientes, and Santa Fé.[2] Many were chafing against the demands. Crucially for the long term, Felipe V seemed intent on rethinking the structures and articulations of Spain's empire. The relatively stable, if fragile, political arrangement that bolstered the mission world was straining.

*   *   *

The Comunero Revolt
"¡Común, común!"

Two decades into the eighteenth century, Paraguay remained at the edge of Spain's empire. Asunción's own citizens described their city as a place of dilapidated buildings and irregular, unhealthy streets.[3] Five thousand inhabitants lived there in 1700, with perhaps as many more in the near hinterlands.[4] Most of the land near the city was held by a few families, often legacy encomenderos, who lived in town and hired foremen to run their estates in the countryside. Villa Rica boasted no more than fifteen hundred residents. The total number of encomiendas had dwindled across the region (from 253 in 1651 to 86 in 1726), and the number of indentured encomendados had dropped by up to two-thirds. Only a handful of pueblos de indios survived by 1717.[5]

And yet, things had changed. Long the domain of encomenderos who could trace their lineage to the sixteenth century, Asunción's affairs had come to be dominated by a small coterie of "outsiders" who ran the brisk yerba trade. These men had arrived from other parts of South America, or even Spain, just as mate exports were beginning to pick up in the Rio de la Plata, Chile, Tucumán, and Peru toward the end of the seventeenth century. With modest capital and strong connections, they had established a transport system of land and water routes, employing carts and boats built in Asunción's shipyard drawn by mules from surrounding ranches. Though metal coin still did not circulate widely in the province, yerba as a reliable export crop had attracted the interest of other merchants trucking in imported goods from Peru and Spain. Some of these lived in Buenos Aires and traveled to Asunción as needed. Together, this small merchant class of yerba and import-export traders alongside the remaining encomenderos established themselves as an economically and politically powerful elite that sat on the cabildo, controlled the militia, and had the ear of the governor. A thin layer of officials attended to government affairs. For the most part, these elites worried chiefly about two issues: the availability of credit, which they needed to recruit yerba workers and to pay boatmen who transported mate from grove to port, and the labor shortage that had plagued Asunción since the sixteenth century.[6]

As trade in yerba had grown, so had the gap between rich and poor and between city and countryside.[7] Just beyond city limits, poor farmers eked out a living by employing as many Indians as they could manage, either by "renting" them from encomenderos or by paying free workers directly. After nearly two centuries of miscegenation and limited inflows of Europeans after 1630, mestizos now vastly outnumbered Spaniards, though any who aspired to respectability might refer to themselves as *españoles*. These folk lived roughly, eager for imported luxury goods from Spain they could barely afford. Mestizos and poor whites rubbed elbows in farm work, the trades, and the yerba groves, forming a small, broadly Spanish and Guaraní-speaking plebeian class. The poor or desperate who ended up in the yerbales were especially susceptible to advances on their wages. Many became debt peons. African slaves were few (their importation had been prohibited by law since 1612), though freedmen and runaways from Brazil also worked in the fields or as carters or boatmen. In everyday life, the barons of yerba and trade shared little with those they saw as their "lessers." They looked down on the plebes of farm, trades, transport, and petty exchanges. These, in turn, bore the condescension,

knowing that they perched but a short fall from those in the lowest eche-
lons. Few of them sat on the cabildo. Nor were they heard there. Cabildo
policy aimed above all to secure the conditions for the yerba trade. Profits from trading activities, as well as taxes levied on imports and exports
from the region, generally flowed from Asunción to Buenos Aires, a matter of pique among small-time merchants and others dependent entirely
on the local economy.

A political crisis in the early 1720s set this tableau into edgy motion.
In 1717, the governor of Paraguay, Diego de los Reyes y Balmaseda, had
attacked a group of unreduced Payaguás Indians who had settled south
of Asunción and whose tubichá had agreed not to raid surrounding villages.[8] In the action, Asunción's militias had taken seventy captives.
Rather than distribute these prisoners in encomienda to settlers, the governor had given them into the care of the Jesuits. Asunceños were incensed. Cabildo elites had disagreed with the attack on the villages, eager to avoid the cost in men and treasure of mounting a campaign. But
the decision to give the Indians to the fathers offended almost everyone.
In particular, members of the rural militia who had done the fighting felt
they had been cheated of a just distribution of scarce resources. Tensions
ran high, though Reyes remained in his post until 1721, when accusations
of self-dealing were leveled against him. A young official, José Antequera
y Castro, replaced him. Antequera reversed Reyes's deference to the Jesuits and sought to exert greater secular control over the missions in accor-
dance with his understanding of royal law.

In the mid-1720s, tensions erupted into conflict. Cabildo minutes from
1723–1724 indicate that economic concerns lay at the heart of complaints.
Council members pointed out that local encomienda Indians were being pulled away from productive labor to defend against "barbarous enemy nations"—unreduced groups like the Payaguás.[9] As a result, "there is
no liberty of [employment] contracts" in the province, no Indians to pay
royal tribute, and no one to restore Asunción's buildings and streets to
their earlier "opulence" (a decidedly rose-tinted view of the past). The Jesuits, said council members, had offered no help, acting as though "their"
Indians were exempt from any contribution to the common good. Adding insult to injury, they had illegally persuaded encomienda Indians to
move to the missions, depriving Asunción's residents of their services.[10]
Worse, declared the council, whereas encomenderos treated their Indians
well, because it is "against natural law to become rich and powerful with

the wealth of others," the Jesuits kept their Indians nearly naked and without food. The fathers have "subjected" and "ruined" the entire province, usurping its "meager riches," with the sole goal of "casting down" its citizens and residents.[11]

Such charges led to open fighting in the summer of 1724. The cabildo, after a public airing of grievances (a *cabildo abierto*), ordered its militia to the Tebicuarí River. The missions, on orders of the viceroy in Lima, responded by mobilizing their militia. A brief encounter went Asunción's way, with three hundred deaths among the mission Guaraní, after which both sides withdrew. Mission towns nearest Asunción dispersed to the forests, fearing an invasion and the beginning of a long season of suffering. While the cabildo expelled the Jesuits from their properties in Asunción, the viceroy now called on Guaraní militias to suppress what had come to be seen as a seditious movement—by the king's Spanish vassals.

By the early 1730s, after a litany of accusations and counteraccusations, the balance of power shifted within Asunción's cabildo. Elite members of the council had begun to tire of the face-off with the missions and knew they could not prevail against the viceroy. They wanted to get back to business and were willing to reinstate the Jesuits to do so. Plebeians, however, for whom little had improved through the years of mobilization, found a champion in a newcomer, Fernando de Mompó y Zayas. Versed in the ideas of the sixteenth-century neo-scholastics (Suárez and Mariana, in particular), Mompó argued that the *común* (the community as a whole) had a right to dissent from unjust royal orders, even to disobey them if it came to that. Father Pedro Lozano, writing after the fact, quoted one incredulous plebeian as saying that he had heard that "sometimes the común has more power than the king, or even the pope."[12] Hundreds among Asunción's poorer residents flocked to Mompó's banner. By 1730, they had begun to call themselves *Comuneros* (Commoners, or those of the community) and had established a "governing committee" without seeking royal permission (a unique occurrence in Spanish America), demanding new cabildo elections. Some sitting council members saved their seats by shifting their allegiances and agreeing to back the upstarts. Others lost their positions to new members. The reconstituted cabildo immediately took control of the militia and set out to make good on Comunero demands.[13] Above all, they wanted to force the missions to transfer control of the Indians to the cabildo, putting an end once and for all to the long nightmare of Asunción's poverty. Most Comuneros doubtless hoped the tens of thousands of Indians would be granted to them in encomienda. But even if they had simply been made available to the local labor market, things could only have improved. If that had happened, it would have been a bonanza.

While the Comuneros saw the missions as the most immediate answer to their umbrage, there may also have been a deeper sentiment in play. Jesuit Pedro de Lozano reported that the Comuneros wanted to establish a new republic that would "enthrone" those who were "not known," people who by status and wealth could claim no place among the "honorable."[14] "Insolents" among the Comuneros, claimed Lozano, said they wanted to destroy all the "noble families" of Paraguay, taking their slaves away, so that even the finest woman would be reduced to a state of poverty and have to fetch her own water from the river, like the young Indian girls who went with jugs on their heads. Of course, Lozano had every reason to deflect Comunero rancor away from the Jesuits and the missions in his recounting of events, so he may have embellished. But in light of Mompó's ideas and given the recent sharpening of inequality in Asunción, plebeians may have harbored as much animus against the local elites as they did against the Jesuits and the Guaraní.

By 1732, the Comuneros were in frank rebellion. As the movement spread, partisans gathered in public squares, shouting "Común, común," calling for their enemies to be clapped in irons.[15] They also began to recruit an army, drawing far and wide from the rural militias charged with fighting unreduced Indians, a burden not shared by elites. The governor in Buenos Aires, acting on orders from Spain, once again mobilized the mission militias to suppress the uprising. The two sides fought pitched battles on and off during the next three years.

Jaguars where men live

Effects of these hostilities on the mission world were catastrophic.[16] Upwards of thirty thousand mission soldiers were drawn into the fray, each one a loss to local agricultural or artisanal production.[17] Fear of invasion led many residents to flee to the forests or to Spanish towns, disrupting communities' capacity to sustain themselves. Large groups of mission folk "wandered through the forest with their wives and children, frantic for something to eat."[18] Some mission refugees took up with unreduced Indigenous groups, who were only too willing to welcome men trained in arms. Reports of theft, property damage, and mayhem soared. Others set out for the eastern *vaquerías* (cattle ranges) in search of sustenance. They were often met by Spanish and Portuguese opportunists, who now rustled herds long protected by the missions. What had been safe spaces when under mission control became danger zones. Hunger and dislocation opened the door to disease. The missions suffered three devastating epidemics (measles and smallpox) between 1730 and 1740.

By the time fighting ceased in 1735, a perfect storm of war, plague, drought, and hunger had scythed through the mission population. From a peak of over 140,000 in 1732, the number of residents had dropped to just over 100,000 by 1735. Missionaries and the many Guaraní who remained set out to rebuild. It was a slow process and for the Jesuits an expensive one. Cattle that had once been for the taking now had to be bought. Among the Guaraní, fields had to be recovered, towns restored, roads reopened. More important, trust between missionaries and residents needed to be reestablished. One thing remained undamaged—the mission Guaraní's reputation for loyalty to the king. For three hard years, they had fought to put down a seditious force. In fact, they had actually battled on two fronts through most of the period. Between 1732 and 1736, six thousand Guaraní troops had been dispatched once again to besiege Colonia del Sacramento in Spain's ongoing territorial and trade disputes with Portugal.[19] Royal officials praised mission troops and recognized the towns' suffering. Even after active fighting stopped, the effects of conflict persisted, with the population bottoming out at seventy-five thousand in 1740, a decline of nearly 50 percent in just eight years.[20] As many as two-thirds of these may have been children who perished from disease and famine.[21] While people did return, total inhabitants did not break one hundred thousand again until 1753–1754, the eve of another violent struggle.

In such circumstances, it is not hard to imagine that mission folk and the Jesuits felt deflated. So much of what they had built over preceding decades had come tumbling down. Residents knew what the Comuneros had wanted and surely breathed a sigh of relief to have avoided a worse fate. Still, a world that had kept predation at bay had cracked open in ways that left them feeling more exposed than they had in a century. One *Annual Letter* noted that, on top of everything else, the cattle herds so crucial to mission survival had been taken by "greedy" Spaniards, who had sold them to Portuguese enemies at a "good price."[22]

A sense of vulnerability may have registered at deeper levels. Another *Annual Letter* reported that in just three mission towns, four hundred people had been "devoured" by jaguars.[23] In some cases, said the Jesuit writer, this appeared to have been a "special punishment" for those who did not attend Mass or had left the community or were "bored by work and discipline." At other times, there were hints that the solidary ethos of mission life was fraying. In one instance, according to the letter, a man from the mission town of Loreto snuck into a neighbor's garden to steal manioc "as a gift" for his accomplice. According to reports, a jaguar prowling the village caught him in the act and mauled but did not kill him, a kind of divine dispensation, said the missionary, so that the perpetrator might have time to repent. The man's wounds were tended to and he did repent. He then died, thankful to have escaped the clutches of the devil. This missionary framing aside—and even if there were many fewer cases than reported—these incidents can only have sparked angst among the Guaraní. Before 1730, there had been little reason for theft, as food had always been abundant. It is understandable, perhaps, that the fathers might have overinterpreted such episodes, worried that those returning from diaspora to the forest would not readjust to mission life. Among the Guaraní, we can imagine that such affronts and brazen attacks by jaguars where humans lived might have been seen as a sign of growing uncertainty about the mission world's prospects.

War in the mission world
"News flew among the towns"

The mission world's recovery from the trauma of the Comunero revolt was interrupted on January 13, 1750, when the Spanish and Portuguese kings signed an agreement to settle long-simmering boundary disputes in South America and Asia.[24] Under the Treaty of Madrid, each side would benefit. In the Pacific, Spain would gain control over the Philippines. In South America, Portugal would receive dominion over the Amazon basin north of Maranhão. In the south, Spain would hold sway over the entire Río de la Plata system, which connected the circuits of Atlantic trade to the South American interior. Portugal would take uncontested possession of Mato Grosso and Goiás, with their promise of gold, and extend its jurisdiction over the wealthy lands east of the Río Uruguay, where seven prosperous mission towns were located.

There was more at stake than sorting out possession in a remote contested zone. During the opening decades of the eighteenth century, Spain found itself in a cramped position vis-à-vis emergent European powers, especially Holland, France, and England. It had not managed to capitalize, as Holland had through the Dutch East India Company, on the broad flows of trade and finance that created a global economy in the seventeenth century. Unlike France, Spain had not been able to correct its "blindness regarding the importance of Commerce," according to one Spanish writer of the time.[25] Nor had it been able to emulate England's combination of maritime strength, private sector investment, and exports of manufactured goods. More broadly, Spain's fiscal position relative to other European powers was worrying. In 1600, Spain's tax receipts (denominated in tons of silver) had trebled France's and been six times England's. By 1700, France had surpassed Spain, while England, with a much smaller population than Spain's, had pulled even (and would overtake it after 1750).[26]

There were two principal reasons for this disparity. First, Spanish tax receipts had flatlined after Andean and Mexican silver output declined in the 1640s—this at a time when much of the silver Spain did receive went to settle debts with other European governments. Second, Spanish shipping during the seventeenth century had been under constant pressure from privateers and contrabandists who at times acted as unacknowledged instruments of rival monarchs.[27] In effect, since the late seventeenth century, the Spanish monarchy had been losing the race to establish the fiscal capacity to compete with its rivals in a commercial world growing by leaps and bounds.

Against this backdrop, Colonia del Sacramento across the Plata River from Buenos Aires was a thorn in Spain's southern flank. For decades, contraband had sloshed through this rough port, evading Spanish revenue collection and playing havoc with Spanish fleets. Under the Treaty of Madrid, Colonia would pass once and for all into Spanish hands, thus protecting the important commercial flows to and from Buenos Aires. England had been challenging Spanish New World commerce and revenues ever since Sir Francis Drake's pirate marauding on the west coast of South America in the sixteenth century. In the Caribbean, England had taken Jamaica from Spain in 1660. This had allowed privateers (pirates, to some) to operate out of Kingston while harassing Spanish shipping, establishing a clandestine trade network that disrupted Spain's commercial and revenue flows from the Caribbean. The Treaty of Madrid finally

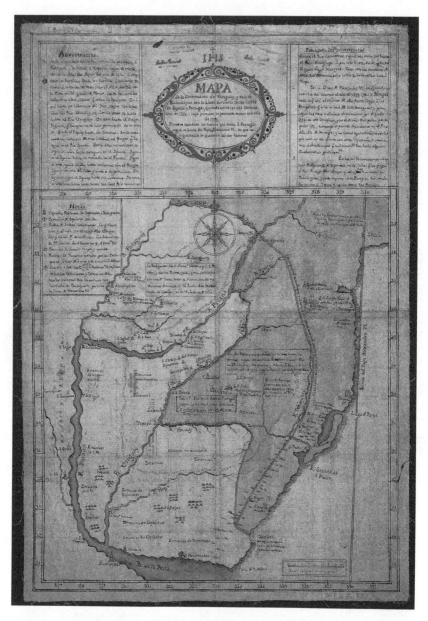

FIGURE 6.1. Proposed Treaty of 1750 boundary line between Spanish (lighter shading) and Portuguese (darker shading) territories, in relation to seven mission communities east of the Uruguay River. *Source:* España. Ministerio de Cultura y Deporte. Archivo General de Simancas, MPD,06,032.

resolved this dispute, awarding England uncontested possession of Jamaica. The Spanish monarchy did not want to face an analogous situation across from Buenos Aires.

Where the Treaty of Madrid promised significant benefits to the Spanish monarchy, it portended upheaval for the mission world. By its terms, Portugal would fix its westernmost border at the Uruguay River, assuming control of an area that included seven wealthy missions that until that time had been under Spain's jurisdiction (Figure 6.1). According to the agreement, residents of these towns had a choice: they could stay put and pass into Portuguese territory, or they could relocate west of the Uruguay, though if they did move, they would forfeit their lands and herds to Portugal. The geopolitical and commercial implications of the proposed exchange sparked controversy in Spanish and Portuguese royal courts.[28] The mission Jesuits reacted immediately, writing to their superiors, to the governor in Buenos Aires, to royal counselors, to the king himself, and even to the king's confessor (a Jesuit). They complained that removal would result in huge economic losses to the communities and to the royal treasury, would destroy the mission world, and would lead the Guaraní to abandon the faith.[29]

News of the treaty did not reach the missions until 1751. Missionaries withheld the information as long as they could, fearing residents' reactions. By 1752, instructions for the treaty's execution had been issued and there was no way to keep the news from the communities any longer. Guaraní leaders received the tidings guardedly, unsure initially how best to respond. On one hand, the king was asking them for a kind of service. During more than a century, mission towns and their militias had answered the monarch's call to arms.[30] They had battled and bested "faithless Indians," repelled Portuguese intruders, and put down rebellious Spaniards. They had besieged Colonia del Sacramento three times between its founding in 1680 and 1735, the latter involving encounters with Portuguese troops and English corsairs. Guaraní soldiers had built fortifications throughout the Plata region. In short, the mission Guaraní had a long history of honoring royal calls. A request from the king was not to be questioned lightly. They were, after all, loyal vassals.

For their service, they had been repeatedly favored. In 1743, recalling Guaraní help during the Comunero revolt and the siege of Colonia that ended in 1736, King Felipe V had affirmed the missions' special jurisdictional status, declaring that "nowhere in the Indies is my sovereignty more recognized" than in the Guaraní reductions.[31] Yet, just seven years later, after King Fernando VI had ascended to the throne, the treaty seemed to backpedal on this reassurance, differing in tone and substance from any previous royal order. By calling on nearly thirty thousand people from seven mission towns to leave their homes, churches, property, and territories, and move elsewhere, this new king demanded that communities agree to their own destruction and the mission world to its dismemberment.

Through 1751 and early 1752, the towns remained divided, within and among themselves. Some took steps to comply, skirring possible relocation sites proposed by royal officers, even building the carts, rafts, and canoes required for any mass exodus.[32] None of the alternative locales proved suitable. The soil was infertile, the trip too perilous, Guaraní scouts reported. Moreover, any new location promised to expose residents to greater dangers from encomenderos or Portuguese raiders. Some groups, not waiting for an official decision, simply voted with their feet, migrating west to join kin in mission towns across the Uruguay River. These movements imposed new burdens on the receiving communities and sapped hometowns of much needed labor. Other communities were defiant. Since kin groups stretched across the Uruguay, all thirty towns were affected by the treaty. As "news flew among the towns" a consensus began to emerge.[33] By late 1752, a position had gelled: the seven would not move and the thirty would stand together. This put the entire mission world at odds with the Jesuits, who had been ordered by their own provincial to persuade the Guaraní to comply with the king's decree.

All of their options were bad. If residents left the seven towns, their lands, churches, herds, and historical connections would be lost. If they stayed after the territory was transferred, they would face Portuguese raids without the protection of Spanish law against enslavement and without any involvement or help from the Jesuits. In response to this Hobson's choice, the seven towns wrote letters of petition to the governor in Buenos Aires, José de Andonaegui, stating their intention to remain. They were not alone. Concepción, a town on the west side of the Uruguay and under no threat of removal, also weighed in. Nicolás Ñeenguyrú, a mburubichá who carried the same name as earlier caciques, a name meaning "he who is with/goes with words," affirmed with an unwavering tone that the Thirty Towns were prepared to make common cause against this assault on their "good way of being."[34] This stance expressed clear bonds of solidarity among the communities while also recognizing that the seven towns constituted the richest and most populous of the mission world as a whole.

"We do not believe it is the King's will"

Penned originally in Guaraní and translated into Spanish, these letters opened by affirming the "great love" that the governor had for the Guaraní and by proclaiming the Guaraní's reverence for Fernando VI, the new king. The king loves us, stated Ñeenguyrú's letter from Concepción, "for our way of being, for our church, and for what we have done in war."[35] Given this, how could the king knowingly undertake such an agreement with the enemy? Felipe V had assured them in 1716 that they were his vassals, stated the missive from San Lorenzo, and he had charged them to take care of his lands and never give them to another king. How is it, asked the epistle from Concepción, that these two declarations "do not correspond to one another and are different?": "Our King does not mistake his words." They were being told to cede their lands to the Portuguese, "enemies of Our King of Spain, as we well know," and go far away "to work, exhaust [our]selves [*câneõ*] and suffer ills and poverty?"—"This is not our will."[36] The epistle continued by proclaiming that they had put themselves into the king's hands "to care for us, free us from evil, help us," and yet now he changes his mind? "We do not know how to believe that our King's saintly heart has ordered us to move."[37] They had "erred in nothing" and had never done anything to lose the king's trust, they said, always paying our tribute and fighting when asked to do so. "We do not believe it is the King's will."[38] As the corregidor of San Juan reminded the governor, the king had publicly thanked the Guaraní for twice chasing the Portuguese out of Colonia del Sacramento, and they were ready to do so again if called upon.[39] They were, said the letter from San Luis, the king's poor, loyal vassals. "How can it be that our King . . . wants to lose us and to put an end to us?" They did not want war, but they were prepared to meet it and would die if they must. "This is what we think."[40]

These dispatches were far more than rhetorical flourishes or plaints to waken the governor's pity. Taken together, they amounted to a clear statement of the Guaraní's understanding of their political and economic role in the Spanish empire, likely the product of deep discussions among mission residents regarding how to confront the crisis of removal. By referring to the governor's love for them, they were reminding Andonaegui of his duty as a royal officer. Their point was that rulers were not entitled to exercise arbitrary power. In referring to the king's affection for them and theirs for him, they were affirming the idea that reciprocal love (*amor*), along with justice as the collective expression of that love, grounded the political order and conditioned the monarch's power. This was straightforward Thomist (and Jesuit) political theology. For Aquinas, love was the natural tendency attracting the many things of the world to one another to form a greater whole. In the world of human sociability, love bound men into a web of sympathies that founded political community, sustained human virtues, and ordained the social world to justice and the common good, much as love ordered Creation itself. Just authority was love applied to the political world.[41]

By asserting the king's love, these Guaraní writers were embracing their role as vassals who bore a reciprocal relationship with the monarch. The king had the power to "make or unmake" his vassals, but in principle he was not entitled to exercise this power without reason: he had no authority to punish vassals who did not "err" in their obligations. Quite the contrary. Saavedra Fajardo had noted in the mid-seventeenth century that the prince is a kind of "victim" or "sacrifice" offered to the "toils and dangers for the common good of his vassals."[42] The *Diccionario de autoridades* (1737) defined sovereignty (*soberanía*) as "power over all," but it immediately noted that kings could and did deprive themselves of their sovereignty "for the greater good of their vassals."[43] The king thus made a gift of his sovereignty by pursuing justice and the common good and by scrupulously respecting custom and acquired rights. Vassals reciprocated through the love and devotion they showed to the king and by their willingness to act accordingly.

These petitions were not merely parroting Spanish ideas. Over a century and a half, the mission Guaraní had cultivated their own understanding of vassalage.[44] They signaled acceptance of their status by reminding the governor of their prompt tribute payments and their repeated military service. The letters also indicate that by 1750, the mission Guaraní had fused vassalage and their own notions of mutuality. Their point regarding the king's obligation did not differ in substance from the Guaraní idea that caciques were under an obligation to perform the reciprocal generosity that maintained the community at large. Of course, the "correlative" quality of vassalage was not the reciprocity of the *pepî*—the invitation to share food, ritual, and company—that had long anchored

Guaraní social life.[45] But the language of these petitions reveals that the mission Guaraní conceived of vassalage as sharing the fundamental principle that human communities were governed by substantive reciprocal obligations in the spirit of *poî*, or "open hand, give to eat . . . share with others," that stretched into open-ended time.[46] From this perspective, vassalage could make good sense as scaling the reciprocity of *poî* to the magnitude of the mission world and its place in the Spanish empire. In other words, the mission Guaraní had found a way to imbue the larger structures in which they had come to live with their own reason. At the same time, it is clear that Guaraní leaders understood vassalage strategically: they knew from experience that humble subjects who honored their obligations were far more likely to be given the benefit of the doubt by a distant king, or at least historically this had been the case.

Written in the crucible of confrontation and forged from Guaraní and Spanish elements, the letters also hinted at a more distinctively Guaraní rationale for rejecting the king's command. In saying that the king could not mistake his words, they may have been doing more than pointing to a contradiction. Among the Guaraní, authority had long been bound up with the power of language itself. The whole point of speech, especially the speech of leaders, was to express the reciprocal relationships that underlay life in common.[47] In Montoya's *Tesoro*, the Guaraní phrase for "a man who does not keep his word" was rooted in a word that meant "twisted, split, cut." By contrast, "the man who is constant in his word" implied someone who would "turn, turn one's body" toward or away from another.[48] From this perspective, a cacique's speech was a kind of gift to his followers, a turning toward them. He spoke the words that constituted the community by reminding its members of what they shared and of the continued need to share it. They reciprocated by granting him a certain prestige vis-à-vis other members of the group, which was the basis for his influence in relation to the community as a whole.[49] For a leader to say a thing and then contradict it for no good reason was to undermine the very idea of his obligation to turn *toward* the community. It was, in fact, a turning away.

Ñeenguyrú's letter from Concepción hints at how ordinary people may have confronted the crisis sparked by the treaty. The "people," said this great cacique, referring to common folk, refused to "hear" the "words" of the corregidores and cabildo and had become "angry with us," using a phrase that conveyed a sense of "becoming alarmed at/giving a blow to."

"This is not God's will," they say, and they will not obey. The "people" are "solely in the hands" of their caciques, insisted Ñeenguyrú, and we cannot speak a "word" about the proposed move.[50] In Guaraní, *to hear* meant "to register sounds" but also "to comprehend or grasp the meaning of something."[51] Assuming Ñeenguyrú accurately reported the state of affairs, he appears to have been making two points. First, that the people simply would not hear those, whether Jesuits, the governor, or even native leaders, who were telling them they had no choice but to move. That is, people refused to credit—"we do not know how to believe"—something so fundamentally at odds with how they understood their role in the Spanish empire and their relationship with the monarchy. Second, he was noting that the treaty had opened a rift between the caciques (leaders of kinship groups) and the corregidores and cabildos elected pursuant to Spanish law and mission practice. The caciques were closest to the intimate churn of day-to-day life and therefore far more exposed to collective sentiment against the treaty. They were the ones whose "words" bore the weight of efforts to interpret the king's demand to abandon lands and lives, an edict contrary to all previous royal declarations.

This casts the claim that the Guaraní did "not know how to believe" that the king had issued the order in a new light. It was not so much a statement of incredulity as a broad refusal to accept diminishment of the fundamental role of words in sustaining society. In the mission world, the speech of corregidores, cabildos, governors, and kings had been layered over those of caciques as spokesmen for kinship groupings. The words of elected officers mattered because they connected everyday life in the missions to the broader political framework of empire. Ñeenguyrú seemed to be saying that ordinary people were holding all leaders—caciques, corregidores, and cabildo members, missionaries, *and* the king—to being constant in their words. Not that the king was somehow just like a cacique; after a century and half under Spanish rule, they knew better. Rather, against the backdrop of vassalage, hearing the king's words as an affront to the binding role of language may have helped them apprehend the enormity of their predicament.

In referring explicitly to "the people," Ñeenguyrú's letter from Concepción not only signaled an attitude toward the proposed transfer. It also bespoke crisis of legitimacy within mission communities: those charged with facing the imperial apparatus—the Jesuits but also corregidores and cabildos—were not in full control of the situation. Of course, such a claim was convenient political cover for someone in Ñeenguyrú's position. Yet his assessment may well have been accurate. One cacique asked Bernardo Nusdorffer, the Jesuit charged with persuading the Guaraní to move, to stop talking about the treaty, since others already "had eyes on him" as one who supported the fathers.[52] By July 1753, many Guaraní had already rejected the missionaries' urgings—"pleas" as well as "threats"—that they abide by the terms of the treaty.[53] Distrust of the Jesuits had grown to the point that a voice began to run within the communities wondering whether the whole affair might be a "fiction" of the priests themselves, rather than the "will of the King." Doubt went beyond words. A few Jesuits reported death threats from Guaraní. One priest met his end and another had to run for his life.[54] Those who remained were marginalized or constantly under watch.

Ñeenguyrú's letter, thus, revealed deeper stakes than imperial officialdom could fathom. Guaraní social organization had long been premised on the negation of concentrated political power. A cacique simply had been in no position to force people to engage in substantive reciprocity. His primary responsibility had been to ensure that society's goods circulated among all its members and to say the words and model the behavior to foster reciprocity within the community. But he had lacked the capacity to command or compel the right way of being, even in the face of war. Or as Clastres put it, "Power is contrary to the group, and the rejection of reciprocity, . . . is the rejection of society itself."[55]

Given what we know of mission life—the emergence of elective office, the mediating role of the fathers, the first stirrings of cacical lineages—it makes no sense to suppose that this political idea had remained unchanged following the foundation of the missions. Nevertheless, as these letters hint, the mission Guaraní may have understood the treaty as menacing not only the mission world but substantive reciprocity itself as a constraint on the role of power in social life. By telling them to move, the king had overstepped the bounds Guaraní political culture had set for him in their willingness to be his vassals; he had broken the circle of mutuality upon which their understanding of vassalage depended and which grounded their pact with him. They had queried him (and the governor), as vassals were entitled and expected to do, and received no satisfactory explanation for the enormity of what was being asked of them. And they had done the same with the Jesuits who, despite all their talk, had refused to stand with the communities when push came to shove. From this vantage, the order to vacate the seven towns, which imperiled the entire mission world, represented an unacceptable inconstancy and a naked exercise of power contrary to reciprocity.

For a time, some may truly have doubted that Fernando VI had issued the order or thought that he was mistaken or had been duped by the Portuguese king, or that the Jesuits had made it up. In the context of the dispute, however, Ñeenguyrú's characterization of people's reaction is perhaps better seen as a refusal to accept at face value a radical reorientation of political and civic common sense. These were people who had lived directly under the Spanish monarch's aegis since the early seventeenth century. They knew that the king of 1753 was not the same person who had promised in 1716 that no one would take their land and that he would always protect them. They had accepted the proposition, long central to European political thinking, that kings' promises carried across time, as did the words of all proper leaders. Their first reaction was to deny subjection to the Portuguese while proclaiming fealty to "the dominion of Spain."[56] In saying that they could not believe the king had ordered them to move and that they had erred in nothing, they were not merely expressing a wounded wonderment. They were acting precisely as aggrieved vassals should: by questioning the justice of the situation. Justice had long consisted of ensuring that each person or group under the king's authority received what properly pertained to them according to their place in the mundane and cosmological order.[57] The king's job was to balance the demands of society's many claimants in light of justice and the common good. The mission Guaraní were arguing that it was not just and made no sense that Fernando VI would force them to surrender the prosperous and peaceful communities they had built to the Portuguese, who were Spain's adversaries, for a matter unrelated to the communities themselves.

It was no accident, therefore, that letters opposing the transfer reminded the governor and the king of the effort mission residents had put into their communities. They had "worked and prepared the land," built their "magnificent church, a nice town, ranches for our cattle, yerba mate and cotton plantations, farms," and made their "poor houses into good ones and with lovely arcades and covered walkways made of stone." They had given "our goods, our animals and even our lives," showing that they were vassals of the king. All of this they had done with "much sweat, much work"—and without pay. Should they "leave behind the sweat of our bodies?" asked one letter. These were not just statements about labor lost. The Guaraní word used over and over again in the letter from Concepción was *aguïyeí*, the state of persistent goodness and worthiness—our aguïyeí church, our aguïyeí village, our aguïyeí way of being. Such statements treated the collective labor of the community as the crucial source of value, of sociality and mutuality made material: "After all the hard work we have done, we should enjoy it, it is not good for the Portuguese to enjoy it." This conceptualization of value in turn enabled a comparative economic perspective that favored mission communities over anything the Spanish or the Portuguese had made. As the letter from Santo Ángel asked: "Why, then, do you give seven beautiful towns to pay for Colonia, which is only one and poor?" and its worth is "not enough to pay for even one of our towns."[58]

In strictly monetary terms, Santo Ángel had a point. The four thousand pesos Portugal offered to indemnify each of the seven towns, even if added to the new lands promised by the Spanish king, did not come close to compensating the economic value of the missions and their estancias and yerba groves. In a back-of-the-envelope calculation, Father Cardiel assessed the value of all San Nicolás's physical assets—houses, buildings, herds, fields—at over a million and a half pesos, and the church of San Miguel alone at a million pesos. Even the Portuguese general who saw San Miguel's church said that just its foundation, which the Guaraní had built without compensation and with "much sweat and fatigue," was worth more than what he was authorized to offer for the whole town.[59] For Spanish officials, Colonia del Sacramento's "value" lay not in its churches, its physical assets, or its beauty but in its strategic importance and its role in transatlantic commerce. By contrast, for the mission Guaraní, value was neither a geopolitical abstraction nor a matter of individual gain but a statement of collective commitment, expressed bodily, to their own communities and between those communities and the Spanish monarchy.

This commitment was why the king's words mattered. If mission residents were reacting from Guaraní understandings about the connection between "words" and the obligations that grounded social relations, the dilemma, shared by caciques, corregidores and cabildo members, and ordinary folk alike, was clear. To acknowledge the treaty was to concede that their understanding of vassalage had cracked. To accept the king's command on this matter—his word—as a legitimate expression of his intent and authority, to believe it for what it purported to be, was to lose the argument before it had begun. A cacique who misused words this way might once have provoked other men to gather followers and leave to start a new community elsewhere. But the king was not a cacique and there was no option without great danger—whether mission residents stayed or went. The challenge they faced, therefore, consisted not simply of what to do in concrete terms: either obey the king's edict or not. The question was whether a principle of substantive reciprocity—within the mission world and in its relationship to the Spanish monarchy—could continue to anchor residents' lives in the empire as they had come to understand it.

This was not Mompó's language of popular sovereignty on behalf of Comuneros claiming a right or power implicit in neo-scholastic theories. Where Mompó had asserted that "the común" was the source of justice and thus ultimately of power and freedom, the Guaraní were claiming that justice was a matter of maintaining reciprocity and keeping the raw exercise of power in check. Here, finally, was the rub. The treaty and the menace of force backing it threatened to push the mission Guaraní into the world of power exercised by the state for its own purposes, with no substantive concern for reciprocal obligations. In light of long experience and of what they knew of human arrangements, their only hope lay in a collective refusal to acknowledge the order as dispositive and to provoke a discussion over its justice. In asserting that they were ready to fight, however reluctantly, they were reminding the king and themselves that an unrepaired breach of reciprocity could be the occasion for vengeance through war. In other words, they were letting the king know that there were consequences for the rupture of mutuality. The king was unmoved. He may not have fully understood, but it may not have mattered.

Reasons of state

As thoughtful a response as these letters were to the crisis, the problem for the mission Guaraní was that by the 1750s new ideas regarding kingship and rule had begun to crystallize within Spanish officialdom. Older Thomist notions of reciprocal love and the common good had weakened in official circles. Among European kings, councils, and advisers, sovereignty increasingly implied untrammeled monarchical authority, especially in matters affecting commercial relations between nations. The Madrid Treaty put reciprocal understandings of sovereignty into direct conflict with the novel claim that vassals faced with a royal command were to obey without hesitation, regardless of how unjust it might seem.

In the minds of royal officials, this tension could be resolved by an idea that had gained traction since the sixteenth century: *Razones de Estado*, or "reasons of state." This term, a matter of anguished debate prior to 1700, became a policy touchstone for the Bourbon monarchy in the mid-eighteenth century. Through the sixteenth century, reason of state had been tied up with an understanding of politics (*policía*) as the art of governing human communities according to justice and reason, which the prince displayed by exercising "prudence"—reasonableness, moderation, and wisdom in action.[60] Reasons of state thus understood had been the basis for legitimate authority.[61] Italian Giovanni Botero, educated in Jesuit colleges, had first popularized the term in 1589 with publication of his *The Reason of State* (*Della ragione di Stato*).[62] Contrary to Machiavelli, said Botero, the prince could assure justice in the kingdom by embracing his rule as the legitimate and moral expression of the people's affection for him. His actions were to be guided and constrained by that affection in line with reason on behalf of the state as the concrete embodiment of the common good. In the sixteenth century, this referred to that state of affairs expressing God's desire that men live peaceably in society. Covarrubias's 1611 dictionary of Spanish (reprinted in 1674) held that *reason of state* was the capacity "to do what is just." Solórzano y Pereira, from his experience in Peru, stated in 1647 that no "reason of state" could be "beneficial" if it elevated human interests above divine ones or if it "trampled . . . rigorous justice."[63]

By 1700, *reason of state* was coming unmoored from such understandings. Royal advisers expressed dismay at Spain's apparent economic and political drift, leading them to rethink *reason(s) of state* in the context of growing imperial and commercial competition. Many looked westward and wondered how the New World could be made more useful (*útil*) to the kingdom. This word and its cousin *utility* (*utilidad*) took on new meanings toward the mid-eighteenth century. In 1647, Solórzano y Pereira had defined *utilidad* in relation to the "common good," as opposed to the "pernicious poison" of "private utility," for those who looked only "to advance their own gain" were the bane of happy republics.[64] But by the 1730s, royal counselors and officials had become more explicitly concerned for economic management in light of the financial burdens of Spain's rivalry with England and France. Position papers and published tracts argued that the kingdom's "utility" would be best served by "the union of industries" and the "liberty of commerce."[65] At a more basic level, according to ideas that began to circulate in policy circles during the 1740s and 1750s, the "good economy of the [Spanish] state" depended fundamentally on improving the economy of the New World by making "the Indians useful and profitable vassals." Only thus could Spain hope to meet European, especially English, commercial and fiscal competition.[66]

Given the stakes, it was clear how the mission Guaraní could be most useful in this particular instance: they could relocate, as the treaty demanded, no questions asked. Or as the governor wrote, if the Guaraní wanted to show that they were "true vassals," they needed to leave their lands without delay, as the king had repeatedly ordered them to.[67] The geopolitical reason was plain. Colonia del Sacramento was the key to controlling the Plata region.[68] Portugal was prepared to cede Colonia, but only in exchange for sovereignty over the territory east of the Uruguay River containing the seven mission towns. They were the linchpin to the entire arrangement. Forcing them to move, however, went against established understandings regarding the treatment of vassals, as the Guaraní were quick to point out. While it had always been lawful for the king to order loyal vassals to leave their villages for good reason, the rationale behind the treaty seemed arbitrary to the Guaraní and in direct conflict with earlier royal declarations. They were not alone. Some Spanish commentators argued that the king's command was unjust, because the Guaraní had always been good subjects, and illegal, because the land belonged either to the Jesuits or to the Indians and therefore was not the king's to give away.[69]

Recalibrated, *reasons of state* allowed Fernando VI to pivot away from older notions of rule to an emerging theory of state interest that would permit the king to back out of promises made by previous monarchs. A term that had figured as an essential background condition of right and just rule, *reason* of state, became a term oriented to the manifold needs of a prosperous state, *reasons* of state. By this logic, the monarchy could undo the "pact" that had allowed the mission world to come into existence and that had enabled it to thrive. Under Hapsburg rule, balancing competing claims within the body politic had been the foundation of good government. Justice did not ask the king to determine a priori how each given person or group ought to behave in relation to the whole, except as their conduct might disrupt social peace. According to emerging views, by contrast, it would be "just" to "make [the Indians] into whatever is required . . . by directing them to their own good and to that of the State." Broadly, what was required was that they contribute to "economic government" as individual producers, consumers, and property owners.[70] This view transformed the role of "Indians" in Spanish imperial thought. Regardless of what previous kings may have done, the monarch was no longer bound to seek justice for his Indigenous vassals in securing the common good. As one writer put it, to ensure the "true interests" of the nation, which were fundamentally "economic," the Indians should be made "useful."[71] This was nothing less than a retreat from the substantive definition of "vassalage" as a reciprocal relationship to one in which subjecthood, now harnessed to economic imperatives, implied unquestioning obedience to royal command above all.

Governor Andonaegui rammed the point home in a May 1753 letter to the communities. After accusing the mission Guaraní of treason against the king, he declared that they were "rebels, traitors, disloyal and disobedient vassals."[72] This verbal fusillade must have been among the more dispiriting and enraging words the mission Guaraní heard during the entire treaty episode. As their letters noted, they had never failed to answer the king's call to fight or serve, and they had always lived up to their tribute obligations—they had "erred in nothing." According to Father José Cardiel, they had even taken personal and collective pride in their service to the king, declaring "I am a soldier of our King," painting his image on their armories and refusing to accept the salary due them for their service.[73] And now to be called disobedient and disloyal because they would not bow to a manifestly unjust request? This alone may have strengthened their resolve, for no king had ever said such things to them during the 130 years of the missions' existence.

It is worth considering as well that the very idea of obedience may have resonated quite differently for the mission Guaraní than for royal officials, or even for Jesuit fathers. In Spanish, the term *obediencia* (obedience) was tied up with a strong principle of hierarchy. Covarrubias defined *obedecer* (to obey) as the "execution of what is commanded of us . . . To give obedience to the higher or superior," a definition fundamentally unchanged in the *Diccionario de autoridades* a century later.[74] In Guaraní, by contrast, Montoya defined the word *aye* as "the doing of a thing, honoring, esteeming, giving content or pleasure, obeying."[75] Except for the last of these, the Spanish equivalents given in the definition do not evoke hierarchy or submission to it as an essential quality of complying with or adhering to a request from a superior or anyone else. Instead, *aye* seemed to imply a willing respect for such a request, an "honoring or treating with reverence" much more like the Spanish *acatar*.[76] What this suggests is that, among the mission Guaraní, the reciprocal qualities of vassalage may have been understood more as *aye* than as *obediencia*. As the Guaraní letters state, they had always honored and revered the king's word, when properly given, as it always had been before. Of course, many among the Guaraní, perhaps especially corregidores and cabildo members elected under Spanish law, may have understood that *aye* and *obedecer* had distinct senses. But since no previous royal request had put them to such a test, the question they faced was how far they could go in acknowledging the latter while remaining true to the former as the basis of their own sense of what it meant to be a good vassal.

Royal dispatches ordering the Guaraní to move employed the language of vassalage, but now to reinforce the will and authority of the king acting pursuant to Reasons of State. The only option presented to them was to obey as one would a superior—the very essence of a command (*mandar*) being that it flows from a superior to an inferior and is backed by the threat of force—rather than to honor a proper request by a leader who kept his word.[77] And so, the mission towns stood by their refusal with an outward resolve that appeared unshakeable. In January 1753, a force of six hundred Indians gathered in the plaza at San Miguel, weapons at their feet, demanding that those who wanted to move as the treaty required step forward.[78] Meanwhile, Spanish officials worried that if Guaraní contumely spread, "there would be no sovereign except in name."[79] One royal official characterized a letter from the towns to the governor, written in Guaraní and opposing transfer, as "seditious" and "fraudulent." The letter made virtually identical points to other missives, stating that mission residents no longer had "confidence" in the king and noting that militiamen from San Luis had burned a royal order of expulsion before the church at San Nicolás.[80] By mid-1753, there was no bridging the ideological and political chasm that had opened between the Guaraní and the monarchy. Guaraní leaders had presented their arguments regarding the justice of the situation. They had been rebuffed. On orders from their superiors, the Jesuits withdrew from the missions.

"Useless vassals"

Through the latter half of 1753, the mission communities presented a united front against the king's command. In August, the letters communicating this stand were dispatched to Governor Andonaegui in Buenos

Aires, despite his minatory missive of May 1753 accusing them of lese majesty. Nothing came of it. Positions had hardened on both sides. Fernando VI's order brooked no questioning and the communities had made it clear they would not back down. Tensions tautened through the early months of 1754. By that time, Ñeenguyrú had assumed political leadership of a movement characterized by one historian as a "stance of radical intransigence before a royal order."[81] This resolve emboldened mission residents in relation to their priests. Tired of harangues by Father Cerdo, the people of San Nicolás sent word to the provincial to remove him or gag him from speaking about the need to abandon their lands and go elsewhere.[82] Perhaps they understood his concern for them, but their minds were made up and his words had become tiresome.

By early 1754, Sepé Tiarayú, a violinist and militia captain from San Miguel, had begun to mobilize an army to resist removal.[83] Captains fanned out in the forest seeking recruits. Mission residents as well as surrounding Indigenous groups joined the growing troop. Kinship relations and reciprocity were critical to consolidating a fighting force. Kin ties stretched from one side of the river Uruguay to the other and bound Christianized Guaraní to unbelieving Indians who lived within or at the edges of the broader territory of the missions. Gifting and invitations to conviviality forged alliances. For example, as allies were still being gathered, a band of patrolling mission warriors paddling their canoes on a river came across another party on a raft, some of whom were recognized as distant kin. The leader of the patrol invited the rafters to stay for a meal. He shared meat and manioc with them and gifted linen and tobacco to their leader. They joined the cause and increased the missions' flotilla of canoes by two.[84] In another instance, Father Nusdorffer noted that nine caciques of non-Christian peoples entered San Luis in late 1753. They were received as old friends, even though just a few years earlier they had fought against mission militias. The fathers suspected they had come to have counsel with Guaraní leaders regarding the situation, which affected all connected with the missions. Once talks were done, the mission captains went to the missionaries and asked them to make a gift of yerba, tobacco, and clothing from the warehouse to their guests. The fathers complied, one of them noting, "We no longer govern here; they govern and we obey."[85]

The Guaraní War, as it is sometimes called, unfolded over the next two years. Initial encounters did not go well for the resisters, but after an initial setback in April 1754, mission troops defeated a combined

Spanish-Portuguese column sent to execute the treaty. Led by Sepé Tia-rayú, the Guaraní prevailed in two confrontations and were able to celebrate their opponents' retreat with a Mass, music, and dancing in November of that year. Believing the matter resolved, Guaraní militias disbanded and men returned to their homes. After a brief lull, the two monarchs redoubled their efforts. In early 1756, a much larger force of three thousand Spanish and Portuguese soldiers, with Tupí allies, attacked the communities again. After opening skirmishes, the two sides met in a pitched battle at Caiboaté, on February 10. Fifteen hundred mission troops died that day, with minimal casualties among the enemy. In the face of such losses, the rebellion fizzled; perhaps memories of the Comunero revolt and its effects on communities were still raw. The missions surrendered and the combined royal armies occupied the seven towns. The mission Guaraní faced the prospect of forcible relocation, dispossession, and perhaps the collapse of the remaining twenty-three towns—the total destruction of the mission world.

Victors suppose they write history. In 1760, Buenos Aires jurist Juan Baltasar Maziel was tapped to produce the post hoc justification of Fernando VI's decision to go to war against his Guaraní subjects. It is a crucial point that Maziel's thorough and learned, if deeply cynical response came after the fact, more ideological cover than substantive inquiry. His argument amounted to a ruthless application of the still-new reasons-of-state logic. He referred explicitly to the "great utility that redounds to the State and the Royal Fisc" from the proposed swap of territory. It suffices to realize the "nonexistent utility" of the seven towns, he wrote, compared to the "maximum prejudice" that Colonia del Sacramento had caused to Spanish commerce in the Atlantic. But more was at stake than the state of treasury and trade. If kings were truly bound by the words and actions of their predecessors—as the Guaraní had argued—it would be, averred Maziel, as if every later king was a mere "subject" of earlier kings or that every earlier king had "jurisdiction [and] empire" over every later monarch. For this reason, the law purporting to forbid the transfer of territory to another sovereign could not apply to Fernando VI but only to his subjects.[86] Of course, writing in 1760, Maziel was interpreting a law nearly two centuries old, one that had seen in any donation of territory a matter of "great harm" to successor kings. In the circumstances of the mid-eighteenth century, as reasons of state were displacing other considerations, allowing past decisions to bind later kings no longer seemed advisable. Failure to see the treaty through would be "enormously prejudicial to the State," Maziel concluded. And as the Indians were nothing but "useless vassals" who had been a drain on royal coffers and a tax on commerce, their complaints should carry no weight against "the common benefit of the whole body of the State."[87]

Maziel's framing of the affair lay bare a profound transfiguration of essential terms, one augured by the way Governor Andonaegui had disparaged the status of the mission Guaraní by referring to them as "disobedient." His position amounted to an effort to alter the meaning of vassalage.[88] By dismissing the mission Guaraní as contributing nothing to the "utility" of the state, Maziel was articulating a legal pretext to assert the primacy of reasons of state over the reciprocal quality of the king's relationship to those he ruled. On this formulation, the Guaraní could be dealt with entirely in terms instrumental to the state's interests, especially economic ones. In the process, mission residents went from being moral subjects to economic objects who might or might not be useful in an imperial regime now anxious over its commercial and fiscal prospects.

The final act in this drama involved a tragic irony. During the years following the war, disagreements over how to draw boundaries between Spanish and Portuguese realms proved insurmountable. In early 1761, with Carlos III barely two years on the Spanish throne, Spain and Portugal signed an accord nullifying the 1750 pact and canceling the proposed transfer of mission towns to Portuguese jurisdiction. For the moment, the mission world had been spared. Despite this formal agreement, Portuguese troops soon trespassed once again on Spanish territory in the Banda Oriental, prompting the governor in Buenos Aires to call up the Guaraní militias. Several mission towns responded eagerly to the opportunity to meet the Portuguese "ambush."[89] They understood that the new treaty meant the mission world would not be dismembered. With Caiboaté and their brush with extinction fresh in mind, they may have concluded that serving "our good King"—a new king—in this way, especially against the hated Portuguese, was a chance to repair their damaged reciprocal relationship with the monarchy. Nothing in the logic of Guaraní reciprocity precluded repair of ruptured mutuality. To the contrary. They knew reciprocity could fail. It could also be restored. Doing so required a specific effort to reengage the open-ended sense of gift and obligation. That said, communities and their leaders were doubtless responding cautiously, given the tribulations of the preceding quarter century.

Regardless, some among the mission Guaraní leapt at the chance to answer the king's call. In light of the struggles of the decade just past, during which their status as vassals had become unsettled, the mission world had nearly been destroyed, and they had come face to face with a Spanish state concerned above all with economic prosperity, doing so may have seemed one of the few reasonable options open to them. And so, when the dust had settled and the Jesuits had returned, the mission Guaraní focused on recovering the world of relative peace, prosperity, and balance they had known up to 1730. It was not to be.

*   *   *

For more than a century after Governor Lariz's official recognition of their vassalage in 1647, mission residents had lived secure in the understanding that they bore a reciprocal relationship to the Spanish monarchy. Broadly speaking, Hapsburg kings had respected the distinctness of the mission world and had repeatedly defended its independence from Spanish settlers who coveted the vast number of Guaraní who made their lives there. During this hundred years, the Guaraní had played a crucial role in securing the southeastern border zone dividing Spanish from Portuguese territory in South America.

This situation changed when Felipe V used his victory in the War of Spanish Succession to "sweep away the fundamental laws, liberties, and institutions" that had allowed the many parts of Spain's composite monarchy to retain separate identities.[90] This change began with Aragon and Catalonia, which had sided with England and the Hapsburgs in the war. Though slow to arrive, the effects of this pivot made their way to South America. In different registers, the Comuneros and the mission Guaraní learned that the symbolic disobedience that had characterized political dispute under the Hapsburgs was no longer an option. The former, panicked that they were being left behind economically, demanded that the missions be broken up and their residents portioned out in encomienda among settlers. Frustrated that the monarch had turned a deaf ear to their plight, they rebelled, invoking theories of popular sovereignty. To meet this crisis, the king had called on his loyal Guaraní subjects to suppress the uprising. Their fidelity came at a tremendous cost, as war, disease, and famine ravaged the mission world.

It was a shock, then, when just a few years on, mission residents learned that seven towns east of the Uruguay would pass into Portuguese hands to settle a boundary dispute between Spain and Portugal. The communities protested to the governor and the king, as they had been entitled to. They were snubbed. A new paradigm of rule held sway. The "good economy of the state" now stood above all other considerations. And so, to preserve the union of their world, they had gone to war against the king. In their staggering loss, they may have feared that the reciprocity bolstering their relationship to the monarchy was crumbling and that their ability to stand apart from the economy of gain, on the ground where aguĭyeí and the common good overlapped, was slipping away.

7

From Community to Liberty

> We do not like the way of being of the Spaniards, in which each
> cares only for himself.
>
> Letter from San Luis, 1768

> What would be a great disgrace for the state of the community
> is . . . a happy outcome for the establishment of liberty.
>
> Protector of the Indians, 1805

AFTER THE DISASTER of the Comunero Revolt and the precipitous loss of
population to 1740, the mission world experienced a slow recovery as residents and missionaries rebuilt. The trend held even during the upheaval
and war of the mid-1750s. By 1760, overall population had once again
broken one hundred thousand and much of the physical destruction of
the 1730s had been repaired. Trust between residents and missionaries remained brittle, a result of the Jesuits' refusal to back the Guaraní during
the Treaty of Madrid episode.

Within officialdom and across a broad transatlantic reading public, the Jesuit order came under a cloud for its supposed role in inciting
the Guaraní to rebellion in 1753–1756. Portugal was the first to act on a
growing animus against the Society of Jesus. In 1759, King José I, "the
Reformer," expelled the Jesuits from Portuguese realms, including Brazil. Their opposition to the Madrid Treaty of 1750, to which they had
ultimately acquiesced, and other perceived affronts to the Portuguese
king had sealed their fate. The missions were central to Portugal's complaints. A Portuguese report noted in 1758 that the fathers had conspired
to "usurp the Indians' liberty" and had aimed to "absorb" the entirety
of "commerce" in South America by an "inhuman and intolerable despotism."[1] More broadly, Jesuits were accused of undermining royal authority, of conspiring to kill the king, of amassing great wealth, of serving only the Pope, of erecting a "powerful Republick" of one hundred
thousand souls on the banks of the Uruguay River—of being, in sum,
a "Machiavellian Fraternity" aiming at nothing less than the "governing

of mankind."[2] With similar complaints, Louis XV suppressed the Society in France in 1764. Carlos III followed suit in February 1767 for all Spanish dominions. In April 1767, royal minister Pedro Campomanes wrote a brief justifying Jesuit expulsion, noting that in Paraguay the fathers had established a "kingdom" apart, "usurped royal authority," and interfered with the advance of Spanish commerce in the region.[3] In stages from 1767 to 1768, the Jesuits in the Plata region were banished. Missionaries were among the last to go, ordered to leave by their own provincial and ushered under guard to ships docked in Buenos Aires. Having been commanded by Pope Clement XIII to comply, they did not resist and left for exile with little more than breviaries and rosaries in their hands, most to Italy. Effects on the mission world were profound.

* * *

"With tears from all of the Indian men, women, and children and especially the poor"

Mission residents were staggered by the expulsion. A letter from the pueblo of San Ignacio Guasú to the governor in Buenos Aires expressed alarm over the missionaries' ouster, worrying that God might punish them, since he had sent the fathers to their lands.[4] Unclear how to react, the residents of San Ignacio promised to respect the king's order and were careful not to oppose what was, by that point, a fait accompli. With memories of the preceding decade's war still fresh, other towns tersely reaffirmed their vassalage.

Such noncommittal responses were in sharp contrast to how residents of San Luis received the news. Urging that the Jesuits not be banished, the cabildo wrote to Governor Antonio María de Bucareli y Ursúa in late February 1768, "with tears from all of the Indian men, women and children and especially the poor."[5] The letter began by apologizing for not delivering a gift of birds they had promised to the king (reminding the king of their reciprocal relationship). They remained "vassals of God and of the King," ready to do royal will; they had fought three times at Colonia and had always paid their tribute, said the missive. Then they got straight to the point. With "humility and tears," they asked that the fathers be allowed "to live with us always," for they "know how to understand our poor manner of being now in so faded a state." The new priests sent to take the missionaries' place (many of them Mercederians) "do not look out for us," stated the letter, and "we do not love them." "We will in-crease tribute" if need be, even give more yerba *caámini*—the finest, most coveted, and most expensive—if that would help. "We are not slaves; our will is that we do not like the way of being of the Spaniards, in which each cares only for himself and does not help others in work and with food." This is a "pure truth," they told His Excellency: if the Jesuits go, the towns would be lost for God and king. Children were already fleeing to the forests. The letter was signed by thirteen cabildo officers on behalf of "the whole town" and forty-one unnamed caciques.

Just two weeks later, in early March 1768, another letter addressed di-rectly to "our good King Don Carlos III" and signed by forty-one corre-gidores and caciques of "the Thirty Towns" struck a decidedly acquiescent stance.[6] They had traveled at the governor's invitation to Buenos Aires, where they had received gifts and reassurance. They were back in their towns now. In a text composed in Guaraní and translated into Spanish, they thanked the king for taking them away from a "poor state of being" and noted that "past errors"—almost surely a reference to the war of the 1750s—were behind them "forever." They thanked Governor Bucareli for receiving them in Buenos Aires and for treating them well: you clothed us, fed us, and called us gentlemen, pleasing us in everything. They con-cluded by asking Bucareli to put their towns in order and "end our afflic-tion and life as slaves." They promised to learn Spanish and said they were content that perhaps their sons would become priests.

It is difficult to parse these two letters, so different in temper and tone. The March missive from the caciques and corregidores has sometimes been read as welcoming the deportation of the Jesuits. Certainly, that is how Spanish officialdom understood it at the time. But there are other in-terpretive possibilities. It is true that the March letter appears to reflect a collective decision by Guaraní leadership across the mission world to ac-cept the Jesuits' exile. But what other choice had they? The nod to "past errors" makes clear that they feared resistance risked sparking another punitive war. By comparison, the earlier San Luis letter seems rawer, writ-ten in the heat of the moment. During their 150-year history, the missions had always honored one of the basic principles predating the Spaniards' arrival: that the community care for all, including widows, orphans, the infirm, the elderly, and newcomers. In referring to the "tears" of every-one, explicitly mentioning children, women, and the poor, the letter re-veals the anxiety of people who for generations had been sheltered from the external economy. It conveys the material and economic agita of ordinary Guaraní by decrying the idea that an individual might "work only for himself" or refuse to help others. Above all, the letter betrays unease at having to confront settlers and the Spanish empire entirely on their own. There is nothing to suggest that San Luis differed in this from other mission communities, save for being explicit about their fears.[7]

None of this dread made it into the March letter. The corregidores and caciques perfunctorily thanked the king and bowed to inevitability. Perhaps this should not surprise us. Guaraní leaders had been in Buenos Aires for a month and had been showered with gifts and been wined and dined. They may have understood this in contrasting ways—as an inducement but also as part of an effort to shore up their reciprocal relationship with the monarchy. Against the nervous uncertainty of the San Luis letter, these officers may have dared a cramped hope: if their sons became priests, they might, in time, fill the Jesuits' roles and ensure their communities' survival amid an epochal change.

Yet there is another, admittedly more cynical possibility. In expressing gratitude for their treatment and contentment at being called "gentlemen," some of these local notables may have been signaling to Governor Bucareli their desire to forge a new relationship with imperial government, as much for themselves as individuals as for their communities. Nicolás Ñeenguyrú, the corregidor of Concepción and author of the 1753 letter declaring the Thirty Towns' unified stance against the Treaty of Madrid, had attended these meetings. He had arrived on a horse—a rare thing for an "Indian"—dressed in the Spanish style and been waited on by a valet. Like the other caciques, he accepted the expulsion as a done deed and seemed eager for the governor's largesse. Shortly after this meeting, he moved to Buenos Aires with his family, where he was supported by the monarchy in a gilded self-exile. It is worth noting that the San Luis letter may have been written while the forty-one caciques and corregidores were gathered in Buenos Aires, but before they had written their letter of thanks. The San Luis cabildo may have dispatched it thinking to support them by making clear how dire the local situation had become. Perhaps it did not occur to them that these officers might come to see things differently. Or perhaps it did and they hoped to sway them.

Regardless, the difference between the two letters is striking. One way to account for it is to consider that the Jesuits' ouster may have opened a gap between the individual and private interests of high-placed community leaders, such as those called to Buenos Aires, and the collective good of the common folk in the communities they served. Those whose names appeared at the foot of the San Luis letter were lower-level officers, not the sort who would be summoned to a conclave with the governor. Their reference to forty-one unnamed caciques may have been an attempt to ensure their concerns came to the governor's attention. If so, the effort seems to have backfired, for the officials in Buenos Aires appear to have turned a deaf ear to what might have seemed a cheeky message.

So long as the mission world had retained its relative autonomy from local Spanish officials, and while town cabildos had engaged with missionaries, opportunities for widespread self-dealing had been constrained. Now caciques, cabildo officers, and corregidores faced new temptations. For instance, cacique Miguel Yeguacá of La Cruz wrote a private letter to the governor in 1768 giving "infinite thanks, with my cabildo, caciques and all my family."[8] What rings loudest in this brief note is a silence. The 1768 letter from the leaders of San Luis had spoken of the "tears" of the entire community. Even the March letter from the caciques and corregidores of the Thirty Towns had invoked the "solace of [the king's] poor vassals." Yeguacá referred only to himself, his caciques and cabildo members, and his family, almost as if he were identifying a separate political class of people seeking preferment.

"In what manner should we conduct ourselves?"

With the Jesuits safely away, royal officials wasted no time in outlining a vision for the one hundred thousand or so residents who still lived in mission communities. In August 1768, Governor Bucareli published *Ordinances for the Government of the Mission Towns of Paraguay*. On their face, the changes, though significant, were not a radical departure. Where the Jesuits had fused spiritual and temporal realms, the *Ordinances* called for a clean separation between them. Newly appointed priests would tend to the spiritual lives of the Guaraní. Secular administrators would oversee towns' economic activities, especially in relations with the wider economy. Meanwhile, Guaraní cabildos would continue to ensure communal production and distribution within the communities, as they long had. But this was to be a transitional phase. At a deeper level, the *Ordinances* proposed nothing short of a revolution for mission communities. "Commerce" rather than "religion" would now hold center stage in the lives of Guaraní vassals, announced the preamble, for nothing is more conducive to "complete happiness" in a republic than "commerce," because it "enriches peoples and civilizes nations." To this end, and because "liberty" is the "soul of commerce," the Indians would need to learn to work individually rather than communally. Land should be parceled out to individuals, thereby "reforming their customs" and promoting "honest ambition." In this way they would be able to enjoy their "natural liberty" and "the benefits of rational society," from which the "despotic government" of the Jesuits had kept them.[9]

These ideas were part of an ongoing ideological transformation within Spanish policy circles. José del Campillo y Cossío's *New Economic System for America* (1743) had explained that "in the Indies, as in other places, there are two components to government, the political and the economic."[10] Politics looked to the "conservation and good conduct of men," economy to "the good order and arrangement of commerce"—that is, the proper disposition of people, lands, and products to the "benefit and utility of the country."[11] "Political government" should not oppose "economic government," where trade was the dominant priority. But there could be no trade without production. And in this Spain fell short of its rivals, noted Campillo. Where England had few Indian vassals in America but many manufactories, Spain had many Indian vassals and no manufactories to speak of. As the bulk of the population and as the ones who worked the land, Indian vassals needed to made "useful." To this end they should enjoy the "liberty" to engage in "the competition between seller and buyer" on equal terms with Spaniards. In earning money, they would become "ambitious for convenience and splendor, which is almost natural in everyone . . . and the mother of industry"—an idea that had been building since the sixteenth century.[12]

This view was gaining support among the king's counselors.[13] Echoing Campillo, royal minister Bernardo Ward stated in *Economic Project* (1762) that the Indians should indeed be made "useful." Though they might lack ambition, providing them the "means . . . to enrich themselves" would, in time, promote the "prosperity of the State."[14] This dictum announced a powerful new principle, one spreading across Europe at the time: the individual pursuit of gain through economic competition could, if properly arranged, ensure the wealth of society as a whole.

A cultural shift in the meaning of *ganancia* (gain or profit) reflected the trend. If during the sixteenth century the term had been inseparable from greed and avarice, by the mid-eighteenth century *ganancia* had all but lost an explicit moral sense. The term was now widely defined in relation to the utility of commercial exchange.[15] Policy proposals, including Ward's, used the word in precisely this way. At a more mundane level, books of "speculative and practical arithmetics," primers in business and accountancy (one by a Jesuit), employed the term *ganancia* in a purely technical register as equivalent to profit. The only hint at a moral meaning in these was the implication that a merchant who failed to act on a legitimate opportunity to earn a profit was either a very poor businessperson or not behaving rationally.[16]

Against this backdrop, reforming the mission communities presented novel challenges. On the surface, Governor Bucareli's *Ordinances* downplayed the effects of the Jesuits' expulsion. By repeatedly referring to established law—especially the *Recopilación* of 1680—they suggested continuity of practice. But this appeal veiled a new theory regarding the king's "Indian" vassals. Where settled jurisprudence held that local custom and acquired rights should be honored when not in conflict with other legal precepts, the *Ordinances* signaled a shift toward the idea that reasons of state would outweigh local arrangements that failed to advance a broader economic agenda. Law, once understood as the guarantor of justice, now became an instrument for promoting private ownership, individual labor, and liberty of commerce—an economic model meant to apply to Indigenous communities regardless of customary practice. The royal minister Count of Campomanes wrote that the Jesuits had prevented the Guaraní from pursuing such opportunities and in so doing had stymied the "political economy" of the region and the kingdom writ large.[17] With these pen strokes, the idea of reciprocal negotiation over the precise contours of royal authority succumbed to Bourbon efforts to secure tighter control over internal dependencies, such as the mission world.[18]

According to twentieth-century historian Víctor Frankl, the Bourbon monarchy ended the missions because the Jesuits had not sought to exploit and organize the Indians according to "rational concepts of an economic state."[19] From the perspective of new notions of political economy, argued Frankl, the mission world represented a "crime against the concentrated sovereignty of [the] State and an economic absurdity." Unlike the Hapsburg monarchy, the Bourbon state would not countenance "intermediate solutions between sovereignty and dependency" that had allowed the mission world to exist and thrive. This concern, not yet fully crystallized, had figured in debates that led to war over the Treaty of 1750 a decade earlier. By 1767, the new understanding had hardened. "Graduated autonomies" such as the mission world needed to be controlled directly if the monarchy were to promote a new economic model that harnessed individual gain to economic progress and fiscal capacity, so that Spain might confront its European rivals on more equal terms.

For the mission Guaraní, whose political perspective had formed in relation to Hapsburg notions of vassalage and good government, and whose economy had been a blend of Jesuit and Guaraní ideas and practices, this turn of events promised upheaval.

The years following the Jesuits' departure were uncertain ones for the Guaraní. At first, some mission towns seemed willing to give new arrangements a try. Days after the *Ordinances* had been issued, the cabildo of Yapeyú thanked Governor Bucareli for his order and noted that everyone continued to labor in the fields, ensuring their "way of being," even if it meant a "few lashes."[20] Yapeyú was not alone in hoping for a good outcome. A Spanish administrator, with every incentive to put a positive spin on events, claimed in a 1769 letter that all the residents of the twenty towns he oversaw were "infinitely grateful" for the king's order and "very satisfied and assured."[21] There may have been reason for guarded optimism at this early stage. Bucareli's *Ordinances* promised that local cabildos would still hold the keys to community warehouses, where common goods were stored, and to community chests, where accounts and important documents were kept. Clear rules aimed to check administrators and priests from pursuing private ends at communal expense. Prices would be regulated to make sure that exchanges "between parties will be reciprocal," for otherwise merchants and employers would cheat mission residents. With such protections in place, stated the *Ordinances*, the Guaraní would be able to enjoy their "natural liberty" and engage in commerce like other men.

It is difficult to know what the Guaraní made of this appeal to "liberty." Though they were no strangers to the term, it had not figured in their responses to recent events. Neither the letters leading up to war in the 1750s nor those following the Jesuits' expulsion referred to explicitly to liberty. The 1768 San Luis letter did pointedly affirm that residents were "not slaves," a statement resonant with the seventeenth-century Spanish idea of liberty (*libertad*) as the absence of arbitrary imposition, but otherwise did not mention liberty. This may have been a deliberate silence.

The *Ordinances* promised a new sort of *libertad*, one insisting that people should seek their own benefit above all else through transactional exchange. On this view, those whose did not readily take up the pursuit of gain could be thought to lack some essential element of humanity, or rationality. By contrast, from the perspective of Guaraní who had spent generations in the missions, with its commitment to the well-being of all, *libertad* may have implied rejecting the notion that individuals should care only for themsevles and "not help others in work and with food," as the San Luis letter protesting the Jesuits' exile had put it in early 1768.

In this light, the ironies of reforming the mission Guaraní take on sharp edges. Beginning in the 1720s, Jesuits themselves had often complained of the Guaraní's lack of initiative, especially in work. Where once they had celebrated residents' desire for communal and reciprocal labor, now the fathers saw an impediment to the missions' increased prosperity. In the 1750s, missionaries had explained to royal officials that they had sought to persuade the Guaraní to accept individual ownership of milk cows and small plots for tobacco and yerba so that they could trade with Spaniards. "But hard as we tried," sighed Father Cardiel, "we could not get them to do so," at least not in significant numbers.[22]

While insisting that seeking gain through commerce was natural, policy makers, like Jesuits before them, equivocated on whether the Guaraní were suited to the liberty envisioned for them, even though their "usefulness" depended on it. The *Ordinances* explicitly warned that exposing the mission Guaraní to the full rigors of gain might lead to harm. Spanish merchants and employers would play on their "rusticity" in any exchange or contract, stated one section. As a result, "complete liberty" might be "fatal and prejudicial to their interests." This was an uncomfortable admission that seemed to cut against the emerging idea of commercial freedom as a human universal. If people were not naturally disposed to gain or could not benefit from it, what could justify reforming them to embrace it or restructuring the world of human relations to enable it? Bucareli resolved this paradox by eclectically blending old and new ideas. According to the *Ordinances'* preamble, temporary limitations on liberty should not be thought "offensive to freedom of commerce when directed to the common good." In time, "free commerce" could unite Guaraní and Spaniards in "friendship," allowing all to act "freely in good faith." "Reform of custom" was admittedly a "most arduous enterprise" that could be achieved only gradually. Until then, the Indians needed to be "conserved" by administrators appointed to defend their "justice and liberty . . . persons and property."[23] It occurred to no one in officialdom to wonder whether the Guaraní might have ideas of their own about how to organize their social and economic lives now that they Jesuits were gone.

After an initial and guarded readiness to consider new possibilities, former mission communities began to strain under multiple pressures. Far more exposed to outsiders than before, the missions drew opportunists. "Indios infieles" (unconverted Indians) entered towns, stole horses, and menaced residents. Portuguese raiders invaded estancias and rustled cattle.[24] Administrators and priests abused their positions, competing with each other, laying bare the practical difficulties of replacing missionaries bound by a vow of poverty with administrators and secular priests.[25] A cabildo officer from Guacuyú wrote in 1768 to say that "his hair had stood on end" when he saw how quickly the town's meager assets vanished from the community warehouse. He did not say whether the Spanish administrator or the Guaraní corregidor—the other two officers who held keys to the warehouse—was behind the theft.[26] Administrators were often to blame. But it was hardly unknown for Native corregidores to leverage their positions, perhaps an augur of growing self-interest among those who held power in the communities. In 1770, for example, the town of Loreto accused their corregidor of saying that he recognized "no superior," including the cabildo and all the caciques. The "sweat of the poorest" flows only to him, cabildo members charged, and they were surrounded by "those who snatch at the King's silver and by Spaniards." They had tried to honor recent laws, they wrote, but surely those laws did not say they must allow themselves to be taken advantage of.[27]

In this spirit, don Antonio Ayrepii, cacique of Nuestra Señora de Itatí, wrote a letter in Guaraní to the lieutenant general in 1770, complaining that Spaniards had entered the village and dragooned dozens of men to work on royal projects in Montevideo and Rio Grande.[28] It had been common practice before 1767 for the missions to send men for such work and to refuse payment for it. But that was then. Now, said Ayrepii, Spaniards had simply taken them "in the King's name," without presenting a royal order and without paying them—with the implication that the men had likely been taken elsewhere pursuant to private ends. With the "most essential and useful men" gone, the town was being "dismembered," warned the cacique. Unable to return when their service ended, these men had "scattered" to the wage labor market, drifters in "remote lands without hope of returning to their villages." These problems, Ayrepii suggested, dated to 1758, the end of hostilities over the seven towns. Since then, he insisted, Itatí had suffered "a poor/afflicted state of being, lacking money/support."[29] Ayrepii's bleak assessment of the wage economy and his reference to a lack of money strongly suggests that Guaraní understood that they were now operating in a fundamentally monetary and commercial reality.

Towns noted their economic travails. At first, they pled general hardship, asking the governor to "console all of us, the poor" with unspecified material or financial help. Soon the requests became sharper, making clear that communities were trying to adapt. In 1772, Concepción asked for eight thousand head of cattle so that people might eat. A year later, San Cosme petitioned for a few ponchos so that rivermen could ply their trade in exchange for wages. An unnamed town asked for iron tools so that they could build canoes with which to transport yerba to market.[30] Such requests indicate that collective resources were short and that local leaders were grasping at straws to keep their communities afloat, recognizing that wage labor and commerce might be necessary for communal survival. "Their warehouses are empty," noted a Spanish lieutenant governor in 1774. Perhaps more worryingly, said this official, people were leaving villages to seek work in the wage economy, a clear sign that the missions' communal labor arrangements were collapsing. One enterprising (or perhaps just desperate) villager explained that he would like to "go to another town where they will pay me in exchange for the work I do so that all of my earnings do not go just to the community."[31] Spanish peddlers and traders flocked to the towns. With the connivance of administrators, they overcharged for goods, underpaid for what they bought, and shorted weights, despite the *Ordinances'* clear prohibitions.

Such trials were not simply corruption and gain run riot. Communities struggled with how to respond to dizzying circumstances, crosscutting forces, and unclear instructions, leaving them to wonder "in what manner should we conduct ourselves?"[32] A concrete example makes the point. In 1780, a dispute arose between the cabildo of San Ignacio Guazú and a cacique named Thomás Abacatú, who swept into the community bearing an order from Buenos Aires apparently appointing him corregidor. The bone of contention was whether and to what extent established practices would be maintained in the town. Cabildo members complained to the governor that they continued to follow "ancient customs," making sure that everyone worked in the fields, "gently" correcting those "who do not want to help in the work of the town." Only in this way, they insisted, could "abundance" be assured for the community as a whole. Abacatú saw things differently. Punishments were causing people to flee the town and seek work among the Spaniards, he said, thereby depriving the community of the labor necessary for communal survival.[33]

This case hints at the tensions defining the post-expulsion era for former mission towns and other communities subject to novel administrative arrangements and the coercive freedom of a wider economy. San Ignacio's cabildo tried to maintain the community as a working unit for all its people, as had been the case before 1767. Whether they resorted to punishment more often or with greater vigor than the Jesuits is impossible to say. The crucial point is that cabildo members saw the world from within San Ignacio. Abacatú, whose easy movement between San Ignacio and Buenos Aires implied familiarity with the world beyond the mission communities, saw San Ignacio at least partly from the perspective of the external economy of *conchabos* (wage contracts), commercial dealings, consumption, and "free trade." His point seems not to have been that San Ignacio should simply lay itself bare to this world. Rather, he seemed to suggest that the invisible cordon around former mission towns was fraying, demanding that older practices be rethought.

Trade has become "prejudicial to the communities"

In 1776, Carlos III established the Viceroyalty of Río de la Plata, with Buenos Aires its administrative center. Split off from the Viceroyalty of Peru, with its capital in Lima, and plugged directly into the circuits of Atlantic trade, Buenos Aires became Spain's most important port and administrative city in the southern hemisphere. Its role only grew after 1778, when Carlos issued the "Rule Regarding Free Trade" that ended the state monopoly on foreign trade in favor of *comercio libre*, or free trade, as a way to foment the Spanish empire's "agriculture, industry, and population."[34] Non-Spanish merchants were now permitted to buy and ship American products on their own ships to destinations of their choosing, subject only to export taxes at ports of exit. From that point forward, Buenos Aires became a cynosure of an increasingly brisk transoceanic trade in leather, cotton, and tobacco exports and imported manufactured goods from Europe.

Despite ideological shifts and the opening of trade, some commodities remained under strict control. Looking to the success Cuban tobacco was enjoying as Europeans took up the smoking habit and eager for the revenues that came with it, Carlos III established a state tobacco monopoly in La Plata in 1778. Under the new law, growers who wanted to sell tobacco had to supply the *estanco* (the monopoly) a certain amount of product at fixed prices. Once processed, this tobacco was sold to foreign merchants for shipment abroad. Beyond that quantity, farmers were free to sell at whatever price they could obtain in the market. While they complained about the government's low prices, they welcomed the steady demand for their product and were happy to be paid in metal currency by monopoly agents or factors acting on their behalf. Though it ran counter to the free-trade trend, the tobacco monopoly became one of Spain's most reliable and bankable sources of revenue across the empire during the late eighteenth century.[35]

On the ground, the appearance of coins sparked deep changes. The fact that tobacco had a ready buyer led many peasant farmers to take up its cultivation. A labor intensive crop, it was amenable to large households, especially those with indentured workers (*yanaconas* still held in encomienda). As tobacco began to be exchanged for money, other products were drawn into an incipient cash nexus. A "cloud of merchants" rolled across the countryside, some buying tobacco and sugar, others selling staples and clothing.[36] Taverns doubling as dry goods sellers sprang up. Indigenous women who lived near Asunción might walk to town on weekends to sell honey, sugar, candies, cheese, corn, and beans for cash to supplement family incomes. Indigenous men drafted from villages for public works projects were known to take advantage of their lunch breaks to earn a few extra coins to supplement their incomes.[37] These money transactions did not displace barter so much as become part of a system with intertwined options for conducting exchange.

While this development created limited opportunities for Indigenous producers, it also subjected them to a broad structural asymmetry in their cash dealings.[38] According to economic historian Carlos Garavaglia, rural producers generally had to take prices from merchants, whether they were selling or buying. In selling cash crops—tobacco, say, or sugar—growers were at a disadvantage. European traders, often farmers' only option for sales, were able to keep prices low. In buying goods, rural people fared no better. Peddlers could hold the line on a high price because, in effect, farmers who lived at the margin were trading away some of the time they would otherwise have spent to feed and clothe themselves. In effect, merchants, especially those with access to credit, negotiated from a position of strength that enabled them to manipulate prices to capture a portion of peasant labor. In the same spirit, yerba proprietors were able to force people into unfavorable terms of exchange. By advancing credit, lowballing piece rates, and jacking up prices for basic necessities—from four to ten times what was charged elsewhere for clothing, ponchos, hats, and knives, all essential for the toil of yerba production—employers could effectively recover all of a worker's wages. A report from the period noted that in one *beneficio* (yerba production site), twenty of twenty-three rural workers were in debt to their employer, who might earn returns of 150 percent on yerba sold in Asunción. Regardless of how it happened, Garavaglia argues, peasant workers were under constant pressure to "transfer their surplus labor and part of their necessary labor" to those who controlled access to money.[39]

The deepening commercial imperative of the latter quarter of the eighteenth century—both as government policy and as private pursuit—had crucial effects on Indigenous communities. The tobacco *estanco*, for instance, like the encomienda before it, relied on a legally mandated labor draft drawing on thirteen non-mission pueblos de indios to bring several hundred Native workers throughout the year to process leaf at a newly established factory in San Lorenzo, near Asunción (at the site of an old Jesuit school).[40] In other words, the commercial "liberty" so highly touted in official circles could be relaxed if larger concerns demanded it. With a division of labor, strict hours, and close discipline, the factory represented a new form of work and productive organization in Paraguay. Though drafted workers received a nominal wage, half of it was deducted and, at least in principle, sent to their town cabildos, creating tensions within home communities already struggling.

As mission territory opened up, individual Spaniards targeted former mission towns for economic plunder. According to a 1788 report, secretly conducted by Francisco Bruno de Zavala at the governor's behest, trade had become "prejudicial to the communities." The books, kept by appointed administrators to track production and purchases on behalf of residents, were "in great disorder and confusion." Administrators might dispatch Indigenous men to private yerba groves, to gather and process the leaf, "without consideration for the effects on the communities." They charged "low rents" to Spaniards for use of mission lands, especially pastures. Renters were less interested in the land itself than in the access it gave them to the vast, untended herds of cattle that had made the missions the largest cattle ranchers in La Plata. Administrators themselves, said the report, sold cattle that belonged to the communities they were charged with overseeing, even inviting futures contracts with merchants that ended up shortchanging communities. In what amounted to a systematic expropriation of mission capital for private ends, herds dropped by a fifth shortly after the Jesuits' expulsion.[41] In some towns, the number was a quarter to a half of what it had been twenty years earlier. These opportunists were responding to commercial cues. European demand for leather skyrocketed toward the end of the eighteenth century—a combination of wars (boots, clothing), new industrial applications (drive belts), and consumption (tack, saddlery, and footwear)[42]—providing a lucrative outlet for local production, now in the context of "free trade."

Some mission towns tried to get in on the hide game, without lasting success.[43] Yapeyú and San Miguel, with easy access to grazing land, were ideal for raising livestock. Before the Jesuits' ouster, they had fed their own communities from these herds and had shared with other mission towns during lean times. But meat and hides involved distinct processes. Producing meat for immediate consumption was a fairly straightforward matter of rounding up and butchering the animals. The production of hides required a fixed abattoir, complex operations, curing time, a robust transportation network, and financial coordination with outside buyers. Before their expulsion, Jesuits had managed the missions' external relations. Now Spanish administrators did, often in ways that diverted income to themselves rather than to the communities they served. And while, technically, mission towns like Yapeyú had property rights in their cattle, in practice they had little recourse against those intent on taking what they could before the herds were completely depleted. Moreover, mission residents do not appear to have been enthusiastic about hide work. Not only did they have to leave their families to do it, depriving the community of their work, but they were paid only in rations, since under the *Ordinances* some portion of their labor was still owed to communal production. It was one thing to work far away when families back home were being provided for in the spirit of leaving no one behind, as had been the case up to 1767. It was quite another to do so as towns strained just to survive, particularly when working for rations alongside *conchabados* (contract workers) earning wages.

Landowners too came to see the former mission communities as a means to commercial ends. In 1793, estancia owner Manuel Antonio Barquín requisitioned fifty Indians from the missions to work on his farm, arguing that the towns had people to spare. He committed to satisfying their tribute and paying them wages to support their families. The royal attorney charged with immediate oversight of the mission towns favored the request, echoing new economic thinking. The circulation of goods was vital to the health of the kingdom, he wrote, and should be promoted whenever possible. To this end, the "ardor of a private individual" working for wages and acting for his own ends was far more likely "to animate the residents in their possessions" than efforts by the cabildo to "infuse the community with spirit."[44]

Leaders of sixteen mission towns, including their appointed Spanish administrators, wrote letters to the attorney strenuously resisting this finding. Granting Barquín's request, one town wrote in May 1794, would subvert the "natural liberty" conceded by the king's grace, "in thanks for which we have served him." If they lost any more people, stated one letter, the communities would be unable to grow crops, tend their livestock, repair their buildings, patrol their borders against "disloyal Indians," send troops to the king's forts to keep the Portuguese at bay, and meet tribute obligations, as good vassals should.[45] No less important, they insisted, removal would open the door to those who wanted to quit the towns for wage work. So many had left already, and every person who "wander[ed] the countryside, in the liberty of their conscience" was one less person to ensure community survival. They had tried to honor such contracts before and had always been "deceived." The "pernicious abuse of labor agreements" by "private individuals" had produced the "disorder" they now suffered. Men would scatter across the land, stated one petition, abandoning their own goods and families and the community's crops. And while at first their choice might seem "voluntary," shortly they would end up "enslaved" by those who would pay them meager wages. Ultimately, they would have nothing to show for their decision except a "libertinage" from which there was no escape once they had fallen into it. Even women spinners might leave the communities for work, until this point a rare thing, returning only when they could bring nothing but "costs and problems." In this way, the towns would in the long run be "depopulated" and reduced to "ruins."[46]

Here was a clear sense of the corrosive power of an economy of gain on communal arrangements that ensured social reproduction. The reasons for so bleak a forecast were manifold. While the missions had maintained a degree of separation from the surrounding economy and while robust institutions and quotidian norms had still grounded mutuality and communal commitment, the communities could tolerate a certain amount of leakage to the outside economy. In the missions, almost everyone had worked, if not with the intensity and desire Jesuits had wished. But they had done so without want snapping at their heels, as in the labor-contract market. Mission residents, including those who could not care for themselves, had been provided for, a social order rooted in the idea that no one should be left strictly to their own fate. For over a century, this is what had allowed the mission world as a community of communities to survive and thrive as a whole. Now outside pressures and internal dynamics were eroding the bonds of mutual obligation and convivial reciprocity. In predicting their own "ruin," the letters from the sixteen towns signaled that they understood the dilemma they faced. Every person who left a community added incrementally to the burden of common obligations on those who remained, which made it that much more likely that people would leave—a death spiral of the model that had sustained the mission world up to 1768.

"The inequality of fortune that makes those communities happy"

By century's end, the mission world was unraveling. In 1792, one Spanish administrator noted that mission corregidores and cabildos were complaining that growing numbers of villagers refused to perform unpaid common labor. This had led some local leaders to punish shirkers. The administrator explained the problem by noting that a lack of "youth education" had deprived the communities of "suitable" people to attend to the "common good."[47] What he appears to have meant is that if ordinary people could only be educated to obedience, all would be well. But the problem ran deeper, for towns were being worn down by the slow bleed of residents to the external economy, despite community officials' efforts to maintain the idea of the common. Mission towns were not alone in this. By one estimate, between 1761 and 1799, the number of people living outside officially recognized Indian villages increased 154 percent, reaching 75 percent of the entire Indigenous population in Paraguay by

1800—whereas three in four Guaraní had lived in the mission world at its zenith. Mission folk were now flooding into the countryside, with no obvious status or means to a livelihood. Between the expulsion in 1767 and 1801, the thirteen Guaraní missions located in what later would become the nation of Paraguay—others were located in what would become Argentine territory—had fallen by two-thirds, to fifteen thousand residents.[48]

A further factor weakening community life had to do with the motives of those who exercised effective control over communal resources. Where individual Jesuits had foresworn worldly possessions, appointed administrators who took their place often pursued material enrichment. Though there were doubtless honest administrators, under the new regime, personal gain had lodged itself at the center of community life. From this perspective, there was a sad irony in towns' opposition to Barquín's request for fifty Indigenous laborers. Each letter was signed by the cabildo, corregidores, *and* the Spanish administrator. Under different circumstances, administrators might have been the target of grievance, intent as they so often were on taking advantage of villagers. Instead, Barquín's petition produced what can only have been a prickly alliance of convenience between Native and Spanish officials. The reason is clear. Both were concerned for community survival, though for diverging reasons. Native leaders continued to bear responsibility for ensuring communal production, caring for those who could not care for themselves, dispensing justice, and organizing festivities. By law, Spanish administrators were supposed to help residents engage the external economy but protect them from being taken advantage of. In practice, administrators often abused their positions for their own profit, the cause of so many complaints against them. Barquín's request for labor threatened both projects: the loss of people would have made it harder for the corregidores and cabildo to conserve community life, but also would have undermined administrators' control over the communities' principal resource, their labor, thereby undercutting gain from office holding. Local leaders appear to have been the prime movers here, and we can only speculate on what arguments and pressures led administrators to sign, given that they might have found ways to profit from brokering Barquín's deal.

By the late eighteenth century, life in the former mission communities—and perhaps other pueblos de indios—seemed woven of just such paradoxes, an index of how desperate the situation had become and an omen for the future. In the Barquín case, the communities knew that far more was at stake than whether fifty men would be sent to work on a distant estate. One former mission town pointedly observed that Barquín's request would be an affront to "our liberty," long ago granted by the king. This would be "prejudicial" to all the residents of the town and to the "good purpose of civilization."[49] It is worth pausing over this statement. By highlighting "our liberty" and following it with a reference to the damage Barquín's request would do to the community—and to civilization—the letter writers were conveying their sense that the liberty to pursue individual economic gain could only come at the expense of the liberty rooted in community autonomy. In other words, they seemed to intuit that the debate was not about whether the Guaraní would have liberty but about what liberty was to mean.

The Spanish lieutenant governor tasked with advocating for the towns also realized that uneven reforms premised on new economic ideas were weakening the towns' communal model. Acceding to Barquín's proposal could only hasten the process, he insisted. Therefore, he argued, so long as the towns remained bound by "an order of fraternity" in which they "help . . . each other" to ensure their common "conservation," the petition should be denied. The general Protector of the Indians, charged with recommending a decision to the governor, agreed. He ruled against Barquín, concluding that individuals should not be separated from the whole, in keeping with the "free will and consent of the Indians." He understood that this outcome contravened the ideological thrust of the day, for he concluded by noting that "these trammels" could not last forever. As their civility and knowledge advanced, he observed, the Guaraní would naturally desire more property, which would "stir and promote the private interest of each . . . from which may result the inequality of fortune that makes those communities happy."[50]

This was the monarchy's goal for the mission communities and ultimately all Indigenous villages: to convert them to an economic system of individual labor, private property, self-interest, and social inequality driven by a desire for status and material accumulation. To this end, insisted Gonzalo Doblas in a 1785 white paper indicting mission governance since expulsion of the Jesuits, the Guaraní should learn the use of money, for money was the "soul of commerce" and the "lifeblood of republics."[51] And yet, the Guaraní still lived in a "fog of ignorance." Unfit for the arena of individual gain, they were easy marks for merchants who "grew rich at public expense" rather than being "useful to society." Nevertheless, said Doblas, who had administered the missions in the 1770s, the chief obstacle to the Indians' "political and civil progress" was that they still lived "in community." What they needed above all was "complete liberty . . . as nature itself demanded." Only in this way would they accept "political and rational ideas that will excite in them the desire for a happiness they have never known."[52]

By pitting community against a particular conception of liberty, Doblas was making a point that had become axiomatic within officialdom as a new century approached: from Mexico to Peru, to Paraguay, collective land and labor within Indigenous communities was a problem demanding a solution. Citing population declines in mission communities during recent decades, Doblas argued that the Guaraní harbored a "repugnance and opposition . . . toward community" because they were unable to work for themselves.[53] Although he acknowledged that this had been a period of epidemic disease, he concluded that the real problem was the idea of community itself: people would work only to the extent it benefited them individually to do so and otherwise would shirk (in modern economic parlance, they were free riders).[54] The chief reason for this, he explained, echoing ideas circulating widely among economic reformers at the time, was that they lacked private property. As Bernardo Ward had noted, an Indian was more likely to work if he had a piece of land to call his own and knew he might lose it than if he had no individual stake in things.[55] The key, for Doblas, was to abolish the communities as collective economic enterprises, "leaving the Indians in full liberty so that each can work for his own utility."[56] "It is patent to the whole world that individuals do not see community goods as their own," he wrote, "and so they seek to dissipate them, because they lack private property in them."[57] There could hardly be a clearer statement of the turn toward an interest-driven theory of human motivation.

Another reason the Guaraní were turning against their communities, said Doblas, was that they saw no benefit from goods deposited in community warehouses. These items—clothing, foodstuffs, and yerba—were produced communally but often ended up in a brisk trade for curtains, tables, fabric, dishware, and cutlery that could be sold to Spaniards who had begun to live on mission lands, paying low rent or nothing at all. This lucrative commercial flow appears to have benefited Spanish administrators and their merchant cronies almost exclusively.[58] As a result, stated Doblas, Guaraní residents "hated everything that is directed to the good of the community."[59] He may have had a point, given the malversations of administrators. Still, he argued, the blame lay chiefly with the Jesuits, because they had instituted the communal system in the first place. The government, concluded Doblas in a later report, had provided no "effective remedy" for the situation.[60] It did not occur to him that the Guaraní may not so much have hated community in principle as that recent events and efforts at reform had transformed their communal practices into a source of woes.

But Doblas was not entirely wrong. Many ordinary mission folk did decamp, hoping for better in the commercial economy. In non-mission towns, people sought "liberation" from encomienda obligations once and for all.[61] Those who left often did not have an easy go of it. Lawsuits from the period indicate that many ended up in debt. Others complained of dishonesty in land deals, "theft of the Indians' sweat" in labor contracts, and the "pernicious consequences of allowing Spaniards, mulattoes, and blacks" into former mission areas.[62] Meanwhile, communities continued to deteriorate. An alarmed administrator from San Joaquín noted in 1789 that the town was experiencing "ruin" and the residents had all but abandoned religion in worrying about material life. Men and women alike refused to work the communal tobacco fields, and "all of the residents are nearly in mutiny."[63]

And yet, mission residents stood against the dissolution of community where it was still possible to do so. In a 1791 report to the viceroy, Doblas noted that mission towns remained in debt to one another, dating from the time of the Jesuits.[64] They refused to pay off these arrears, he said, even when new administrators took office. This made it easy for corrupt officials to fudge accounts and defraud the people they served, said Doblas, a problem Buenos Aires had been unable to solve. Of course, this was hardly a novel development. Mission towns since the seventeenth century had been in debt to one another, part of the reciprocal circulation of goods within the mission world, a matter the missionaries too had left unsettled.[65] While the communities worried about corruption, they may have had their own reasons for refusing to clear these debts. Doblas himself noted in 1805, that mission towns preserved "a kind of brotherhood."[66] The persistence of unpaid monetary and in-kind debt among them—which Doblas saw as a problem regarding the circulation of goods and money—strongly suggests they strove to maintain intercommunal mutuality decades after the Jesuits had gone. A settling of the accounts would have broken this circle of solidarity.

Relationships of mutuality also persisted in everyday life, though not without certain incongruities. In his 1785 report, Doblas complained that mission Indians did not know how to sell their own labor. By way of example, he observed that when someone needed shoes, they would go to the cobbler, give him the materials, and ask him to fashion a pair of shoes. The cobbler would make them, "and if the recipient gave him something, he received it, if not he left without asking for anything."[67] This had been common through the mission years, as Cardiel himself had noted. The same thing happened with many other common needs. As had the Jesuits before him, Doblas saw only a failure to understand the logic of commercial exchange, for it allowed those who needed shoes and other goods to suppose they could get them for free and did little to encourage people to think of their labor as a commodity. Moreover, he complained, the cobbler's attitude could provoke a perverse contest between priest and administrator over who would be able to capture the value of the cobbler's labor. For his part, the priest might pay the cobbler a wage to make shoes and then sell them at markup. Seeing this, the administrator might order the cobbler to the communal fields in order to recapture some of the cobbler's work.[68] This vignette identifies one of the thorniest problems facing reforms aiming to push the mission Guaraní into commerce: who would control the Indians' labor now that it had clear economic value and access to it was untrammeled?

Here lay the tragedy of the system of "community," as far as Doblas was concerned. Whether under the Jesuits or now Spanish administrators and priests, the Guaraní had been denied the freedom to pursue individual initiative. The only answer was to abolish the community system in toto. Once it had been eliminated, he argued, the Guaraní would be able to fend for themselves—or be forced to by circumstances. Certainly, we can imagine the cobbler might have wanted to escape the pressure to provide his labor for free to fellow townspeople. Yet Doblas did not consider that the shoemaker and his clients may have been acting pursuant to the logic of gift and reciprocity, entirely bypassing the question of economic "value" that animated the competition between priest and administrator over the cobbler's labor.

Substantive mutuality, in other words, and the values underlying it could serve as a refuge from the demands raining down on ordinary mission residents. In towns where appointed Spanish officials and even some caciques or mayordomos pursued self-interest cloaked in communal obligation, it is perhaps no wonder that reciprocal relationships and an egalitarian spirit continued to make sense to ordinary people. We have only glimpses, but women may have been central to this effort. Doblas noted, for instance, that in matters of dress, the Guaraní had long promoted equality, at least among ordinary folk. He attributed this to the Jesuits. He recounted the tempest that arose when he ordered Guaraní women to stop wearing the traditional *tipoy* (a white smock-like dress) and instead wear Spanish clothes. He had told them that those who did so would be treated with greater "distinction" than those who did not. He was flummoxed when the women balked, "being concerned with the equality with which they had been raised."[69] There is little to go on here, but given that female voices do not often emerge from the records, might this be a hint of the role Guaraní women played in shoring up the foundations of substantive mutuality, as they had almost surely been doing all along? Of course, from Doblas's perspective, their reaction made little sense. He assumed that these women would naturally seek "vanity" in order to "distinguish" themselves.[70] That they should "refuse to allow anyone to stand out from the others" was one of those things that required reform. And in the end, he noted, they had come around and "disabused themselves of this error."

"The new system of liberty, abolishing that of community"

At the dawn of a new century, the regional economy was bustling. With the advent of free trade in 1778, silver remittances to Spain had been rerouted from Cuzco to Buenos Aires.[71] This financial flow, though diminished from Potosí's glory days, made Buenos Aires into a funnel through which passed a thickening stream of exports and imports. Asunción too had seen gains, exporting tobacco, timber, furniture, and hides. For many within Spanish officialdom, the former mission communities were the means of accelerating this trend. To this end, the king issued a 1798 decree abolishing "the system of community" that, it was said, had stymied Guaraní progress.

In early 1800, Viceroy Marqués de Avilés in Buenos Aires prepared to implement the edict. He solicited input on his proposal from underlings.[72]

Some argued that ending the communal regime would expose the Indians to the "vice of greed so dominant in our times," leaving nothing between them and raw exploitation by Spaniards, who had always resented their lack of access to Native workers.[73] Others backed Avilés. Friar Joaquín Corcio insisted that the system of community was "prejudicial" to God, king, and the Indians, for it denied them "liberty," man's greatest good. Only by eliminating it could the Indians become civilized and prove their "utility" to "state and society."[74] Having heard these views, Avilés proclaimed the "liberation of the community regime," ending the missions' communal system.

Initially, 323 families (of 45,000 or so remaining residents) were exempted from communal labor and given small plots of land, a few cows, seed, and tools.[75] Word traveled fast. Before long, communities were calling for the law to be extended quickly to cover all mission towns. Residents of San Xavier asked the viceroy to "liberate" them from community work, so that "each might earn the sweat of his brow."[76] Communities that had been "liberated" wrote in apparent gratitude. A September 1800 letter, translated from Guaraní into Spanish by a Franciscan priest, referred to the "recently liberated sons" of Itapúa as giving "repeated thanks" for the new law. According to the Spanish version of the letter, they were "happily" carrying out the "act of their liberty" as his majesty had commanded. In October 1800, the corregidor and cabildo of Santa María la Mayor claimed that they were enjoying the "valuable liberty" that had "removed us from oppression during which time we have been forgotten, without the paternal love of a true father."[77]

These letters might seem to suggest broad Guaraní support for elimination of the communal land and labor regime in favor of individual commercial liberty. But this too readily concedes the conventional narrative regarding the "transition" to a modern, market-oriented economic regime. In fact, reality was more complex. Rereading the letters through modern Spanish retranslations of the original Guaraní raises intriguing interpretive possibilities. Thus, where the original Spanish version of the Itapúa letter (translated from Guaraní by a Franciscan priest) referred to the "pleasure and happiness" with which the town was now carrying out the "act of their liberty," a modern Spanish retranslation of the Guaraní text refers vaguely to following "this order" and says only that they are thankful the viceroy has recognized them as his vassals.[78] In light of political principles of vassalage still recognized by the Guaraní, this amounted to little more than a bland acknowledgement of the new decree.[79] Similarly, a retranslation of the Santa María letter indicates that the original Spanish translation (it is not known who did it) overstated the Guaraní embrace of liberty and rejection of community. The opening paragraph of the original eighteenth-century Spanish translation refers to "all those who . . . now enjoy valuable liberty." The modern Spanish retranslation of the same Guaraní text renders a quite different sense. It says nothing of "valuable liberty" but instead offers the thanks of "we who have enjoyed your good love, for having removed us from the great darkness in which we have lived for many years." And where the original Spanish translation refers to having ended the "oppression in which we have lived," the modern retranslation speaks only of "a desolating poverty/anguish" and asks the viceroy to "take pity on us, as our father, as the savior from our poverty."[80]

These differences are subtle but telling. The modern retranslations do not suggest that the Guaraní wholeheartedly embraced the new system for its supposed virtues, or at least the ones Spanish officials imagined they were being thanked for. The letters clearly express relief that the king and the viceroy are finally paying attention to the adversities—*poriahú*, meaning "anguish, misfortune, affliction" as well as "poverty"—they had suffered during many years of reform.[81] And while both letters refer to townspeople as "liberated," the term appeared as a Spanish loanword in the original Guaraní versions. Historical linguist Capucine Boidin has proposed that the Guaraní may have employed this usage to describe the concept of individual economic liberty as understood by Spaniards, without any implication of acceptance.[82]

In short, there appears to have been a gap between what Spanish officials read and what writers from the mission towns may have meant. In the Itapuá case, it is clear that the Franciscan priest who translated the Guaraní did so loosely and in such a way as to make it seem that the Indians had eagerly embraced the new arrangements. Perhaps that is how he understood it. Perhaps he worried that a less positive reaction might be taken amiss by officials. There is no indication of who translated the Santa María letter. But whether a Spanish interpreter, a local priest, or even a Guaraní translator, we do not have to speculate too freely to understand how Spanish officials read these missives. In 1806, Miguel Lastarria, a royal officer charged with reforming "the abusive Jesuitical government," wrote a policy brief of the mission communities since 1768. The

Itapuá and Santa María letters were included in the report. The section heading under which they were grouped speaks volumes: "Letters from various Cabildos of Guaraní Indians, . . . that manifest jubilation and give thanks for the change in the oppressive Government of Community."[83] In other words, officials who received these documents, already so convinced by new economic ideas, could only imagine that the Guaraní shared their contempt for "oppressive" community and desired only liberty in an individual register.

There is no denying that some Guaraní did. In August 1800, a cacique from San Francisco de Atira dispatched a memorandum to Viceroy Avilés.[84] José Sapí, a carpenter by trade, began by observing that since the law had already freed eight mission towns to "subsist on their own, with independence from the Community," this "admirable providence" should be extended to his own town of Atira, which was not of the missions. Communities were the "owners" of everything, he argued, leaving nothing for "private individuals." Under the circumstances, this was politic language. Rather than lay the plight of the Guaraní to the encomenderos and their "mistreatments," or more proximately to Spanish administrators, Sapí blamed the "system of community" itself, echoing the recent law "liberating" mission towns. And so, while the warehouses were filled with clothes and the herds were numerous, families went about hungry, unclothed, and unwell, noted Sapí. Their situation was worse than that of slaves, who at least were cared for so that their "price" not be lost. "Many individuals," noted this carpenter, had used their time away from community labor to accumulate goods and thereby "notably distinguish themselves from others." More often, whether because they lacked the capacity or because of the "misery" they suffered, Indigenous folk were gripped by a "servile way of thinking" and had no goods of their own. The only solution, concluded Sapí, was for "each to work for himself, just as the Spaniards do it."

It is hard to imagine a statement more closely aligned with the tone and substance of recent official pronouncements regarding Indigenous communities. Or one further removed from the 1768 missive sent by the mission town of San Luis, which had rejected "the way of being of the Spaniards, in which each works only for himself." Atira had experienced all the harshness of the encomienda, said Sapí, and its residents had always had to balance communal labor against the unrelenting demands of encomenderos. By contrast, San Luis, and other mission towns, had been insulated from the encomienda since the early seventeenth century, allowing Guaraní notions of mutuality to reseat themselves within the system of communal labor and land. Thus, rather than criticize such arrangements, as Sapí later would, the San Luis letter expressed a broad anxiety regarding the community's survival and the fate of deeper principles of mutuality. In 1768, however, San Luis's residents could not know how things would end up. By 1800, in towns like Atira, some Guaraní, like Sapí, could see advantage in "liberty." Having mastered the language of the new economic ideology, he could tell the viceroy precisely what he wanted to hear. Under the new law, Sapí observed, Indians would be able to "make good use of their work," which will be of "incalculable benefit to the State." Moreover, as Guaraní married Spaniards, the label "Indian" would fade away and the contempt in which Indigenous people had so long been held would end.

Sapí's letter has been offered as evidence that the Guaraní broadly had turned against the principle of community and yearned only to be "free."[85] But Sapí had already accepted the proposition that human beings were individuals first and members of larger communities second—and then only if they chose to be. In this regard, it is noteworthy that his petition did not speak for his community; it asked only that he, his family, and five other named individuals who were "ready" be granted the liberty promised by law. These five were tradesmen as well: a mason, two carpenters, a weaver—privileged workers all and the most likely to find stable employment in a labor market. Though he pointed out that many others were "suited" to similar treatment, his reference to "servility" indicates that he was speaking through his status rather than from his membership in a collective or his duties as a cacique. If Viceroy Avilés liked what he read in Sapí's letter, it is little wonder: Sapí affirmed commercial exchange as a matter of human nature and proposed a solution to the problem of the Indians—their extinction by miscegenation and economic integration.

Although many Guaraní leaders must have been tempted by this understandings of liberty, we must not suppose they shared Sapí's unreserved enthusiasm for the new state of affairs. And we must not confuse resignation with "free" choice. Preceding decades had been defined by a tug between two official tendencies: to promote individual economic pursuits and to regulate just how exposed the Guaraní would be to raw gain.[86] These were meant to be parts of a larger transition to a new economic model. But botched reforms and sharp contradictions had backed communities against a wall, and the situation was more complicated than whether mission residents, or Guaraní generally, broadly accepted or rejected the viceroy's order. The failures of reforms after 1768 and the steadily increasing pressures of everyday life had so eroded community bonds and forced so many to react in individualistic ways just to survive that ordinary people may have seen few realistic alternatives to accepting the inevitable. In essence, the very conditions of what was realistic had changed. Here is one of the secrets of the transformation to an economy of gain and of reforms to bring it about: it makes its own milieu by eroding solidarities and giving people few options beyond acquiescing to a certain kind of liberty and calling it a matter of human nature.

By 1803, roughly six thousand mission residents had been "liberated" pursuant to the edict of 1800.[87] A new royal decree in March of that year ordered all remaining towns—roughly forty thousand people—be put into "the new system of liberty . . . abolishing that of community." Under its terms, individual Indian men were to enjoy the same freedom as Spaniards to engage in economic activity so that they might pass from "a rude and ignorant state to another enlightened and free."[88] To this end, communal labor would be extinguished. Common lands would finally be divided up among residents, who would receive deeds to their parcels, so that they could pass it to descendants. Subsequent instructions acknowledged that the Indians remained vulnerable to exploitation and so forbade Spaniards from purchasing lands around the towns and prohibited Indians from selling their plots to Spaniards. There would be no more administrators, since once the "system of liberty" was in place, they would be unnecessary. The government would ensure that the Indians did not fall victim to false contracts. Schools would be established so that all the Indians could learn Spanish and how to protect themselves from opportunists.[89]

On paper, it all seemed quite straightforward, as arguably had the 1768 *Ordinances* before them. But an enormous problem loomed over the entire enterprise. For decades, mission towns had used communal property—often held in Buenos Aires—as collateral to secure loans to blunt the effects of changing conditions. According to one royal official in 1804, these debts represented the chief impediment to liberty among the mission towns.[90] The reason was clear. Once land was in private hands, there would be no assets against which to satisfy creditors' claims. The answer, argued this official, was to sell community-held property in Buenos Aires, still on the books from Jesuit days, in order to liquidate the arrears. If that was not enough, collective assets of the former mission towns—such as "unused" community lands—could be sold to pay down the balance. And if this too fell short, a modest per capita annual fee (above tribute) could be levied on the communities.

It was at this point that Gonzalo Doblas reentered the debate. In an 1805 proposal, he agreed that the communities' debts, especially those held by outside creditors, needed settling. He saw no problem with charging them against mission towns' Buenos Aires assets or against "idle" community lands. But rather than proceed town by town, officials should treat these debts as common liabilities shared among the former mission communities. Echoing one of his earlier statements, Doblas noted that "they have conserved a kind of brotherhood, mutually helping and aiding each other" in meeting misfortunes of weather, accident, or greed.[91] As it stood, towns that were owed the most refused to force less fortunate communities to pay up.[92] Doblas, in other words, recognized that intercommunal mutuality had continued to exert a powerful influence within and among the former mission communities.

The conclusion he drew from this fact demonstrates how far official thinking had drifted from older ideas of good government and established custom. Because towns had extended aid without expectation of immediate return, said Doblas, and because the "extinction of community" would benefit all, better-off towns should help the poorer ones clear their arrears. Once communities were no longer bound by these obligations, the Guaraní would be allowed to own property only within a three-kilometer radius of their towns. Spaniards would be excluded from ownership within this zone, ensuring that Indians and Spaniards alike possessed just what land they could make productive. Remaining lands, especially distant estancias and yerba groves that had constituted the vast wealth of mission community holdings, would be absorbed by the monarchy, to be sold or rented to "well-off people" who could populate them with cattle, or cultivate cash crops on them. Proceeds from these transactions would be used to satisfy remaining debts, in what would have amounted to a forced appropriation of Guaraní capital.

The tragic irony of this idea is stunning. By clearing inter-community debts and satisfying the claims of "private creditors" against common property, Doblas proposed to rely on the history and structures of intercommunal reciprocity within and among mission communities to extinguish the "brotherhood" these towns had so consciously maintained after expulsion of the Jesuits. Creditors would be made whole by drawing down collective assets, and the system of community would finally be abolished in favor of economic liberty by the mechanisms of communal reciprocity and solidarity themselves.

Following years only muddied the broad economic situation of Indigenous communities. Although mission towns had been the first to be "liberated," by late 1804 pueblos de indios, home to Indians still under the encomienda or subject to personal service, were also put into "liberty with individual property."[93] But there was no clear process to implement these blueprints. Thus, while an 1804 "Instruction" laid out twenty-five chapters detailing what was to be done, little of this found its way into practice.[94] Nor did Doblas's proposal of 1805 see the light of day. Some towns were "liberated"; others remained under the control of administrators. Meanwhile, debts appear not to have been cleared in any systematic fashion. The situation remained fluid and uneven. The number of mulattoes, mestizos, and poor Spaniards, many of them "free" peasants or laborers, continued to grow, giving rise to a proletariat or semi-proletariat of agricultural peons, tree fellers, shipbuilders, river and road transport folk, and tobacco processors.[95] Few owned or controlled land. Those who found wage labor, generally poorly paid, faced limited options for survival.

Partly for this reason, those who got their livings in the wage economy, Indians and non-Indians alike, tended to locate in or near Indigenous communities. Proximity to Indian towns, especially former mission communities, seemed to be a broad strategy among wage laborers, recognition that such collectivities, for all their troubles, might still buoy those who otherwise bobbed alone in the churn of an unsettled economic world.[96] Because they represented concentrated pools of labor, these communities attracted employers seeking workers, which gave an incentive to mestizos and other non-Indians to live nearby. In the final analysis, most Indigenous people—those who still resided in former mission towns as well as residents of pueblos de indios—inhabited a tangled reality in which the individual liberty of having to shift for oneself overlapped with the continued clout (and corruption) of Spanish administrators and even encomenderos, in a context of uncertain individual prospects and increasingly fragile community obligations.

Meanwhile, those with capital had been snapping up property for decades, often at the expense of Indigenous towns. Spaniards were "concentrating generation by generation on Indian lands . . . occupying more and more space to the detriment of the Indians," one report had observed in 1781.[97] This was not supposed to have happened, but the trend was unmistakable and much advanced by 1800, driven by changes in the broader economy, especially the new emphasis on trade in wheat, leather, and sugar for export. Within Indian communities, by contrast, most production continued to be for subsistence or at most local exchange, and family farming remained central, though rarely without the need to seek paid labor in the expanding *conchabo* market.[98]

For a growing number of ordinary people, *liberty* implied a life of roaming the countryside, alternately working for wages and living off the land. When most Indigenous folk had been anchored in mission towns or tied to an encomienda, elites had been unconcerned by those who seemed adrift in the economy. Now landowners and officials saw something else: idleness and vagrancy. They began to worry that ordinary people were finding ways to "live almost without working."[99] Although depleted by opportunists, herds of feral cattle allowed many to eat relatively well without having any obvious fixed residence or obligation. Responding to these concerns in the 1790s, Governor Rivera had introduced a new system of labor control, requiring all persons of working age to carry an employment card stating their employer's name and subjecting them to arrest if they could not produce it upon demand.[100] Officially, the point was to make sure people were working rather than playing at dice, drinking, or otherwise wasting time. It was a myth, of course, that people could live without working, but fear of it demonstrates the gathering anxieties of elites as an economy in flux continued to move toward liberty understood as the necessity to seek wage labor.

Amid the upheaval, former mission communities plunged into a desperate state. In 1805, the Protector of the Indians urged attention to their plight. People were dying for lack of hospitals, healers, and medicines. Communities were being worn down by overwork and hunger, one reason so many wanted to leave, he said. In two years, there will not be a head of cattle left for them to eat. And yet, claimed the Protector, there was a bright side to their despair: "What would be a great disgrace for the state of the community is in part a happy outcome for the establishment of liberty, because lacking any help with rations or animals, the Indians

are having to cultivate their fields with the work necessary for their subsistence."[101] In other words, things were dire indeed, but liberty might be
achieved by the threat of starvation. Or as the new governor of the former
mission towns put it in a letter to the viceroy in late 1805, without the help
of the community and experiencing "all the effects of slavery, this miserable situation has done the good of forcing them to seek their subsistence
through personal labor."[102]

The mission Guaraní appear not to have shared his optimism or his
sangfroid. Yet they seemed to understand that the die had been cast. They
had no choice but to seek their chances in the economic chaos created
by reform. In 1807, letters from leaders of the communities raised "a sad
clamor" against the "demoralizing servitude under greedy and despotic
administrators" and asked that "full liberty" finally be extended to all,
so that they might be *useful* to themselves, the town, the state," echoing the new mantra of the times.[103] Every day that passes without liberty
brings us closer to misery, they complained. Similarly, the cabildo of Itatí
wrote to the governor noting that one half of the town had been put into
liberty, while the other half had not, which was leading the whole town
"to ruin." There simply were not enough residents any longer, and all the
tradesmen had already been "freed," though even they were unable to
make a go of it in the wider economy.[104]

The bishop of Buenos Aires echoed these concerns in 1810, though
with a studied dispassion.[105] Many had left their towns to sign on as peons to Spaniards, wrote the prelate, abandoning their assigned lands and
forgetting the "prosperity" of their own families. Yet few had flourished
after separating from their communities. This did not "weaken the general principles" of economic liberty, he hastened to add. Those who had
stayed in the communities lacked the "condition and temperament" to
succeed individually, because they would not work hard enough. None of
which is particularly surprising, said the bishop. The Jesuits had understood how to govern these people. Reforms had failed to reproduce their
success. Now "liberty" was the only way forward. All the Indians must be
put to the same fate, he declared, extinguishing the community system in
its entirety, so that each and every one of them "will experience the benefit that is promised, or suffer the work and calamity which perhaps will
make them more miserable to the extent they long for liberty."

This statement, like the protector's and the governor's, did not come
out of the blue. It resonated with ideas advanced in England by Joseph

Townsend in *A Dissertation on the Poor Laws* (1786) (and later extended and systematized by Thomas Malthus). Against the backdrop of English enclosure, the narrowing of subsistence options, and a massive displacement of people from countryside to cities, Townsend had put it bluntly: the poor should have no alternative to facing the "struggle for existence." Like Juan Fernandez Island in the South Seas, where goats and dogs came to a bloody equilibrium by the workings of predation and population, the poor should have only the option to survive, or not, without succor in the fight. And in this ordeal, averred Townsend, one force alone could be counted on above all others to make people work: "In general, it is only hunger which can spur and goad them on to labour."[106] Thus would work, or rather the physical capacity to labor, come to be imagined as a commodity distinct and separate from any particular social arrangement, thereby subjecting the Guaraní to the freedom of those with the means to truck and trade in the lives of others.

There is every reason to believe that these and related ideas were influencing policy in Spanish America. Though Townsend's text was not translated into Spanish at the time, his ideas were likely familiar to many within Spanish officialdom. Townsend had traveled through Spain in the late 1780s, meeting the Count of Campomanes, then the highest minister to the king, and other officials.[107] Campomanes read English and had a keen interest in such matters. He had referred to "political economy" in 1750, its first recorded use in Spanish. In 1764, he had called for an end to price controls on grain, even during periods of severe shortage. Controls did not work, he argued, and private parties were under no obligation of "commutative justice" or "in conscience" to obey them.[108] He had also written the brief justifying the Jesuits' ejection in 1767. He was part of a generation of leading figures in Spanish administration and thought and of a younger generation in the colonies who read Adam Smith's *Wealth of Nations* in English and French, and later in Spanish, when a translation cleansed of moral and religious errors came out in 1794.[109] During these years, political economy had become the subject of "polite conversations" in Madrid.[110]

So, when the bishop of Buenos Aires stated flatly that Spaniards must be allowed to live in Indian towns so as to promote competition and rowel the Guaraní to productive work, regardless of the dangers this might present to the Indians, he was not saying anything especially controversial. Here, ultimately, was the *liberty* so long touted as the answer to economic woes, the other side of the coin of gain: people should have no refuge from shifting for themselves, even when conditions promised little more than hardship or worse. Only thus, concluded His Excellency, will the Indians awaken from "their simple inaction and natural passivity."[111]

*   *   *

Of course, the mission Guaraní had been anything but passive. By 1810, communities had spent over five decades trying to conserve themselves in the face of radical disruption. Reforms had failed because the ideas behind newly drafted laws were never quite equal to the economic free-for-all that the expulsion of the Jesuits had unleashed. Before 1767, the mission world had been a materially successful pact between the Guaraní, the Jesuits, and the Spanish monarchy. That accord, premised on Hapsburg openness to mediated outcomes, came apart after the Jesuits' exile, as Bourbon concern for reasons of state took center stage. The mission Guaraní were not consulted on the substance of proposed reforms, and their complaints were registered case by case, at best, rather than in their totality. Policy makers sought not an equilibrium between the missions and the monarchy but their submission to an economic agenda premised on new conceptions of property, labor, utility, competition, exchange, consumption, liberty, individualism, emulation, and inequality.

The point of reform had been to convert the Guaraní into factors of production and consumption, a means to economic ends. New opportunities for individual gain were supposed to motivate and educate the Guaraní to what they needed to do. In fact, they empowered those—administrators, priests, well-off Spaniards, and perhaps a few Indigenous men—who were poised to profit from the missions' collapse. Though some in official circles recognized that administrators' venality and opportunists' greed contributed to the failure of reforms, the emergent consensus blamed the Guaraní: where once the mission residents had been considered exemplary vassals contributing to the common good, now Spanish officials saw lazy and inconstant Indians, susceptible only to the prod of hunger, an attitude toward peasants and workers increasingly common among elites in Europe as well. Instead of ensuring a smooth transition to the new regime, reforms had exposed the towns to raw private gain from within and without. The outcome had been a chaos from which almost everyone, save the Guaraní, stood to benefit.

The dilemma facing communities, therefore, was not a stark matter of accepting the system of liberty over the system of community. Ex-mission towns, and even pueblos de indios by this time, almost surely did not see the world in such binary terms. A simple complaint of corruption by a Guaraní mayordomo helps make the point. In 1808, the cabildo of Santa Rosa de Lima, once a prosperous mission community, accused Tomás Esperati, the Guaraní mayordomo, of irregularities.[112] There were three charges. One involved straightforward abuse of position: Esperati had taken community property for himself, appropriating the town's milk cows, as well as many of its mules, horses, and oxen, and he had grossly underpaid the bakers so that he could control the sale of bread. The second allegation raised the problem of accounting for "value." "Where is the real value of the celeste linen that *our* warehouse bought for our priest and where are the five pesos that the same priest gave to [Esperati] for a burial?" asked the cabildo (my emphasis). They should have been used to buy cloth for residents and silver for the church. Here was an understanding of value in distinct but overlapping registers—things could be denominated in money and, at the same time, be a matter of communal ritual obligations. Many other things have gone missing, stated the petition. They had had abundant wheat before "liberty"; but now they had no idea where it was. "The value of what enters [the warehouse] we do not see," said the complaint, because Esperati refuses to keep an accurate ledger. He looks out "only for himself and his own good," which is why he took the position. In effect, the mayordomo stood accused of pursuing private accumulation at community expense. His control of accounts and the value they represented along with his lack of responsibility to the wider community gave him a power in the emerging economy of gain that caciques could not claim. The final charge advanced a different concern: Esperati had failed in his reciprocal duties. He had eschewed common labor, refusing "to come with us on jobs outside of town, nor has he gone with us to the division of calves and foals." And he had held the festivities of the patron saint "without the customary pomp and the gifts of invitation" lavished on guests from other towns. Festivities and the gifts that went with them, though frowned on by Spanish reformers as profligate, remained crucial to Guaraní communal life. To have given them short shrift, as Esperati had, likely to save himself the expense of putting them on, constituted as important a breach of responsibility as abuse of position and the hiding of value.

The willingness to complain equally about matters falling within the transactional sphere and concerns rooted in substantive mutuality suggests that Guaraní communities and their people may have sought above all to find their own point of balance between these realms in elaborating their economy—though they had to do so in the face of a worldview that acknowledged only one as a matter of human nature.

8

The Only Example in the
History of the Universe

The whole bent of what they do is to strengthen those natural ties
by which society is principally cemented.

Edmund Burke, 1770

He denies that they have any right in morality to the assistance of
their neighbors.

William Godwin, 1820

IN THE EARLY 1790S, an embittered, sleep-deprived Jesuit, weary from
prayer and devotions decided to set the record straight on the Paraguay
missions. Father José Peramás had spent over a decade in the missions between 1755 and the Jesuits' expulsion in 1767. Exiled to the Italian town
of Faenza, he and a handful of companions kept to themselves, avoiding other clergy. When he was not on his knees or in bed, Peramás was
at his writing desk. He died in May 1793. His brother, also a Jesuit, posthumously published Peramás's curious tract called *Commentaries on Guaraní Government Compared to Plato's Republic.*[1] Other than the fact that
the missions had become reality and the Republic had remained a fig-
ment of Plato's imagination, Peramás found little to distinguish the two.
In hasty pages alternating between Plato's description of the Republic and
his own portrayal of the missions, Peramás railed against "liberal philosophers" of "these times" who raise "self-love" above virtues and morals
and in this "century rich of excess . . . absolve themselves of all blame and
judge it to be the greatest good."[2]

By the 1790s, Peramás was whispering to the wind. For half a century,
the remote mission world of South America had shone brightly in the firmament of European thought. Philosophers, historians, novelists, play-
wrights, encyclopedists, poets, political economists, wags, and not a few
middlebrow autodidacts with philosophical pretensions had held up the
Paraguay missions as a mirror to Europe itself. During these decades, Europeans too were experiencing the vertigo of accelerated transformation,
not least the triumph of a social order premised on gain as a mainspring

of social life. Large questions hung in the air. If all individuals pursued only their self-interest, a notion clearly at odds with once-dominant understandings of virtue and morality, what would restrain worst impulses? Put another way, could individual self-love be unleashed without sparking social and moral chaos? Such questions were hardly new, but with the technological, social, and cultural changes of the latter half of Europe's eighteenth century—rural enclosure, urbanization, steam engines, factories, rising levels of inequality, widespread precarity among the poor in cities and countryside alike—they were newly urgent.

*   *   *

Of friendship and self-love

In the realm of ideas, such concerns trace to Machiavelli and Hobbes. Machiavelli had proposed in *The Prince* (1513) that human nature had become so intractable that Christian morality, by itself, could no longer guide rulers. Princes therefore needed to lead by the dictates of power, informed by a wider prudential understanding of men's actual conduct in the world, especially their selfishness. This notion had provoked fierce opposition, especially from Jesuits, fearing that if rulers could not be counted on to act according to Christian charity, morality and even religion might be doomed.[3] In the mid-seventeenth century, Thomas Hobbes, reacting to the chaos of the English civil war (1642–1651), argued that civic order resulted not from a divinely ordained predisposition to social life but from fear of a war of "all against all"; "Man is a wolf to man," he claimed, after Plautus. In a covenant "extorted by fear," men in a state of nature surrendered their liberty to the state—the Leviathan—to avoid death at each other's hands.[4] While neither Machiavelli nor Hobbes spoke explicitly of a society of gain, both recognized the growing tendency in early modern Europe for individual self-concern and the use of money to corrode morals and solidarities.

By the late seventeenth century, a dwindling number of thinkers continued to insist with any vigor that human nature remained rooted in sociability. For these, Hobbes's Leviathan did not solve the problem of human conflict so much as naturalize it and root it within social order. In 1699, for example, the Earl of Shaftesbury argued against a foundational selfishness. Human beings, he wrote, naturally seek "social love, friendship, gratitude, or whatever else of a generous kind" over "self-interesting passions." People are at bottom "rational and sociable" and their end is "society." The appeal to self-interest, claimed Shaftesbury, hid a ruthless logic in which "Kindness of every sort, Indulgence, Tenderness, Compassion, and . . . all natural Affection, should be industriously suppressed [as] mere folly, and weakness of nature."[5] In essence, Shaftesbury rejected Hobbes's claim that there was no human impulse to society except insofar as fearful individuals yielded their freedom to the state to save themselves from each other.

Even those who disagreed with Shaftesbury were not invariably convinced that a covenant of fear could solve the problem of self-interest unleashed. John Locke, relying on notions of natural rights, argued that making each individual the "proprietor of his own person" might restrain the free-for-all a universal "state of war" implied, so long as government ensured private property.[6] Others considered that self-love might be led to curb itself, apart from political arrangements. Directly repudiating Shaftesbury, Bernard Mandeville in 1705 compared human society to a "grumbling hive" of bees, where "every Part was full of vice, / Yet the whole Mass a Paradise." From this paradox, he drew the insight that "private vices"—including avarice, prodigality, luxury, and even fraud—might result in "publick benefits." Indeed, without vices, Mandeville seemed to say, society could not prosper, for "Lust" and "Vanity" were "Ministers of Industry." He did not completely deny the need for a restraining reason—"Vice is beneficial found, / When it's by Justice lopt and bound"—but he did not explain how justice should be discerned and administered. Nevertheless, he concluded, circumstances in Europe were such that any effort to ground social order in "Bare Vertue" was "a vain Eutopia seated in the Brain."[7]

Over following decades, the vaporous notion that self-interest might check itself began to condense into a solid idea.[8] Alexander Pope wondered whether man's "self-love" might not "become the cause / of what restrains him . . . / 'Til jarring int'rests of themselves create / Th' according music of a well mixed State," allowing "Self-Love and Social be the same."[9] Pope's view was neither a total surrender to Hobbes nor a complete rejection of Shaftesbury, for it was reason aligned with virtue that would assure individual self-control and lead "jarring int'rests" into concert. But by allowing a positive role for self-love, Pope seemed to confirm that deep change was afoot.

The philosophical baseline for these debates, as it had been for those who criticized gain in the sixteenth and seventeenth centuries, was Aristotle's notion that human beings were by nature inclined to live together. Society, in turn, rested on friendship, the highest expression of which was the pursuit of life in common among those alike in virtue and who wished each other well in all things. Social life and its politics were the means to educate men in the virtues that would promote "the good life, or felicity" of individuals and the whole. This could happen only through the right actions of virtuous lawmakers and citizens. Virtue was easily subverted. Those who occupied themselves "wholly in the making of money," the desire for which was "unlimited," had little thought for the wider impact of their actions.[10] The pursuit of wealth for its own sake—what Aristotle called "chresmatics"—tended to corrupt men and incline them to the "art of acquisition." Aquinas had accepted this idea but modified it. Recognizing that men were naturally sociable, he understood that they were also driven by practical interests. This material and commercial impulse could be beneficial, he allowed, but only if governed by virtuous action—specifically, Christian charity—oriented to the common good. This, ultimately, was the stance adopted by the Jesuits.

What Machiavelli, Hobbes, Shaftesbury, Mandeville, Pope, and many others were debating was whether and to what extent some version of the Aristotelian (and for Catholics, Thomistic) paradigm could or should continue to serve as a ground of European social relations. By the late seventeenth century, self-love, especially that oriented to commerce and the accumulation of money, had so suffused collective life in parts of Europe as to color all thinking about social order. The question of how to maintain the "harmony" necessary for social unity remained up for grabs through the eighteenth century.[11] Broad opinion had not so much turned against morality and virtue as that men seemed to behave as though they no longer mattered in practical affairs, particularly in the face of unprecedented opportunities for individual enrichment in the commercial sphere. This is what led Spinoza, Vico, and later Rousseau to accept what amounted to a new axiom of political theory: that men should be considered "as they are" rather than as they ought to be.[12] Of course, what men actually were who gave no thought to morals and virtue could be discerned only by observing their actions in the world. What could be glimpsed was not encouraging. During the first decades of the eighteenth century, the picture coming into focus was of men, typically men of commerce, who gave free rein to individual material self-interest, heedless of the state of their souls or the effects of their actions on a shared human world. It was to this fact that Pope and Mandeville proposed the idea that perhaps the very vices condemned by an increasingly languid morality could, somehow, check themselves in service of the greater good.

David Hume took an important step toward formalizing this notion. In the section of *A Treatise on Human Nature* (1739) entitled "On Morals," he acknowledged that the self-regarding "avidity . . . of acquiring goods and possessions" bore a uniquely ruinous potential because, as a motivation, it was "insatiable, perpetual, universal, and directly destructive of society"—and "there is scarce anyone" who is not driven by it. Nothing in the human mind, neither affection nor reason, was strong enough to "counter-balance the love of gain, and render men fit members of society." Restraining gain, therefore, could not be a matter of "the wickedness or goodness of human nature," insisted Hume. Rather, the "passion of self-interest" would have to restrain itself. He is less than clear on how this would happen, though the "stability" of private property might allow for "mutual restraint and forbearance."[13] Regarding those who had little or no property, he was silent.

The broad idea that the pursuit of gain could palliate its own ills was quickly taken up by thinkers eager to promote prosperity while ensuring social order. The payoff was obvious: self-interested commercial pursuit promised to increase society's overall wealth. And yet, in the traditional view, the pursuit of gain for its own sake amounted to the deadly passion of avarice, reflecting a moral intuition that unchecked self-interest trampled human sociability. But a new sensibility centuries in the making was emerging in Europe. For instance, Hume argued that commercial striving could be distinguished from other baneful "passions" by two facts. First, the desire for money was less dangerous than the pursuit of power, so long as moneymaking did not mix with politics. Second, the acquisition of money seemed rational in ways politics did not. As Hume put it, because "avarice, or desire of gain, is a universal passion which operates at all times, in all places, and upon all persons," it was unlike the baser and more fickle passions, which varied by person and circumstance.[14] "Avarice" could thus serve as the "spur to industry" and the "desire of gain" be redefined as a calculable "interest" sharing none of the moral and practical inconveniences of the inconstant passions or the caprices of politics.[15]

And because, on this view, commercial interests were universal and predictable, their interplay might of itself check excess and so avert the moral chaos implicit in the idea that individuals would pursue their gain heedless of pernicious effects on wider society.

"Paraguay can furnish [an] example"

These questions, as well as the anxieties they betrayed, were the opening through which the mission world of Paraguay entered European intellectual life for several decades between the 1730s and the early nineteenth century. Texts on the missions had gained a learned readership by the end of the seventeenth century. John Locke knew of Father Montoya's *Spiritual Conquest* (1639), as well as the writings of Fathers Anton Sepp and Nicolás del Techo, who had spent time in the missions.[16] In these accounts, Locke read of martyrdom-seeking Jesuits who had braved unimaginable conditions to peaceably bring bellicose cannibals to Christianity and civilization. After 1700, such accounts piqued a more general interest in Paraguay. Techo's *History of the Provinces of Paraguay of the Society of Jesus* (1673) was translated from Latin and Spanish into French in 1703 and English in 1732. In 1717, French royal engineer Amédée-François Frezier published a chronicle of his voyage to South America between 1712 and 1714. An English translation appeared almost immediately, and another, updated, in 1735.[17] In the original French version, Frezier detailed the "genius and constitution" of South America's inhabitants, "Indians as well as Spaniards," and discussed the trade South America had with Europe. Readers of the 1735 English version would have come across a final chapter absent from the French original (and from the 1717 English version) entitled "An Account of the Settlement, Commerce and Riches of the Jesuits in Paraguay."

To this point, Paraguay had been little known beyond erudite circles. The English version of Frezier's book changed that, sparking broad interest in the missions. The added chapter was a fevered account. In a dozen pages, it laid out many of the tropes that came to dominate how Europeans thought about the missions: their wealth, the commanding role of the Jesuits, the meekness of the Guaraní, and the need to "free" them to engage in trade. According to the chapter, three hundred thousand families lived in the missions (as many as 1.5 million people), a gross exaggeration—though the scale of it was part of what astonished. The Indians were "laborious and tractable," controlled in "entire Submission" with "Supreme Command" by forty missionaries. Each priest governed ten thousand families, who obeyed "with the exactest Regard and Awe." The region was abundant in gold and silver (also false), and the Jesuits reaped all the benefits of the Indians' labor, earning the "Revenue of a Sovereign," by making themselves "Absolute Lords and Masters" and the Guaraní "so many slaves." The Indians would be "free" and "improve their talents," said the writer, only if they had property and used money so that the "Circulation of Trade" could begin in earnest—a point made and disputed repeatedly over succeeding decades.[18]

In the early 1740s, Jesuits began to respond in print to such accusations. Lodovico Muratori's *Il cristianesimo felice* (Happy Christianity; 1743) was the first book-length text to exert lasting impact in European intellectual circles. From his desk in Modena (he never visited South America), Father Muratori described the missions in elegiac terms, detailing their civil and ecclesiastical government. Portraying them as a kind of Christian utopia, he lavished attention on economic arrangements and daily lives of mission residents. Among the first to use the missions to comment on contemporary European life, he offered small asides to prick readers' consciences through comparisons that did not always favor Europe. For instance, he noted that Europeans, unlike the Guaraní, believed themselves happy only if they possessed many things and much money, dressed pompously, and ate extravagantly. By contrast, the missions boasted hospitals that served all, schools for the children, and apothecaries for those needing medicine, unlike so much of Europe. Spaniards, he noted, used slaves, but the Guaraní never had. And whereas in Europe, property and greed had led to a "disorder that disturbs society," in Paraguay the lack of gold and silver and the absence of money and property allowed the Indians to conserve "peace, friendship, and unity." For their part, the Jesuits acted disinterestedly and respected each person, ensuring the "harmony" and "public good" essential to community.[19]

After Muratori's book, the missions became a vehicle for commenting on Europe's dire moral circumstances. In his *Spirit of the Laws* (1748), an essential text of modern constitutional theory, Montesquieu compared the Paraguayan missions to Sparta, finding in them a vital lesson in good government, the only such example amid the "dregs and corruption" of modern times when men of affairs spoke only of manufactures, commerce, finance, wealth, and luxury. Government there had been made to serve human happiness in a spirit of virtue and "public interest." Any future effort to do the same in Europe would need to emulate the missions: establish the community of goods (as Plato himself had counseled, Montesquieu noted), protect citizens from those who ruin their morals, and ensure that commerce be carried on only by the community and not by private persons. It was especially important, stated Montesquieu, to forbid the circulation of money, for money simply multiplied desires infinitely and led men to "corrupt one another," as the dark panorama of contemporary European life demonstrated.[20]

Montesquieu advanced this comparison as part of his larger argument regarding the sources of republican government: "Paraguay," as he put it, "can furnish [an] example" of how to govern well and "render men happier." Morality should guide "ordinary passions." Virtue, because it sought to elevate the common good above private interests, remained foundational for any republic: when "virtue ceases . . . avarice enters everywhere."[21] This understanding shared much with Aristotle's account of virtue (as well as his suspicion of money and wealth) and with Aquinas's concern for the common good. But Montesquieu shifted subtly into a new register. For Aristotle, the virtues implied no particular sacrifice. The pursuit of virtue had defined what it was to be human and to live in human society, for it was only through the cultivation of the virtues that men learned to recognize the good and conduct themselves correctly in the world and in relation to power. Amid the ruckus of the unabashed pursuit of gain in the commercial realm, Montesquieu sought primarily to protect society against self-interest unbound. He did not oppose "the spirit of commerce" as such, for it could conduce to peace among nations. But it did not always do so among individuals. For in places where people were moved only by gain, there was a "traffic of all the humane, all the moral virtues," such that things were done "only for money." In such places, a certain "sentiment of exact justice" led people to adhere too "rigidly to the rules of private interest," to the neglect of others.[22] The answer to this dilemma in any given society was to instill "political virtue" among those who governed, which required a "renunciation of self, . . . always a painful choice."[23] In Paraguay, said Montesquieu, the self-renunciation of Jesuits, who dressed in rags and died penniless, was a triumph of virtue that had allowed the missions to achieve an extraordinary prosperity unknown among Spaniards and other Europeans captivated by gain. In short, while he bore no great love for the Jesuits, Montesquieu admired them for their willingness to use power in the service of "human happiness," a rare enough thing, he felt, and necessary for any viable political order.[24]

"Sublime ideas"

Montesquieu's concern for the fate of morality and virtue in public life was widespread in the middle of the eighteenth century. In 1754, Rousseau published his *Discourse on the Origin of Inequality*. A year later, he followed with the *Discourse on Political Economy*, initially published as an entry in the *Encyclopédie* as "Economy: Moral and Political." In the first, Rousseau offered a scathing critique of a contemporary Europe where "avarice" had allowed the "few to gorge themselves with trifles, while the starving multitude want the bare necessities of life." For Rousseau, this was not a result of a predatory human nature à la Hobbes— men were not "naturally wicked"—but an outcome of social processes themselves. "Savage men" had not known good or evil nor "rivalry and competition" or "opposition of interests." Society, by contrast, might have an "air of harmony" but was in fact riven by the universal effort to "profit at the expense of others." Society was a "horrible state of war"—"a new state of nature"—that had destroyed "natural liberty" and fixed the law of "property and inequality . . . for the advantage of a few ambitious individuals."[25]

Where the *Discourse on Inequality* proceeded from first principles, the *Discourse on Political Economy* spoke to historical conditions. Economy, claimed Rousseau, connoted nothing more than the wise and legitimate government of the whole, whether the household or the state. But urbanization, a stress on commerce over agriculture, on industry over craft, and the fact that human relations had ceased to have any "sinews other than money" had brought society to the point that "private interest" had supplanted "public interest." "Opulence and misery" had led to the "mutual hatred of citizens" so that the "fundamental conventions" of "social union" had collapsed, leaving only force to prevent "dissolution of the civil state."[26] Here Rousseau was reacting to parallel concerns. His references to money and private interest reflected a deep worry for the direction and role of "economy" in society: he feared that "self-love" would run riot as inequality slouched over European social life. At the same time, he was also trying to answer Hobbes's notion that the Leviathan could contain the war-of-all-against-all. For Rousseau, *economy* was necessarily moral as well as political, since individuals needed to act in morally responsible ways in order to sustain the substance of social life.

Rousseau was hardly alone in his disquiets. In September 1755, the *Journal Oeconomique* (perhaps the first journal of political economy) published a short essay addressing similar worries. In "A Project for a Singular Establishment," an anonymous author sought to defend the idea of community against the storm battering society.[27] "The greater part of men," stated the short article, lacked a "union of fraternity and concord" and so were "not as happy as they could be." Against this "general disorder," men should "join . . . amongst themselves" in order to "help each other reciprocally" in the spirit of the "mutual aid common to all societies." In these intentional communities, people would work to "lessen their pains and seek the pleasantness and sweetness of life." Money would not circulate. Children would be raised in common. The community would remain under the authority of the king, who would shelter it from harm. Already there were ten such establishments in France, noted the author. The article did not mention the Paraguay missions, but it might as well have, given how the reading public was coming to understand them. Of course, Rousseau in 1754–1755 and the article's author were operating at completely different scales. Rousseau was speaking of society writ large. The article seemed resigned to thinking small. The distance between the two views posed deep questions: Could the course of society as a whole still be shaped, or had scale so changed and things gone so far down the path of individual self-interest that only small, contrarian gestures might any longer be imagined? How could human beings avoid the "thousand disorders" of a turbulent, competitive, money-soaked Europe?

To answer these questions, Rousseau articulated a radical alternative to Hobbes's bleak view of human possibility.[28] Drawing on nearly two centuries of writing about the New World's Indigenous people, he argued that primitive men had lived in a "state of nature *in its first purity*."[29] They differed from modern men in lacking both the instinct to inequality and the capacity for it; "wandering up and down the forests" in oblivious and solitary liberty, they had had no ties among themselves, not even to fight with each other. Even so, they had possessed one "natural virtue" prior to all reflection, reason, morality, or law: a desire and capacity to assist "those we see suffering."[30] This primeval state of nature had at a certain point given way to social life. Only *within* society had the thickening of exchange taught men to seek individual advance at each other's expense. In this new social arrangement, competition and inequality had vanquished "notions of good and all principles of equity," delivering men to "the law of the strongest."[31] The challenge was to figure a stance that would allow human beings to thrive in this second, social state of nature. Put another way, Rousseau was asking how "men being taken as they are" could learn to live together in community rather than be as wolves to each other.[32] His answer, given in two books published in 1762—*The Social Contract* and *Émile*—was education. In *The Social Contract*, he argued that a viable human order required that men be bound into a social unity. To bring about this "general will," men had to learn their obligations to each other and to the whole of society amid the "universal competition" of "private interests" that had made social life so fractious. *Émile* amounted to a pedagogy that would allow social man to recover the empathy of "nature in its first purity," now within society as "a new state of nature."[33]

Although Rousseau knew of the missions, they did not figure in his texts. There are two likely reasons for the this. First, the times were against it. Animus against the Jesuits rose to a pitch across Europe and with it suspicion of the missions. Despite Montesquieu's praise for them and even though the *Encyclopédie* entry on Paraguay had lauded them as a "masterwork of competence and politics," the mission world had come under intense criticism in France as Rousseau was writing. One sensational tract claimed the fathers had fomented the Guaraní War of 1755 and had installed "Nicholas I, Emperor of the Mamelucs" to rule over all of South America.[34] Rousseau's nemesis Voltaire mocked the missions and depicted the Jesuits as self-serving theocrats in his play *Candide*. And in what appears to have been an effort to undermine Rousseau's broad reliance on primitive men as a vehicle for philosophical reflection, Father Louis-Bertrand Castel (a Jesuit) explained that missionaries never really detached "savages" from lives poor, incommodious, laborious, and dull. At best, even in Paraguay, they might succeed in getting them to accept the rudiments of religion and thereby save their souls.[35] A second, deeper reason for not engaging the missions may have been that they did not fit well with Rousseau's argument. If, as Voltaire claimed, the Jesuits had succeeded in subduing the Guaraní by despotism, and if the Guaraní, as Castel implied, had followed meekly out of a religious impulse, there was little hope that education to reason and moral capacity would have the desired effect. Rousseau's goal was to establish a new social order anchored by a common set of values he called "civil religion," not to establish a Christian utopia à la Muratori. Both politically and philosophically, in other words, the missions may have seemed poor grist for Rousseau's mill.

Unease over the "general disorder" of mid-eighteenth century Europe was not limited to the rarefied circles of Enlightenment philosophes. In England, which had no "Jesuit problem" to speak of, middlebrow readers became avidly interested in Paraguay as a mirror for reflecting on their own angst regarding society's direction. In 1753, London's *Gentleman's Magazine and Historical Chronicle* ran a series of pieces on the "Jesuit's polity in Paraguay." Readers learned of the most "extraordinary commonwealth" in faraway South America. Established under almost impossibly difficult circumstances, the jungle missions of the Jesuits might offer "counsel and instructions" to the English in relations with their own "savages" in North America.[36] A few years on, Edmund Burke's widely read *An Account of the Settlements of America* devoted a chapter to the missions, concluding that they possessed "some extraordinary perfection" that had "unit[ed] a perfect subjection to an entire content and satisfaction of the people," a lesson, perhaps, for those who "seldom think of using any other instruments than force or money."[37] In this, the Guaraní were not unlike Indigenous people in North America, of whom Burke noted that "the whole bent of what they do is to strengthen those natural ties by which society is principally cemented."[38] Excerpting Jorge Juan's account of the missions, the *Gentleman's Magazine* of London noted in 1763 that the "commonwealth of the Jesuits" in Paraguay was a "prudent oeconomy" wholly dominated by the fathers.[39] Ambitious readers might peruse *The Modern Part of an Universal History*, a multivolume history of the world from earliest times, which contained a significant chapter on Paraguay. The Jesuits had converted the Guaraní "without shedding a drop of blood . . . something quite new to the world."[40] These Indians lived in a "system of civil policy, not to be paralleled in the annals of mankind," that had inspired in them "a love of order, society, temperance, frugality, and every other virtue, which can humanize the mind and conduct to temporal and eternal happiness." That the Jesuits had of late been undone by their own "pride and haughtiness" was no reason to condemn the excellence of what had been accomplished in so distant a place with such unpromising people.

Despite growing rancor against the Jesuits, some French writers continued to take lessons from Paraguay. In 1758, Melchior Grimm, Rousseau's good friend, noted that while the Paraguay missions threatened to become "a powerful empire" that might subjugate all of South America and thereby "nullify the authority of Europe's kings in those climes," it was important to keep in mind that "the people of Paraguay [are] one of happiest living on earth." If there was any consolation for Europeans who could not count themselves so content, said Grimm, it was a prospective schadenfreude befitting Europe's moment, for even the fortunate Guaraní "will become corrupt one day like all the other people of the world, and their turn will come, as ours has."[41] A few years later, the Marquis d'Argenson's *Considerations on the Ancient and Present Government of France,* published posthumously in 1764, also offered a long chapter on Paraguay. It began by noting that there was in the New World "a country where the government might serve as an example for Europe, if the world were still in a state of innocence." Without great natural riches, the inhabitants of the missions had contrived to meet the "real needs" and satisfy "any wise and moderate object of desire," without the "ambition and avidity of Europeans."[42] What is striking about these two views is how they hedged their enthusiasm to head off any accusation that they were proposing Paraguay as an actual model for present European life—Grimm by prophesying the missions' unavoidable decline and d'Argenson by characterizing the missions in terms of an age of innocence long surpassed in Europe.

With such writers, a broad reading public continued to look to the missions as a way of confronting deep moral upheaval. In 1764, readers of Manchester's *The Polite Miscellany: containing a variety of food for the mind; being an elegant collection of moral, humorous, and improving essays* could finish a short piece entitled "Humorous reflections on the instability of worldly grandeur" only to encounter an article on the Paraguay missions. In it, gentle readers learned that in "The Country of the Missions," everything was "in common" and the Indians knew nothing of gold, silver, or money, as had once been the case in the ancient government of Sparta. This "odd, and out-of-the-way constitution in another hemisphere" was "perhaps the only example . . . to be found in the history of the universe."[43] Similarly, the *London Magazine, or Gentleman's Monthly Intelligencer* ran a series of articles in 1769 entitled "The State of the Jesuits in Paraguay." Drawing on Father Pierre Charlevoix's multivolume history of Paraguay, these monthly installments observed that among the Guaraní "*mine* and *yours* are unknown words." The absence of private property had allowed them to be bound in a "perfect union," where quarrels and lawsuits were unknown and the first virtue was charity. Everyone was employed and enjoyed true human liberty—that is, the capacity to live morally, more "taken up with the concerns of others than one's own." Put another way, in Paraguay, individual freedom and social concert had been harmonized, unlike what was happening among supposedly more civilized people. As though to drive the point home, these articles were interspersed with others pointing to the depravities of contemporary England, where even in Parliament there was a "public market . . . for conscience" that endangered virtue, liberty, and social unity, leaving "only prostitutes" where once there had been "free men."[44]

These juxtapositions suggest that the mission world provoked such intense interest because its very existence seemed to tack against the winds of self-love that had been whipping across Europe for some time. Machiavelli had proposed that morality was too slender a reed to bear the weight of power itself. Hobbes had worked his way from the unbridled violence of the English Civil War to a myth about human origins: men, left to their natural inclinations, would kill each other unless restrained. And yet, in the eighteenth century, self-interest seemed to have come into its own, occasioning a broad moral panic. Rousseau had responded by articulating an alternative to the seeming unavoidability of avarice and inequality: though easily corrupted in society, human beings could learn to construct a moral life together. The question was whether they would and, if so, how? Against this debate over the nature and future of human prospects, some saw in the Paraguay missions a hope that men might pass from a pre-social to a peaceful social existence without experiencing Europe's moral wreck. If this was true, then perhaps Hobbes had been wrong. So long as men were capable of improvement, morality might still have a spark of life. This left open the possibility that some program of political, legal, or educational reform—à la Shaftesbury, Montesquieu, or Rousseau—could ignite human society against the onslaught of self-interest.

From this vantage, Paraguay could seem as close to an actual idyl as modern humanity was likely to see—in the sense of an intentional community formed on the basis of first principles. The English translator (or perhaps the marketing folk?) of Charlevoix's *History of Paraguay* certainly thought so, emblazoning the frontispiece with the assurance that the book was "a Full and Authentic Account" of the establishments that had "realized the Sublime Ideas of FENELON, Sir THOMAS MORE, and

PLATO."[45] As Stelio Cro has noted, the mission world became "the first and only instance of a modern project" in which a "classical myth" came to be perceived as "historical reality."[46] Implications for social and political thought were profound. At a moment when the balance between individual (especially economic) freedom and social unity seemed menacingly unresolved, the missions' apparent virtue and harmony was comforting to many Europeans. If savage men could be brought to such a state, perhaps a virtuous society was not a "Eutopia seated in the Brain" after all.

This was the hope expressed in the myth of the Noble Savage, that shorthand for theories of human nature and the origins of society so widespread in European letters at this time.[47] The trope can be traced to Montaigne's essay "Of Cannibals." With wry wit, Montaigne had commented on contemporary European conditions by noting that the Tupinambá people of Brazil's Atlantic coast were no more "barbarous and savage" than any other nation, including European ones, notwithstanding the fact that from time to time they ate each other. Lacking arts or vices, they did not suffer the avarice or envy of Europeans and were perfectly adapted to their circumstances, surpassing in happiness and harmony "the fancy and even the wish and desire of philosophy itself."[48] According to Stephen Toulmin, Montaigne saw the world as consisting of "a multiplicity of people . . . with idiosyncratic viewpoints and life stories," one in which difference represented no threat, intellectual, cultural, or otherwise. In the context of eighteenth-century Enlightenment thought, however, particularity and heterogeneity had become problematic, for they could not so easily be reduced to stark reason nor readily harnessed to a universalizing narrative. Instead, a blander consternation with stubborn differences among human beings held sway.[49] And so it was that many who looked on the missions now saw only indolence among the Guaraní, who the Jesuits, by some genius, had managed to govern. Few paused to wonder what role the Guaraní themselves might have played in their own situation. Discourse about the missions, in other words, was a story Europeans were telling themselves about themselves through an imagined relationship to others, not a story that had an actual role for those others.

"Is there nothing beyond avarice?"

As the Jesuits came under deeper suspicion, the missions were drawn inescapably into Europe's political, theological, and intellectual struggles.

Champions of Enlightenment ideas then sweeping the continent—that cluster of concepts, intuitions, theories, and conceits that have grounded modern social and political thought ever since—found in the missions a convenient target. Voltaire described them sardonically as a "masterpiece of reason and justice" in which the Jesuits were "masters of everything, [while] the people have nothing."[50] Others took aim at the missions because they contravened new notions of individual liberty, especially from ecclesiastical tyranny. If mere savages could be brought to social unity and prosperity while retaining morality and virtue under the tutelage of Jesuits, as was often claimed, what did this imply of efforts to loosen the hold of religion and morality on social life as a precondition of human progress?

This was the question that led Jean d'Alembert, coeditor of the *Encyclopédie* until 1759, to write an anonymous tract against the Jesuits in 1765. Though concerned with conditions in France, d'Alembert explicitly invoked the missions. Europe, he noted, was on the cusp of a new era "not only in the history of the human mind, by the revolution which seems to be preparing itself in our opinions, but also in the history of states and empires." The Jesuits had opposed this reformation of the human order, revealing the breadth of their ambitions most clearly in Paraguay. Though the fathers had converted the Guaraní without violence, he allowed, the result had been pernicious, for the priests had established an illegitimate sovereignty aimed at the "governing of mankind" through the imposition of religion. Had they encountered as few obstacles to "domination" in Europe as in America, they might well have conquered France. This would have been a loss because "philosophy"—individual freedom, reason, progress—"has penetrated for the happiness of mankind." More barbarous men, like the Guaraní, could not enjoy this good fortune, asserted d'Alembert, for they knew only "the necessities of nature" and could aspire only to satisfy them. Thus, "liberty is a good not made for [the Indian]," because "he does not know how to profit from it." The Jesuits had fed the Guaraní, kept them busy, and blinkered them so they would not see their own "chains." Such people, "docile and meek," might benefit from the sort of rule the Jesuits had exercised in Paraguay, but Europeans born to individual liberty were another story.[51]

By denying the Guaraní any capacity or need for liberty, d'Alembert was directly challenging the savage man/noble savage as a point of departure for thinking about the contemporary European situation. Rousseau had argued that men had been free in a state of nature, concerned only with solitary subsistence. That liberty had become corrupted when they entered society. His goal in *The Social Contract* had been to reconcile liberty and social life for all human beings. D'Alembert began from a different premise. Precisely because they did not aspire to anything beyond subsistence, the Guaraní were incapable of profiting from liberty. In this view, to qualify for freedom, the Guaraní needed to do something with it, beyond attending to "the necessities of nature." They had failed to do so. Whatever had happened at the missions, the fathers, not the inert Guaraní were responsible for it. And since the Jesuits were opposed to the new "philosophy," it followed that what might appear to be a kind of perfection in the missions' government in no way bore on the circumstances of contemporary Europe. In declaring the Guaraní unfit for "liberty"—that quintessential "prerogative of man," according to the *Encylopédie* entry for the term[52]—d'Alembert made two points. First, liberty was not simply an inborn quality of being human; liberty befit only those who used it to progress. Second, by their failure, the Guaraní had placed themselves and all primitive peoples outside the pale of relevant humanity for purposes of political and philosophical reflection. His bottom line was clear: henceforth, Paraguay and other parables of primitive men should be ignored in debates about Europe's future.

D'Alembert's was hardly the final word on this subject, though his stance made clear that the missions and all references to savage peoples had become a sharp bone of ideological contention. Philosopher-historian Abbé Mably, for instance, critiqued the notion that liberty had meaning only in relation to the arrangements of a commercial society. In *Doubts Proposed to the Political Economists on the Natural and Essential Order of Political Societies* (1768), he rejected the assumption that private property and the inequality attending it were part of the "natural order." This point, Mably said, "remained unclear for a great number of readers." He began by asking what grounded the political economists' argument that personal liberty—which could be understood as property in one's own person—depended on the institution of private property in land. Land had not always been held privately and the appearance of private landed property was a historical occurrence, he wrote. Given this fact, what reason was there to suppose the property regime could not now be changed? The Iroquois and the Huron did not divide up land this way. Nor had the Spartans, who had usufruct rather than ownership. He pressed the point by noting that in Paraguay, the Jesuits had ensured that property was held in common, so that everyone had "useful" work and "the state" was the owner of all. "Who would not want to live in this Platonic society; and which of its citizens believes they have lost the property of their person, because they do not have patrimony of their own?" If, as the political economists say, the greatest happiness of the social body consists in the greatest abundance possible, how is it, asked Mably, that the inhabitants of Paraguay cannot be said happy?[53]

These were rhetorical questions. With them, Mably was challenging the assumption that only private property, competition, and gain could induce people to work. What proof did the political economists offer? Can it really be that only the "avidity to have, acquire and multiply" goods can make the land fertile? "Is there nothing beyond avarice . . . capable of moving the human heart?" Well-made laws could encourage citizens to work, rewarding each with their share of what was produced. The "natural order" championed by the political economists, argued the Abbé, was in reality a product of positive laws, no more natural than any other set of institutional arrangements. Moreover, once private property was established, inequality of fortunes invariably followed, interests became opposed, and the vices of wealth and poverty besotted the public spirit and corrupted civic mores. Is this what our Philosophers pin their hopes on for the world? After all, Mably insisted, history tells us that inequality of fortune is the torment of the people. For the rich always look down on those who "are condemned to work that they might live." And from this was born unjust and tyrannical government, partial and oppressive law—in short, "the calamities under which the people groan."[54]

Debates regarding liberty, morality, and political economy were the tinder onto which Abbé Raynal tossed his incendiary *A Philosophical and Political History of the Settlements and Trade of Europeans in the Two Indies*. First published in Paris in 1770, three years after the Jesuits' exodus from South America, this history of the "two Indies" opened a new, global front in discussions about Europe's past, present, and future. The book went through multiple editions in French during its first decade and was translated into English in 1777.[55] A compendium of pieces by various authors, the book was digressive, polemical, and contradictory. Its critique of European imperialism reached a wide public. Partly for this reason, it was denounced in the French parliament, banned, and publicly burned in 1781, its author hounded to exile in Geneva.

The work advanced several points. Among them, interspersed with commentary on contemporary European conditions, was a historical account of European expansion in the world since the sixteenth century. It acknowledged that "the refinement of European barbarity" in the name of trade and commerce had been inconsistent with good morals and had inflicted enormous suffering on non-European peoples across the globe (though, paradoxically, in a section authored by Diderot, it argued that commerce, properly framed and pursued, could bring about an era of peace in Europe). It noted the "immense differences" separating the savage, who had been "born in the center of liberty," and the civilized man, who had been "born in the shackles of slavery. " The savage man's "aversion . . . for our cities," arose from "the improper manner in which we have introduced ourselves into his forests."[56] There was much of Rousseau in this, except that now the savages were flesh-and-blood human beings in the flow of history, not mere chimeras of the philosophical imagination.

The "savage" thus became a crucial pivot for understanding the emerging role of economy, gain, and commerce in human affairs. The book made its case by establishing a clear contrast between Europeans and the Indigenous people of South America, especially regarding the instinct to avarice. In a deeply Rousseauian and anti-Hobbesian vein, Raynal argued that it was not "in the midst of forests, but in polished society, that we learn to despise and to distrust mankind." Whereas European merchants could be counted on to cheat the unsuspecting, savages "unrestrained by laws" treated others fairly in trade, a truth redounding "to the disgrace of our religion, of our policy, and of our morals." The dancing and singing of forest peoples bore an "almost natural expression of concord and friendship, of tenderness and pleasure," an empathy that allowed them to "feel what we affect to feel."[57] Here was the moral fantasy underlying the idea of the noble savage as a counterpoint to European depravity.

Raynal, trained by Jesuits, deepened this analysis by defending the Paraguay missions from detractors like d'Alembert, who dismissed their relevance to debates over European prospects. The Jesuits were far from blameless, he admitted, and in recent times they had pursued their own "sordid interest."[58] But allegations directed against the missions themselves and against the Guaraní had missed the mark. To those who said the Jesuits had tyrannized the Guaraní through religion, Raynal countered that the mission world had healed a deep division in modern society. Where Europe had long ago created a "discord" between civil and religious government that had "disturbed the harmony of all states," the Jesuits had found a way to unite the two to "promote a sturdy good in America." Like the Incas, they had established a social order free of money and without crime and punishment, a place where morals were "beautiful and pure," gentler even than in ancient Peru.[59]

Given the tenor of the times, Raynal felt compelled to respond to those who claimed that the Jesuit system had "retard[ed] the progress of population" among the Guaraní. This was an accusation rooted in the growing concern for political economy in Europe. The objections were of two sorts. The first claimed that the Jesuits had limited population growth among the Guaraní by imposing celibacy on them. At the time, wide opinion held that the only way to increase society's prosperity was to expand the population of laboring people. By forcing chastity on the Guaraní, it was said, the Jesuits had curbed economic growth in the whole Plata region and weakened imperial trade. Raynal answered by noting that it simply was not the true that the Jesuits had stymied Indian procreation—to the contrary. If population had not grown as smartly as it might have, climate, disease, and, frankly, the rapacity of ordinary Spaniards were to blame.[60] The second complaint came from "politicians" who asserted that slow growth among the Guaraní sprang "from their having no property." These naysayers argued that the Guaraní had been reduced to a "state of equality" and so had been unable to form any desire for "emulation" and any motive to "excel another"—the essential drivers of individual gain. Raynal agreed that property could serve as a "source of increase both of men and subsistence." But when "attended with avarice, ambition, luxury, a multitude of imaginary wants, and various other irregularities arising from the imperfections of our governments," it could have the opposite effect. In Paraguay, unlike Europe, "plenty was universal, and the public stores were filled"—no one went hungry and none were pushed to compete just to live. True, the Guaraní were not as industrious as they might have been, given as they were to "idleness, eating, and dancing." But they could be counted "happy" to the extent they had not suffered "want" as a goad to work and had no interest "in the multiplicity of enjoyments that our wants require." In other words, their wants, so different from Europeans', not the absence of property, explained why their economic progress had been slower than might be hoped.[61]

Raynal did not limit himself to responding to critics on their own terms. After refuting their charges, he made a final point that cut against all previous writing on Paraguay and the Guaraní and, by implication, all Indigenous people who had come under European domination in recent centuries. After all the objections had been met—the imposition of religion, the retardation of population growth, Guaraní lassitude—one fundamental question remained: Can it be supposed that the Guaraní retained nothing of their savage state of liberty? This might seem a nodding reference to the noble savage's liberty in the state of nature. For Raynal it was more, enough so that he flagged it for close attention: "Let the reader take no account of what hath been written, and reflect only upon the few lines I now shall add." The Jesuits' supporters and enemies alike had failed to take the Guaraní themselves much into account, said Raynal. Too many had supposed that the missions were entirely the work of the fathers. In fact, the Guaraní had never believed that they "owed" so very much to "the care" of their "legislators" and had all the while been well aware of the Jesuits' "despotism." Like men generally, the Guaraní understood that "all manner of authority is more or less odious." So when the Society had been expelled, the Guaraní had "readily persuaded themselves that they should be free, and that their happiness would not be diminished by it."[62]

This statement bore an enormous moral weight. Raynal was insisting that Europeans had much to answer for in their treatment of non-Europeans since the sixteenth century. More to the point, he was proposing that the Guaraní not be reduced to simple objects of manipulation but be understood as free human beings capable of making their own decisions. Intentional or not, this was a direct riposte to d'Alembert's denial of liberty to the Guaraní and to Jesuit writers like Muratori and Charlevoix, who never really questioned the idea of a civilizing project. The implications were profound: it was not for Europeans to decide how the Guaraní should live; they could choose for themselves, if only they were left to do so. Never before, and not often since, had Indigenous political autonomy been the kernel of a European argument regarding historical developments. Implicitly, Raynal was proposing that the world might accommodate diverse principles of social, political, and economic organization, a diversity grounded in a fundamental liberty available to all people and to all peoples. Of course, the specific idea of liberty that underwrote his position sprang from European thought and the changes it was undergoing. This realization, however, was probably a bridge too far for Raynal. Nevertheless, it allowed him to conclude that something would be lost if "the most beautiful edifice that has been raised in the New World" were overthrown.[63]

"Progress from savage state to highest civilization"

Despite his sensitivity, Raynal could not escape what was becoming the mastering trope of his age: that commerce represented "the universal spirit of modern politics" and "the new soul of the moral world," as he put it.[64] While discussing eighteenth-century settlements on the banks of South America's Orinoco River, a place where Spaniards, Dutch, Africans, mestizos, mulattoes, Jesuits, Capuchins, Franciscans, and Indigenous people of various nations met and collided, Raynal expressed hope that these "vast and fertile regions" would someday emerge from the "state of obscurity into which they are plunged." But he noted the difficulties involved: "Between a savage life and a state of society, there is an immense desert to pass: but from the infancy of civilization to the full vigor of trade, there are but a few steps to take."[65] He did not say on which side of the civilizational line the world of the Orinoco rested. The most important point is that he understood society as proceeding from savage life to a state of society, to an infant civilization, to the "full vigor of trade." In employing this evolutionary schema, Raynal was conjuring an idea that, in its way, was no less philosophically imprisoning than d'Alembert's denial of liberty to Indigenous people: that human collectives ascended through particular stages on their way to civilization and that European society had reached the apex of an arc the rest of the world had yet to traverse.

The idea of stages was hardly new. Rousseau had seen society as advancing through three steps—a pre-social existence rooted in natural liberty, a first social order that had created unfreedom, and a second social order that would recover liberty while enshrining morality. Yet he was concerned for a moral rather than commercial order and his was a philosophical rather than historical point. In the late eighteenth century, "stadial" theories privileged a growing commercial sphere. Members of the Scottish Enlightenment pushed a self-congratulatory narrative purporting to explain Europe's economic rise vis-à-vis other societies. Lord Kames's *Sketches of the History of Man* (1774) identified four supposedly universal stages of human development: (1) small, relatively isolated hunter-gatherer peoples; (2) somewhat larger groupings of pastoralists; (3) still larger concentrations of sedentary agriculturalists, requiring laws to ensure labor and distribution; and (4) fully realized commercial societies of connected market towns. For many late-eighteenth-century Europeans, this proved an especially persuasive model. It seemed to describe Europe's trajectory in recent centuries and augured an end to the process, with all its dislocations. At the same time, it explained why the rest of the world lagged as Europe summitted civilization's pinnacle.

Fundamentally, Kames's *Sketches* told the story of humanity's "progress from the savage state to its highest civilization and improvement." Though claiming "only to state facts," Kames shaped his account by scaffolding historical events. Transitions from stage to stage were typically turbulent, sometimes violent. Human motivations were complex and varied. Selfishness spanned history from the rudest to the most polished social arrangements, competing throughout with men's natural "appetite for society." This was the central tension of human progress: "What can be more averse to concord in society than dissocial passions?" he asked, "and yet these prevail among men." Trade was a natural though not well-developed propensity among primitive peoples. It had been with the introduction of money and commerce that "avarice" had entered prominently into human affairs and risked the equipoise between selfishness and sociability. This was especially so between stages three and four, the very transition in which Europe found itself when Kames was writing. Money, he noted, had made men "industrious" but had also "produced a great alteration in the human heart," promoting inequality and "artificial wants without end." Commercial society was therefore especially prone to "dissocial" behavior. "Avarice" could "threaten the total dissolution of society" by the "[slow] poison of commercial opulence." Against this backdrop, said Kames, the "epidemic distempers of luxury and selfishness are spreading wide in Britain." And yet, modern industrial society provided a "cornucopia of plenty" the likes of which no society had ever seen.[66] Here was the dilemma of the modern age.

Though uneasy about this development, Kames offered no solution. The closest he came to proposing an escape from the predicament might be called the stiff-upper-lip theory of social life. In a 1778 edition of *Sketches*, he noted that while society was riven by selfish instincts, misfortune could become familiar and experience would "harden" people to the "distress" they caused.[67] The alternative was worse. Without "agitation," humanity would be reduced to lethargy and life "would be altogether insipid." This, he said, had been the fate of the Guaraní under the Jesuits. The very perfection of the missions, Kames insisted, had sunk these people into a "listless state of mind." They had adored the fathers but had not resisted the fathers' expulsion in 1767. They were so apathetic that they did not even regret dying. The reason for this inertia was that the Jesuits had kept them "without ambition, without property, without fear of want, and without desires."[68] In other words, the Guaraní had not learned that the only sensible response to the spur of competition and want was individual self-interested behavior. Raynal's notion that the Guaraní's reaction might be understood in terms of their natural liberty and capacity to decide for themselves how best to live ill fit Kames's idea that the stages of human progress culminated in commercial civilization.

Broadly speaking, stadial histories found it difficult to accommodate the mission world in their explanatory schema. William Robertson's *The History of America* (1777), totally misapprehending Guaraní ways, insisted that "the government of the Jesuits" was "most irksome" to the Guaraní, because "the rights of private exclusive property" they had known before the Jesuits had been destroyed by "the community of property" the fathers had imposed. Quoting French explorer and mathematician Charles Marie de La Condamine, who spent a decade in Ecuador measuring a degree of latitude at the equator, Robertson allowed that little was lost in this, as the mission Guaraní, like all other peoples of that part of South America, were "stupid" and hardly different from "the brute creation."[69]

More pointedly for our purposes, Adam Smith did not mention the Paraguay missions, though he knew of them well. It is worth reflecting a bit on this lacuna, given Smith's centrality to subsequent economic thought. Unlike Kames, who claimed to be "stating facts," Smith sought to elaborate a theory of commercial society. Stadial histories were useful to this project to the extent they provided a clear pivot for distinguishing savages from contemporary Europeans, while recognizing that certain deep structures of human nature could develop over historical time. This allowed the history of humanity to be understood as the move away from primitive conditions toward an ever-thickening culture of "truck, barter, and exchange."

For Smith, or at least the Smith of *The Wealth of Nations*, the driving force of such exchange was not benevolence but each person's "regard to their own interest," an appeal not to their humanity but to their "self-love."[70] Though not as anxiously as Kames, Smith did worry that this powerful impulse might slip from control as the inequality of competitive outcomes deepened. But he did not believe that any force external to self-love could prevent it. Instead, following Mandeville's suggestion that from vice might come virtue, he proposed the famous notion of "an invisible hand"—a phrase he employs once in *The Theory of Moral Sentiments* (1759) and once in *The Wealth of Nations* (1776). More simile than explanatory mechanism, the idea implied that the aggregate of self-interested behavior—in a society not of individuals but of estates, rooted in human "sympathy"—could mutually check each person, thus avoiding chaos and ensuring the public good without need for coordination or state interference. Or as the translator of the first Spanish edition of *The Wealth of Nations* put it in 1794, "the common good," which must inspire the actions of the "public man," does so even as it dispenses "private benefits."[71]

Theories abhor counterexamples, and the mission world did not square well with the intellectual and ideological project in *The Wealth of Nations*—that of elevating transactional exchange to the level of a universal premise of self-organization as the destination of history's developmental march.[72] On one hand, if the Guaraní remained "primitive," their very existence posed a conundrum for the stadial idea (as did all persistently primitive peoples), for nothing in the framework explained why people might fail to progress (racial thinking was already beginning to fill that gap). But if the Jesuits had civilized them, whatever they had become was out of step with the march from aboriginal state to commercial society. After all, the internal life of the missions had been organized around collective land and work, broad redistribution of goods, and the absence of money, not around individual labor, private property, and the circulation of currency. Which implied a second difficulty: by all reports, the missions were large and unusually prosperous, or in 1776 recently had been, without suffering the moral derangement so commonly bemoaned in Europe. For Smith, this was not supposed to be possible under primitive conditions, or under circumstances of common property and a lack of commercial markets. These inconvenient facts might be passed off by insisting that the Jesuits had been tyrants and the Guaraní sheep, so that the Paraguay missions simply did not bear on Smith's ideas, which were predicated on the free actions of free men. This was a frequent accusation, as we have seen. No less plausibly, the missions so jarred with Smith's ideological project—amounting to a countercase—that he left them aside as contributing nothing to the social order he envisioned.

In 1771, the *London Magazine, or Gentlemen's Monthly Intelligencer* published a series of communications debating humanity's prospects. Amateur philosophers assuming Greek pen names argued over whether human beings were at bottom selfish (Hobbes) or benevolent (Shaftesbury). Hobbes's claim that men were nothing more than wolves to other men and that "the ruling passion of mankind is a desire of self-preservation" was "absurd," said one. Amid the "dissoluteness of the time," asked another, how would "virtue" stand before the "pliancy of conscience?" Could society cohere if there were "no real friendship" or "social felicity," only "spoil and power"? As though to answer, one pundit offered a clumsy parable of a pilgrim on the road to Utility. He ends up in a palace called Commodity, loses all moral bearings, and finishes in the grave, reminded that vanitas, vanitatum, omnia vanitas (vanity of vanities, all is vanity). Against this angst, it was still possible to speak admiringly of the "wonderful mode of legislation" known only in Paraguay, which by banishing "mine and thine" had created a "moral people."[73]

From the late 1770s forward, however, the mission world of Paraguay, once a shining city in Europe's tropical imagination, began to fade from broad discussions about the future. When mentioned at all, it was increasingly to dismiss it or to use it as a negative reference in support of some polemical position. Explorer Lewis de Bougainville, during his 1766–1769 circumnavigation of the globe, said the Guaraní were little more than "a race of savage, inconstant men" who had been mistreated by the Jesuits.[74] In a 1771 pamphlet, Denis Diderot, once Raynal's collaborator and an editor of the *Encyclopédie*, cited Bougainville's *Voyage* to claim that the "cruel" Jesuits had enslaved the Guaraní and left them without the right to property.[75] Across the channel, Josiah Tucker in *A Treatise Concerning Civil Government* (1781) argued against Locke's idea that while human beings might elect to join civil society, they had "no natural desire or inclination" to do so. Locke had made his point, Tucker claimed, by arguing that the Indians of America were "universally acknowledged" as living in a state of equality and freedom, without need for jurisdiction or legislation of any kind. Tucker disagreed. The Indians of America, he proclaimed, were "universally the disgrace of Human Nature." They did not choose how to conduct their lives and thus had nothing to offer those searching for "Models of Government worthy of Imitation." Nor, he asserted, did the Paraguay missions prove anything. Despite Jesuit efforts to improve them, the Guaraní remained "mere savages." Irrational, intemperate, and indolent, they, and all other Indians, were a "defective race" unfit for "a liberal plan of civil government," notwithstanding the "ravings of Rousseau."[76]

It is striking how far this was from Raynal's willingness to consider that the Guaraní might decide for themselves how to face posterity. For Tucker, there was one right way of government and Europeans had discovered it. Savage peoples like the Guaraní, it seemed, could or would not progress. How to explain their failure? Stage theory had no response, for "progress" could not simultaneously be a matter of choice and the universal fate of mankind. Tucker's answer to this dilemma was clear: Indigenous people were, to all intents and purposes, beyond the pale of proper Human Nature, a "defective race" with no real place in the world.

Some pushed back against this obdurate stance, if with bland conviction. Professor Dunbar of Aberdeen chided Tucker for saying the Guaraní were "destitute of every human virtue." Surely, said Dunbar, Tucker could be more charitable and "correct the rancour of his Philosophy." He cannot really have meant to deny "some glimmerings of Humanity and some decisive indications of a moral nature" to such people.[77] But this was weak tea. Even while objecting, Dunbar effectively conceded Tucker's view of the Guaraní as a "defective race," arguing only that the glint of a moral nature might turn them to European understandings of the world if properly tutored.

But tutelage presumed the efficacy of education and rational persuasion. By the mid-1780s, a powerful, not-altogether-new idea was taking root: want, rather than fussy reason, might change the behavior of the unenlightened and ensure the triumph of a commercial civilization. This was the gist of Joseph Townsend's *A Dissertation on the Poor Laws* (1786). By allowing people to live without working, England's parish relief system had encouraged the poor to idleness. This, claimed Townsend, was "inconsistent with the most established principles of political economy," for labor is the foundation of individual happiness. And if they refused to work—that is, if they would not earn a wage—then the "peaceable, silent, unremitted pressure" of hunger would correct them. For "the poor know little of the motives which stimulate the higher ranks to action—pride, honor and ambition," stated Townsend. To seal this point, he noted that the Jesuits' practice of feeding villagers living near their establishments had been charity "misapplied." Only "useful labour" is the friend of the poor. "They should have no hope" other than to earn the "friendship of their employers," which would make them obedient and productive.[78]

Such sentiments were thick in the intellectual air. By the 1790s, those who continued to speak well of the mission world were hedging their bets, perhaps sensing they were losing the moral contest over the shape of modern society. Louis Genty, who traveled to the Americas in the 1780s, argued that the Indians might be introduced gradually to "work and social virtues" until the "well-being of each individual" made them "useful." The missions did not speak to this prospect: if the Guaraní had been "the happiest of all the savages of America after conquest," it was only in comparison to those who had been "the victims of our avarice, our cruelty, and our tyranny."[79] In 1793, anonymous author A. R. D. S. published a pamphlet in English, purportedly translated from Italian (where exiled Jesuits lurked) entitled *An Essay on Civil Government, or Society Restored*.[80] The editor's introduction explained that it sought to bring public attention to "our striking deficiencies" in social organization. The *Essay* lamented the "present wretched state of vicious individuality," which rejected any notion of "mutual assistance." Nothing had been done to address this concern because a "too general belief" held man to be "so far sunk, as impossible to be raised." Times were dire. Within and between societies, said A. R. D. S., virtues and vices were "arming . . . dreadful enmity against each other," threatening to "ruin the whole edifice of human happiness." The only solution was to recognize that liberty, property, interest, and money were so intertwined that "society is thus made to begin by its dissolution, . . . amidst the barbarous tumult of opposing and inimical interests." Communities should therefore be divided into small units, the "sordid, selfish" system of private property abolished, and money banished, an arrangement reflecting the "true nature of man." The book said nothing of Paraguay, a silence the editors found odd, for they included a series of letters from readers noting that the author's ideas bore an uncanny resemblance to the "system" and "principles" governing the missions there.[81]

That same year, the exiled Father Peramás, from his garret in Faenza, wrote to set the record straight and ensure the missions' mark on history. Though comparable to Plato's Republic, the Guaraní commonwealth should not be implanted in Europe, he said, for any effort to do so would only sow "disorder" and "confusion." Even in Paraguay, the Guaraní were perishing because the spirit of "mutual aid" and "reciprocal charity" was succumbing to the view that mutual competition remained the only commonality among men. Two years later, English philosopher James Monboddo, in *Antient Metaphysics; or the Science of Universals*, noted that while the "wonders in Paraguay" were gone, the missions had been a "renewal of antient times," and the Indians had been "as happy as any people that ever existed, while they continued under the government of the Jesuits."[82]

These were but dying echoes of earlier efforts to speak to European developments through the experience of the missions. Genty could account for the Guaraní's happiness only against the backdrop of European cruelty to all other Indians. A. R. D. S. refused to acknowledge Paraguay, though readers clearly saw the parallels. Peramás was content to make sure the mission world not be forgot. Monboddo invoked Paraguay only in a wistful past tense. Most others had moved on, bored with the story of the missions. J. G. Herder, generally sympathetic to other peoples, even "primitive" ones, referred to the mission Guaraní as "degenerated" and childlike in *Outline of a Philosophy of the History of Man* (1784).[83] In 1787, responding to the king's question "Of what does the well-being of people consist, and what are the means to attaining it?" a French essayist invoked the missions only to say that it was hard to imagine anyone would abolish "all forms of property" and dedicate themselves exclusively to agriculture. "God forbid we should adopt such a regime."[84]

Even middlebrow culture, once as likely to cheer as condemn the missions, turned against them, less for reasons of political economy than to signal acceptance of commercial civilization's dynamism. London's *Anecdotes, Memoirs, Allegories, Essays, and Poetical Fragments: Tending to amuse the fancy, and inculcate morality* published a short article entitled "On Intellectual Exercise" in 1795. (From its brevity and lack of cogency, it is unclear whether it was intended to amuse or inculcate.) Exercise of the mind, it proclaimed, was no less important than exercise of the body, something impossible to accomplish in a state of "uniform peace and tranquility." To bolster this stance, the article pointed to the people of Paraguay, who were "mere children in understanding." This had been the fault of the Jesuits, who had kept them "without ambition, without property, without fear of want, and without desires."[85] Perhaps some readers noticed that this language had been lifted directly from Kames's *Sketches*, which had found no place for the missions in a universal history that proceeded by stages.

"A stage of development happier than what he has attained"

Joseph-Marie Degérando's *The Observation of Savage Peoples* (1800) may provide a fitting epitaph to the mission world's transit across the Western philosophical firmament. Writing at the dawn of a new century, Degérando published a manual for French "philosophical travelers" who were setting out to map Australia, the next prize in the globe-girding commercial competition between France and Britain. This was to be field work in service of empire and trade, acknowledged Degérando, though it might also serve a more humanist impulse. For in an "age of egoism," he wrote without a hint of irony, the study of others was a means to "studying ourselves."[86]

According to Degérando, a true science of man could not answer to a "single overarching standard of values, in terms of which all cultures, characters and acts can be evaluated."[87] While humans belonged to a "universal society" and a "common family," difference would not yield to abstract thought: "The time for systems is past," he stated. Rather, learning must pursue "the way of observation" and meaningful comparisons. These, in turn, would allow European man to recognize "the bonds that unite us to our fellows" and to say, without reservation, "I am a man, and nothing human is alien to me." To this end, Degérando framed an inventory of questions the observer should ask of savage people, implying that he be content to hear their answers: how they live, their customs, habits, ways, signs, reciprocities, hierarchies, and languages, which would reveal their political, intellectual, and moral state.[88]

Eschewing a comprehensive schema of values, he nevertheless proclaimed that "trade is a means of leading the people to civilization," for it will "inspire in the Savage some new desires which will bring him closer to us." If well treated, savages might "witness of our happiness, of our riches, and at the same time of our superiority" and from "gratitude" join in an alliance "to reach our own condition." Through the "gentle and useful influence" of trade, it might even be possible to reproduce in the Southern Seas "the astonishing revolution of Paraguay!"[89] What had long impressed European observers about the mission world, including its detractors, was that the Jesuits had brought the Guaraní to prosperity and civilization without violence. By invoking the missions, Degérando seemed to suggest that "gentle commerce" might now accomplish in Australia what he assumed religion had in Paraguay. Here may have been the fondest hope of Europeans who went to the world in the nineteenth century: that the savage would become aware of "his inferiority" and seek "a stage of development happier than what he has attained" by engaging in the one activity that promised to unite all human beings: trade.[90]

Such an idea could make sense only on two conditions. First, that commerce be narrowly conceived as the truck in goods—no mention of labor or land. Second, that it take the form of voluntary exchange rather than a coercive pursuit of gain by some at the expense of others. That is, Degérando's proposal for a science of "observation" abetted by trade depended on a myopic understanding of recent history. For as Raynal had made clear twenty years earlier, commerce in service to empire had not been kind to Native folk, a point later historians tacitly agreed to forget for a long season. Put another way, Indigenous peoples, like the Guaraní, had come face to face with individual self-interest long before commerce had contrived to call itself "doux"(sweet, gentle) and before markets were assumed to conjure the common good from the chaos and amorality of self-interest. As I have argued, the Guaraní had reacted by adapting substantive mutuality to produce the relative prosperity and stability of the mission world, which Degérando misunderstood as proof that the suasion of commerce could bring savages to civilization without travail.

Like Raynal before him, Degérando could not escape trade and commerce as a mastering human desire and stadial history as the means to its realization. Even as he warned philosophical travelers against their own "egoism" and exhorted them to friendship with savage others, it simply did not occur to him that Indigenous people might not ultimately be motivated by trade, acquisition, accumulation, and emulation—that is, gain. So, while Degérando's manual bore the imprint of the eighteenth century's egalitarian impulse to encompass all humanity, it also represented the moment when an ethnographic "science of man" was strangled at birth by its umbilical connection to Western commerce, all but ensuring Europeans would have no constructive way during the next century of relating to non-European others who seemed to defy "Progress," especially along its economic axis.

*   *   *

The mission world had captivated European letters because, for a time, it represented such a vivid contrast to the great transformation that had been preparing itself in Europe, in Paraguay, and other places touched by Western presence since the sixteenth century. By the early nineteenth century, commerce, rooted in the pursuit of gain and the unavoidability of competition, had come to be accepted as the way of the world, at least among Europeans. The implications for social life were vast. As political philosopher William Godwin put it in his 1820 diatribe against Thomas Malthus's

An Essay on the Principle of Population, a dispassionate willingness to see the idle suffer for their own good and for society's had got "possession of the public mind." Extending Townsend's insights to their logical extreme, Malthus had concluded (in an 1803 edition of his original 1798 essay) that a person whose labor was not wanted "has no claim of right to the smallest portion of food, and in fact has no business to be where he is. At nature's mighty feast . . . she tells him to be gone, and will quickly execute her own orders." Otherwise, warned Malthus, the banquet of commercial civilization would be beset by the many who would seek a plate, or even crumbs, while refusing to work for them.[91]

With so odious a doctrine, charged Godwin, Malthus had undertaken to "annul" the very foundations of "political society" and "the happiness of mankind."[92] By leaving the poor to be culled by the "agency of vice and misery" and the "punishment of want," Malthus could only "bring our human nature into hatred and contempt," a condition utterly at odds with any "care to perpetuate the commonwealth." Godwin canvassed diverse historical examples—China, India, Rome, Sparta, Aztec Mexico, Incan Peru—to demonstrate how out of keeping Malthus's position was in the annals of humankind. Among these exemplars, he pointed to the missions of Paraguay, "one of the most memorable establishments in the history of the world." Here, Malthus had been especially disingenuous: he "passes over the affair of Paraguay in a smooth and quiet manner," observed Godwin, because its example "would . . . alone be sufficient to decide the question of Mr. Malthus' theory."[93] (Certainly, the mission world's general abundance and universal care for the poor belied the proposition that "no possible form of society could prevent the almost constant action of misery upon a great part of mankind, if in a state of inequality, and upon all, if all were equal."[94]) But the matter ran deeper. Malthus had complained that the mission communities would have perished by nature's swift stroke *"but for the assistance of their neighbours"* during times of scarcity.[95] In other words, their crime had not been that they lacked money or property, as others had complained, but that mutuality and solidarity had buffered residents from extremity. This, lamented Godwin, was Malthus's grave new world: whether Guaraní or Englishmen, ordinary folk had no "right in morality" to human reciprocity or solidarity in matters of economy.[96]

By 1800, reasoned arguments regarding Europe's moral and social direction had begun to seem moribund, bled by political economy's subtle razor. Reality had tipped toward those prepared to accept that self-interest, with its acknowledged dissocial qualities, was a fact of human nature driving an economic world premised on competition, abundance for some, and "fear of want" for the rest. To maintain this illusion, human sociality, even neighborly mutual aid, needed to be put away as a childish thing. For those who remained unsure, the message seemed to be, as Kames had said, that everyone should just harden to the change and carry on and not be too eager to tally human costs or engage in a vain effort to understand those who did not see things the same way. And so, it was time that Paraguay, the mission world, and the Guaraní be forgot, along with Indigenous people generally. In Europe's new lattice of sensibilities, the Western mind had moved on to a triumphal mode of historical reflection capable of recognizing only the stadial procession of a world of gain long in the making—leaving society, and those who might still insist on it, to the margins of moral and practical reason.

CONCLUSION

Reflections

DURING THE LATTER HALF of the eighteenth century, reformers sought to reorient the economy of Spain's New World possessions toward greater circulation and accumulation within Spanish territories and beyond. For Atlantic-facing South America, this meant ensuring Buenos Aires's primacy as a commercial port. In the 1750s, this concern had led the Spanish monarchy to agree to swap seven mission towns for control over Colonia del Sacramento, then under Portuguese jurisdiction. The mission Guaraní had gone to war to defend what they had built. They lost, though a quirk of monarchical succession spared the mission world for a season.

The reprieve did not last long. After the Jesuits were cast out of Spanish territories in 1767, hopes had been high among settlers in Paraguay. From their perspective, for the first time since the seventeenth century, no one stood in the way of making the mission Guaraní into productive workers and "useful" vassals. After royal legislation had failed to countervail raw gain at Guaraní expense by the early seventeenth century, the mission world had thrived at the intersection of Indigenous sociality and substantive mutuality and Jesuit notions of charity and the common good. But where Jesuit missionaries had leveraged their connections to imperial power to shelter the Guaraní from settlers and local officials, former mission communities at the turn of the nineteenth century faced dangers on all sides, without a chart to navigate their situation. Bungled reforms had made Indigenous communities more vulnerable by undermining their capacity to respond collectively to the demands of local criollos. By 1810, Guaraní "freed" from the System of Community faced uncertain prospects under the System of Liberty, as local elites wanting a dependent workforce clashed with royal officials who envisioned an Indigenous yeomanry.

Guaraní communities—mission and non-mission alike—confronted independence movements from this deeply conflicted position. The crisis of royal authority following Napoleon's invasion of Spain in 1808 complicated matters. In 1810, the provisional governmental junta in Buenos Aires deposed the viceroy, arguing that when the king could not govern, sovereignty returned to the people. At Asunción, by contrast, royalists sided with the viceroy, claiming that the colonies belonged to Spain as a political entity—rather than to the Crown—implying that American subjects could make no separate claim of sovereignty or self-government. At the same time, the Portuguese court of João VI, located in Rio de Janeiro since 1808, had entered into an alliance of convenience with Spanish royalists at Montevideo, threatening Brazilian incursions into what had been Spanish mission territory east of the Uruguay River.

Amid these tensions, the Guaraní faced a renewed challenge. General Manuel Belgrano, dispatched by the Buenos Aires junta in 1810, arrived in former mission territories to persuade the Guaraní and their militias to acquiesce to criollo sovereignty. In two proclamations, he promised the Guaraní to "restitute to you your rights [*derechos*] of liberty, property, and security," supposedly long denied by the Jesuits. To this end, he abolished personal service, as the king had done repeatedly for nearly two centuries, and pronounced the end of tribute.[1] The Guaraní would now be "free" men. The message, for all that it sought to reassure, was delivered with an explicit threat to "unleash the sword of justice" if they did not accept his offer of help.

Written originally in Spanish, these proclamations were translated into Guaraní, clearly with the intention that they be read out to mission inhabitants, as had long been done with royal orders. According to historical linguist Capucine Boidin, it is impossible to know with certainty who undertook the original Spanish-to-Guaraní translations, though lexical differences suggest a Guaraní mission resident may have done so. By retranslating the Guaraní into Spanish, Boidin is able to show telling gaps between what Belgrano was saying and what mission Guaraní would likely have heard. For instance, while Belgrano's Spanish texts stated that he would assure mission inhabitants their "rights" of "property" and "liberty," the Guaraní version spoke only of "*teko aguĭyeipe*," the state of persisting goodness promoting health and "happiness [good way of living]" at a collective as well as individual level, a far cry from Enlightenment notions of individual rights claimed against the social whole.[2] The retranslated Guaraní version of the text suggests that mission residents did not think in terms of lacking rights and liberty. Rather, they wished to be "removed from the power of those who impoverish [. . . and] oppress you," a reference to administrators, priests, and merchants who had pursued their gain at community expense for nearly half a century after expulsion of the Jesuits. Only thus, stated the Guaraní version, could inhabitants return to the "way of being the king desired for you," to the "good life that you have given yourselves with your own sweat." Similarly, while Belgrano's Spanish text announced that the junta had shown "wise providence" in recognizing the Guaraní "as our brothers," proffering a social contract rooted in Buenos Aires's uncontested political authority, the Guaraní version has Belgrano promising to "make you see that we are your kin [*parientes*]," seemingly accepting the reciprocal obligations and "eternal love" implicit in kinship, while reserving to the Guaraní the decision whether or not to accept the proposed relationship.[3]

Belgrano was trying to thread a political needle: he aimed to convince the mission Guaraní to accept Buenos Aires's sovereignty over them while reassuring them that their fundamental relationship to political authority would not change. For their part, torn between Spaniards who claimed to rule in the king's place and others who insisted that the monarchy's authority still held, Guaraní leaders may have sought to keep their options open, not overtly disagreeing with the general but refusing to accept his framing of what was at stake, all while trying to avoid panic within the communities. After all, they had gone to war in the 1750s to protest a rupture of royal reciprocity and had sought to repair the relationship afterward. They could not know what Belgrano's words implied for them. Was he promising a renewed political mutuality, or was this to be something entirely different? The general himself may not have known precisely. The stakes of this encounter are apparent in the gulf between the exhortatory, even minatory tone of Belgrano's Spanish letters and the same language rendered in Guaraní. So when Belgrano threatened in Spanish to "unleash the sword of justice" upon them if they "forgot what you owe to the Fatherland [*patria*] and the king," the Guaraní version had him offering "to correct you if you forget our land and our king." In the Guaraní, this latter phrase employed the inclusive *our* (*ñande*, which explicitly includes speaker and hearer, as opposed to *ore*, which refers only to the speaker and others, excluding the hearer).[4] Thus, in Guaraní, the land belonged to the Guaraní no less than to the criollos, as against the abstraction of a *patria* ruled by Europeans from Buenos Aires. In Guaraní, this "land" was ruled by "our" (inclusive) king, a construction that came close to contradicting the junta's claim to sole sovereignty.

By 1813, the tension between Buenos Aires and Spain broke in favor in independence. The Constituent Assembly immediately extinguished tribute, personal service, and the labor draft. Guaraní vassals who bore a reciprocal relationship to the king were to become citizens subject to Buenos Aires, "perfectly free men; equal in rights to all other citizens."[5] Yet no ready-made word existed in Guaraní to convey the novel status of citizen. As a result, a clumsy neologism had to be coined: *citizen* (*ciudadano*) was rendered as "those who are the same as Spaniards in the city."[6] This implied a curious, subtly inflected equality, whether devised by a Spanish writer and translator, or by a Guaraní translator. For while Spaniards assumed themselves free without need of justification (by having declared themselves to be so), Indians were "perfectly free men" because they had been "liberated" by those who took their own freedom for granted—even though Spaniards and Guaraní alike had been vassals. The lack of clarity surrounding citizenship was compounded by the fact that even in Spanish the word *ciudadano* remained unsettled, mingled with the older word *vecino*, a voting member of a city "who enjoys its privileges and is obliged to its responsibilities."[7] The new idea of *ciudadano* as a rights-bearing individual citizen of a nation-state with undefined obligations represented a dramatic inflation of what had been a grounded sense of belonging defined by community and place but also a diminishment of what was expected of those who lived there.[8] Among the Guaraní, the notion of citizen remained up in the air. Letters circulating within Guaraní towns from 1816 forward indicate that rights were still understood in terms of communities as places of protection and shelter (*amparo*) and justice in ways that were continuous with the earlier language of vassalage, with its thick overlay of kinship, mutuality, and political reciprocity as foundational principles of sociable life.[9] At the same time, the Guaraní now faced a new and different kind of state, one that needed to engulf them strictly as citizens rather than relate to them as members of society who might live, at least partly, on their own terms.

Ensuing decades did little to dispel the confusion. Liberal elites who declared independence from Spain argued that new nations should position themselves to respond to British "unbounded commerce."[10] Just as colonial authorities of the late eighteenth century had wanted Indians to become useful vassals, new leaders in Argentina wanted them to become productive citizens, helping build modern, commercial republics through their labor. Guaraní fates thus came to depend on where people stood in relation to the boundaries of newly independent nations. Elites in Buenos Aires set out to secure a property regime and trading system centered in that city, subduing interior provinces to "the rights of capital" in relation to foreign markets.[11] For a season, Paraguay resisted incorporation into a liberal, trade-driven Atlantic model. President José Gaspar Rodríguez de Francia set Paraguay onto a distinctive path through mid-century, expropriating Paraguay's small but powerful landed oligarchy and enacting an agrarian reform radical for its time, redistributing land to the poor, and reorienting the economy away from Buenos Aires's export-import model. In 1814, he had even mandated that European men not marry women "known as European," instead requiring they marry Indigenous, mixed-race, or black Paraguayan women. In undercutting Paraguay's merchant class and creating state-owned enterprises surpassing even the missions' vast holdings, Paraguay became, according to one historian, "the most egalitarian society yet know in the Western hemisphere."[12] This situation held until the devastating War of the Triple Alliance (1864–1870), pitting Argentina, Brazil, and Uruguay against Paraguay. When the dust had settled, Paraguay had lost significant territory and upwards of 60 percent of its pre-war population had perished. Nine in ten Paraguayan men, mostly Guaraní, had lost their lives, a "providential and useful extermination" that was the price of "progress," according to Argentine president Domingo Sarmiento.[13]

By the end of the nineteenth century, liberal ideologues in Buenos Aires had succeeded in creating a "Republic of capital," with its promise of progress, inequalities, competition, and dependencies.[14] Trade had become the order of the day, and wages, with their insecurities, the enveloping condition of quotidian life for many ordinary folk. Like Jesuits of the eighteenth century, European-descended elites (many of them mestizos) decried the "indolence" of Native workers. And yet, Asunción's Chamber of Commerce, whether out of pity or perverse admiration, marveled at the capacity of Paraguay's Indigenous people to suffer under inhuman conditions in producing the yerba that assured 60-percent dividends in La Industrial Paraguayana, Paraguay's most highly capitalized company into the late nineteenth century. "No day laborer in the world would be able to survive that life of labor, of privations, and of dangers," stated the Chamber's secretary.[15] It was to their credit, he continued, that under such difficult conditions, they had been able to maintain "ties like those of a family and they esteem one another, they care for and mutually aid one another," a recognition, perhaps, that gain for some may depend on the very human solidarity it undermines among others.

In 1894, Australian socialists who had immigrated to Paraguay a year earlier to establish their own free colony found this solidarity baffling.[16] When they went to Villa Rica's market in search of provisions, they discovered that Indigenous women effectively controlled proceedings. Among the many vendors selling rice, manioc, sweet potatoes, lemons, oranges, cheese, and cabbages, the cost did not vary. The price of a good at one mat or stall was exactly as at any other. When the white men tried to bargain, the women of the market refused to reduce an asking price to compete with others, even though they might have earned more had they done so. They might even recommend the products at another stall, losing a sale. Nor would they try to lure a customer away from someone else. A report in the colony's English-language newspaper noted, with some exasperation, that it was "mysterious to a foreigner, this fixing of prices," and "irritating" that a "multitude of bare-footed women, largely unknown to one another" should be able to hold so firm. And yet, said the writer, by "cling[ing] stubbornly to Guaraní" customs, these women were expressing a "solidarity . . . that makes the European way look hateful indeed. . . . Who is to say the Guaraní is not right?"[17]

There is a connection between these women of the Villa Rica market who at the twilight of the nineteenth century refused to compete on price and the residents of mission San Ignacio in 1630 who complained to the king that Spaniards were treating them as "animals that are hunted." Two and a half centuries apart, both were making the same point: people should not behave toward other people as predators do prey, whether it is "hunting" them down and dragging them off to the yerba mines at Mbaracayú, or, more subtly, trying to gain at the expense of a neighbor by dropping a price. It was, rather, for people to find ways to live together, to give and to receive and give again through open-ended time. There is also a link between Spanish settlers who pressed Guaraní into service and Australian socialists baffled by the market women: an impulse still uncouth if no longer precisely new among Europeans in 1630 had become by 1894 a drive so universal that even those who recognized it as "hateful" took it for an unalterable fact of human nature.

These strands of historical experience are entwined. In Paraguay, the moral and motivational transformation implicit in Spaniards' pursuit of individual gain at the expense of Guaraní bodies and communities from the sixteenth century forward met a principled affirmation of substantive mutuality by the Guaraní during the decades and centuries following their initial encounter. But what can the Guaraní be said to have accomplished? An answer to this question must begin by acknowledging the strangeness of what befell them: the shame of the woman lost in a game of chance who was stripped naked because her clothes were not part of the wager; the consternation when Spaniards accepted daughters, sisters, and nieces but refused to live up to the obligations of brothers-in-law; the bewilderment at women being treated as currency; the despair unleashed by settlers' raids in the name of accumulation and liberty; the oddness of confronting what we now recognize as a tragedy of the commons with respect to their own bodies; the fear that wage labor might "vex all" more thoroughly than even the encomienda; the realization that appeals to "free choice" could be just a ruse; the failure of law to "conserve" the Guaraní because Spaniards would not heed conscience. None of this could have made much sense from the perspective of Guaraní social relations before the advent of Europeans. Nor did it resolve to clarity from the viewpoint of Spaniards' own moral framework regarding social life, for during most of this period, gain was a motivation acted upon but not fully legitimized—indeed, still pointedly questioned. In the New World, ordinary men faced a theater of action with few limits, where war, trade, coexistence, enslavement, conversion, exploitation, and abuse blurred to indistinctness. If in the Old World the impulse to pursue material gain could be seen chiefly among merchants, in the New World common men could imagine exploiting other people, regardless of calls to justice.

Facing this challenge, Guaraní survived by learning to live precariously amid the devastation of what had once been vibrant and interconnected communities. But they were also attentive to opportunity. And so, when they encountered Europeans who seemed to lack a driving concern for worldly profit and who by their actions seemed motivated by a somewhat more generous sense of social possibility, Guaraní responded with energy, creativity, and hope.

One implication of the account I have offered here is that Europeans, broadly, were hardly alone in reflecting anxiously on what was coming to seem as a generalized condition of war or predation, depending on one's point of view and cultural context, within society itself. If Hobbes wrote from a deep concern that an economic free-for-all seemed to be rending England's seventeenth-century social fabric, the San Ignacio petitioners of the same period could be said to have laid their concerns before the king on the theory that predatory behavior by Spanish vassals was undermining the prospects for a shared social order upon which the reciprocity of the Guaraní's vassalage and their conversion to Christianity were premised.[18]

In becoming an inevasible condition of everyday life and by operating simultaneously at all levels of social existence, individual material gain-seeking imperiled society's weave of interdependence in both seventeenth-century England and seventeenth-century Paraguay. In the emergent order of things, human beings, or at least some among them, were emboldened to seek their own advantage at others' expense. Here lay the deeper meaning of gain's upthrust at the center of collective life: it permitted, encouraged, and legitimized individual behavior that threatened commitments to human sociality and thereby "menace[d] . . . social existence"—that is, it promoted an "unsociable sociability."[19] Even before market relations were fully theorized in the nineteenth century, Europeans were coming to see everyday life as a sphere of self-interested, possessive, competitive economic actors under no moral or political obligation to consider the wider consequences of their actions vis-à-vis others, even when their conduct was socially ruinous. From this perspective, the idea that gain could be set loose and justified within the social order subjected human life in common to an ontological aporia. In this new world of gain, society had to face the reality that its own internal organization and motivational structures—rather than some external threat—might lead to its destruction, a prospect that became the background condition for all subsequent social and political conflict.

For Hobbes, this meant that only the unhampered authority of the Leviathan could prevent cataclysm and ensure the continuity of social life. A truculent human nature had to be taken as such and the state given the power to control it. As universal economic struggle came to be accepted as the norm, or at least as unavoidable, society itself became an arena of mutual combat, barely contained. The Guaraní saw the problem differently. If they were to live *with* Europeans, as they had sought to early on and as Spanish theology and political theory demanded, how could they escape the unsocial condition in which settlers felt free to prey upon them? From their point of view, the issue was not human nature, for men might or might not act as predators toward each other, depending on whether they shared social life—that is, whether they were within society or on their own in the forest, where being preyed upon was an ever-present risk. For the Guaraní, the challenge was to ensure sociality through time—society against predation, to take a liberty with one of Pierre Clastres's central ideas.[20]

Anthropologist Carlos Fausto has argued that one of the long-term consequences of the missions was the "dejaguarization" of the Guaraní cosmos. He means by this that the Guaraní incorporated elements of Christianity to reject the ritual of vengeful cannibalism, reciprocity in its negative form. In its place, claims Fausto, the Guaraní embraced *mborayhu* (loving) as a general condition of "social reproduction," expressed through Native concepts of generosity and reciprocity.[21] Initially, argues Fausto, this appears to have been less a wholesale acceptance of Christian morality than an effort by Guaraní shamans to appropriate the "imagery and power" of the missionaries in cosmological matters. Over the longer term, however, it involved definitively renouncing the predator position, always at odds with the demands of kinship and openness to others, in favor of recognizing a shared vulnerability as prey. For Fausto, this transformation unfolded at the point of intersection between cosmological understanding and day-to-day matters of diet and ritual practice.

But there were other forces in play. I have argued that the Guaraní reaffirmed reciprocity to preserve the possibility of *tecó aguïyeí*, or state of good living, in the face of those who would prey upon them. They came to the conclusion that while exchange always implicates the natural and human substance of society, gain as outright predation needed to be banished from the place where people lived together. In so doing, they rejected the proposition that to avoid being prey, it was necessary to become predators within social life. The mission world stood for this powerful idea. It was a community where substantive mutuality and Jesuit notions of the common good converged just as the practice of gain was condensing in the European imagination. The idea that men might "hunt" other men while living alongside them could make no social or moral sense to the Guaraní. This understanding of society as the place where jaguars do not roam, in other words, asks what exchange is for, for whose benefit, and with what implications for social life.

Godwin's early-nineteenth-century critique of Malthus expressed this concern in language calibrated to the times, invoking the Paraguay missions to do so. The economy of gain, which allowed some men to draft others to their desires, could work only by jettisoning the precept that all people were owed dignity and survival by dint of their humanity. According to Godwin, Malthus had concluded that this required not only a refusal of institutions to support the poor but even a repudiation of mutual aid among people. There was to be nothing beyond the infinitesimal sociality of the immediate gainful transaction to govern human relations, especially in regard to labor. That is, reciprocity, generosity, and solidarity had no acknowledged place in the new order of things; they might be asserted, but always from a position of doubt that they could matter at all. From that point forward, ordinary folk were to be on their own as they faced the "fear of want," the reverse side of gain's coin. They might reciprocate with others who shared their plight, be generous and solidary toward them. But among the champions of the new economy, these attitudes came to be seen as refusals to confront economic reality, little more than defensive postures, throwbacks to earlier and less dynamic times. Those advantaged by this arrangement could unsee the social implications of their position by peering nearsightedly through the spectacles of "bourgeois" virtues and dignity.[22] Moral myopia and facile notions of scientific necessity led them to conclude that human nature had been ever thus. Blinkered in this way, they could imagine with equanimity and incuriosity that progress always justified the human costs incurred in pursuing it (much as Spanish settlers had stilled the voice of conscience centuries earlier).

The idea that fear of want might discipline the lower classes had a long history by the time Godwin wrote. Spanish humanist Juan Luis Vives first questioned medieval understandings of charity in relation to the poor and their care in the sixteenth century.[23] By the eighteenth century, a growing number of European thinkers were prepared to say that society owed nothing to those who did not, would not, or could not work. By the early nineteenth century, this view could admit no counterinstance if it was to bear the moral weight of its implications. This, said Godwin, was why Malthus had failed to mention the Paraguay missions, where for a hundred and fifty years it had been a point of pride and principle that no one go hungry. The missions' expurgation from history thus flowed into the broader intellectual current that relegated Indigenous people, and with them ideas of substantive mutuality, to the edges of Western consideration. It was another century before anthropologists—Malinowski, Mauss, Polanyi—began to take up "primitive" economics once again in ways that could trouble embedded assumptions of gain-driven behavior.

When in the late eighteenth and early nineteenth centuries, European writers looked to the mission world of Paraguay, they were disputing whether *economy* could be thought of as a sphere of human activity largely free of normative constraint regarding relations between individual and collective life. Prior to this time, despite the expanding reach of gain in everyday life among Europeans, these two strands of human experience had remained bound up with one another and, at least in Spain, continuous with axioms of good government. The Enlightenment-period debate signaled the moment at which a new matrix of ideas, intuitions, and feeling regarding exchange had become strong enough to produce open disagreement about the future of social relations, and even society itself. As I have argued, the mission world, seen from afar and by people most of whom never traveled to South America, became a kind of Rorschach, signaling different perspectives on the question of whether gain could serve as an organizing idea for human life in common.

Dispute over the mission world thus informed the eighteenth century's self-conscious public argument over what role moral considerations would play in the economy of gain. Sixteenth-century Catholic theologians, Jesuits notably among them, had also raised such concerns about money and exchange and had done so by reflecting on conditions in the New World. At that time, economy and morality were not yet thought of as occupying distinct spheres. Those who took up this issue sought to divine the balance point for self-interest, on the assumption that morality still had the power to move individual conscience in public life. By the eighteenth century, the question was another: how could society hold together if economy were "disinfested of intrusive moral imperatives?"[24] This question sparked anxious debates regarding the moral and social implications of an emergent economic order. European political economists of the late eighteenth and nineteenth centuries concluded that the riddle required no explicit answer: the individual pursuit of self-interest was a matter of human nature and the action of competition itself made unnecessary any introspection on gain's role in social life.

Since the late twentieth century, moral economy has been a conceptual tool for pushing back against this understanding. It is not the name for an autonomous normative force against economic thinking. It insists, instead, that people whose lives have been upended by gain also have much to say about the "economy." If the market economy is less a clockwork mechanism than a Rube Goldberg contraption powered by gain, then moral economy might be said to represent the ghost in the machine, the animating sociality of all exchange—even when it is forgot. Economy, in other words, is not just system effects, something that happens only in aggregates to abstract individuals. It is also what happens between people with regard to the most basic things in life, including the question of how human beings should live together. Put another way, economy is and has ever been a moral arrangement that answers to society, no more or less so than any other human institution. All economy, therefore, is moral economy, for it prescribes the role of exchange in collective life and through transactions quickens regulative principles that specify the obligations, greater or lesser, that people owe one another.

This means humans must be careful of which exchanges we enshrine as normal and dominant. Polanyi made the point in referring to a "self-regulating market" driven by the pursuit of individual gain as unrealizably "utopian." The idea that people should respect the outcomes of a system of exchange that would destroy them (or even kill them by starvation, as Townsend and Malthus had it) strained the moral principles governing "harmony and conflict" to the point of "complete contradiction."[25] While Europeans did not arrive in Paraguay with a fully worked-out justification for their behavior, the Guaraní came to understand that they were being asked to acquiesce to their own ruin in the face of gain. This led Guaraní to a deep collective reflection on social life, undertaken in the heat of disruption and suffering, as such things generally are.

This framing implies a different story about economic relations than the one bequeathed us by the last two centuries years of human ingenuity and ruthlessness. This other story, as told here, rejects the notion that gain, as well as its later sacralization in the market, represents the unfolding of a singular human nature. It challenges the "mystical readiness to accept the social consequences of economic improvement, whatever they might be."[26] Before economy could be about efficiencies, aggregates, and the supposedly impersonal forces of markets, human relations had to be transformed. Men had to learn that gain operated at all levels of interaction in the sphere that came to be known as economic. And, ultimately, beyond. In the logic of that realm, every man was potentially prey to every other, even within society, a reality that would force all men to behave as predators, if able, and otherwise accept their lot as prey. For this to happen, all other modes of exchange—substantive mutuality rooted in gift and reciprocity—needed to be pushed to the margins of everyday interactions. This is necessarily a global story, one that seeks not grand generalizations but a richly described, globally distributed history of (moral) economy, with all its differences and misalignments but also its commonalities and comparisons across time and place.

In the spirit of this endeavor, I tentatively proffer four propositions that might illumine other moments of early clashes between gain and mutuality. First, nineteenth-century European resistance to market relations, which Polanyi referred to as a "protective countermovement," appear to have had an earlier chapter in the Guaraní's persistent efforts to make settlers into brothers-in-law, in the Spanish monarchy's failed attempt to restrain gain by legal means, and in the Guaraní's considered alliance with Jesuit missionaries. These were not merely momentary responses to base necessity. With different intonations and inflections, all expressed visions of how people should live in the world, conditioned by shared, if contested, material realities. Here was a precocious version of Polanyi's "double movement"—as gain-before-markets spread across the globe through European expansion, it called forth efforts to check it.[27] And while the Guaraní suffered and provoked their share of convulsions as they confronted the disorienting reason of gain, their story indicates that responses can also unfold over long periods through deep deliberation over how to accommodate necessity without sacrificing the essential.

Second, the Guaraní's rejection of predation within social life signals that historical accounts of economy have not given enough attention to gain itself as a motive in transactional exchange and to its effects on collective life. This is not because gain has been thought irrelevant. Rather, gainful conduct has been so taken for granted as describing how human beings naturally behave as to require no elucidation. Consequently, most stories of the "great transformation" begin in the late eighteenth century, recounting the convergence of money, capital, and supposedly self-regulating markets. Yet even in Paraguay, with none of these and with institutions that might otherwise be dismissed as non-economic, we can see the broad pursuit of material gain in action, with effects every bit as concrete as those that later befell the English working class of the late eighteenth and early nineteenth centuries—or Vietnamese peasants in the twentieth century, for that matter.[28]

Third, the fact that sixteenth-century Spanish theologians and lawyers, seventeenth-century Jesuits and mission residents, and eighteenth-century European savants and armchair philosophers railed against gain's corrosive effects on social life argues that the individual pursuit of self-interest is a general human problem demanding reflection and response. As I have shown, there was room for overlapping and even mutually reinforcing perspectives on the dilemma, across philosophical and cultural divides.

Finally, the Guaraní's tortuous path into the world of gain involved repeated refusals to abandon what they understood to be a proper way of being. The heavy cost they paid in doing so hints that narratives culminating in disruptive catharses marking the "final demise" of old ways may not get the story quite right, at least not always.[29] People like the Guaraní have strained to preserve their understanding of how life should be lived, not because it is old or because they cannot think of anything else to do, but because it is, from their perspective, right and, at a minimum, better and more humanly true than the alternatives they have faced. This strategy, because it involved compromise, demanded they attend to what mattered most at any given moment. Such thinking, when the individual pursuit of gain was still new in the world, has been a critical if understudied part of modern economy's story—and not just among Indigenous people.

Recent times have been no kinder to the Guaraní than were the initial decades of their encounter with Europeans. There are fewer Guaraní now (under one hundred thousand) than lived in the mission world at its zenith in the early decades of the eighteenth century. Forests have been taken, stripped, and enclosed to make way for agroindustry. Guaraní have been pushed into corners of space where it is all but impossible for them to maintain a meaningful relationship to the forest or to other communities. Wage labor, now as then, is a trap from which most are unable to escape and few able to profit, at the cost of their own production systems and cultural commitments. Some have found ways to engage in commercial gathering to generate revenues in support of communities and to make the case for the preservation of forests.[30] They remain the exception.

It should hardly seem surprising that the Land Without Evil as a point of reference has begun to reflect these crosscurrents and hardships. Recent tellings among the Guaraní have expressed a desire for the conditions that can guarantee "cultural life": not only shared food but also the inspiration to dance and sing in each other's company.[31] For some, the ruins of the mission world represent a point of passage and potential respite. According to stories collected from Guaraní writers, a culture leader equal parts Guaraní shaman and Jesuit missionary may live beyond the sea, waiting for people to come. Contemporary variations on the theme of the Land Without Evil have looked to Guaraní phrases meaning "bounteous earth, land of perfect space-time," where people are able to develop physically, socially, and spiritually in relation to forest, field, village, and each other, a state of being where people are good-humored, greet each other with joy, and do not fight. Alongside other Indigenous ethical and moral principles—live well (*buen vivir*), good life, harmonious living—Land Without Evil has been framed in wider political, philosophical, ideological, and institutional contexts. It has been enshrined in the Bolivian constitution of 2009 and the right to it is guaranteed by the United Nations.[32] These ideas have become foundational in the emergence of an increasingly vocal Indigenous movement across the globe, one with links to other transnational initiatives, including the Vía Campesina, the International Peasants' Movement, which began in Latin America but now embraces two hundred million farmers and peasants on every continent. These mobilizations represent efforts to confront and question dominant assumptions of economic, social, and political life at a scale to match the global magnitude of the hazards they face.[33]

Broadly, this was the spirit of Avá-Guaraní priest Guillermo Rojas's "Message to the King of Spain" in 1992. Drawing on oral histories and principles condensed from the experience of living through the long ordeal of gain, Rojas observed that the Guaraní do not leave anyone aside, because all are brothers. Though war was long ago waged against them, he said, they do not fight for anything, like white men do. These men sell trees and do not pay the Guaraní for their work. But people must care for each other in mutual joy and reciprocity, he stressed. And so Guaraní dance and pray for all humanity. If they do not, the Blue Jaguar, destroyer of the world, will devour everything, exterminating people and all that exists.[34] Rojas's statement bespeaks a deep reserve of moral sentiment and reason. "It is one thing to dance as though nothing has happened;

it is another to acknowledge that something singularly awful has happened . . . and then decide to dance," as Jonathan Lear said of the reintroduction of the Crow Sun Dance in 1941, after its suspension decades earlier.[35] And yet, Rojas's call cannot be assumed a universal Guaraní stance. A recently recorded Mbyá-Guaraní narrative envisions a world laid waste and then re-created, but without white people in it, because their "bodies are dirty" and they have "ruined" the earth.[36]

This ambivalence and the present-day situation of the Guaraní might thus be seen as a late chapter in the encounter that has been at the core of this book—one that has threatened to end their world for five centuries. One of my goals has been to suggest that contemporary efforts among Indigenous people to reaffirm their own ideas regarding human life have a history. My point is not that their views represent some special insight possible only for Indigenous people. It is, simply, that the lives they have lived, and their reflections on them, have been left out of the history of the modern economic world. Since their unwilled insertion into Western historical time, the Guaraní have continually professed their way of being in the face of a practice and later an ideology that would erase it. The fragility of that accomplishment is clear from what happened to the mission Guaraní after expulsion of the Jesuits.[37]

Their achievement is not a matter of abstract morality so much as a way of thinking and acting that has allowed them to insist that the world of gain is not all there is or ever can be. Yet, the Guaraní, like the Crow and other Indigenous people, may have scant reason to care what historians say about them or any relationship they might bear to historical time.[38] Still, current circumstances may favor novel encounters, alignments, and alliances. Especially as humanity turns toward the calamities of our century, there is urgent need for an intercultural historical, philosophical, and ethical inquiry rooted in the spirit of giving and receiving as a way of human living, one that looks to an economy of "social reciprocation" rooted in a "cosmopolitan sociality."[39]

The main obstacle to such an investigation has not been Indigenous people but natives of the West who have bowed so long and so low to the illusion that the intrinsic value of economic progress obviates any concern for its destructive effects and that competitive self-interest is "man's natural state but also his optimal strategy for economic success."[40] Western thinkers imagined collective life as the realm of the Invisible Hand writ large, where self-interest as predation on others supposedly works itself out at the scale of whole societies, whole countries, and finally the world entire, without need for a visible hand of restraint, a politics of the common good, a substantive notion of sociality, an obligation of reciprocity, or a totting up of costs. And this in the face of Adam Smith's own warning that "society," the name of a moral arrangement, "cannot subsist among those who are at all times ready to hurt and injure one another."[41] From this perspective, the story told here is a reminder that modern economy emerged not just from European technology or any particular gift of rational thought but also from an achieved moral nescience, a casual, almost flinty indifference to the prospects of others, society, and the world, a behavior that came to be explained away as human nature.

And in this, Western history, as a way of thinking, has been complicit. By assuming that the human passage through time is above all about increasing the ambit of individual freedom, we historians have continually made the case, witting or not, for refusing to ask sharper questions about the role substantive mutuality plays in binding societies— what Polanyi called "the reality of society." We have not done enough to consider the extent to which social life is "a history that must be remade every day."[42] The Guaraní have understood only too well the burden of insisting on reciprocity in the world of gain. With eyes fixed on the horizon where the Land Without Evil may be glimpsed, they appear to have judged the cost of losing it to be greater still. Perhaps they are not alone.

Notes

MCE—Montoya, Antonio Ruiz de, *Conquista espiritual* (in Bibliography)
MSC—Montoya, Antonio Ruiz de, *Spiritual Conquest* (in Bibliography)
ML—Montoya, Antonio Ruiz de, *Lexicon Hispano-Guaranicum* (in Bibliography)
Montoya, *Tesoro*—Montoya, Antonio Ruiz de, *Tesoro de la lengua guaraní* (in Bibliography)
LANGAS—Lenguas generales de América del Sur (https://langas.cnrs.fr/#/description)
MCA—*Manuscritos da Coleção de Angelis* (in Bibliography)
RAED—Real Academia Española, *Diccionario de la lengua constellana* (in Bibliography)
RAH—Real Academia de la Historia
ST—Aquinas, *Summa Theologica* (in Bibliography)
SP—Solórzano y Pereira, Juan, *Política indiana* (in Bibliography)

Introduction

1. Montoya, *Tesoro*, 7v, 130v. Guaraní myths contain a "cataclysmology" referring especially to floods and fires. See Nimuendajú, *Lendas*. The term *Guaraní* refers to various contemporary peoples that (1) share a linguistic family, (2) share elements of culture, (3) share a history of contact with European colonizers, (4) and include groups that over time have been "guaranized" by linguistic and colonial absorption. Chamorro, "Imagens," 79.

2. Polanyi, *Great Transformation*, 43.

3. Polanyi, *Great Transformation*, 31.

4. I draw on Polanyi for this definition and have made it somewhat more precise by looking to Graeber, *Anthropological Theory*, 219–20. I have not followed Pierre Bourdieu's pessimistic take on gift-reciprocity, which concedes too much to transactional culture and in effect sees gift through gain. See Dufy and Weber, *Más allá*, 43–44.

5. Polanyi, *Great Transformation*, 30.

6. Polanyi, *Great Transformation*, 46, 127, 258A; Block and Somers, *Power*, 228.

7. Poley, *Devil's Riches*; Sahlins, *Western Illusion*, 112.

8. Clendinnen, *Ambivalent Conquests*; Restall, *Seven Myths*.

9. Thompson, "Moral Economy," 76–77, 78. He first used the term *moral economy* in *The Making of the English Working Class*, 548.

10. Scott, *Moral Economy*; Booth, "On the Idea"; Arnold, "Rethinking Moral Economy"; Edelman, "Bringing the Moral Economy"; Götz, "'Moral Economy'"; Palomera and Vetta, "Moral Economy"; Carrier, "Moral Economy"; Adelman, "Introduction."

11. Bloch and Parry, "Introduction," 10.

12. Shenk, "'I Am No Longer Answerable,'" 241–46.

13. Thompson, *The Making*, 78, 548.

14. Beckert, *Empire of Cotton*.

15. As I argue in chapter 8, substantive mutuality was largely banished from accounts of modern economy toward the beginning of the nineteenth century, along with references to Indigenous economy. It was another century before anthropologists began to recover gift-reciprocity from that oblivion. See note 20.

16. White, *Middle Ground*; Hämäläinen, *Comanche Empire*; Mallios, *Deadly Politics*.

17. Karatani, *Structure*; Carrier, *Gifts*.

18. Tutino, *Mexican Heartland*, 9; Ali, *Local History*, 10; Sartori, *Liberalism*; Stoll, *Ramp Hollow*, xv. The Mexican historiography has made much of "moral economy" in recent decades. See Mora Muro, "Resistencia."

19. Polanyi, *Great Transformation*, 31.

20. The project begins with Bronislaw Malinowski (*Argonauts*, 1922), Marcel Mauss (*Gift*, 1924), and Polanyi (*Great Transformation*, 1944). Polanyi was the only one of them who advanced a historical argument. Most of the work since that time has been done by economic anthropologists and sociologists. See P. Clastres, *Society*; Sahlins, *Stone Age Economics*; Gudeman, *Economics*; Gudeman, *Anthropology*; Graeber, *Anthropological Theory*; Sahlins, *Western Illusion*; Zelizer, *Economic Lives*. Essential work along these lines has been done specifically on the Guaraní. See, e.g., Melià and Temple, *El don*; Fogel and Scappini, "A través del don."

21. On the economy and society of the Guaraní and early Paraguay, I have relied on historians Carlos Garavaglia and Florencia Roulet; anthropologists Bartomeu Melià and Dominique Temple, Ramón Fogel and Gloria Scappini, Branislava Sušnik, and Guillermo Wilde; and geographer Jan Kleinpenning. On the Guaraní within and outside the missions, I am indebted to contemporaries such as anthropologists Lia Quarleri and Guillermo Wilde and historians Julia Sarreal, Eduardo Neumann, Shawn Austin, and Norberto Levinton. I confess to having passed over many topics dealt with in greater depth by these and other scholars. I owe an enormous debt to historical linguist Capucine Boidin for her help in reading Guaraní sources, especially A. Montoya's *Tesoro* and *Lexicon*, but crucially LANGAS's growing corpus of translated (and retro-translated) Guaraní documents. The trope of utopia and dystopia is a bright thread running through the literature on the missions since at least the late eighteenth century. See, e.g., Muratori, *Cristianesimo*; Peramás, La República *de Platón*. In the twentieth century, the missions still held this allure. See Graham, *Vanished Arcadia*; Caraman, *Lost Paradise*; Neto, *Utopia*; Garavaglia, "Misiones."

22. Fasolt, *Limits*, xvi.

23. Fasolt, *Limits*, xiv.

24. Chamorro, *Teología*; Nimuendajú, *Lendas*.

25. Nimuendajú, *Lendas*; Métraux, "Migrations"; H. Clastres, *Land-Without-Evil*.

26. Villar and Combès, "La Tierra"; Noelli, "Curt Nimuendajú"; Melià, "La Tierra-sin-mal,"; Chamorro, *Teología*, 176–86; Barbosa, "'Terra sem Mal'"; Chamorro, "Imagens," 99–102; Sušnik, *Los aborígenes*, 2:10; Shapiro, "From Tupã." See Melià, "La novedad" for detailed bibliography of the Guaraní between the late 1980s and the early 2000s.

27. Schaden, *Aspectos*, argues for closer attention to the variants in the myth as understood by different Guaraní subgroups, the Ñandeva, Mbüá, and the Kayová. See also Chamorro, "Imagens."

28. Montoya, *Tesoro*, 209v. In offering Guaraní terms, I have adopted the spelling and diacritics in Montoya's *Tesoro*, though these can be inconsistent.

29. Gândavo, *Tratado*, 153; D'Evreux, *Voyage*, 350.

30. See Pompa, "Profetismo," 167.

31. Villar and Combès, "La Tierra."

32. Boidin is right to be cautious of the phrase, especially with regard to the debate over migration. See Boidin, "Teko aguyjei." To set the idea aside altogether, however, would be to nullify a crucial concept from which insight may yet be wrung. Given epistemological condescension toward Indigenous ideas, I believe scholars have an obligation to bring such ideas to bear in analytical ways.

33. Lacombe, *Guaranis*, 16.

34. Melià and Temple, *El don*, 27.

35. Melià's work has been the tonic to the overeagerness of earlier Western scholars to depict the Land Without Evil in predominantly transcendental terms. Such meanings are present, but the notion of the Land Without Evil as a flight beyond reality ignores a crucial aspect of its power as an idea. Chamorro, "Imagens," 102.

36. Melià and Temple, *El don*, 29.

37. Melià and Temple, *El don*, 32; Chamorro, *Teología*, 185–86. See Pompa, "Profetismo," 162.

38. Chamorro, "Imagens."

Chapter 1

1. Polanyi, *Great Transformation*, 47–48.

2. Politis, "Pampas," 255–56; Noelli, "Tupi Expansion," 659–70; Noelli, "As hipóteses"; Moore, *Prehistory*, 371–72.

3. Silverman and Isbell, *South American Archaeology*, 255.

4. Noelli, "Curt Nimuendajú"; Sušnik, *Los aborígenes*, 2:11, 38; P. Clastres, *Society*, 213; Nordenskiöld, "Guaraní Invasion."

5. Noelli, "La distribución," 17; Wright, "Destruction," 317–18; Melià, *El Guaraní*, 48–51; Kleinpenning, *Paraguay*, 1441–42.

6. Montoya, *Tesoro*, 376r.

7. Montoya, *Tesoro*, 258v.

8. Souza, "O sistema," 224.

9. Souza, "O sistema," 234.

10. Sušnik, *Los aborígenes*, 2:19–20; Montoya, *Tesoro*, 258v; Sušnik, *Los aborígenes*, 5:127–30.

11. Souza, "O sistema," 239.

12. P. Clastres, *Archeology*, 165.

13. P. Clastres, *Archeology*, 166.

14. Sušnik, *Los aborígenes*, 5:127.

15. Souza, "O sistema," 234.

16. Soriano, "Imagen"; Montoya, *Tesoro*, 107r, 261r.

17. P. Clastres, *Archeology*, 154–62; H. Clastres, *Land-Without-Evil*, 25–42.

18. Schmidel, *Viaje*, 171–75, 205–13, 250–54.

19. Montoya, *Tesoro*, 183v.

20. P. Clastres, *Society*, 192–94; Sahlins, *Stone Age Economics*, 1–39; P. Clastres, *Archeology*, 193.

21. Sahlins, *Stone Age Economics*; P. Clastres, *Archeology*, 193.

22. P. Clastres, *Archeology*, 195.

23. Souza, "O sistema," 246.

24. Noelli, "Curt Nimuendajú," 143.

25. Murra, *Reciprocity*; Murra, *Economic Organization*; Alberti and Mayer, *Reciprocidad*.

26. Mauss, *The Gift*, 81.

27. Mauss, *The Gift*, 72.

28. Godbout, *World of the Gift*, 173.

29. H. Clastres, *Land-Without-Evil*, 88.

30. Souza, "O sistema," 232.

31. Pierre Clastres called it an "ontological dimension." P. Clastres, *Society*, 41–42.

32. Montoya, *Tesoro*, 307r-v.

33. Melià and Temple, *El don*, 48–49; Montoya, *Tesoro*, 307r-v, 313v-r. I have benefited from Melià and Temple's analysis of Montoya's entries, though I have rooted the analysis in my own reading of the source. Austin, Boidin, Wilde, and others have taken a similar approach. Montoya's *Tesoro* was critical to Jesuit evangelization of the Guaraní in the early seventeenth century. Many entries inflected Guaraní words with Christian notions. Just as many, or likely more, did not. A challenge in using this source to get at early contact or precontact meanings is that Montoya published it in 1639. By then, Guaraní and Europeans had been living side by side for over a century. Earlier meanings may have changed. An answer to this caution is twofold. First, Spaniards generally and certainly Jesuits commonly learned Guaraní rather than the other way round. Second, many of the Guaraní the Jesuits contacted during 1620s and 1630s had not lived in close contact with Spaniards, suggesting that original meanings (especially those without obvious theological import) may have remained current. In short, while Montoya's *Tesoro* is an imperfect source, carefully employed it provides a crucial lens onto Guaraní understandings.

34. Cardim, *Tratados*, 173.

35. MCE, 198.

36. Montoya, *Tesoro*, 321v, 268v.

37. Souza, "O sistema," 231, 243; Montoya, *Tesoro*, 313v.

38. Montoya, *Tesoro*, 268v.

39. Melià and Temple, *El don*, 24–25; Montoya, *Tesoro*, 196v, 268v, 307r, 313v, 321v; Schmidel, *Viaje*, 61, 172

40. Melià and Temple, *El don*, 20–22; Montoya, *Tesoro*, 363.

41. Melià and Temple, *El don*, 24–25; Vanaya, *Mitos*, 87–91. See also Clendinnen, *Aztecs*; and Clendinnen, *Ambivalent Conquests*.

42. Léry, *Histoire*, 293.

43. Cabeza de Vaca, *Relación*, 222.

44. Roulet, *La resistencia*, 85. See also Wilde, *Religión y poder*, 142.

45. D. Torres, *Cultura guaraní*, 120.

46. Montoya, *Tesoro*, 71r, 219v.

47. Montoya, *Tesoro*, 307r-v.

48. Montoya, *Tesoro*, 5r, 63v, 146r, 326r–v.

49. Montoya, *Tesoro*, 6r–v.

50. Covarrubias, *Tesoro*, 209v; ML, 161, 191, 277

51. Montoya, *Tesoro*, 29r.

52. Melià and Temple, *El don*, 141.

53. Melià and Temple, *El don*, 143.

54. Viveiros de Castro, *From the Enemy's Point of View*, 154.

55. Melià and Temple, *El don*, 142–43.

56. Melià and Temple, *El don*, 148.

57. Cf. Clendinnen, *Aztecs*, 94–95.

58. Viveiros de Castro, *From the Enemy's Point of View*, 4.

59. P. Clastres, *Archeology*, 237–77.

60. Quarleri, "Lógicas," 187; Fernandes, *A função social da guerra*, 357.

61. Viveiros de Castro, *From the Enemy's Point of View*, 286–87.

62. Schmidel, *Viaje*, 172.

63. Chakravarti, *Empire of Apostles*, 135–37.

64. Kleinpenning, *Paraguay*, 594–95, Nordenskiöld, "Guaraní Invasion," 104–5; Alconini, *Southeast Inka Frontiers*, 134, 144

65. Candela, "Las mujeres," 10.

66. Sušnik, *Los aborígenes*, 2:22–26.

67. Montoya, *Tesoro*, 20v–21r. As to the last of these, given in Montoya as "escusarse," it is worth noting that Covarrrubias's *Tesoro* of Spanish gives as a definition of *escusarse* the act of "explaining why one cannot do what was asked of one." Covarrubias, *Tesoro*, 370v.

68. Montoya, *Tesoro*, 21r.

69. Montoya, *Tesoro*, 20v–21r, 161v, 313r–v.

70. Montoya, *Tesoro*, 363v.

71. Sušnik, *Los aborígenes*, 2:19–20.

72. P. Clastres, *Archeology*, 198; P. Clastres, *Society*, 206–7.

73. MCE, 48. See also Boidin, *Mots guarani*, 378.

74. MCE, 48.

75. Austin, "Guaraní Kinship," 551.

76. P. Clastres, *Society*, 214–15. My emphasis.

77. P. Clastres, *Society*, 215–16; H. Clastres, *Land-Without-Evil*.

78. Montoya, *Tesoro*, 364r.

79. Viveiros de Castro, "Cosmological Deixis," 469.

80. It is worth noting that Montoya's Spanish-to-Guaraní *Vocabulario* uses *tecocatú* far more conventionally to describe the man who keeps his word. ML, 142.

81. Haraway, *Staying with the Trouble*.

82. ST, I-II, q. 94, art. 2.

83. Aristotle, *Nicomachean Ethics*, Book 8, sec. 4, 12.

84. ST, II-II, q. 23, art. 1.

85. ST, II-II, q. 23, art. 1; I, q. 38, art. 2.

86. Aquinas, "On Kingship," 192–93.

87. RAH, *Las siete partidas*, 3:145, 148 (part. 4, tit. 27); Burns, *Las Siete Partidas*, 3:1003–4.

88. Dueñas, *Espejo*, 38–39.

89. Bodin, *Les sixes livres*, 345.

90. Davis, *The Gift*, 14–15.

91. Howell, *Commerce*, 146–47.

92. Algazi, "Introduction."

93. Bijsterveld, "The Medieval Gift," 130–35, 139, 144.

94. Bijsterveld, "The Medieval Gift," 142.

95. P. Clastre, "Échange," 54.

96. RAH, *Las siete partidas*, 1:18; 2:351 (1.1.10; 3.1.2); Burns, *Las Siete Partidas*, 1:4; 3:534.

97. Levi, "Reciprocidad mediterránea," 111.

98. Seneca, *Proverbios*, vii r–v. The Proverbs with comments likely by Pedro Díaz de Toledo, were first published in 1482 and saw subsequent editions, including Cromberger's from Seville [1512, 1528, and 1535], to 1555.

99. Levi, "Reciprocidad mediterránea," 105. For a German case involving transformation of customary obligations, see Algazi, "Feigned Reciprocities," 119, 125.

100. Covarrubias, *Tesoro*, s.v. "*don* (gift)," 1:326v.

101. Guerreau-Jalabert, "Caritas y don."

102. Commerce within smaller towns may have been more considerable than once thought. Milton, *Market Power*, 1–6.

103. Bloch, *Feudal Society*, 1:67.

104. Polanyi, *Great Transformation*, 58.

105. Howell, *Commerce*, 17, 159–71.

106. Parker, "El surgimiento," 425.

107. Milton, *Market Power*.

108. Mercado, *Summa*, 97v, 320v.

109. A. Guevara, *Reloj*, 775; Valentini, *Opera*, 440, 444; Covarrubias, *Tesoro*, 2:12r. My emphasis.

110. Muldrew, *The Economy of Obligation*, 123.

111. Covarrubias, *Tesoro*, 1:229v; 2:52v; Nicot, *Thresor*, 134.

112. Muldrew, *The Economy of Obligation*, 43.

113. Mercado, *Summa*, 196r.

114. Azpilcueta Navarro, *Manual*, 328; Calle, *Instrucción*, 10.

115. Bracciolini, *De Avaritia*, 117

116. Bracciolini, *De Avaritia*, 113, 115, 227, 118, 134.

117. Bracciolini, *De Avaritia*, 103, 106, 110, 114, 117, 118, 120, 123, 132.

118. Vilches, *New World Gold*, 145–209.

119. Villalón, *El vallisoletano*, 41.

120. Wilson, *Arte*, 25; Mercado, *Summa*, Prologue, 17v, 128v.

121. Mercado, *Summa*, 18r.

122. Mercado, *Summa*, 112v, censure by Diego Rodríguez, 32r, 119v, 120v, 121v.
123. Maravall, *Estado moderno*, 2:60, 81, 121.
124. Mercado, *Summa*, 17v.
125. Maravall, *Estado moderno*, 2:114, 117.
126. Quevedo, "Poderoso caballero."
127. Villalón, *El crotalón.*
128. 1 Timothy 6:10. See also Ecclesiastes, 5:10; Hebrews 13:5; Luke 12:15; Matthew 6:24; James 5:1–6.
129. Aquinas, *De Regno*, ¶¶ 8, 38, 139; Aquinas, "De regimine," 50.
130. Aquinas, "De regimine," 6.
131. Aquinas, "De regimine," 50.
132. Alighieri, *Divine Comedy*, 185.
133. Howell, *Commerce*, 265–68.
134. Azpilcueta Navarro, *Comentario*, 58.
135. Grice-Hutchinson, *Early Economic Thought*, 105–6.
136. Mercado, *Summa*, 65v.
137. Mercado, *Summa*, 18v, 31r.
138. Monsalve, "Economics and Ethics," 495–519.
139. F. Camacho, *El pensamiento económico*, 205–40.
140. Monsalve, "Economics and Ethics," 496.
141. Todeschini, *Richesse franciscaine*, 31; Howell, *Commerce*, 277–78.
142. Mercado, *Summa*, 61r, 65v, 66v.
143. Muldrew, *The Economy of Obligation*, 47.
144. Aquinas, *De Regno*, ¶ 14.
145. Alonso-Lasheras, *Luis de Molina's* De Iustitia, 106.
146. Aquinas, "De regimine," 1, 9.
147. Figueroa, *Varias noticias*, 221r.
148. Hespanha, "Las categorías," 66.

Chapter 2

1. Torre Revello, *Documentos*, 453.
2. Roulet, *La resistencia*, 164.
3. Nowell, "Aleixo Garcia."
4. Kleinpenning, *Paraguay*, 149.
5. Kleinpenning, *Paraguay*, 162.
6. Lockhart and Otte, *Letters*, 15.
7. Gandía, *Historia.*
8. Garavaglia, "Crises and Transformations," 25.
9. Roulet, *La resistencia*, 112–16.
10. Sušnik, *Los aborígenes*, 2:127.
11. Blanco, *Historia*, 627.
12. Schmidel, *Viaje*, 312–13.
13. Roulet, *La resistencia*, 118.

14. Schmidel, *Viaje*, 174.

15. Schmidel, 313; Roulet, *La resistencia* 120.

16. Guzmán, *Argentina*, 183.

17. Roulet, *La resistencia*, 123–24, 127–28.

18. Roulet, *La resistencia*, 135.

19. Service, *Spanish-Guaraní Relations*, 21; Sušnik, *Los aborígenes*, 2:54–55.

20. Sušnik, *Los aborígenes*, 2:54.

21. Kleinpenning, *Paraguay*, 164–69.

22. AGI, "Relación de Don Domingo Martínez de Irala," Autos fiscales, Charcas Justicia 1131, Pieza 13.

23. Cabeza de Vaca, *Relación*, 59–60.

24. Roulet, *La resistencia*, 153–55.

25. Roulet, *La resistencia*, 155–56.

26. Montoya, *Tesoro*, 377r–v.

27. Roulet, *La resistencia*, 153.

28. Roulet, *La resistencia*, 161.

29. Sušnik, *Los aborígenes*, 2:55; Roulet, *La resistencia*, 164–65.

30. Roulet, *La resistencia*, 164.

31. Cabeza de Vaca, *Relación*, 205.

32. Roulet, *La resistencia*, 165.

33. Guzmán, *Argentina*, 183–84; Schmidel, *Viaje*, 176.

34. Roulet, *La resistencia*, 90.

35. Schmidel, *Viaje*, 172.

36. Torre Revello, *Documentos*, 449.

37. Torre Revello, *Documentos*, 453.

38. Service, *Spanish-Guaraní Relations*, 33–34.

39. Torre Revello, *Documentos*, 417.

40. Schmidel, *Viaje*, 322, 489.

41. Torre Revello, *Documentos*, 449.

42. Torre Revello, *Documentos*, 449.

43. Roulet, *La resistencia*, 180.

44. Cabeza de Vaca, *Relación*, 34.

45. Lockhart and Otte, *Letters*, 16; "Dos Cartas al Consejo de Indias," por J. Ochoa Eizaguirre, de 1545, in Roulet, *La resistencia*, 96n13.

46. Roulet, *La resistencia*, 183–86.

47. Machaín, *El gobernador*, 415–16.

48. Roulet, *La resistencia*, 189n32.

49. Xerez, *Verdadera relación*, 107.

50. Kleinpenning, *Paraguay*, 600–1; CBG, 250.

51. Roulet, *La resistencia*, 190n33; Perusset, "Reglamentación," 1004.

52. Torre Revello, *Documentos*, 449; Candela, "Las mujeres."

53. Torre Revello, *Documentos*, 417; Ministerio de Fomento, *Cartas*, 609.

54. Schmidel, *Viaje*, 333.

55. Schmidel, *Viaje*, 474–75. ANA, NE, 574, 1r–3r. I thank Guillaume Candela for his transcription of this document and permission to cite it here.

56. "Fray Bernardo de Armenta 10 octubre 1544," AGI, Autos fiscales, Charcas, Justicia 1131, Pieza 15.

57. Candela, "Las mujeres," 24; Covarrubias, *Tesoro*, 2:142r.

58. Schmidel, *Viaje*, 474.

59. Machaín, *El gobernador*, 415–16.

60. Torre Revello, *Documentos*, 449.

61. Roulet, *La resistencia*, 188n31, 190n33.

62. Blackburn, *Making of New World Slavery*; Monteiro, *Blacks*.

63. Austin, *Colonial Kinship*, 36, 38–39.

64. Montoya, *Tesoro*, 213v, 377r–v.

65. Covarrubias, *Tesoro*, 364r.

66. Montoya, *Tesoro*, 377v.

67. CBG, 249–52.

68. Roulet, *La resistencia*, 171.

69. García Santillán, *Legislación*, 354, 347–56.

70. García Santillán, *Legislación*, 354.

71. Schmidel, *Viaje*, 340, 345–46.

72. CBG, 48.

73. Schmidel, *Viaje*, 346.

74. Schmidel, *Viaje*, 229; *CBG*, 11, 13–14.

75. Schmidel, *Viaje*, 347.

76. Schmidel, *Viaje*, 232.

77. Mercado, *Summa*, 112v.

78. Guevara, *Reloj*, 646.

79. Alba, *Diálogos*, 16.

80. Villalón, *El crotalón*, 367, 377.

81. Villalón, *El crotalón*, 377; Maravall, *Estado moderno*, 1:423–25.

82. Schmidel, *Viaje*, 348–49, 353.

83. Cabeza de Vaca, *Relación*, 1:343–344.

84. Schmidel, *Viaje*, 230.

85. Torre Revello, *Documentos*, 448.

86. Schmidel, *Viaje*, 469–70.

87. Roulet, *La resistencia*, 196; Cabeza de Vaca, *Relación*, 351.

88. CBG, 11; "Abusos de españoles contra los indios, Martin Gonzalez, 1 de julio de 1556," AHN, Colección de documentos de Indias, 24, no. 17; Roulet, *La resistencia*, 63–64.

89. CBG, 264–65.

90. Schmidel, *Viaje*, 353, 356.

91. Schmidel, *Viaje*, 351.

92. Roulet, *La resistencia*, 203–20.

93. Schmidel, *Viaje*, 232.

94. Schmidel, *Viaje*, 353.

95. Schmidel, *Viaje*, 469–70.

96. Schmidel, *Viaje*, 332–33.

97. Schmidel, *Viaje*, 171–72.

98. Strathern, *Gender*, 338.

99. Roulet, *La resistencia*, 278.

Chapter 3

1. Lockhart and Otte, *Letters*, 49.

2. Las Casas, *Brevísima*, 41.

3. "Leyes y ordenanzas."

4. Las Casas, *Brevísima*, 124, 144.

5. Las Casas, *Brevísima*, 41; Mann, *1491*, 147.

6. The debate on Indigenous depopulation has been enduringly intense. For an overview, see Mann, *1491*, 107–48.

7. RAH, *Las siete partidas*, 2:7 (2.1.5); Burns, *Las Siete Partidas*, 2:27; Covarrubias, *Tesoro*, 311v; 569v.

8. "Leyes y ordenanzas"; Las Casas, *Brevísima*, 32, 152.

9. Levi, "Reciprocidad mediterránea," 126.

10. Hespanha, "Las categorías," 83–84; Covarrubias, *Tesoro*, 523v.

11. Covarrubias, *Tesoro*, 65r; Saavedra Fajardo, *Idea*, 251.

12. Garavaglia, "Crises and Transformations," 9.

13. Covarrubias, *Tesoro*, 230r.

14. Soto, *Tratado*, 147–48, 151.

15. Scattola, "La virtud."

16. Soto, *Tratado*, 132, 136.

17. Covarrubias, *Tesoro*, 496v.

18. Soto, *Tratado*, 211.

19. Bellarmine, "De officio," 223.

20. Lira, "Dimensión," 1158.

21. Soto, *Tratado*, 27.

22. "Leyes y ordenanzas."

23. I have avoided the word *Crown* (*corona*) in the book. The term was rarely employed in documents of the period with regard to the Iberian monarchy. Its use by historians has been a carryover from the English context and conflates distinct notions of sovereignty and the origins of royal power. Monod, *Power of Kings*, 42–43; Grafe, *Distant Tyranny*, 121.

24. García Santillán, *Legislación*, 347–50.

25. Machaín, *El gobernador*, 425–26, 429–32, 433–35.

26. García Santillán, *Legislación*, 325–26.

27. C. Pastore, *La lucha*, 83.

28. Sušnik, *El indio colonial*, 22; Roulet, *La resistencia*, 235.

29. "Informe de um jesuíta anônimo, 1620."

30. Roulet, *La resistencia*, 235.

31. Machaín, *El gobernador*, 484.

32. Souza, "O sistema," 234.

33. "Carta del factor Dorantes," 80.

34. Machaín, *El gobernador*, 483–85.

35. Machaín, *El gobernador*, 485–87.

36. Machaín, *El gobernador*, 487–90.

37. Machaín, *El gobernador*, 489.

38. M. Pastore, "Coerced," 31; Nonneman, "On the Economics." More generally, see Ostrum, *Governing the Commons*.

39. Kleinpenning, *Paraguay*, 1444–45.

40. Service, *Spanish-Guaraní Relations*; M. Pastore, "Coerced," 29, 31.

41. Roulet, *La resistencia*, 247.

42. Lockhart and Otte, *Letters*, 49.

43. CBG, 281–85.

44. Zavala, *New Viewpoints*, 85–86.

45. M. Pastore, "Coerced," 9.

46. Machaín, *El gobernador*, 511–24.

47. Machaín, *El gobernador*, 514.

48. Machaín, *El gobernador*, 513, 521.

49. "Abusos de españoles contra los indios, Martin Gonzalez, 1 de julio de 1556," AHN, Colección de documentos de Indias, 24, no. 17, 1r–2v, 3r.

50. CBG, 255.

51. García Santillán, *Legislación*, 330–31.

52. Service, *Spanish-Guaraní Relations*, 58–62.

53. Lockhart and Otte, *Letters*, 16.

54. Sušnik, *Una visión*, 61.

55. CBG, 163–64; Kleinpenning, *Paraguay,* 1045–46.

56. López, "Shipbuilding," 31–37.

57. Service, *Spanish-Guaraní Relations*, 50–51.

58. Candela, "Paraguay."

59. Garavaglia, *Mercado*, 218.

60. Sušnik, *Los aborígenes* 2:81–83; Sušnik, *Una visión*, 61.

61. Perusset, "Dinámicas," 15, 21–22.

62. Quoted in Roulet, *La resistencia*, 248n35.

63. Machaín, *El gobernador*, 512.

64. Machaín, *El gobernador*, 522–23.

65. Machaín, *El gobernador*, 514.

66. Service, *Spanish-Guaraní Relations*, 54; Kleinpenning, *Paraguay*, 1438.

67. Service, *Spanish-Guaraní Relations*, 41; Sušnik, *Los aborígenes* 2:83.

68. Sušnik, *Los aborígenes* 2:83.

69. Necker, "La réaction," 78.

70. "Informes del Cabildo," 32.

71. Necker, "La réaction," 78

72. Machaín, *El gobernador*, 389–92.

73. "Real cédula pidiendo el buen tratamiento de los indios por parte de los encomenderos," ANA, SH 1n37 (1582); "Real cédula por que se ponga freno a los malos tratamientos y extorciones a los indios por encomenderos y administradores, con pena de privación de cargos y encomiendas," ANA, SH 8n9 (1608).

74. Carta de Martín González, 3 mayo 1575, Madrid. AGI, Charcas 143.

75. Candela, "Influences," 410–15.

76. Kleinpenning, *Paraguay*, 1439.

77. Necker, *Indiens*, 64; Kleinpenning, *Paraguay*, 206–12.

78. Kleinpenning, *Paraguay*, 211–12.

79. Necker, *Indiens*, 66, 141–43.

80. Necker, *Indiens,* 87–88.

81. Clendinnen, *Ambivalent Conquests*, 49.

82. Austin, "Guaraní Kinship," 556–58.

83. ANA, CJ 1451n1, 1–15 (1574).

84. Austin, *Colonial Kinship*, 66–71.

85. ANA, CJ: 1963n6, 1–11 (1564); 2117n7, 1–8 (1588); 2202n2, 1–6 (1590); 2031n7, 1–6 (1600).

86. Austin, "Guaraní Kinship," 557.

87. ANA, CJ 1987n2 (1590).

88. ANA, CJ 1987n2, 4–5.

89. ANA, CJ 1987n2, 9–10, 12.

90. Garavaglia, "Un capítulo," 20–25.

91. Lane, *Potosí*, 89–91.

92. Garavaglia, "Un capítulo," 20.

93. Necker, "La réaction," 79; Morales, "Los comienzos," 53–54.

94. "Ordenanza de Juan de Garay," 197–98.

95. García Santillán, *Legislación*, 356.

96. García Santillán, *Legislación*, 373–74.

97. "Real cédula al Virrey del Perú."

98. García Santillán, *El gobernador*, 376.

99. García Santillán, *Legislación*, 377–80, 382.

100. "Expediente sobre los informes del fiscal Francisco de Alfaro de 24 y 26 de febrero de 1606." AGI, Charcas, 18, R. 3, N.5, 1–8 (1r–4v), 19.

101. "Real cédula aprobatoria."

102. Garavaglia, *Mercado*, 218.

103. Garavaglia, *Mercado*, 161, 163; Garavaglia, "La demografía," 25–27.

104. Kleinpenning, *Paraguay*, 697.

105. "Real cédula aprobatoria," 592.

106. Gandía, *Francisco de Alfaro*, 460.

107. "Testimonio de los autos," AGI, Charcas 33, 1v-2r.

108. Kleinpenning, *Paraguay*, 697.

109. "Testimonio de los autos," AGI, Charcas 33, 2v.

110. "Testimonio de los autos," AGI, Charcas 33, 3v, 4v, 5v, 7r, 8v, 11v, 13r, 14r, 18v.

111. The document represents the Indians' voices in the third person plural.

112. Gandía, *Francisco de Alfaro*, 568.

113. Gandía, *Francisco de Alfaro*, 451–526.

114. "Testimonio de los autos," AGI, Charcas 33, 4v.

115. Austin, *Colonial Kinship*.

116. "Testimonio de los autos," AGI, Charcas 33, 13r.

117. RAH, *Las siete partidas,* 3:135 (4.25.6); Burns, *Las Siete Partidas*, 4:994.

118. Gandía, *Francisco de Alfaro*, 465.

119. Austin, *Colonial Kinship*, 74, 76.

120. Gandía, *Francisco de Alfaro*, 456.

121. "Testimonio de los autos," AGI, Charcas 33, 5v. My emphasis.

122. "Testimonio de los autos," AGI, Charcas 33, 5v, 13r.

123. Gandía, *Francisco de Alfaro* 510–12.

124. Page, "Relación," 135.

125. Las Casas, *Brevísima*, 150.

126. Ostrum, *Governing the Commons*, 177–78.

127. "Testimonio de los autos," AGI, Charcas 33, 4v.

128. Gandía, *Francisco de Alfaro*, 512–13.

129. "Real cédula aprobatoria," 566.

130. Kleinpenning, *Paraguay*, 697.

131. Page, "Relación," 133, 136.

132. Lira, "Dimensión," 1157.

133. Las Casas, *Avisos*, ii–iii, v–vi.

134. Rodrigues, *Summa*, preface of Sebastián de Cormellas.

135. Lozano, "Instrucción para las conciencias de los encomenderos," *Historia de la Compañía*, 95–96, 344–46.

136. "Real cédula aprobatoria," 3:11, 600.

137. Morales, "Los comienzos," 52.

138. "Real cédula por que se ponga freno a los malos tratamientos y extorciones a los índios por encomenderos y administradores, con pena de privación de cargos y encomendas," ANA, SH vol. 8n9 (1608).

139. Owensby, *Empire*.

Chapter 4

1. Kleinpenning, *Paraguay*, 235–43, 253–57.

2. Lozano, *Historia de la Compañía,* 309–13; Page, "Relación," 128–57.

3. Lozano, *Historia de la Compañía*, 313.

4. The words attributed to Tabacambí in Lozano appeared in nearly identical form in a 1677 official report on the state of the Jesuit missions. As Capucine Boidin has argued, Tabacambí's statement there bore Indigenous intonations, suggesting that if his speech was a paraphrase, it was at least a faithful one. Boidin, *Mots guarani*, 367–71,

quoting a statement taken in a 1677 court case, found at AGN, Archivo y colección Andrés Lamas, Leg. 6, *Relación sumaria de los servicios presentados a la Corona por los indios guaraníes de las misiones*, 7r–v.

5. Montoya, *Tesoro*, 217r, 326r.

6. Montoya, *Tesoro*, 329v.

7. Techo, *Historia*, 357–58, 361–62.

8. Hernández, *Misiones*, "Primera instrucción," 580–84, 585–89.

9. ST, 1:370–72 (I, q. 76, art. 1).

10. Mariana, *De rege*, 113–14.

11. Turner, *Thomas Aquinas*, 51–56, 58. Italics in the original.

12. *Constitutions*, 3–13.

13. J. M. Molina, *To Overcome Oneself*, 44.

14. Loyola, *Ejercicios*, 90 (§102), 91 (§106), 107 (§166), 114 (§185), 127 (§214).

15. *Ratio Studiorum*, 62.

16. *Ratio Studiorum*, 86, 87, 190.

17. ST, IV:1264–65, 1267 (II-II, q. 23, art. 2, art. 3, art. 6); IV:2048, 2031 (III, q. 4, art. 4; III, q. 2, art. 5); IV:661 (I-II, q. 17, art. 9).

18. ST, IV:2230 (III, q. 40, art. 1).

19. Nadal, *Pláticas*, 89.

20. J. M. Molina, *To Overcome Oneself*, 47; Chakravarti, *Empire of Apostles*; Clossey, *Salvation and Globalization*.

21. Alencastro, *Trade*, 153.

22. Jesuit views were flexible enough to allow for variable outcomes, depending on circumstances. Cushner, *Lords of the Land*; Cushner, *Farm and Factory*; Cushner, *Jesuit Ranches*.

23. MSC, 116.

24. Cardiel, *Las misiones*, 67.

25. Fúrlong, *Justo van Suerck*, 85.

26. Storni, *Catalogo*, 296–297.

27. Covarrubias, *Tesoro*, 1:313.

28. MSC, 131, 152; MCE, 64r, 76r.

29. Hernández, *Misiones*, 385.

30. Mallios, *The Deadly Politics*; MCE, 169.

31. Acosta, *De promulgando*, 433.

32. ST, I:417–21 (I, q. 83).

33. MacGregor, *Luis de Molina*; L. Molina, *On Divine Foreknowledge*; R. Camacho, "Francisco Suárez," 79–101.

34. Montoya, *Tesoro*, 17r, 61v, 62r, 113r, 126r, 159v, 183v, 184v, 284v, 285v, 286v, 287r, 289r, 308v, 310r, 333v, 338v, 339r, 341r, 350r, 375r, 378r.

35. Montoya, *Tesoro*, 349v–350r, 378r.

36. ST, II:1140–41 (I-II, q. 112, art. 1, art. 2).

37. ST, II:619 (I-II, q. 6, art. 4).

38. *Cartas anuas, 1632 a 1634*, 156–57.

39. Viveiros de Castro, *Inconstancy*, 50.

40. MSC, 145.

41. Austin, *Colonial Kinship*, 131–42.

42. *Cartas anuas, 1632–1634*, 179, 184.

43. MSC, 163–64.

44. MSC, 39–40.

45. Page, "Relación," 136.

46. Lozano, *Historia de la Compañía*, 199.

47. *Documentos*, 436–438.

48. MSC, 93–94; MCE, 41r. The Spanish version says the cacique wondered whether the Jesuits were "*intratable*" (hard to deal with; incapable of being spoken to). It is close to the English word *intractable*, though with greater emphasis on incommunicability. Covarrubias's *Tesoro* defines *tratar* as "having knowledge of someone and having conversation" (52v [2]).

49. *Cartas anuas, 1632 a 1634*, 104.

50. Kleinpenning, *Paraguay*, 242. I have emphasized the lowest number here. Others range up to 100,000.

51. Zavala, *Orígenes*, 478.

52. Garavaglia, *Mercado*, 293.

53. MSC, 43.

54. Garavaglia, *Mercado*, 48–54.

55. Garavaglia, *Mercado*, 293–94.

56. MSC, 31.

57. Austin, "Guaraní Kinship," 590.

58. MCA, 1:291–92.

59. Garavaglia, *Mercado*, 126.

60. MCA, 1:352–61.

61. MSC, 40–41.

62. Garavaglia, *Mercado*, 245–49.

63. Boidin, *Mots guarani*, 63–80.

64. Boidin, *Mots guarani*, 350–51.

65. Boidin, *Mots guarani*, Annexe, 75.

66. Montoya, *Tesoro*, 87v.

67. Montoya, *Tesoro*, 340r.

68. Montoya, *Tesoro*, 31v. I thank Capucine Boidin for confirming and refining this characterization.

69. Montoya, *Tesoro*, 258v.

70. Boidin, *Mots guarani*, 342–45.

71. MCA, 1:356–60.

72. Boidin, *Mots guarani*, 331–65.

73. Boidin, *Mots guarani*. Annexe, 74, 79.

74. ST, II, 1009–10 (I-II, q. 94, art. 2.)

75. Maravall, "Saavedra Fajardo," 227.

76. Kleinpenning, *Paraguay*, 244–45; Monteiro, *Blacks*, 56–57.

77. Mintz, *Sweetness*, 29–30.

78. Alencastro, *Trade*, 104.

79. Monteiro, "From Indian to Slave"; Alencastro, *Trade*, 187–91.

80. Monteiro, *Blacks*, 60–61.

81. Monteiro, *Blacks*, 62.

82. MSC, 169–70.

83. Montoya, *Tesoro*, 230r–v; MSC, 169–70.

84. MSC, 190; Monteiro, *Blacks*, 60–61.

85. MSC, 170.

86. Fausto, *Warfare*, 5–6.

87. MSC, 101.

88. MSC, 181.

89. MCA, 243–44.

90. MSC, 116.

91. Bartra, *Tercer concilio*, 27.

92. Cushner, *Why Have You Come*, 105–6.

93. *Cartas anuas, 1663–1666*, 184–85, 237, 242, 244, 245.

94. MCA, 1:261–64.

95. MCA, 1:319.

96. MCA, 1:366.

97. MCA, 1:364.

98. MCA, 1:368.

99. Other communities also resisted Jesuit counsel to abandon their lands. Sušnik, *Los aborígenes*, 2:147.

100. MCA, 1:363.

101. *Cartas Anuas, 1632–1634*, 136–37.

102. MCE, 48v–53r.

103. I lean heavily on the Annual Letters (*Litterae annuae; Cartas anuas*) of 1632–1634. Missionaries wrote reports on their activities and passed them on to superiors, who compiled "edifying" missives that found their way across the Jesuit world. Orschel, "'Uniting the Dispersed Members,'" 402. The letters also informed benefactors of the Society's doings. *Cartas Anuas, 1632–1634*, 21. Tone, content, level of detail, and emphasis varied from year to year and writer to writer. The Paraguay Annual Letters of 1632–1634 have been described as somewhat drier than others of roughly the same period. These rich sources require careful handling.

104. *Cartas anuas, 1632–1634*, 128.

105. *Cartas anuas, 1632–1634*, 124, 128.

106. *Cartas anuas, 1632–1634*, 121, 129, 134, 137–38. Numbers vary. Métraux claimed that about 4,000 survived the journey. Métraux, "The Guaraní," 78. The Annual Letters suggest the number was higher. Eight thousand are said to have passed through Acaray before moving on.

107. MCE, 52v.

108. *Cartas anuas, 1632–1634*, 124.

109. MCE, 52v.

110. *Cartas anuas, 1632–1634*, 130.

111. MCE, 52v.

112. Wilde, *Religión y poder.*

113. Cushner, *Why Have You Come*, 105.

114. Melià and Temple, *El don*, 24. Some contemporary Guaraní myths say that the blue jaguar will come to devour the stars and men. See Métraux, "The Guaraní," 93; Goeje, *Philosophy*, 41.

115. Sušnik, *Los aborígenes*, 2:150–51.

116. Wilde, "Political Dimension," 75; Levinton, *El espacio.*

117. MSC, 142; Sušnik, *Los aborígenes*, 2:146–47.

118. Viveiros de Castro, *Inconstancy*, 16.

119. Overing and Passes, "Introduction," 5–6. In the same book, Peter Gow argues that for the contemporary Piro, "nothing is more important than everyday sociability." Gow, "Helplessness," 60.

120. Melià and Temple, *El don.*

121. Lozano, *Historia de la conquista*, 1:391; Melià and Temple, *El don*, 148–149.

122. Montoya, *Tesoro*, 207v, 208v. The *Tesoro* also has an entry for *guarînî* = "war/guerra" and *aguarînî* = "to make war/guerrear." This definition is descriptive and lacks the value-laden qualities of *maramôna*. Montoya, *Tesoro*, 130v.

123. Montoya, *Tesoro*, 363v.

124. Covarrubias, *Tesoro*, 2:44r.

125. Montoya, *Tesoro*, 208v.

126. Viveiros de Castro, *Inconstancy*, 31, 47, 58–63; Viveiros de Castro, *From the Enemy's Point of View.*

127. Overing and Passing, "Introduction," 6; Melià and Temple, *El don*, 142–145.

128. Montoya, *Tesoro*, 363r, 364r, 365r.

129. Lozano, *Historia de la conquista*, 391.

130. MSC, 93–94.

131. Montoya, *Tesoro*, 8v–9r, 191r; ML, 390.

132. Viveiros de Castro, "Cosmological Deixis," 469–88.

133. Montoya, *Tesoro*, 8r, 364r.

134. Sušnik, *Los aborígenes*, 2:147.

135. Noelli, "Curt Nimuendajú," 143.

136. Ganson, *The Guaraní*, 46.

137. Lear, *Radical Hope*, 56–57, 104.

138. Melià, "La Tierra-sin-mal," 501–5; Melià and Temple, *El don*, 32.

Chapter 5

1. MCE, iv.

2. Aquinas, "On Kingship," 120.

3. MCE, 100r.

4. MCE, 65v–66r, 95v–96r.

5. Ganson, *The Guaraní*, 46–47.

6. Kleinpenning, *Paraguay*, 273.

7. Ganson, *The Guaraní*, 46–47; Quarleri, *Rebelión*, 88–89.

8. "Autos sobre la visita," 52–54.

9. Montoya, *Tesoro*, 381v.

10. Zeballos, *Arte real*, 156r.

11. *Cartas anuas, 1632–1634*, 117.

12. Avellaneda, "Orígenes," 173–200.

13. Boidin, *Mots guaraní*, 367.

14. Techo, *Historia* 5:277–80.

15. Montoya, *Tesoro*, 192v.

16. Montoya, *Tesoro*, 364r.

17. Covarrubias, *Tesoro*, 134v.

18. Montoya, *Tesoro*, 35r, 38r, 41v, 302r, 340r.

19. LANGAS, "Respuesta que dieron los indios a las reales provisiones, Cabildo de San Ignacio del Ypaumbuçu" (1630), ¶3, 7; Boidin, *Mots guaraní*, 76, 77.

20. Montoya, *Tesoro*, 343r-v.

21. Montoya, *Tesoro*, 343v. The specific reference comes after a series of exemplary phrases invoking *tupã*, the word the Jesuits used to name the Christian God but which in Guaraní meant "thing worthy of admiration." The cited example does not refer to *tupã*, following two entries referring to a generalized kind of "confidence" or "trust." Caution is in order, since the idea of being confident in the shelter of God's embrace would have been perfectly in keeping with what the Jesuits wanted the Guaraní to learn.

22. MCE, 72r.

23. Avellaneda, "Orígenes."

24. Austin, *Colonial Kinship*, 111–12.

25. Montoya, *Tesoro*, 191r.

26. Sarreal, *Guaraní*, 49; Kleinpenning, *Paraguay*, 1473; *Cartas anuas, 1681–1692*, 267.

27. Kleinpenning, 268–74, 303.

28. Garavaglia, *Mercado*, 353; Kern, "O processo," 33; Sušnik, *Los aborígenes*, 2:90–91.

29. Austin, *Colonial Kinship*, 213–15.

30. Salinas, *Dominación colonial*, 101; Austin, *Colonial Kinship*, 214.

31. ANA, NE-324, 135v–150v (1670).

32. ANA: CJ-1953 n. 5 (1674); CJ-1969 n. 7 (1692); CJ-1952 n. 3 (1689); NE-151, 56r–62v (1709); CJ-1970 n. 12 (1691); CJ-2051 n. 9 (1693).

33. Sušnik, *Los aborígenes*, 2:224.

34. MCE, IV, 6r.

35. *Cartas anuas 1644*, 68.

36. Levinton, *La arquitectura*, 9–10.

37. Wilde, *Religión y poder*; Takeda, "Los padrones," 67.

38. Levinton, "Las estancias," 35–36.

39. Hernández, *Misiones*, 580–84, 585–89.

40. Rodríguez, *Ejercicio*, 165, 330.

41. *Cartas anuas, 1663–1666*, 50, 81, 85–86; MCE, 65v; "Preceptos de Nuestros padres generales y provinciales," AGN-BN 140, 3r.

42. MCA, 214.

43. MCE, 64r.

44. *Cartas anuas, 1645–1646*, 39.

45. MCE, 53v.

46. *Cartas anuas:1644*, 67, 69, 85–86; *1645–1646*, 39 46–47; *1650–1652*, 33–34; *1663–1666*, 75, 76–77.

47. Fúrlong, *Antonio Sepp*, 42–43.

48. *Cartas anuas 1658–60*, 112.

49. *Cartas anuas 1644*, 84–85.

50. Montoya, *Tesoro*, 381.

51. Fausto, "Se Deus."

52. Covarrubias, *Tesoro*, 68v.

53. Montoya, *Tesoro*, 268v.

54. *Cartas anuas 1663–1666*, 114.

55. Masy, "La propiedad," 114–17; Sarreal, "Jesuit Missions," 7.

56. ML, 174; Montoya, *Tesoro*, 127r, 182v, 183v.

57. Masy, "La propiedad," 114–16.

58. *Cartas anuas 1681–1692*, 268–70.

59. *Cartas anuas 1681–1692*, 163.

60. *Cartas anuas 1681–1692*, 161–62.

61. "Carta del P. Provincial Thomas Donvidas de 10 de diciembre de 1685," in "Cartas de los PP. generales y provinciales de la Compañía de Jesús a los misioneros jesuitas de Paraguay, Uruguay y Paraná," BNE, Sala Cervantes, Mss/6976, 125 [123–132].

62. "Ordenes para todas las reducciones aprobados por el P Genl Juan Paulo Oliva," ARSI, Paraq. 12, 169v–170r.

63. Cardiel, *Las misiones*, 83.

64. Bailey, *Art*, 155–56.

65. Levinton, *La arquitectura*, 96.

66. Mörner, *Political and Economic Activities*, 204.

67. Bataille, *Accursed Share*, 38–39.

68. Kleinpenning, *Paraguay*, 293.

69. Fúrlong, *José Cardiel*, 153.

70. Echevarri, *Reyno jesuítico*, 196.

71. Fúrlong, *Misiones*, 629; Pastells, *Historia*, 1:294.

72. Maeder and Bolsi, "La población"; Conzelmann, *Wirtschaftswachstum*, 95–96.

73. Kleinpenning, *Paraguay*, 1476–79; Sarreal, *Guaraní*, 49.

74. Kleinpenning, *Paraguay*, 1458–59.

75. "Carta del Pe Provincial Blas de Silva para todas las doctrinas, 22 diciembre 1707," BNE, Sala Cervantes, Mss/6976, 212; Montoya, *Tesoro*, 402r–v; ML, 361.

76. Cardiel, *Las misiones*, 87.

77. "Carta del Pe Provincial Blas," BNE, Sala Cervantes, Mss/6976, 212.

78. Sepp, *Jardín*, 179.

79. Sušnik, *Los aborígenes*, 2:204, 242.

80. Garavaglia, *Mercado*, 342.

81. Levinton, *El espacio*, 16.

82. Sarreal, *The Guaraní*, 86.

83. "Carta del Pe Gregorio Horozco provincial desta province, 6 de febrero de 1689," in "Cartas," BNE, Sala Cervantes, Mss/6976, 149.

84. ST, II-II, 3:1435 (q. 58, art. 9, obj. 3).

85. Maravall, "Saavedra Fajardo," 227.

86. Alonso-Lasheras, *Luis de Molina's* De Iustitia, 104–16.

87. Melià and Temple, *El don*, 70–72.

88. "Carta del Padre Provincial Lauro Nuñez a los PPes Missioneros, 3 de julio de 1694," in "Cartas de los PPes," BNE, Sala Cervantes, Mss/6976, 171 [169–71].

89. Wilde, *Religión y poder*, 83.

90. Vassberg, *Land*; Penry, *People*, 73. I'm grateful to Julia Sarreal for bringing this connection to my attention.

91. Oliver, "Breve noticia," 109; Montoya, *Tesoro*, 92v.

92. Pe Luis de la Roca, "Disposiciones dejadas en su visita al pueblo de San Miguel" (1714–1715), AGN, Sala IX: 6-9-5.

93. Cardiel, *Las misiones*, 91. Though Cardiel wrote this text after the Jesuits had been expelled from the missions in 1767, he drew on previous works he had written in 1747 and 1758, while still in the missions.

94. Mantilla, "La ociosidad."

95. Wilde, *Religión y poder*, 69–73; Sarreal, *The Guaraní*, 68–70.

96. Sepp, *Relación*, 219.

97. AGN, Sala IX: 6-9-5 Compañía de Jesús, 29.10.1714; 6-9-6 Compañía de Jesús, San Luis, 13.7.1727.

98. Cardiel, *Declaración*, 293.

99. Cardiel, *Declaración*, 293.

100. Oliver, "Breve noticia," 103.

101. Sepp, *Relación* 121; Levinton, *El espacio*, 197–98.

102. Pe Luis de la Roca, "Disposiciones dejadas en su visita al pueblo de San Miguel" (1714–1715), AGN, Sala IX: 6-9-5.

103. "Ordenes del P. Prov. Luis de la Roca para las doctrinas del Paraná y Uruguay en la visita de 1724," in "Cartas," BNE, Sala Cervantes, Mss/6976, 237 [236–240].

104. Adoue, Orantin, and Boidin, "*Diálogos*."

105. The document is the subject of promising anthropological and linguistic research. See especially Orantin, "La cloche."

106. Montoya, *Tesoro*, 217r, 331r–v.

107. Melià y Temple, *El don*, 41–42.

108. "Carta del P. Antonio Betschon," 246.

109. Montoya, *Tesoro*, 116v–117r.

110. Cardiel, *Las misiones*, 60, 67.

111. Cardiel, *Las misiones*, 68; Sarreal, *The Guaraní*, 70. Much remains to be learned about the nature of work in the missions.

112. "Memorial del pe provincial Antonio Machoni, 1742," in "Cartas de los PP. Generales," BNE, Sala Cervantes, Mss/6976, 297.

113. "Memorial del pe provincial Antonio Machoni, 1742," in "Cartas de los PP. Generales," BNE, Sala Cervantes, Mss/6976, 297.

114. Cardiel, *Las misiones*, 89–90.

115. Fúrlong, *José Cardiel*, 186; Kleinpenning, *Paraguay*, 1340.

116. AGN-BN 140, "Preceptos," 22v.

117. Orantin, "La cloche," 76.

118. Hernández, *Misiones*, 242.

119. Sarreal, *The Guaraní*, 90–91.

120. Fúrlong, *José Cardiel*, 185–86.

121. Wilde, *Religión y poder*, 73.

122. Wilde, *Religión y poder*, 58–61, 73–78.

123. AGN-BN 140, "Preceptos," 29r,

124. Wilde, *Religión y poder*, 74.

125. Cardiel, *Las misiones*, 95–96.

126. AGN-BN 140, "Preceptos," 28v.

127. Oliver, "Breve noticia," 115; "Memorial del provincial Antonio Machoni, 1742," in AGN-BN 140, "Cartas de los PP. Generales," 297.

128. AGN-BN 140, "Preceptos," 1r, 2r, 7r, 12r, 20v, 21r, 36r–38r.

129. "Memorial del pe provincial Antonio Machoni, 1742," in "Cartas de los PP. Generales," BNE, Sala Cervantes, Mss/6976, 297–98.

130. Sarreal argues that some caciques had become "placeholders" rather than active leaders in the mission communities. Sarreal, "Caciques," 224–51. Takeda has argued that caciques remained important throughout and that a kind of status sorting may have been underway in the eighteenth century. Takeda, "Los padrones."

131. Oliver, "Breve noticia," 112.

132. LANGAS, Carta al gobernador de Buenos Aires, Neenguyru, 1753, ¶ 51; Montoya, *Tesoro*, 321v. Melià y Temple, *El don*, 48–49. It is crucial to point out that Montoya's *Tesoro* gives the verb in this phrase, *moatyrõ* (put straight/restored), as denoting the action of fixing or curing a thing that had been broken. Montoya, *Tesoro*, 223r.

133. 1 Corinthians 4:12. The original Spanish translation of the letter refers to "work," though the word does not appear in the Guaraní text other than as an allusion to things done with the hand.

134. Melià and Temple, *El don*, 57; Popescu, *El sistema*, 45.

135. Cardiel, *Las misiones*, 93–94; Kleinpenning, *Paraguay*, 1458–59.

136. ANA, ACA, Acuerdo capitular del 7-8-1724; ANA, ACA 21, 19, 52.

137. "Carta del P. Pedro Lozano al Sr Procurador general Sebastian de San Martin," in Córdoba del Tucuman, 30 de enero de 1732, BNE, Sala Cervantes, Mss/12977/34, 10v–11r, 13r.

Chapter 6

1. Vieira, "Las reducciones," 318–27.
2. ANA, ACA 20 [257], 24-9-1723, 29–31.
3. ANA, ACA 20 [245], 24-9-1723, 31.
4. López, *Revolt*, 69; Kleinpenning, *Paraguay*, 1452, 1458, 1460–61.
5. Kleinpenning, *Paraguay*, 674; López, *Revolt*, 67.
6. Kleinpenning, *Paraguay*, 1223.
7. López, *Revolt*, 68.
8. Saeger, "Origins."
9. ANA, ACA 20 [245], 24-9-1723, 29–31.
10. ANA, ACA 20 [245], 24-9-1723, 29–31. The accusation was not without foundation. See ANA, NE vol. 151 (1678), 113–21.
11. ANA, ACA 21 [257], 4-12-1724, 67–68.
12. Lozano, *Historia de las revoluciones*, 2:4.
13. López, *Revolt*, 114–15.
14. Lozano, *Historia de las revoluciones*, 2:286, 289.
15. Lozano, *Historia de las revoluciones*, 2:175.
16. Avellaneda, "Conflicto."
17. *Cartas anuas 1714–1720*, 534.
18. *Cartas anuas 1714–1720*, 535.
19. Kleinpenning, *Paraguay*, 1480.
20. Kleinpenning, *Paraguay*, 1479; Avellaneda, "Conflicto," 14–15.
21. Conzelmann, *Wirtschaftswachstum*, 94.
22. *Cartas anuas 1714–1720*, 619.
23. *Cartas anuas 1714–1720*, 593–94.
24. "Tratado de la línea divisória de los estados de las coronas de España y Portugal en Asia y América, firmado en Madrid a 13 de enero de 1750," AGN-BN 5676.
25. Uztáriz, *Theorica*, 241.
26. Piketty, *Capital*, 365.
27. Elliot, *Empires*, 224–26.
28. Quarleri, *Rebelión*, 127–34.
29. Nusdorffer, "Relación," 7:139 et seq. See also Urquijo, "Clima," 36–37.
30. See Avellaneda and Quarleri, "Las milicias," 109–32.
31. "Cédula Real previendo lo que han de observarse en las Misiones y pueblos de indios . . . a cargo de los Padres de la Cia de Jesús," ANA, SH vol. 55–21 (1743); "Copia de real cedula al provincial . . . para el bien de aquellos indios," ARSI, Paraq. 13, 273r–274v.
32. Nusdorffer, "Relación," 148–253.
33. Neumann, "Mientras volaban correos."
34. References to the letters are from Mateos, "Cartas," 547–72; Ganson, *The Guaraní*, 192–97. See especially LANGAS. I thank Capucine Boidin for the interpretation of Neenguyru's name.
35. LANGAS, Carta, Neenguyru, 1753: ¶ 8.

36. LANGAS, Carta, Neenguyru, 1753: ¶¶ 86–87.

37. LANGAS, Carta, Neenguyru, 1753: ¶¶ 3, 16, 17, 19, 22.

38. LANGAS, Carta del pueblo de Santo Angel: ¶ 38; Carta de San Miguel: ¶¶ 5, 24.

39. LANGAS, Carta del pueblo de San Juan: ¶ 24.

40. LANGAS, Carta del pueblo de San Luis: ¶ 26.

41. Hespanha, "Las categorias," 66–67.

42. Fajardo, *Empresas politicas*, 259 [emp. 39].

43. RAED, 3:124.

44. The Portuguese claimed the letters were Jesuit propaganda. "Relação abbreviada," 59–79. Careful work by historical linguists with the LANGAS project indicate that they were written in Guaraní by Guaraní and translated into Spanish, probably by missionaries.

45. Melià and Temple, *El don*, 48, 49, 57, 214; Covarrubias, *Tesoro*, 2:65r.

46. Montoya, *Tesoro*, 307r–v.

47. Melià and Temple, *El don*, 64, 163, 207.

48. Montoya, *Tesoro*, 75r, 133v, 143v. I am grateful to Capucine Boidin for the nuances of this phrasing.

49. P. Clastres, *Society*, 27–47, 189–218.

50. LANGAS, Carta, Neenguyru, 1753: ¶ 29, 79; Montoya, *Tesoro*, 322r–v.

51. Montoya, *Lexicon*, 278r; Montoya, *Tesoro*, 151r.

52. Nusdorffer, "Relación," 144.

53. BNE, Papeles Varios, Mss/1101, "Memorial q el P. Provincial de la Provincia de Paraguay presentó al Sr. Comisario Marqués de Valdelirios, 19 julio 1753," 108v.

54. BNE, Papeles Varios, Mss/1101, "Memorial," 111r–v, 112r.

55. P. Clastres, *Society*, 41–42. Primitive societies, argued Clastres, came to a "very early premonition" that power as an organizing principle posed a "mortal risk for the group." This idea has been criticized as saying more about Western than indigenous social orders. See Moyn, "Of Savagery"; Bessire and Bond, "Ontological Anthropology." Cf. Viveiros de Castro, "Introduction".

56. Nusdorffer, "Relación," 146.

57. RAH, *Las siete partidas*, 3:351 (3.1.3); Burns, *Las Siete Partidas*, 3:535.

58. LANGAS: Carta, Neenguyru, 1753: ¶¶ 5, 51, 53, 55; Carta del pueblo de San Juan: ¶ 28; Carta del pueblo de Santo Angel: ¶ 32.

59. Cardiel, *Las misiones*, 82.

60. Pujol, "La razón"; A. García, "El dilema."

61. Höpfl, *Jesuit Political Thought*, 106–7, 126–30.

62. Botero, *Botero*.

63. Covarrubias, *Tesoro*, s.v. "razón" (pt. 2: 11r–v); Solórzano y Pereira, *Política indiana*, 1:399 (2.17.14); 3:2186 (5.15.4).

64. Solórzano y Pereira, *Política Indiana*, 3:2194 (5.15.22).

65. AGN-BN, Leg. 126 (pieza 0109), *Estado político del reyno del Peru, gobierno sin leyes, ministros relaxados, tesoros con pobreza, &c.* (1730), 134r–135v, 204v–205r; Uztáriz, *Theorica*.

66. Campillo, *Nuevo Sistema*, 4, 284; AGN-BN 108, "Relacion del origen o establecimiento del comercio de Inglaterra, Londres, 1 mayo 1753."

67. Pastells, *Historia*, 81–82.

68. Quoted in Quarleri, *Rebelión*, 133.

69. Herzog, *Frontiers*, 127.

70. Campillo, *Nuevo Sistema*, 92.

71. Campillo, *Nuevo Sistema*, 10, 72.

72. Quoted in Quarleri, *Rebelión*, 206.

73. Fúrlong, *José Cardiel*, 159.

74. Covarrubias, *Tesoro*, 566r; RAED, 3:1.

75. Montoya, *Tesoro*, 25v.

76. Covarrubias, *Tesoro*, 1:8r.

77. Montoya, *Tesoro*, 25v; Covarrubias, *Tesoro*, 535v–536r; RAED, 2:474.

78. Nusdorffer, "Relación," 180.

79. BNE, Mss/18650/5, "Reflexiones sobre la oposición de los Jesuitas al Tratado y motivos secretos que tienen," 37r.

80. AGNM, Instituciones Coloniales: Inquisición, vol. 104, assig. 12844: "República Jesuita del Paraguay. Copia de la carta sediciosa fraudulenta . . . al gobernador de Buenos Ayres . . . con motivo de les hazer creer todos los engaños que en ellas se contienen traducidos fielmente de la lengua Guarany."

81. Quarlieri, *Rebelión*, 225.

82. Nusdorffer, "Relación," 156.

83. On the war, see Quarleri, *Rebelión*; Golin, *Guerra*.

84. Wilde, *Religión y poder*, 169–70 (quoting Nusdorffer); Quarleri, *Rebelión*, 227–38.

85. Nusdorffer, "Relación," 231.

86. *Recopilación de las leyes de destos reynos*, 299r–300r [lib. V, tit. X, leyes 2,3].

87. Maziel, *De la justicia*, 116, 118, 119, 127 (¶¶ 101–3, 105, 107, 110, 125, 126).

88. Covarrubias, *Tesoro*, 2:65r. RAE, *Diccionario*, 3:426.

89. LANGAS, Carta al Gobernador Pedro Cevallos, 1761.

90. Elliot, *Empires*, 230.

Chapter 7

1. *Relação abbreviada*, 31, 33. The book was translated into Spanish, Italian, German, English, and Latin within a year of its Portuguese release.

2. *Full, Clear, and Authorised Account*, 56; D'Alembert, *Sur la destruction*, 10.

3. Campomanes, *Dictamen*, 130, 135.

4. LANGAS, Carta al Señor Gobernador, San Ignacio Guasu, 1768.

5. LANGAS, Carta al Señor Gobernador, San Luis, 1768, ¶¶ 10, 12, 20, 21, 22.

6. LANGAS, Carta al Rey Carlos III, corregidores y caciques de los treinta pueblos, 1768, ¶¶ 16, 18, 27, 28.

7. Wilde, *Religión y poder*, 194.

8. Wilde, *Religión y poder*, 194–95.

9. AGN-BN, Ordenanzas para el gobierno de los pueblos de misiones del Paraguay, s.7 v. 1 e. 14 n. 4: 10v, 12r, 20v, 46r, 47v. (Hereafter AGN-BN, Ordenanzas)

10. Campillo, *Nuevo Sistema*, 65.

11. RAED, 3:312.

12. Campillo, *Nuevo Sistema*, 127, 130–31, 162, 300.

13. Gándara, *Apuntes*, 124–25, 130.

14. Ward, *Proyecto*, 214, 251, 275; RAED, 2:623 (entry for "Estado"). Ward wrote the text in 1762. It was published in 1779.

15. RAED, 2:17.

16. Puig, *Arithmetica*; Biel, *Aritmética*. Among the earliest of these was Moya's *Arithmetica* (1569), indicating that shift of the term began gradually.

17. Campomanes, *Dictamen*, 135, 138; Campomanes, *Bosquejo*, 139, 181–82.

18. Elliot, *Empires*, 230.

19. Frankl, "Idea," 68–69.

20. LANGAS, Carta al Gobernador, Guirabo Narciso, 1768, ¶¶ 16, 17.

21. Wilde, *Religión y poder*, 195.

22. Cardiel, *Las missiones*, 65–67, 92.

23. AGN-BN, Ordenanzas, 5r, 25r, 48r.

24. LANGAS, Carta a los tenientes de Yapeyu, 1768, ¶ 5.

25. Cardiel, *Compendio*, 223.

26. LANGAS, Carta al Gobernador Bucareli, Guacuyu, 1768, ¶ 12.

27. LANGAS, Carta del pueblo de Loreto al Gobernador y Capitán general Juan José de Vertiz y Salcedo, Guirayu, 1770.

28. LANGAS, Carta desde Nuestra Señora de Itatí al Teniente General, 1770, ¶¶ 6, 9, 10.

29. Montoya, Tesoro, 131v, 329r.

30. LANGAS: Carta al Gobernador don Francisco Bucareli, Tañuira, 1768; Carta al Administrador General Juan Angel Lezcano, Pueblo de Concepción, 1772; Carta del piloto de San Cosme al Gobernador, Chandi Hipolito San Cosme, 1773; ANA, NE, 518, 4r–v.

31. Ganson, "Our Warehouses," 51.

32. LANGAS, Carta del pueblo de Loreto, 1770, ¶ 91.

33. LANGAS, Carta de San Ignacio Guasu al T. de Gobernador relativa al Corregidor, Yabe Ignacio, 1780. It is possible he was a pretender who had produced a fake order appointing him.

34. Ramírez and Ortiz, *Reglamento*.

35. Kleinpenning, *Paraguay*, 937.

36. Garavaglia, *Mercado*, 478–81.

37. Garavaglia, *Mercado*, 341.

38. Garavaglia, *Mercado*, 479–80.

39. Garavaglia, *Mercado*, 478–82.

40. Kleinpenning, *Paraguay*, 934–38.

41. AGI Buenos Aires 142, 1r-v, 3r-v, 4r–5v.

42. Sarreal, *The Guaraní*, 193.

43. Sarreal, *The Guaraní*, 205–16.

44. AGN, Interior, Leg. 34, exp. 4 (30.5.1) (2630), Indios de Misiones, Manuel Antonio Barquín solicita cincuenta indios de las misiones para cultivo de sus tierras, Año 1793, 7. (Hereafter AGN, Barquín.)

45. AGN, Barquín, 14, 19.

46. AGN, Barquín, 18, 20, 31, 33, 41, 60.

47. ANA, NE, 376, 63r–v.

48. White, *Paraguay's Autonomous Revolution*, 26; Garavaglia, *Mercado*, 203.

49. AGN, Barquín, 15, 18.

50. AGN, Barquín, 70, 91.

51. Doblas, *Memoria histórica*.

52. Doblas, *Memoria histórica*, 11, 13, 18, 81.

53. Doblas, *Memoria histórica*, 78.

54. Doblas, *Memoria histórica*, 31.

55. Ward, *Proyecto*, 268.

56. Doblas, *Memoria histórica*, 77.

57. Doblas, *Memoria histórica*, 34.

58. AGN, Interior, Leg. 30, exp. 25. "Obrando sobre varios puntos de policía y gov[no] de todos los pueblos de misiones de indios guaraníes," 21. (Hereafter AGN, Obrando.)

59. Doblas, *Memoria histórica*, 34.

60. AGN, Obrando, 14–15.

61. ANA: NE-76, 1r; NE-149, 107r–121r.

62. ANA: NE-376, 95–105; NE-519, 835; NE-439, 7r; NE-313, 28r, 29r; CJ, 1358.6 (1786); CJ 1316.9 (1799); CJ, 1308.1 (1804); CJ, 1901.4 (1798); CJ, 1999.8 (1794).

63. ANA, NE-600, 76r–87v.

64. AGN, Obrando, 16.

65. AGN BN 140, "Preceptos de Nros PPes generals y provincials," 22v; AGI Buenos Aires, 142, 8.

66. Doblas, *Memoria sobre una nueva forma*, 7.

67. Doblas, *Memoria sobre una nueva forma*, 27.

68. Doblas, *Memoria sobre una nueva forma*, 27.

69. Doblas, *Memoria sobre una nueva forma*, 15, 39.

70. Ward, *Proyecto*, 268.

71. Elliot, *Empires*, 357.

72. Sušnik, *El rol*, 2:83.

73. Sušnik, *El rol*, 2:84–85. Lastarria, *Documentos*, 39.

74. AGN Div. Colonia, sec. Gobierno, Sala IX, Leg. 18.3.1, Fray Joaquín Corcio al virrey Áviles, San Francisco Javier, 19 de julio de 1800, 1r–v.

75. Ganson, *The Guaraní*, 152.

76. Lastarria, *Documentos*, 3:364.

77. LANGAS: Carta al Señor Virrey Marques de Aviles, Tapiae, 1800; Carta al Sr. Virrey, Chememba, 1800.

78. LANGAS, Carta al Señor Virrey Marques de Aviles, Tapiae, 1800, ¶¶ 5–6.

79. LANGAS, Carta al Señor Virrey Marques de Aviles, Tapiae, 1800, ¶¶ 8–9.

80. LANGAS, Carta al Señor Virrey, Chememba, 1800, ¶¶ 3–4.

81. Montoya, Tesoro, 317v.

82. Boidin, "Teko aguyjei," 41–42.

83. Lastarria, *Documentos*, 363. See also Couchonnal and Wilde, "De la política."

84. Lastarria, *Documentos*, 374–76.

85. Sušnik, *El rol*, 2:88.

86. Quarleri, "El 'beneficio.'"

87. Guillermo Wilde says that of 42,885 Guaraní remaining in former mission communities at the end of the eighteenth century, 6,121 had been "freed" by 1801. Wilde, *Religión y poder*, 271.

88. AGN Interior Leg. 450, exp. 1129, "Expediente obrado para el cumplimiento de Real Cedula de 17 de marzo de 1803 por la qual se manda que los 30 pueblos de Misiones del Uruguay, . . . se reduzcan al nuevo sistema de livertad de sus naturales, aboliendo el de comunidad en que hasta ahora han vivido," 0004–0005. (Hereafter AGN, Expediente.)

89. AGN, Expediente, 0026–0030, 0040–0043.

90. AGN, Expediente, 0031–0033.

91. Doblas, *Memoria sobre una nueva forma*, 7–8

92. Doblas, *Memoria sobre una nueva forma*, 7.

93. AGN, Expediente, 0060–062; "Declaraciones y expresas resoluciones soberanas . . . se proponen en 55 art⁰ˢ," in Lastarria, *Colonias*, 72–143.

94. AGN, Expediente, 0036–0056.

95. Garavaglia, *Mercado*,353.

96. Rivarola, "Castas y clases," 63.

97. ANA, SH, 147, no. 6. Kleinpenning, *Paraguay*, 806–10.

98. Garavaglia, *Mercado*, 353–70.

99. ANA, SH, 147, no. 6.

100. Garavaglia, *Mercado*, 369–70.

101. AGN, Expediente, 0078.

102. AGN, Expediente, 0093.

103. AGN, Expediente, 0118–0123. My emphasis.

104. AGN, Expediente, 0125.

105. AGN, Expediente, 0160–0167.

106. Townsend, *Dissertation*, 11, 27.

107. Townsend, *Journey*, 1:279–82.

108. Campomanes, *Bosquejo*; Campomanes, *Respuesta*, 63–64.

109. R. Smith, "*Wealth*." See A. Smith, *Investigación*.

110. Mackay, "*Lazy. Improvident People*," 150–51. See also R. Smith, "*Wealth*," 110.

111. AGN, Expediente, 0160–0167.

112. ANA, NE 2900, 124v–125r, 121r. I am grateful to Capucine Boidin for a personal communication and for supplying me with an early, unpublished version of her own translation of this document.

Chapter 8

1. Peramás, La República *de Platón*.

2. Peramás, La República *de Platón*, 20, 43–44.

3. In England: Starkey, *Dialogue*. In France: Gentillet, *Anti-Machiavel*. For Jesuits: Ribadeneyra, *Tratado*.

4. Hobbes, *Leviathan*, 110.

5. Cooper, *An Inquiry*, 80.

6. Locke, *Second Treatise*, 79 (sec. 138).

7. Mandeville, *Fable*, 3, 9, 23, 24.

8. Sheehan and Wahrman, *Invisible Hands*.

9. Pope, *Essay*, 69.

10. Aristotle, *Nicomachean Ethics*, Books 8 and 9; Aristotle, *Politics*, 22–29 (1257a–1258b).

11. Aristotle, *Politics*, 51 (1263b). Aristotle's polis assumed a society in which unequals could be harmonized by the operation of virtue upon the souls of men. See MacIntyre, *After Virtue*, 231.

12. Hirschman, *Passions*, 12–14.

13. Hume, *Treatise*, 255–56, 261.

14. Hume, *Essays*, 113.

15. Hume, *Essays*, 93; Hirschman, *Passions*, 48–56.

16. See Locke, *Works*, 9:564, "The catalogue and character of most books of voyages."

17. Frezier, *Voyage*.

18. Frezier, *Voyage*, 323, 325, 334.

19. Muratori, *Il cristianesimo*, chaps. 14, 15. BNE, Recoletos: Gen: 3/70093.

20. Montesquieu, *De l'Esprit*, 1:61–62.

21. Montesquieu, *De l'Esprit*, 1:34, 62.

22. Montesquieu, *De l'Esprit*, 2:254–55.

23. Montesquieu, *De l'Esprit*, 1:57.

24. Montesquieu, *De l'Esprit*, 1:66.

25. Rousseau, *Discours sur l'origine*, 65, 68, 129, 131, 174, 207, 254.

26. Rousseau, *Discours sur l'économie*, 9, 25, 30, 34, 46.

27. Boudet, *Journal*, 97–105.

28. Rousseau, *Discours sur l'economie*, 42.

29. This first state of purity has been thought of as a "referential allegory" rather than an actually occurring historical state. See Cro, *Noble Savage*, 160.

30. Rousseau, *Discours sur l'origine*, 69.

31. Rousseau, *Discours sur l'origine*, 91.

32. Rousseau, *Du Contrat*, 105.

33. Rousseau, *Du Contrat*, 168–218; Cro, "Classical Antiquity," 415; Rousseau, *Discours sur l'origine*, 90; Rousseau, *Émile*.

34. Anonymous, *Histoire*.

35. Castel, *L'homme*, 232.

36. *Gentleman's Magazine*, 23:23–25.

37. Burke, *Account*, 1:286.

38. Burke, *Account*, 1:181–82.

39. *Gentleman's Magazine,* 23:23–25

40. *Modern Part,* 39:153, 198, 201.

41. Grimm, *Correspondance,* 2:228.

42. D'Argenson, *Considérations,* 109, 111.

43. *Polite Miscellany,* 203–11.

44. *London Magazine,* 38: 263–65, 461–65, 512–15, 568–751, 613–16, 662–66.

45. Charlevoix, *History.* For Charlevoix's influence on Rousseau, Diderot, Voltaire, and Raynal, see Cro, "Classical Antiquity."

46. Cro, "Classical Antiquity," 417.

47. Ellingson, *Myth.*

48. Montaigne, "Of Cannibals," ch. 30.

49. Toulmin, *Cosmopolis,* 41–42.

50. Voltaire, *Candide,* 164.

51. D'Alembert, *Sur la destruction,* 24–27.

52. *Encyclopédie,* 9:462.

53. Mably, *Doutes,* 1–2.

54. Mably, *Doutes,* 9–13.

55. Raynal, *Philosophical and Political History.*

56. Raynal, 3:145; 2:300. Raynal and Diderot both wrote about Paraguay, the missions, and the Guaraní. I shall refer to Raynal because he was widely recognized as the author of the entire work and its many subsequent editions.

57. Raynal, *Philosophical and Political History,* 2:260, 366.

58. Raynal, *Philosophical and Political History,* 2:285.

59. Raynal, *Philosophical and Political History,* 3:264, 328.

60. Raynal, *Philosophical and Political History,* 3:236, 254, 344.

61. Raynal, *Philosophical and Political History,* 3:288, 476.

62. Raynal, *Philosophical and Political History,* 2:289.

63. Raynal, *Philosophical and Political History,* 2:290.

64. Combe, *Le triomphe,* 2:288; Raynal, *Philosophical and Political History,* 4:722.

65. Raynal, *Philosophical and Political History,* 4:212.

66. Kames, *Sketches,* 1:1, 71, 376, 398, 400, 404, 415, 428, 475, 477; 2:33, 511, 523.

67. Kames, *Sketches,* 1:405.

68. Kames, *Sketches,* 1:409.

69. Robertson, *History of America* 1:313. On La Condamine in Ecuador, see Ferreiro, *Measure.*

70. A. Smith, *Inquiry,* 1:41–42.

71. A. Smith, *Investigación.*

72. Sheehan and Wahrman, *Invisible Hands.*

73. *London Magazine,* 40:294–95, 316, 349, 373, 395–97, 397–98, 402–4, 494.

74. Bougainville, *Voyage,* 56, 58.

75. Diderot, "Supplément."

76. Tucker, *Treatise*, 82, 83, 87, 93.

77. Tucker, *Treatise*, 154.

78. Townsend, *Dissertation*, 23, 25–26.

79. Genty, *L'influence*, 12, 16, 98.

80. A. R. D. S., *Essay*.

81. A. R. D. S., *Essay*, 1, 5, 8, 80, 83, 90, 91, 103, 162, 188.

82. Peramás, La República *de Platón*, 216–17; Monboddo, *Antient g*, 101–2.

83. Herder, *Outlines*, 285.

84. Gosselin, *Reflexions*, 21–22. See Imbruglia, *Jesuit Missions*, 262.

85. Addison, *Collection*, 30–32.

86. Degérando, *Observation*, 61.

87. Berlin, "Herder," 430.

88. Degérando, *Observation*, 61, 63, 64, 77.

89. Degérando, *Observation*, 97.

90. Degérando, *Observation*, 87.

91. Godwin, *Of Population*, viii; Malthus, *Essay*, 531.

92. Godwin, *Of Population*, 1.

93. Godwin, *Of Population*, 71, 72–75, 104, 105.

94. Godwin, *Of Population* 543; Malthus, *Essay*, 11.

95. Godwin, *Of Population*, 75. Emphasis in Godwin.

96. Malthus, *Essay*, 42.

Conclusion

1. LANGAS: "Proclama a los Naturales de los Pueblos de las Misiones" (1810), ¶¶ 4, 16; "Proclama al Pueblo Paraguayo," (1810); Boidin, "Textos".

2. Boidin, "Textos," 6-7.

3. LANGAS: "Proclama a los Naturales," ¶¶ 9, 10, 11; "Proclama al Pueblo Paraguayo," ¶¶ 7, 12.

4. LANGAS, "Proclama a los Naturales," ¶¶ 14,16; Boidin, "Textos," 5–6.

5. LANGAS, "Ratificación del decreto que libertó a los indígenas del tributo, abolición de la mita, encomiendas, etc." (1813), ¶ 4.

6. Boidin, "Textos," 11–12.

7. RAED, 1:364.

8. Lempérière, *Entre Dieu*, 50–60. Boidin, "Textos," 11–12.

9. Couchonnal and Wilde, "De la política," 19–20.

10. Robertson and Robertson, *Letters*, 94, 103.

11. Adelman, *Republic of Capital*, 290.

12. E. Burns, *Poverty*, 128.

13. Whigham and Potthast, "Paraguayan Rosetta Stone"; "Letter to Bartolomé Mitre," 1872.

14. Adelman, *Republic of Capital*.

15. Warren, *Rebirth*, 184–85.

16. *Cosme Monthly*; Wilding, *Paraguayan Experiment*, 18.

17. *Cosme Monthly.*

18. MacPherson, *Political Theory*, 61–70, 78–87.

19. Sahlins, *Western Illusion*, 112; Karatani, *The Structure*, 299.

20. This is not the place to take up that sense of "society" among Amerindians that included all of the other-humans (animals) that made/make up the world. See Viveiros de Castro, "Cosmological Deixis," 469–88.

21. Fausto, "If God," 83, 93–94.

22. McCloskey, *Bourgeois Dignity*; McCloskey, *Bourgeois Virtues.*

23. Michielse and Krieken, "Policing the Poor."

24. Thompson, "Moral Economy," 90.

25. Polanyi, *Great Transformation*, 89, 144.

26. Polanyi, *Great Transformation*, 35.

27. Polanyi, *Great Transformation*, 79.

28. Scott, *Moral Economy.*

29. Thompson, "Moral Economy," 132, 136.

30. Reed, *Prophets*, 212.

31. Chamorro, "Imagens," 79–107.

32. Bolivia's Plurinational Constitution of 2009, ch. 2, art. 8. See Lalander "Ethnic Rights"; United Nations, *Declaration of Indigenous Human Rights.*

33. Giraldo, *Utopías*; Villar and Combès, "La Tierra"; Edelman, "Bringing the Moral Economy."

34. Rojas, "Sacerdote."

35. Lear, *Radical Hope*, 97, 153.

36. Pierri, "Como Acabará, 167.

37. Melià, *Mundo guaraní*, 176–80.

38. Hoxie, *Parading through History*, 7.

39. Danowski and Viveiros de Castro, *Ends of the World*; Raworth, *Doughnut Economics*, 61–78, 89–91; Overing and Passes, "Introduction"; Karatani, *The Structure*, 291.

40. Raworth, *Doughtnut Economics*, 89.

41. A. Smith, *Theory*, 86 (II.ii.3.3).

42. Melià and Temple, *El don*, 29.

Bibliography

Acosta, José de. *De promulgando evangelio apud barbaros: Sive de procuranda indorum salute, libri sex.* 9th ed. London, 1670.

Addison, Joseph. *A Collection of Interesting Anecdotes, Memoirs, Allegories, Essays, and Poetical Fragments: Tending to Amuse the Fancy, and Inculcate Morality.* London, 1793.

Adelman, Jeremy. "Introduction: The Moral Economy, Careers of a Concept." *Humanity: An International Journal of Human Rights, Humanitarianism, and Development* 11, no. 2 (Summer 2020): 187–92.

———. *Republic of Capital: Buenos Aires and the Legal Transformation of the Atlantic World.* Stanford, CA: Stanford University Press, 1999.

Adoue, Cecilia, Mikhaël Orantin, and Capucine Boidin. "*Diálogos en guaraní,* un manuscrit inédit des réductions jésuites du Paraguay (XVIIIᵉ siècle)." *Nuevo Mundo/Mundos Nuevos.* Posted December 1, 2015. https://journals.openedition.org/nuevomundo/68665.

Alba, Diego Núñez. *Diálogos de la vida del soldado.* Madrid, 1890. First published Salamanca, 1552.

Alberti, Giorgio, and Enrique Mayer, eds. *Reciprocidad e intercambio en los andes peruanos.* Lima: Instituto de Estudios Peruanos, 1974.

Alconini, Sonia. *Southeast Inka Frontiers: Boundaries and Interactions.* Gainesville: University Press of Florida, 2016.

Alencastro, Luiz Felipe de. *The Trade in the Living: The Formation of Brazil in the South Atlantic, Sixteenth to Seventeenth Centuries.* New York: SUNY Press, 2018.

Algazi, Gadi. "Feigned Reciprocities: Lords, Peasants and the Afterlife of Late Medieval Social Strategies." In *Negotiating the Gift: Pre-modern Figurations of Exchange,* edited by Gadi Algazi, Valentin Groebner, and Bernhard Jussen, 99–127. Göttingen: Vandenhoeck & Ruprecht, 2003.

———. "Introduction: Doing Things with Gifts." In *Negotiating the Gift: Pre-Modern Figurations of Exchange,* edited by Gadi Algazi, Valentin Groebner, and Bernhard Jussen, 9–27. Göttingen: Vandenhoeck & Ruprecht, 2003.

Ali, Tariq Omar. *A Local History of Global Capital: Jute and Peasant Life in the Bengal Delta.* Princeton University Press, 2018.

Alighieri, Dante. *The Divine Comedy 1: Hell.* Translated by Dorothy Sayers. New York: Penguin, 1950.

Alonso-Lasheras, Diego. *Luis de Molina's* De Iustitia et Iure: *Justice as Virtue in an Economic Context.* Brill, 2011.

Anonymous. *Histoire de Nicolas I, Roy du Paraguai, et Empereur des Mamelus.* Saint Paul, 1756.

Aquinas, St. Thomas. "De regimine principum." In *St. Thomas Aquinas: Political Writings,* edited by R. W. Dyson, 3–51. Cambridge: Cambridge University Press, 2002.

———. *De Regno ad regem Cypri: On Kingship to the King of Cyprus.* Translated by G. B. Phelan. Toronto: Pontifical Institute of Medieval Studies, 1949.

———. "On Kingship." In *The Political Ideas of St. Thomas Aquinas,* edited by Dino Bigongiari, 175–96. New York: Free Press, 1997.

———. *Summa Theologica.* Vols. 1–5. Allen, TX: Christian Classics, 1981.

A. R. D. S. *An Essay on Civil Government or Society Restored.* London, 1793.

Aristotle. *The Nicomachean Ethics.* Translated by David Ross. London: Oxford University Press, 1925.

———. *The Politics of Aristotle.* Edited by Ernest Barker. London: Oxford University Press, 1946.

Arnold, Thomas C. "Rethinking Moral Economy." *American Political Science Review* 95, no. 1 (March 2001): 85–95.

Atlas Histórico do Brasil. "A Igreja católica e as Missões." FGV CPDOC. https://atlas .fgv.br/marcos/igreja-catolica-e-colonizacao/mapas/missoes-jesuitas-na-bacia-do -paraguai.

Austin, Shawn Michael. *Colonial Kinship: Guaraní, Spaniards, and Africans in Paraguay.* Albuquerque: University of New Mexico Press, 2020.

———. "Guaraní Kinship and the Encomienda Community in Colonial Paraguay, Sixteenth and Early Seventeenth Centuries." *Colonial Latin American Review* 24, no. 4 (2015): 545–71.

"Autos sobre la visita de las reducciones del Paraná y Uruguay, que hizo el gobernador don Jacinto de Lariz el año de 1647." *Revista del Archivo General de Buenos Aires* 2 (1870): 35–144.

Avellaneda, Mercedes. "Conflicto y disputas territoriales entre jesuitas y asunceños: La Revolución de los Comuneros y sus consecuencias en el espacio de las misiones." Academia, online. https://www.academia.edu/3558977/Conflicto_y_disputas _territoriales_entre_jesuitas_y_asuncenos_la_Revolución_de_los_Comuneros_y _sus_consecuencias_en_el_espacio_de_las_misiones.

———. "Orígenes de la alianza jesuita-guaraní y su consolidación en el siglo XVII." *Memoria Americana: Cuadernos de Etnohistoria* 8 (1999): 173–200.

Avellaneda, Mercedes, and Lía Quarleri. "Las milicias guaraníes en el Paraguay y Río de la Plata: Alcances y limitaciones (1649–1756)." *Estudos Ibero-Americanos* 33, no. 1 (2007): 109–32.

Azpilcueta Navarro, Martín de. *Comentario resolutorio de usuras*. Salamanca, 1556.

————. *Manual de confesores y penitentes*. Salamanca, 1556.

Bailey, Gauvin Alexander. *Art on the Jesuits Missions in Asia and Latin America, 1542–1773*. Toronto: University of Toronto Press, 2001.

Barbosa, Paulo Antunha. "A 'Terra sem Mal' de Curt Nimuendajú e a 'Emigração dos Cayuáz' de João Henrique Elliot: Notas sobre as 'migrações' guarani no século XIX." *Tellus* 13, no. 24 (January–June 2013): 121–58.

Bartra, S. J., Enrique. *Tercer concilio limense, 1582–1583*. Lima: Publicaciones de la Facultad Pontificia y Civil de Teología, 1982.

Bataille, Georges. *The Accursed Share: An Essay on General Economy*. Vol. 1. New York: Zone Books, 1988.

Beckert, Sven. *Empire of Cotton: A Global History*. New York: Vintage Books, 2015.

Bellarmine, Robert. "De officio principis Christiani." In Bk. 1, Ch. 6, *Jesuit Writings of the Early Modern Period, 1540–1640*, edited by John P. Donnelly, S.J., 221–30. Indianapolis: Hackett, 2006.

Berlin, Isaiah. "Herder and the Enlightenment." In *The Proper Study of Mankind: An Anthology of Essays*. 359–434. New York: Farrar, Straus and Giroux, 1997.

Bessire, Lucas, and David Bond. "Ontological Anthropology and the Deferral of Critique." *American Ethnologist* 41, no. 3 (2014): 440–56.

Biel y Aznar, José. *Aritmética especulativa y práctica para lo mercantil*. Zaragoza, 1789.

Bijsterveld, Arnoud-Jan. "The Medieval Gift as Agent of Social Bonding and Political Power: A Comparative Approach." In *Medieval Transformations: Texts, Power and Gifts in Context*, edited by E. Cohen and M. B. de Jong, 123–56. London: Brill, 2001.

Blackburn, Robin. *The Making of New World Slavery: From the Baroque to the Modern, 1492–1800*. New York: Verso, 1997.

Blanco, José María. *Historia documentada de la vida y gloriosa muerte de los padres Roque González de Santa Cruz, Alonso Rodríguez y Juan del Castillo de la Compañía de Jesús, mártires del Caaró y Yjuhí*. Buenos Aires: Sebastián de Amorrortu, 1929.

Bloch, Marc. *Feudal Society*. Vol. 1. London: Routledge & Kegan Paul, 1965.

Bloch, Marc, and Jonathan Parry. "Introduction: Money and the Morality of Exchange." In *Money and the Morality of Exchange*, edited by Marc Bloch and Jonathan Parry. Cambridge: Cambridge University Press, 1989.

Block, Fred, and Margaret R. Somers. *The Power of Market Fundamentalism: Karl Polanyi's Critique*. Cambridge, MA: Harvard University Press, 2016.

Bodin, Jean. *Les six livres de la République*. Lyons, 1587. First published 1576.

Boidin, Capucine. "Mots guarani du pouvoir: Pouvoir des mots guarani. Essai d'anthropologie historique et linguistique (XIX–XVI et XVI–XIX)." Unpublished manuscript. Paris, Universités Sorbonne Nouvelle Paris 3 (2017): 63–80.

————. "Teko aguyjei, 'derechos,' 'vida buena,' un concepto político central de las proclamas y cartas del general Belgrano traducidas al guaraní." *HAL* (2016): 25–51. https://halshs.archives-ouvertes.fr/halshs-01716477/document.

————. "Textos de la modernidad política en guaraní (1810–1813)." *Corpus* 4, no. 2 (2014): 2–18.

Booth, William James. "On the Idea of the Moral Economy." *American Political Science Review* 88, no. 3 (September 1994): 653–67.

Botero, Giovanni. *Botero: The Reason of State*. Edited by Robert Bireley. Cambridge: Cambridge University Press, 2017.

Boudet, Chez Antoine. *Journal Oeconomique, ou Memoires, Notes et Avis sur les Arts, l'Agriculture, le Commerce*. Paris, septembre 1755.

Bougainville, Lewis-Antoine de. *A Voyage around the World*. London, 1772. First published Paris, 1771.

Bracciolini, Poggio. *De Avaritia (Dialogus contra Avaritiam)*. Translated by G. Germano. Livorno: Belforte Editore Livraio, 1994.

Burke, Edmund. *An Account of the European Settlements in America*. 5th ed. Vol. 1. London, 1770. First published 1757.

Burns, E. Bradford. *The Poverty of Progress: Latin America in the Nineteenth Century*. Berkeley: University of California Press, 1983.

Burns, Robert, ed. *Las Siete Partidas: Medieval Law; Lawyers and Their Work*. Vol. 3. Translated by Samuel Parsons. Philadelphia: University of Pennsylvania Press, 2001.

Cabeza de Vaca, Alvar Núñez. "Estatutos y ordenanzas que mandó publicar el gobernador D. Alvar Núñez Cabeza de Vaca, sobre el trato y gobierno de los indios." In *Legislación sobre Indios del Río de la Plata en el siglo XVI*, edited by Juan Carlos García Santillán, 347–56. Madrid, 1928.

———. *Relación de los naufragios y comentarios*. Tomo 1. Madrid: Librería General de Victoriano Suárez, 1906.

Calle, Saravia de la. *Instrucción de mercaderes muy provechosos*. Madrid: Colección Joyas Bibliográficas, 1949. First published 1544.

Camacho, Francisco Gómez. *El pensamiento económico en la Escuela de Salamanca*. Edited by Ricardo Robledo. Salamanca: Universidad de Salamanca, 1998.

Camacho, Ramón Kuri. "Francisco Suárez, teólogo y filósofo de la imaginación y la libertad." *Revista de Filosofía* 25, no. 58 (2008): 79–101.

Campillo y Cossío, José del. *Nuevo Sistema de gobierno económico para la América*. Madrid, 1789.

Campomanes, Pedro Rodríguez de. *Bosquejo de política económica española, delineado sobre el estado presente de sus intereses*. Edited by Jorge Cejudo. Madrid: Editora Nacional, 1984. First published 1750.

———. *Dictamen fiscal de expulsión de los Jesuítas de España (1766–1767)*. Edited by Jorge Cejudo and Teofanes Egido. Madrid: Fundación Universitaria Española, 1977.

———. *Respuesta fiscal: Sobre abolir la tasa y establecer el comercio de granos*. Madrid, 1764.

Candela, Guillaume. "Influences of the Lascasian Discourse in Paraguay (Sixteenth Century): the Itinerary of Martín González." In *Bartolomé de las Casas, O.P.: History Philosophy, and Theology in the Age of European Expansion*, edited by David Thomas Orique and Rady Roldán-Figueroa, 392–420. London: Brill, 2019.

———. "Las mujeres indígenas en la conquista del Paraguay entre 1541 y 1575." *Nuevo Mundo Mundos Nuevos* (September 2014): 4–15. http://journals.openedition.org/nuevo mundo/67133.

————. "Paraguay and Iberian Empires: Contacts, Connexions, and Migrations (1538–1575)." Unpublished paper presented at the 9th Rio de La Plata Workshop, William and Mary College, Williamsburg, Virginia, 20 March 2018.

Caraman, Philip. *The Lost Paradise: The Jesuit Republic in South America*. London: Sidgwick and Jackson, 1975.

Cardiel, José. *Compendio de la historia del Paraguay (1780)*. Edited by José M. Mariluz Urquijo. Buenos Aires: Fundación para la Educación, la Ciencia y la Cultura, 1984.

————. *Declaración de la verdad: Obra inédita*. Buenos Aires: Impr. de J. A. Alsina, 1900.

————. *Las misiones del Paraguay*. Edited by Héctor Sáinz Ollero. Madrid: Historia 16, 1989.

Cardim, Fernão. *Tratados da Terra e Gente do Brasil*. Rio de Janeiro: J. Leite & Cia., 1925. First published 1584.

Carrier, James G. *Gifts and Commodities: Exchange and Western Capitalism since 1700*. New York: Routledge, 1995.

————. "Moral Economy: What's in a Name." *Anthropological Theory* 18, no. 1 (2018): 18–35.

"Carta de Antonio Betschon a R.P. Javier Am-Rhin provincial de Alemania superior," Paraguay, 1719. "El Río de la Plata visto por viajeros alemanes del siglo XVIII, según cartas traducidas por Juan Mühn." *Revista del Instituto Histórico y Geográfico del Uruguay* 7 (193): 241–49.

"Carta del factor Dorantes, 5 marzo 1545." In *Correspondencia de los oficiales reales de Hacienda del Río de la Plata con los reyes de España,* edited by Roberto Levillier, 1:80. Madrid: Est. tip. "Sucesores de Rivadeneyra," 1915.

Cartas anuas de la Provincia Jesuítica del Paraguay, 1632 a 1634. Edited by Ernesto Maeder. Buenos Aires: Academia Nacional de la Historia, 1990.

Cartas anuas de la Provincia Jesuítica del Paraguay, 1644. Edited by Ernesto Maeder. Resistencia, Chaco: Instituto de Investigaciones Geohistóricas—Conicet, 2007.

Cartas anuas de la Provincia Jesuítica del Paraguay, 1645–1646 y 1647–1449. Edited by Ernesto Maeder. Resistencia, Chaco: Instituto de Investigaciones Geohistóricas—Conicet, 2007.

Cartas anuas de la Provincia Jesuítica del Paraguay, 1650–1652 y 1652–1654. Edited by María Laura Salinas and Julio Folkenand. Resistencia, Chaco: Instituto de Investigaciones Geohistóricas—Conicet, 2008.

Cartas anuas de la Provincia Jesuítica del Paraguay, 1658–60 y 1659–62. Resistencia, Chaco: Instituto de Investigaciones Geohistóricas—Conicet, 2010.

Cartas anuas de la Provincia Jesuítica del Paraguay, 1663–1666, 1667–1668, 1669–1672, 1672–1675. Edited by María Laura Salinas and Julio Folkenand. Asunción: Centro de Estudios Antropológicos de la Universidad Católica, 2013.

Cartas anuas de la Provincia Jesuítica del Paraguay, 1681–1692, 1689–1692, 1689–1700. Edited by María Laura Salinas and Julio Folkenand. Asunción: Centro de Estudios Antropológicos de la Universidad Católica, 2015.

Cartas anuas de la Provincia Jesuítica del Paraguay, 1714–1720, . . . 1756–1762. Edited by María Laura Salinas and Julio Folkenand. Asunción: Centro de Estudios Antropológicos de la Universidad Católica, 2017.

Castel, Père Louis-Bertrand. *L'homme moral opposé à l'homme physique de Monsieur R***: Lettres philosophiques, où l'on refute le déisme du jour.* Toulouse, 1756.

Castro e Silva, Marcos Araújo, et al. "Genomic Insight into the Origins and Dispersal of the Brazilian Coastal Natives" *Proceedings of the National Academy of Sciences of the USA* 115, no. 5 (February 4, 2020): 2372–77.

Chakravarti, Ananya. *The Empire of Apostles: Religion, Accommodation, and the Imagination of Empire in Early Modern Brazil and India.* New Delhi: Oxford University Press, 2018.

Chamorro, Graciela. "Imagens espaciais utópicas: Símbolos de liberdade e desterro nos povos guarani." *Indiana* 27 (2010): 79–107.

———. *Teología guaraní.* Quito: Ediciones Abya-Yala, 2004.

Charlevoix, Pierre Francis-Xavier. *The History of Paraguay.* 2 vols. London: Lockyer Davis, 1769.

Clastres, Hélène. *The Land-Without-Evil: Tupí-Guaraní Prophetism.* Chicago: University of Illinois Press, 1995.

Clastres, Pierre. *The Archeology of Violence.* Los Angeles: Semiotext(e), 2010.

———. "Échange et pouvoir: Philosophie de la chefferie indienne." *L'Homme* 2, no. 1 (January–April 1962): 51–65.

———. *Society against the State.* New York: Zone Books, 1989.

Clendinnen, Inga. *Ambivalent Conquests: Maya and Spaniard in Yucatan, 1517–1570.* Cambridge: Cambridge University Press, 1987.

———. *Aztecs: An Interpretation.* Cambridge: Cambridge University Press, 1995.

Clossey, Luke. *Salvation and Globalization in Early Jesuit Missions.* Cambridge: Cambridge University Press, 2008.

Combe, Joseph André Brun de la. *Le triomphe du nouveau monde.* Vol. 1. Paris, 1785.

The Constitutions of the Society of Jesus and Their Complementary Norms: A Complete English Translation of the Official Latin Texts. St. Louis: The Institute of Jesuit Sources, 1996.

Conzelmann, Paulwalter. *Wirtschaftswachstum und -entwicklung im jesuitenstaat von Paraguay.* Köln: Kölner Dissertation, 1958.

Cooper, Anthony Ashley (Earl of Shaftesbury). *An Inquiry Concerning Virtue, or Merit: The Moralists: A Philosophical Rhapsody.* Vol. 2. London, 1711.

Cosme Monthly (Colonia Cosme, Caazapa, Paraguay, 1894). State Library of South Australia, Digital Collections. PRG 1343/3.

Couchonnal, Ana, and Guillermo Wilde. "De la política de la lengua a la lengua de la política: Cartas guaraníes en la transición de la colonia a la era independiente." *Corpus: Archivos virtuales de la alteridad americana* 4, no. 1 (2014): 1–32.

Covarrubias Orozco, Sebastián de. *Tesoro de la lengua castellana, o española.* [Pt. 1 to 602v is cited as <page number>; Pt. 2 starts again with 1r and is cited as <page number>(2)]. Madrid, 1611.

Cro, Stelio. "Classical Antiquity, America, and the Myth of the Noble Savage." In *European Images of the Americas and the Classical Tradition*, edited by Wolfgang Haase and Meyer Reinhold, 379–418. Vol. 1, part 1 of *The Classical Tradition and the Americas*. Berlin, 1993.

———. *The Noble Savage: Allegory of Freedom*. Waterloo, Canada: Wilfrid Laurier University Press, 1990.

Cushner, Nicholas P. *Farm and Factory: The Jesuits and the Development of Agrarian Capitalism in Colonial Quito, 1600–1767*. New York: SUNY Press, 1983.

———. *Jesuit Ranches and the Agrarian Development of Colonial Argentina, 1650–1767*. New York: SUNY Press, 1984.

———. *Lords of the Land: Sugar, Wine, and Jesuit Estates of Coastal Peru, 1600–1767*. New York: SUNY Press, 1980.

———. *Why Have You Come Here?: The Jesuits and the First Evangelization of Native America*. New York: Oxford University Press, 2006.

D'Alembert, Jean Le Rond. *Sur la destruction des Jésuites en France, par un auteur désintéressé*. Edinburgh, 1765. https://archive.org/stream/surladestructio01alemgoog#page/n8/mode/2up/search/paraguai.

Danowski, Déborah, and Eduardo Viveiros de Castro. *The Ends of the World*. Translated by Rodrigo Guimarães Nunes. Cambridge, UK: Polity Press, 2017.

D'Argenson, Marquis. *Considérations sur le Gouvernement de la France*. Amsterdam, 1764.

Davis, Natalie Zemon. *The Gift in Sixteenth-Century France*. Madison: University of Wisconsin Press, 2000.

Degérando, Joseph-Marie (Baron). *The Observation of Savage Peoples*. Translated by F. C. T. Moore. London: Routledge and Kegan Paul, 1969. First published Paris, 1800.

Diderot, Denis. "Supplément au voyage de Bougainville." In Vol. 2 of *Oeuvres complètes*, 193–250. Paris, 1875–77. http://classiques.uqac.ca/classiques/Diderot_denis/voyage_bougainville/Supplement_bougainville.pdf.

Doblas, Gonzalo de. *Memoria histórica, geográfica, política y económica sobre la Provincia de Misiones de indios guaranís*. Buenos Aires, 1836. First published 1785.

———. *Memoria sobre una nueva forma de gobierno para la provincia de Misiones, con arreglo al sistema de libertad de los indios y abolición de las comunidades* (Concepción, 1805). In *La Revista de Buenos Aires* 8, no. 85, 1–28. Buenos Aires, 1870.

Documentos para la historia de Argentina. Vol. 19. Buenos Aires, 1927.

Dueñas, Juan. *Espejo de consolación de tristes*. Part 3. Barcelona, 1580. First published 1542–1548.

Dufy, Caroline, and Florence Weber. *Más allá de la gran división: Sociología, economía y etnografía*. Buenos Aires: Antropofagia, 2009.

Eagleton, Terry. *Materialism*. New Haven, CT: Yale University Press, 2017.

Echevarri, Bernardo Ibáñez de. *Reyno jesuítico del Paraguay*. Vol. 4. Madrid: 1770.

Edelman, Marc. "Bringing the Moral Economy Back in . . . to the Study of 21st-Century Transnational Peasant Movements." *American Anthropologist* 107, no. 3 (September 2005): 331–45.

Ellingson, Ter. *The Myth of the Noble Savage*. Berkeley: University of California Press, 2001.

Elliot, John. *Empires of the Atlantic World: Britain and Spain in America, 1492–1830.* New Haven, CT: Yale University Press, 2006.

Encyclopédie, ou dictionnaire raisonné des sciences, des arts et des métiers, etc. Autumn 2017 edition. Vol. 9, no. 462. Original edited by Denis Diderot and Jean le Rond d'Alembert. 2017 version edited by Robert Morrissey and Glenn Roe. University of Chicago: ARTFL Encyclopédie Project. http://encyclopedie.uchicago.edu/.

D'Evreux, Yves. *Voyage dans le Nord du Brésil fait durant les années 1613 et 1614.* Paris: Librairie A. Franck, 1864. First published 1615.

Fasolt, Constantin. *The Limits of History.* Chicago: University of Chicago Press, 2004.

Fausto, Carlos. "Se Deus fosse jaguar: Canibalismo e cristianismo entre os Guaraní (séculos XVI–XX)." *MANA* 11, no. 2 (October 2005): 385–418.

———. *Warfare and Shamanism in Amazonia.* Cambridge: Cambridge University Press, 2012.

Fernandes, Florestan. *A função social da guerra na sociedade tupinambá.* São Paulo: Museu Paulista, 1952.

Ferreiro, Larrie. *Measure of the Earth: The Enlightenment Expedition that Reshaped Our World.* New York: Basic Books, 2011.

Figueroa, Cristóbal Suárez de. *El pasajero: advertencias utilísimas a la vida humana.* Madrid: Biblioteca Renacimiento, 1913. First published Madrid, 1617.

———. *Varias noticias importantes a la humana comunicación.* Madrid, 1621.

Fogel, Ramón, and Gloria Scappini. "A través del don y la expoliación de la Economía Guaraní." In *Proceso histórico de la economía paraguaya,* edited by Luis Rojas Villegas, 20–57. Asunción: Cultura, 2012.

Frankl, Victor. "Idea del imperio español y el problema jurídico-lógico de los estados misiones en el Paraguay." In *Estudios de historia de América,* edited by Pedro M. Arcaya. 31–70. Mexico, 1948.

Frezier, Amédée François. *A Voyage to the South-Sea and along the coasts of Chili and Peru, in the Years 1712, 1713, and 1714.* London, 1735.

A Full, Clear, and Authorised Account of the Late Conspiracy in Portugal: The Horrid ATTEMPT upon the LIFE of his Most Faithful Majesty; The real Manner of discovering the PLOT; And the dreadful Execution of the CONSPIRATORS. London, 1759.

Furlong Cárdiff S.J., Guillermo. *Antonio Sepp S.J., y su Gobierno Temporal (1732).* Buenos Aires: Ediciones Theoria, 1962.

———. *José Cardiel, S.J., y su Carta-relación (1747).* Buenos Aires: Librería del Plata, 1953.

———. *Justo van Suerck y su carta sobre Buenos Aires, 1629.* Buenos Aires: Ediciones Theoria, 1963.

———. *Misiones y sus pueblos guaraníes.* Buenos Aires: s.n., 1962.

Gándara, Miguel Antonio de la. *Apuntes sobre el bien y el mal de España.* Edited by Jacinta Macias Delgado. Madrid: Instituto de Estudios Fiscales, 1988. First published 1762.

Gândavo, Pedro de Malgalhães. *Histoire de la province de Sancta Cruz.* Lisbon, 1576.

———. *Tratado da Terra do Brasil.* Vol. 100. Brasília: Edições do Senado Federal, 2008.

Gandía, Enrique de. *Francisco de Alfaro y la condición social de los indios.* Buenos Aires: "El Ateneo," 1939.

————. *Historia de la conquista del Río de la Plata y del Paraguay: Los gobiernos de don Pedro de Mendoza, Alvar Núñez y Domingo de Irala, 1535–1556.* Buenos Aires: A. García Santos, 1932.

Ganson, Barbara. *The Guaraní under Spanish Rule in the Río de la Plata.* Stanford, CA: Stanford University Press, 2003.

————. "Our Warehouses Are Empty: Guaraní Responses to the Expulsion of the Jesuits from the Rio de La Plata, 1767–1800." In *Missões Guarani: Impacto Na Sociedade Contemporânea,* 4:41–54. São Paulo: EDUC-FAPESP, 1999.

Garavaglia, Juan Carlos. "Un capítulo del mercado interno colonial: El Paraguay y su región (1537–1682)." *Nova Americana* 1 (1978): 11–55.

————. "The Crises and Transformations of Invaded Societies: The La Plata Basin (1535–1650)." In vol. 3, pts. 2 and 9 of *The Cambridge History of the Native Peoples of the Americas,* edited by Frank Salomon and Stuart B. Schwartz, 1–58. Cambridge: Cambridge University Press, 1999.

————. "La demografía paraguaya: aspectos sociales y cuantitativos (siglos XVI–XVIII)." *Suplemento Antropológico* no. 19 (1984): 19–85.

————. *Mercado interno y economía colonial.* México City: Grijalbo, 1983.

————. "Las misiones jesuíticas: utopía y realidad." In *Economía, sociedad y regiones,* 121–81. Buenos Aires: Edición de la Flor, 1987.

Garay, Blas, ed. *Colección de documentos relativos a la historia de América y particularmente a la historia del Paraguay.* Tomo 1. Asunción: Talleres Kraus, 1899.

García, Antonio Rivera. "El dilema de Saavedra Fajardo: Entre el espíritu católico y la razón de estado." In *Pensar lo público: Reflexiones políticas desde la España contemporánea,* edited by Francisco Colom González, 59–94. Medellín: Universidad Pontificia Bolivariana, 2005. http://www.saavedrafajardo.org/archivos/respublica/hispana/documento21.pdf.

García, José Barrientos. *Un siglo de moral económica en Salamanca (1526–1629).* Vol. 1. Salamanca: Universidad de Salamanca, 1985.

García Santillán, Juan Carlos. "Consulta. Advertencias de cosas de indios que tienen necesidad de remedio. 12 de agosto de 1581." (89–392). Archivo General des Indias.

————. *Legislación sobre Indios del Río de la Plata en el siglo XVI.* Madrid: Imp. del Asilo de Huérfanos del S.C. de Jesús, 1928.

————. "Ordenanzas dadas por el gobernador D Juan Ramírez de Velasco, sobre el gobierno y trato de los indios. 1 de enero de 1597." In Juan Carlos García Santillan, *Legislación sobre Indios del Río de la Plata en el siglo XVI,* 356–75. Madrid: Imp. del Asilo de Huérfanos del S.C. de Jesús, 1928.

————. "Ordenanzas dadas por el gobernador y capitán general justicia mayor y juez de residencia de las provincias del Río de la Plata Don Hernán Arias de Saavedra, sobre el tratamiento de los indios. 29 de diciembre de 1603." In Juan Carlos García Santillan, *Legislación sobre Indios del Río de la Plata en el siglo XVI,* 376–88. Madrid: Imp. del Asilo de Huérfanos del S.C. de Jesús, 1928.

Gentillet, Innocent. *Anti-Machiavel: Édition de 1576.* Edited by C. Edward Rathé. Genève: Librairie Droz, 1968.

Gentleman's Magazine, and Historical Chronicle. Vol. 23. London, January 1753.

Genty, Louis. *L'influence de la découverte de l'Amérique sur le bonheur du genre humain.* Paris, 1788.

Giraldo, Omar Felipe. *Utopías en la era de la supervivencia: Una interpretación del Buen Vivir.* México: Itaca, 2014.

Godbout, Jacques. *The World of the Gift.* Montreal: McGill-Queen's University Press, 1998.

Godwin, William. *Of Population: An Enquiry Concerning the Power of Increase in the Numbers of Mankind.* London, 1820.

Goeje, C. H. de. *Philosophy, Initiation and Myths of the Indians of Guiana and Adjacent Countries.* Leiden: Brill, 1943.

Golin, Tau. *A Guerra Guaranítica: Como os exércitos de Portugal e Espanha destruíram os Sete Povos dos jesuítas e índios guaranis no Rio Grande do Sul 1750–1761.* 2nd ed. Passo Fundo, Brasil: EDIUPF, Universidade de Passo Fundo, 1999.

Gosselin, Charles Robert. *Réflexions d'un citoyen adressées aux notables sur la question proposée par un grand Roi.* Paris, 1787.

Götz, Norbert. "'Moral Economy': Its Conceptual History and Analytical Prospects." *Journal of Global Ethics* 11, no. 2 (2015): 147–62.

Gow, Peter. "Helplessness—The Affective Preconditions of Piro Social Life." In *Anthropology of Love and Anger,* edited by Joanna Overing and Alan Passes, 46–63. London: Routledge, 2000.

Graeber, David. *Towards an Anthropological Theory of Value: The False Coin of Our Own Dreams.* New York: Palgrave, 2001.

Grafe, Regina. *Distant Tyranny: Markets, Power, and Backwardness in Spain, 1650–1800.* Princeton, NJ: Princeton University Press, 2012.

Graham, R. B. Cunninghame. *A Vanished Arcadia. Being Some Account of the Jesuits in Paraguay, 1607–1767.* London: William Heinemann, 1924.

Grellard, Christophe. *De la certitude volontaire: Débats nominalistes sur la foi à la fin du Moyen Âge.* Paris: Publications de la Sorbonne, 2014.

Grice-Hutchinson, Marjorie. *Early Economic Thought in Spain, 1177–1740.* Indianapolis: Liberty Fund, 2015.

Grimm, Friedrich Melchior. *Correspondance littéraire, philosophique et critique de Grimm et de Diderot depuis 1753 jusqu'en 1790.* Tome 2. Edited by Jules-Antoine Taschereau and A. Chaudé. Paris, 1758. https://artflsrv03.uchicago.edu/philologic4/grimm/navigate/2/40/.

Gudeman, Stephen. *Anthropology of Economy: Community, Market, and Culture.* Oxford: Blackwell, 2001.

———. *Economics as Culture.* London: Routledge & Kegan Paul, 1986.

Guerreau-Jalabert, Anita. "Caritas y don en la sociedad medieval occidental." *Hispania* 60, no. 1 (January–April 2000): 103–26.

Guevara, Antonio de. *Reloj de príncipes.* Valladolid, 1529.

Guzmán, Ruy Díaz de. *Argentina: historia del descubrimiento y conquista del Río de la Plata*. Edited by Silvia Tieffemberg. Buenos Aires: EFFL, 2012.

Hämäläinen, Pekka. *Comanche Empire*. New Haven, CT: Yale University Press, 2008.

Hamilton, Earl J. *American Treasure and the Price Revolution in Spain, 1501–1650*. Cambridge, MA: Harvard University Press, 1934.

Haraway, Donna. *Staying with the Trouble: Making Kin in the Chthulucene*. Durham, NC: Duke University Press, 2016.

Herder, Johann Gottfried Von. *Outlines of a Philosophy of the History of Man*. Vol. 1. Translated by T. O. Churchill. London, 1803. First published 1784–1791.

Hernández, P. Pablo. *Misiones del Paraguay: Organización social de las doctrinas guaraníes de la Compañía de Jesús*. Vol. 1. Barcelona, 1913.

Herzog, Tamar. *Frontiers of Possession: Spain and Portugal in Europe and the Americas*. Cambridge, MA: Harvard University Press, 2014.

Hespanha, António Manuel. "Las categorías del político y de lo jurídico en la época moderna." *Ius fugit: Revista interdisciplinar de estudios histórico-jurídicos* 3, no. 4 (1994): 63–100.

Hirschman, Albert O. *The Passions and the Interests: Political Arguments for Capitalism before Its Triumph*. Princeton, NJ: Princeton University Press, 1977.

Hobbes, Thomas. *Leviathan*. Edited by Michael Oakeshott. New York: Simon & Schuster, 1997.

Höpfl, Harro. *Jesuit Political Thought: The Society of Jesus and the State, c. 1540–1630*. New York: Cambridge University Press, 2004.

Howell, Martha C. *Commerce before Capitalism in Europe, 1300–1600*. Cambridge: Cambridge University Press, 2010.

Hoxie, Frederick E. *Parading through History: The Making of the Crow Nation in America 1805–1935*. Cambridge: Cambridge University Press, 1995.

Hume, David. *Essays, Moral, Political, and Literary*. Edited by Thomas H. Grose and Thomas H. Green. London: Green & Co., 1875. First published 1777.

———. *A Treatise on Human Nature*. Edited by L. A. Selby-Bigge. Oxford: Clarendon Press, 1896. First published 1739.

Imbruglia, Giralamo. *The Jesuit Missions of Paraguay and a Cultural History of Utopia (1568–1789)*. Leiden: Brill, 2017.

"Informe de um jesuíta anônimo, 1620." In vol. 1 of *Manuscritos da Coleção de Angelis: Jesuítas e Bandeirantes no Guairá (1549–1640)*, edited by Jaime Cortesão and Pedro de Angelis, 162–74. Rio de Janeiro: Biblioteca Nacional, 1951.

"Informes del Cabildo y de los Gobernadores del Paraguay." Edited by J. D. Bareiro. *Guarania* 2, no. 20 (June 1935).

Iriarte, José, et al. "Out of Amazonia: Late-Holocene Climate Change and the Tupi-Guarani Trans-continental Expansion." *Holocene* 27, no. 7 (July 1, 2017, posted online November 26, 2016): 967–75.

Kames, Lord Henry Home. *Sketches of the History of Man*. Vol. 1. 3rd ed. Dublin, 1779.

Karatani, Kojin. *The Structure of World History: From Modes of Production to Modes of Exchange*. Durham, NC: Duke University Press, 2014.

Kern, Arno Álvarez. "O processo histórico platino no século XVII: Da aldeia guaraní ao povoado missioneiro." *Estudos Ibero-Americanos* 11, no. 1 (1985): 23–41.

Kleinpenning, Jan. *Paraguay, 1515–1870: Una geografía temática de su desarrollo.* Vols. 1 and 2. Madrid: Iberoamericana, 2003.

Lacombe, Robert. *Guaranis et jésuites: Un combat pour la liberté (1610–1707).* Paris: Société de'Ethnografie, 1993.

Lalander, Rickard. "Ethnic Rights and the Dilemma of Extractive Development in Plurinational Bolivia." *International Journal of Human Rights* 21, no. 4 (2017): 464–81.

Lane, Kris. *Potosí: The Silver City That Changed the World.* Oakland: University of California Press, 2019.

Langholm, Odd. *Economics in the Medieval Schools: Wealth, Exchange, Value, Money and Usury according to the Paris Theological Tradition, 1200–1350.* Leiden: Brill, 1992.

Las Casas, Bartolomé de. *Avisos y reglas para los confesores de españoles.* 1552.

———. *Brevísima relación de la destruición de las Indias.* London, 1822. First published Seville, 1552, 1542.

Lastarria, Miguel. *Documentos para la Historia Argentina: Colonias orientales del Río Paraguay o del Plata.* Tomo 3. Buenos Aires: Universidad de Buenos Aires, Facultad de Filosofía y Letras, 1914.

Lear, Jonathan. *Radical Hope: Ethics in the Face of Cultural Devastation.* Cambridge, MA: Harvard University Press, 2006.

Lempérière, Anick. *Entre Dieu et le Roi, La République: Mexico, XVIe–XIXe siècles.* Paris: Les Belles Lettres, 2005.

Levi, Giovanni. "Reciprocidad mediterránea." *Hispania* 60, no. 204 (January–April 2000): 103–26.

Léry, Jean de. *Histoire d'un Voyage Fait en la Terre du Bresil.* La Rochelle, 1578.

"Letter to Bartolomé Mitre, 1872." *La Nacional* (Buenos Aires). November 25, 1876.

Levinton, Norberto. *La arquitectura jesuítico-guaraní: Una experiencia de interacción cultural.* Buenos Aires: Editorial SB, 2008.

———. *El espacio jesuítico-guaraní: La formación de una región cultural.* Asunción, 2009. https://www.academia.edu/26182354/El_espacio_jesuitico_guaran%C3%AD_doc.

———. "Las estancias de Nuestra Señora de los Reyes de Yapeyú: Tenencia de la tierra por uso cotidiano, acuerdo interétnico y derecho natural (Misiones jesuíticas del Paraguay)." *Revista Complutense de Historia de América* 31 (2005): 33–51.

"Leyes y ordenanzas nuevamente hechas por S.M." 1542. http://www.cervantesvirtual.com/servlet/SirveObras/06922752100647273089079/p0000026.htm.

Lira, Andrés. "Dimensión jurídica de la conciencia: Pecadores y pecados en tres confesionarios de la Nueva España, 1545–1732." *Historia Mexicana* 55, no. 4 (April–June 2006): 1139–78.

Locke, John. *Second Treatise of Government.* Edited by Thomas P. Peardon. New York: Liberal Arts Press, 1952.

———. *The Works of John Locke.* Vol. 9. London: C. and J. Rivington, 1824.

Lockhart, James, and Enrique Otte, eds. *Letters and People of the Spanish Indies: Sixteenth Century.* Cambridge: Cambridge University Press, 1976.

London Magazine, or Gentleman's Monthly Intelligencer. Vols. 38 and 40. London, 1769, 1771.

López, Adalberto. *The Revolt of the Comuneros, 1721–1735: A Study in the Colonial History of Paraguay.* Cambridge, MA: Schenkman, 1976.

———. "Shipbuilding in Sixteenth-Century Asunción del Paraguay." *Mariner's Mirror* 61, no. 1 (2013): 31–37.

Lowe, Lisa. *The Intimacies of Four Continents.* Durham, NC: Duke University Press, 2015.

Loyola, Ignacio. *Ejercicios espirituales.* Edited by Candido de Dalmases, S.J. Santander: Sal Terrae, 1987.

Lozano S.J., Pedro de. *Historia de la Compañía de Jesús en la provincia del Paraguay.* Tomo 2. Madrid, 1755.

———. *Historia de la conquista del Paraguay, Río de la Plata y Tucuman.* Tomo 1. Edited by Andrés Lamas. Buenos Aires, 1873–1875.

———. *Historia de las revoluciones de la provincia del Paraguay (1721–1735).* Tomo 2. Buenos Aires, 1905.

Mably, Abbé Gabriel Bonnot. *Doutes proposés aux philosophes économistes, sur l'ordre naturel et essentiel des sociétés politiques.* Paris, 1768.

MacGregor, Kirk R. *Luis de Molina: The Life and Theology of the Founder of Middle Knowledge.* Grand Rapids, MI: Zondervan, 2015.

Machaín, Ricardo de Lafuente. *El gobernador Domingo Martínez de Irala.* Buenos Aires: Librería y editorial "La Facultad," Bernabé y cía., 1939.

MacIntyre, Alasdair. *After Virtue: A Study in Moral Theory.* 3rd ed. Notre Dame, IN: University of Notre Dame Press, 2007.

Mackay, Ruth. *"Lazy, Improvident People": Myth and Reality in the Writing of Spanish History.* Ithaca, NY: Cornell University Press, 2006.

Macpherson, C. B. *The Political Theory of Possessive Individualism: Hobbes to Locke.* Oxford: Oxford University Press, 1962.

Maeder, Ernesto, and Alfredo Bolsi. "La población de las misiones guaraníes entre 1702–1767." *Estudios Paraguayos* 2, no. 1 (1974): 111–38.

Malinowski, Bronislaw. *Argonauts of the Western Pacific.* New York: E. P. Dutton, 1922.

Mallios, Seth. *The Deadly Politics of Giving: Exchange and Violence at Ajacan, Roanoke, and Jamestown.* Tuscaloosa: University of Alabama Press, 2006.

Malthus, Thomas. *An Essay on the Principle of Population.* London: J. Johnson, 1798, 1803.

Mandeville, Bernard. *The Fable of the Bees; or, Private Vices, Publick Benefits.* 2nd ed. London: Edmund Parker, 1723.

Mann, Charles. *1491: New Revelations of the Americas before Columbus.* New York: Knopf, 2005.

Mantilla, Gorki Gonzales. "La ociosidad natural del indio como categoría jurídica en el siglo XVI." *Ius et Veritas* 7, no. 12 (1996): 133–42.

Manuscritos da Coleção de Angelis, Jesuítas e bandeirantes no Guairá (1549–1640). Vol. 1. Edited by Jaime Cortesão and Pedro de Angelis. Rio de Janeiro: Biblioteca Nacional, 1951.

Maravall, José Antonio. *Estado moderno y mentalidad social: Siglos XV a XVII.* 2 vols. Madrid: Revista de Occidente, 1972.

———. "Saavedra Fajardo: Moral de acomodación y carácter conflictivo de la libertad." In *Estudios de historia del pensamiento español,* 225–56. Madrid: Ed. Cultura Hispánica, 1984.

Mariana, Juan de. *De rege et regis institutione.* Translated by George A. Moore into English as *On the Education of the King.* Washington, DC: Country Dollar Press, 1948. First published Toledo, 1598.

Martín, José-Luis. *Economía y sociedad en los reinos hispánicos de la baja Edad Media.* Barcelona: El Albir, 1983.

Masy, Rafael Carbonell de. "La propiedad comunitaria en las reducciones guaraníes." *Suplemento Antropológico* 27, no. 2 (1992): 99–130.

Mateos S.J., Francisco. "Cartas de indios cristianos del Paraguay." *Missionalia Hispánica* 6, no. 16 (1949): 547–72.

Mauss, Marcel. *The Gift.* Chicago: Hau Books, 2016.

Maziel, Juan Baltazar. *De la justicia del tratado de límites de 1750.* Edited by José M. Mariluz Urquijo. Buenos Aires, 1988. First published 1760.

McCloskey, Deirdre N. *Bourgeois Dignity: Why Economics Can't Explain the Modern World.* Chicago: University of Chicago Press, 2010.

———. *The Bourgeois Virtues: Ethics for an Age of Commerce.* Chicago: University of Chicago Press, 2006.

Melià, Bartomeu. *El Guaraní conquistado y reducido: Ensayos de etnohistoria.* Asunción, 1988.

———. *Mundo guaraní.* Asunción: Centro de Estudios Antropológicos, Universidad Católica, 2006.

———. "La novedad Guaraní (viejas cuestiones y nuevas preguntas)." *Revista de Indias* 64, no. 230 (2004): 175–226.

———. "La Tierra-sin-mal de los Guaraní: Economía y profecía." *América Indígena* 49 (July–September 1989): 491–507.

Melià, Bartomeu, and Dominique Temple. *El don, la venganza y otras formas de economia guaraní.* Asunción: Centro de Estudios Paraguayos "Antonio Guasch," 2004.

Mercado, Tomás de. *Summa de tratos y contratos.* Seville, 1587.

Métraux, Alfred. "The Guaraní." *Handbook of South American Indians* (Washington, DC) 3 (1948): 69–94.

———. "Migrations historiques des Tupi-Guarani." *Journal de la Société des Américanistes* 19 (1927): 1–45.

Michielse, H. C. M., and Robert van Krieken. "Policing the Poor: J. L. Vives and the Sixteenth-Century Origins of Modern Social Administration." *Social Service Review* 64, no. 1 (March 1990): 1–21.

Milton, Gregory B. *Market Power: Lordship, Society, and Economy in Medieval Catalonia (1276–1313).* New York: Palgrave, 2012.

Ministerio de Fomento, España. *Cartas de Indias.* Madrid, 1877.

Mintz, Sidney W. *Sweetness and Power: The Place of Sugar in Modern History*. New York: Penguin, 1985.

The Modern Part of an Universal History . . . Complied from Original Writers. Vol. 39. London, 1763.

Molina, J. Michelle. *To Overcome Oneself: The Jesuit Ethic and Spirit of Global Expansion, 1520–1767*. Berkeley: University of California Press, 2013.

Molina, Luis de. *On Divine Foreknowledge: Part IV of the Concordia*. Translated and edited by Alfred Freddoso. Ithaca, NY: Cornell University Press, 1988.

Monboddo, James Burnett. *Antient Metaphysics*. Vol. 4., *Containing the History of Man*. Edinburgh, 1795.

Monod, Paul Kléber. *The Power of Kings: Monarchy and Religion in Europe, 1589–1715*. New Haven, CT: Yale University Press, 1999.

Monsalve, Fabio. "Economics and Ethics: Juan de Lugo's Theory of the Just Price, or the Responsibility of Living in Society." *History of Political Economy* 42, no. 3 (2010): 495–519.

Montaigne, Michel de. "Of Cannibals." In *Essays of Montaigne*, chap. 30, edited by William Carew Hazlitt and translated by Charles Cotton. London, 1877. https://www.gutenberg.org/files/3600/3600-h/3600-h.htm#link2HCH0030.

Monteiro, John M. *Blacks of the Land: Indian Slavery, Settler Society, and the Portuguese Colonial Enterprise in South America*. Edited by James Woodard and Barbara Weinstein. Cambridge: Cambridge University Press, 2018.

———. "From Indian to Slave: Forced Native Labour and Colonial Society in São Paulo during the Seventeenth Century." *Slavery and Abolition* 9, no. 2 (1988): 105–27.

Montesquieu, Charles de Secondat. *De l'Esprit des lois*. Vols. 1 and 2. Paris, 1759. First published 1748.

Montoya, Antonio Ruiz de. *Conquista espiritual hecha por los padres de la Compañía de Jesús*. Madrid, 1639.

———. *Lexicon Hispano-Guaranicum: "Vocabulario de la lengua Guaraní."* Edited by Paulo Restivo [1639]; Edited by Christiani Frederici Seybold [1722]. Stuttgart, 1893.

———. *The Spiritual Conquest*. Translated by C. J. McNapsy, S.J., et al. St. Louis: Institute of Jesuit Sources, 1993.

———. *Tesoro de la lengua guaraní*. Madrid: Iuan Snchez, 1639.

Moore, Jerry D. *A Prehistory of South America: Ancient Cultural Diversity on the Least Known Continent*. Boulder: University Press of Colorado, 2014.

Morales S.J., Martín. "Los comienzos de las reducciones de la provincia del Paraguay en relación con el derecho indiano y el Instituto de la Compañía de Jesús. Evolución y conflictos." *Archivum Historicum Societatis Iesu* 67 (January 1998): 3–129.

Mora Muro, Jesús Iván. "Resistencia campesina en la historiografía mexicana: Del marxismo economicista a la economía moral." *Revista Enchiridion* 5, no. 10 (July–December 2018): 38–45.

Mörner, Magnus. *The Political and Economic Activities of the Jesuits in the La Plata Region*. Stockholm: 1953.

Moya, Juan Perez de. *Arithmetica practica y specvlatiua del Bachiller Iuan.* Salamanca, 1562.

Moyn, Samuel. "Of Savagery and Civil Society: Pierre Clastres and the Transformation of French Political Thought." *Modern Intellectual History* 1, no. 1 (2004): 55–80.

Muldrew, Craig. *The Economy of Obligation: The Culture of Credit and Social Relations in Early Modern England.* New York: St. Martin's Press, 1998.

Muratori, Lodovico Antonio. *Il cristianesimo felice nelle missione de' padre della Compagnia di Gesù nel Paraguai.* Venezia, 1752.

Murra, John V. *The Economic Organization of the Inka State.* Greenwich: Jai Press, 1980.

———. *Reciprocity and Redistribution in Andean Civilizations: The 1969 Lewis Henry Morgan Lectures.* Chicago: Hau Books, 2017.

Nadal, Gerónimo. *Pláticas espirituales del P. Jerónimo Nadal, S.J., en Coimbra.* Granada, 1945. First published 1561.

Necker, Louis. *Indiens Guarani et chamanes franciscains: Les premières réductions du Paraguay, 1580–1800.* Paris: Anthropos, 1979.

———. "La réaction des Indiens Guarani à la Conquête espagnole du Paraguay, un des facteurs de la colonisation de l'Argentine à la fin du XVI siècle." *Société Suisse des Américanistes*: 71–77. https://www.sag-ssa.ch/bssa/pdf/bssa38_11.pdf.

Neto, Miranda. *A Utopia Possível.* Brasília: Fundação Alexandre de Gusmão, 2012.

Neumann, Eduardo. "Mientras volaban correos por los pueblos: Auto-governo e práticas letradas nas missões Guaraní—Século XVIII." *Horizontes Antropológicos* 10, no. 22 (July–December 2004): 93–119.

Nicot, Jean, Aimar de Ranconnet, and Hadrianus Junius. *Thresor de la langue françoyse, tant ancienne que moderne.* Paris, 1606.

Nimuendajú, Curt Unkel. *As lendas da criação e destruição do mundo como fundamentos da Religião dos Apapocúva-Guaraní.* Edited by Juergen Riester. São Paulo: HUCITEC, USP, 1987. First published 1914.

Noelli, Francisco Silva. "Curt Nimuendajú e Alfred Métraux: A invenção da busca da 'terra sem mal.'" *Suplemento Antropológico* (Asunción) 34, no. 2 (1999): 123–66.

———. "La distribución geográfica de las evidencias arqueológicas guaraní." *Revista de Indias* 64, no. 230 (2004): 17–34.

———. "As hipóteses sobre o centro de origem e rotas de expansão dos Tupi." *Revista de Antropología* 39, no. 2 (1996): 7–53.

———. "The Tupi Expansion." In *Handbook of South American Archaeology*, edited by Helaine Silverman and William Isbell, 659–70. New York: Springer, 2008.

Nonneman, Walter. "On the Economics of the Socialist Theocracy of the Jesuits in Paraguay 1609–1767)." In *The Political Economy of Theocracy*, edited by Mario Ferrero and Ronald Wintrobe, 119–42. New York: Palgrave Macmillan, 2009.

Nordenskiöld, Baron Erland. "The Guaraní Invasion of the Inca Empire in the Sixteenth Century: An Historical Indian Migration." *Geographical Review* 4, no. 2 (August 1917): 103–21.

Nowell, Charles E. "Aleixo Garcia and the White King." *Hispanic American Historical Review* 26, no. 4 (November 1946): 450–66.

Nusdorffer, Bernardo. "Relación de todo lo sucedido en estas Doctrinas en orden a las mudanzas de los siete Pueblos del Uruguai." In Vol. 7 of *Manuscritos de la Coleção De Angelis*, edited by Jaime Cortesão and Helio Vianna, 139–91. Rio de Janeiro: Biblioteca Nacional, 1969.

Oliver S.J., Jaime. "Breve noticia de la numerosa, y florida Xptiandad Guaraní." *Archivum Romanum Societatis Iesu (ARSI)*. Buenos Aires.

Orantin, Mickaël. "La cloche, le rabot et la houe: Fragments d'un quotidien de travail dans les missions jésuites du Paraguay (ca. 1714)." Master's thesis, IHEAL, Université Paris III Sorbonne Nouvelle, June 2017.

"Ordenanza de Juan de Garay, 17 octubre 1578." In "Diario del capitán de fragata Don Juan Francisco Aguirre." *Revista de la Biblioteca Nacional* tomo 1, 1ª pte. (Buenos Aires, 1948–1951): 197–98.

Orschel, Vera. "'Uniting the Dispersed Members': The 'Annual Letters' of the Irish Jesuits." *Studies: An Irish Quarterly Review* 103, no. 412 (Winter 2014–15): 402–13.

Ostrum, Elinor. *Governing the Commons: The Evolution of Institutions for Collective Action*. Cambridge: Cambridge University Press, 1990.

Overing, Joanna, and Alan Passes, eds. "Introduction: Conviviality and the Opening Up of Amazonian Anthropology." In *Anthropology of Love and Anger*, 1–30. London: Routledge, 2000.

Owensby, Brian P. *Empire of Law and Indian Justice in Colonial Mexico*. Stanford, CA: Stanford University Press, 2008.

———. "Pacto entre rey lejano y súbditos indígenas: Justicia, legalidad y política en Nueva España, siglo XVII." *Historia Mexicana* 61, no. 1 (2011): 59–106.

———. "The Theater of Conscience in the 'Living Law' of the Indies." In *New Horizons in Spanish Colonial Law: Contributions to Transnational Early Modern Legal History*, edited by Thomas Duve and Heikki Pihlajamäki, 125–50. Berlin: Max Planck Institute for European Legal History, 2015.

Page, Carlos A. "Relación de las misiones del Paraguay del P. Marciel de Lorenzana (1621)." *IHS: Antiguos Jesuitas en Iberoamérica* 6, no. 1 (January–June 2018): 128–57.

Palomera, Jaime, and Theodora Vetta. "Moral Economy: Rethinking a Radical Concept." *Anthropological Theory* 16, no. 4 (2016): 1–21.

Parker, Geoffrey. "El surgimiento de las finanzas modernas en Europa (1500–1700)." In vol. 2 of *Historia económica de Europa*, edited by Carlo M. Cipolla, 410–64. Barcelona: Ariel, 1979.

Pastells, F. Mateos, ed. *Historia de la Compañía de Jesús en la provincia del Paraguay*. Vol. 8. Madrid: V. Suárez, 1948.

Pastore, Carlos. *La lucha por la tierra en el Paraguay*. Montevideo: Editorial Antequera, 1972.

Pastore, Mario H. "Coerced Indigenous Labor and Free Mestizo Peasantry: A Property-Rights, Rent-Seeking View of Colonial Paraguay." *Munich Personal RePEc Archive* (MPRA), paper no. 27150, December 8, 2010 [1990]. http://mpra.ub.uni-muechen.de/27150/.

Penry, S. Elizabeth. *The People Are King: The Making of an Indigenous Andean Politics.* Oxford: Oxford University Press, 2020.

Peramás, José Manuel. La República *de Platón y los guaraníes.* Edited by Juan Cortés del Pino. Buenos Aires: Emecé Editores, 1946.

Perusset, Macarena. "Dinámicas socio-culturales entre los grupos guaraníes frente a la violencia del régimen de encomienda: Paraguay (siglos XVI–XVII)." *ANPHLAC* (2011): 1–24. https://revista.anphlac.org/anphlac/article/view/1292/1159.

———. "Reglamentación jurídica vs. usos y costumbres en el Paraguay colonial temprano (1542–1612)." *Antíteses* 2, no. 4 (July–December 2009): 991–1004.

Pierri, Daniel. "Como acabará essa terra? Reflexões sobre a cataclismologia Guarani-Mbyá, à luz da obra de Nimuendajú." *Revista Tellus* 13, no. 24 (January–June 2013): 159–88.

Piketty, Thomas. *Capital and Ideology.* Translated by Arthur Goldhammer. Cambridge: Belknap Press, 2020.

Polanyi, Karl. *The Great Transformation: The Political and Economic Origins of Our Time.* Boston: Beacon Press, 1957.

Poley, Jared. *The Devil's Riches: A Modern History of Greed.* New York: Berghahn, 2016.

The Polite Miscellany: containing a variety of food for the mind; being an elegant collection of moral, humorous, and improving essays. Manchester: R. Whitworth, 1764.

Politis, Gustavo. "The Pampas and Campos of South America." In *Handbook of South American Archaeology*, edited by Helaine Silverman and William Isbell, 235–60. New York: Springer, 2008.

Pompa, Cristina. "O Profetismo Tupi-Guarani: A Construção de um Objeto Antropológico." *Revista de Indias* 64, no. 230 (2004): 141–74.

Pope, Alexander. *An Essay on Man.* London: John and Paul Knapton, 1745.

Popescu, Oreste. *El sistema económico en las misiones Jesuitas.* Bahía Blanca, Argentina: Ed. Pampa-Mar, 1952.

Puig, Andrés. *Arithmetica especulativa y practica y arte de algebra* [. . .]. Barcelona, 1715.

Pujol, D. Xavier Gil. "La razón de estado en la España de la contrarreforma: Usos y razones de la política." In *La Real Sociedad Económica de Amigos del País de Valencia y el Departamento d'Historia Moderna de la Universitat de València*, 355–74. Valencia: Real Sociedad Económica de Amigos del Paieis de Valencia, March 1999.

Quarleri, Lía. "El 'beneficio de la libertad': Objetivos y límites de las políticas reformistas en los pueblos guaraníes (1784–1801)." *Folia Histórica del Nordeste* (Resistencia) no. 21 (2013): 7–32.

———. "Lógicas y concepciones sobre trabajo, acumulación y bienestar en los pueblos de indios guaraníes (siglos XVII y XVIII). *Anos 90* 20, no. 37 (July 2013): 177–212.

———. *Rebelión y guerra en las fronteras del Plata: Guaraníes, jesuitas e imperios coloniales.* Buenos Aires: Fondo de Cultura Económica, 2009.

Quevedo, Francisco de. "Poderoso caballero es don Dinero," 1603. https://www.biblioteca.org.ar/libros/123.pdf.

Ramírez, Bibiano Torres, and Javier Ortiz de la Tabla, eds. *Reglamento para el comercio libre, 1778.* Seville: CSIC, 1979.

The Ratio Studiorum: *The Official Plan for Jesuit Education.* Translated by Claude Pavur, S.J. St. Louis: Institute of Jesuit Sources, 2005.

Raworth, Kate. *Doughnut Economics: Seven Ways to Think Like a 21st-Century Economist.* White River Junction, VT: Chelsea Green, 2017.

Raynal, Abbé Guillaume Thomas. *Histoire philosophique et politique, des établissements et du commerce des Européens dans les deux Indes.* La Haye, 1774.

———. *A Philosophical and Political History of the Settlements and Trade of the Europeans in the East and West Indies.* Translated by John Obadiah Justamond. London: The Strand, 1783.

Real Academia de la Historia. *Las siete partidas del rey don Alfonso el Sabio.* 4 vols. Madrid, 1807.

Real Academia Española. *Diccionario de la lengua castellana (Diccionario de autoridades).* 3 vols. Madrid: Gredos, 1979.

"Real Cédula al Virrey del Perú, Don Luis de Velasco, sobre lo que se ordena acerca de los servicios personales de los indios." In Vol. 14 of *Gobernantes del Perú, cartas y papeles, siglo XVI: Documentos del Archivo de Indias,* edited by Roberto Levillier, 302–22. Madrid: Sucesores de Rivadeneyra, 1921.

"Real Cédula aprobatoria de las Ordenanzas de Alfaro con inserción de las mismas. San Lorenzo, septiembre 8 de 1618." *Revista de la Biblioteca Nacional* 3, no. 11 (1939): 566–603.

Recopilación de las leyes destos reynos, hecha por mandado . . . (Castilla y León). Alcala Henares, 1591.

Recopilación de leyes de los reynos de las Indias, 1680. Madrid: Iulian Paredes, 1681.

Reed, Richard K. *Prophets of Agroforestry: Guaraní Communities and Commercial Gathering.* Austin: University of Texas Press, 2014.

Relação abbreviada da Republica, que os religiosos Jesuitas das províncias de Portugal e Hespanha estabelecerão nos Domínios Ultramarinos das duas Monarchias. John Carter Brown Library, Brown Digital Repository. 1757. https://repository.library.brown.edu /studio/item/bdr:16009/.

Restall, Matthew. *Seven Myths of the Spanish Conquest.* New York: Oxford University Press, 2003.

Ribadeneyra, P. Pedro de. *Tratado de la religión y virtudes que deue tener el Príncipe Christiano para gouernar y conseruar sus estados: contra lo que Nicolas Machiavelo y los políticos deste tiempo enseñan.* Madrid, 1595.

Rivarola, Milda. "Castas y clases: Una lectura de la estructura social paraguaya." In *Desigualdad y clases sociales: Estudios sobre la estructura social paraguaya,* edited by Luis Ortíz, 61–74. Asunción: ICSO, 2016.

Robertson, William. *The History of America.* Dublin, 1777.

Robertson, John Parish, and William Parish Robertson. *Letters on Paraguay: Comprising an Account of Four Years' Residence in That Republic, Under the Government of the Dictator Francia.* Vol. 1. London, 1838.

Rodrigues, Manuel. *Summa de casos de consciencia: . . . en la qual se resuelue lo mas ordinario de todas las materias morales.* Barcelona, 1596. First published 1595.

Rodríguez, Alonso. *Ejercicio de perfección y virtudes cristianas.* Vol. 1. Barcelona, 1834. First published 1609.

Rojas, Guillermo. "Un sacerdote guaraní se dirige al rey de España." *Boletín de Antropología Americana* 25 (July 1992): 173–78.

Roover, Raymond de. "The Scholastic Attitude toward Trade and Entrepreneurship." In *Business, Banking and Economic Thought in Late Medieval and Early Modern Europe,* 336–45. Chicago: University of Chicago Press, 1974.

———. "Scholastic Economics: Survival and Lasting Influence from the Sixteenth Century to Adam Smith." *Quarterly Journal of Economics* 69, no. 2 (May, 1955): 161–90.

Roulet, Florencia. *La resistencia de los guaraní del Paraguay a la conquista española (1537–1556).* Posadas: Editorial Universitaria, 1993.

Rousseau, Jean-Jacques. *Du contrat social.* Paris, 1903. First published 1762.

———. *Discours sur l'économie politique.* Amsterdam, 1763. First published 1756.

———. *Discours sur l'origine et les fondements de l'inégalité parmi les hommes.* Amsterdam, 1755.

———. *Émile, ou de l'Éducation.* 3 vols. Amsterdam, 1762.

Saavedra Fajardo, Diego de. *Empresas políticas.* Madrid: Planeta, 1988. First published 1640.

———. *Idea de un príncipe político christiano representada en cien empresas.* Monaco, Milan, 1640.

Saeger, James Schofield. "Origins of the Rebellion of Paraguay." *Hispanic American Historical Review* 52, no. 2 (1972): 215–29.

Sahlins, Marshall. *Stone Age Economics.* New York: Aldine de Gruyter, 1972.

———. *The Western Illusion of Human Nature.* Chicago: Prickly Paradigm Press, 2008.

Salinas, María Laura. "Dominación colonial y trabajo indígena: Un estudio de la encomienda en Corrientes colonial." *Centro de Estudios Antropológicos de la Universidad Católica (CEADUC)* 81 (May 2010): 297–99.

Sarreal, Julia. "Caciques as Placeholders in the Guaraní Missions of Eighteenth Century Paraguay." *Colonial Latin American Review* 23, no. 2 (2014): 224–51.

———. *The Guaraní and Their Missions: A Socioeconomic History.* Stanford, CA: Stanford University Press, 2014.

———. "Jesuit Missions and Private Property, Commerce, and Guaraní Economic Initiative." *Oxford Research Encyclopedia of Latin American History,* October 2015. https://doi.org/10.1093/acrefore/9780199366439.013.313.

Sartori, Andrew. *Liberalism in Empire: An Alternative History.* Berkeley: University of California Press, 2014.

Scattola, Merio. "La virtud de la justicia en la doctrina de Domingo de Soto." *Anuario Filosófico* 45, no. 2 (2012): 313–41.

Schaden, Egon. *Aspectos fundamentais da cultura guaraní.* São Paulo: Difusão Européia do Livro, 1962.

Schmidel, Ulrich. *Viaje al Río de la Plata (1534–1554).* Buenos Aires, 1903.

Scott, James C. *The Moral Economy of the Peasant: Rebellion and Subsistence in Southeast Asia.* New Haven, CT: Yale University Press, 1977.

Seneca, Lucius Annaeus Philosophus. *Proverbios de Seneca (traducidos y comentados)*. Seville: Jacobo Cromberger, 1535.

Service, Elman R. *Spanish-Guaraní Relations in Early Colonial Paraguay*. Ann Arbor: University of Michigan Press, 1954.

Sepp S.J., Antonio. *Jardín de flores paracuario*. Vol. 3. Edited by Werner Hoffmann. Buenos Aires: Eudeba, 1974.

———. *Relación de viaje a las misiones jesuíticas*. Buenos Aires: Eudeba, 1971. First published 1696.

Shapiro, Judith. "From Tupã to the Land without Evil: The Christianization of Tupi Cosmology." *American Ethnologist* 14, no. 1 (February 1987): 126–39.

Sheehan, Jonathan, and Dror Wahrman. *Invisible Hands: Self-Organization and the Eighteenth Century*. Chicago: University of Chicago Press, 2015.

Shenk, Timothy. "'I Am No Longer Answerable for Its Actions': E. P. Thompson after Moral Economy." *Humanity: An International Journal of Human Rights, Humanitarianism, and Development* 11, no. 2 (Summer 2020): 241–46.

Silverman, Helaine, and William H. Isbell, eds. *Handbook of South American Archaeology*. New York: Springer, 2008.

Smith, Adam. *An Inquiry into the Nature and Causes of the Wealth of Nations*. Edited by Edwin Cannan. London: Methuen, 1904.

———. *Investigación de la naturaleza y causas de las riquezas de las naciones*. 4 vols. Translated by Josef Alonso Ortiz. Valladolid, 1794–1806.

———. *The Theory of Moral Sentiments*. Edited by D. Raphael and A. Macfie. Oxford: Clarendon Press, 1976.

Smith, Robert Sydney. "*The Wealth of Nations* in Spain and Hispanic America, 1780–1830." *Journal of Political Economy* 65, no. 2 (April 1957): 104–25.

Solórzano y Pereira, Juan. *Política indiana*. 3 vols. Madrid: Biblioteca Castro, 1996.

Soriano, Rosa Tribaldos. "Imagen y representación de las mujeres guaraníes: Conflictos y resistencias en las misiones jesuitas (siglos XVII–XVIII)." In *Conflicto, negociación y resistencia en las Américas*, edited by Izaskun Álvarez Cuartero, 197–214. Salamanca: Ediciones Universidad de Salamanca, 2018.

Soto, Domingo de. *Tratado de la justicia y del derecho*. Vol. 1. Translated by J. T. Ripoll. Madrid: Reus, 1922. First published 1552.

Souza, José Otávio Catafesto de. "O sistema econômico nas sociedades indígenas Guarani pré-coloniais." *Horizontes Antropológicos* 8, no. 18 (December 2002): 211–53.

Starkey, Thomas. *A Dialogue between Reginald Pole and Thomas Lupset*. Edited by Kathleen M. Burton. London: Chatto & Windus, 1948. First published ca. 1532.

Stoll, Steve. *Ramp Hollow: The Ordeal of Appalachia*. New York: Hill and Wang, 2018.

Storni S.J., Hugo. *Catálogo de los jesuitas en la Provincia del Paraguay (Cuenca del Plata), 1585–1768*. Rome: Institutum Historicum S.I., 1980.

Strathern, Marilyn. *The Gender of the Gift*. Berkeley: University of California Press, 1988.

Sušnik, Branislava. *Ciclo vital y estructura social*. Vol. 5 of *Los aborígenes del Paraguay*. Asunción: Museo etnográfico Andrés Barbero, 1979–1980.

———. *Etnohistoria de los guaraníes, época colonial.* Vol. 2 of *Los aborígenes del Paraguay.* Asunción: Museo etnográfico Andrés Barbero, 1979–1980.

———. *El indio colonial del Paraguay: El guaraní colonial.* Asunción: Museo etnográfico Andrés Barbero, 1965.

———. *El rol de los indígenas en la formación y en la vivencia del Paraguay.* Tomo 2. Asunción: Instituto paraguayo de estudios nacionales, 1982.

———. *Una visión socio-antropológica del Paraguay, XVI–1/2 XVII.* Asunción: Museo etnográfico Andres Barbero, 1993.

Takeda, Kazuhisa. "Los padrones de indios guaraníes de las misiones jesuíticas (1656–1801): Análisis dinámico y comparativo desde la óptica de los cacicazgos." *Dossier: Surandino Monográfico* 1 (2016): 66–105.

Techo, Nicolás del. *Historia de la provincia del Paraguay de la compañía de Jesús.* Vol. 5. Madrid, 1897. First published 1673.

Thompson, E. P. *The Making of the English Working Class.* New York: Vintage, 1963.

———. "The Moral Economy of the English Crowd in the Eighteenth Century." *Past and Present,* no. 50 (February 1971): 76–136.

Todeschini, Giacomo. *Richesse franciscaine: De la pauvreté volontaire à la société de marché.* Paris: Verdier, 2008.

Torre Revello, José, ed. *Documentos históricos y geográficos relativos a la conquista y colonización rioplatense.* Tomo 2. Buenos Aires: Talleres, S.A., 1941.

Torres, Dionisio González. *Cultura guaraní.* Asunción: Editora Litocolor, 1987.

Torres Ramírez, Bibiano, and Javier Ortiz de la Tabla, eds. *Reglamento y aranceles reales para el libre comercio de España a Indias de 12 octubre 1778.* Seville: Escuela de Estudios Hispano-Americanos, 1979.

Toulmin, Stephen. *Cosmopolis: The Hidden Agenda of Modernity.* Chicago: University of Chicago Press, 1992.

Townsend, Joseph. *A Dissertation on the Poor Laws: By a Well-Wisher to Mankind.* Berkeley: University of California Press, 1971.

———. *A Journey through Spain in the Years 1786 and 1787.* Vol. 1. London, 1791.

Tucker, Josiah. *A Treatise Concerning Civil Government, in Three Parts.* London: The Strand, 1781.

Turner, Denys. *Thomas Aquinas: A Portrait.* New Haven, CT: Yale University Press, 2013.

Tutino, John. *Making a New World: Founding Capitalism in the Bajio and Spanish North America.* Durham, NC: Duke University Press, 2011.

———. *The Mexican Heartland: How Communities Shaped Capitalism, a Nation, and World History, 1500–2000.* Princeton, NJ: Princeton University Press, 2018.

United Nations. *Declaration of Indigenous Human Rights.* 2007. https://www.un.org/development/desa/indigenouspeoples/declaration-on-the-rights-of-indigenous-peoples.html.

Urquijo, José M. Mariluz. "Clima intelectual rioplatense de mediados del setecientos: Los límites del poder real." In Juan Baltazar Maziel, *De la justicia del tratado de límites de 1750.* Buenos Aires: Academia Nacional de la Historia, 1988. First published 1760.

Uztáriz, Geronymo de. *Theorica, y practica de comercio y de marina.* 2nd ed. Madrid, 1742. First published 1727.

Valentini, Joannis Ludovici Vivis. *Opera omnia, distributa et ordinata.* Tomo 4. Edited by Gregorio Majansio. Valencia, 1783.

Vanaya, Marta, ed. *Mitos y leyendas guaraníes.* Buenos Aires: Jamkana, 1986.

Vassberg, David. *Land and Society in Golden Age Castile.* Cambridge: Cambridge University Press, 1984.

Vieira, Antonio Arango. "Las reducciones de los Jesuitas en el Paraguay." *Revista Javeriana* 16, no. 80 (1941): 318–27.

Vilches, Elvira. *New World Gold: Cultural Anxiety and Monetary Disorder in Early Modern Spain.* Chicago: University of Chicago Press, 2010.

Villalón, Cristóbal de. *El crotalón de Christophoro Gnophoso.* Madrid, 1871. First published ca. 1550.

———. *El vallisoletano Cristobal de Villalón y su provechoso tratado de cambios y contratación de mercaderes y reprobación de usura.* Madrid, 1945. First published Valladolid, 1546.

Villar, Diego, and Isabelle Combès. "La Tierra sin Mal: Leyenda de la creación y destrucción de un mito." *Revista Tellus* 13, no. 24 (January–July 2013): 201–25.

Viveiros de Castro, Eduardo. "Cosmological Deixis and Amerindian Perspectivism." *Journal of the Royal Anthropological Institute* 4, no. 3 (September 1998): 469–88.

———. *From the Enemy's Point of View: Humanity and Divinity in an Amazonian Society.* Translated by C. V. Howard. Chicago: University of Chicago Press, 1992.

———. *The Inconstancy of the Indian Soul: The Encounter of Catholics and Cannibals in Sixteenth-Century Brazil.* Chicago: Prickly Paradigm Press, 2011.

———. "Introduction." In *The Archeology of Violence,* edited by Pierre Clastres, 9–51. Translated by Jeanine Herman. Cambridge, MA: Semiotext(e), 2010.

Voltaire. *Candide, ou l'optimisme.* Paris, 1877. First published 1759.

Ward, Bernardo. *Proyecto económico: En que se proponen varias providencias, dirigidas a promover los intereses de España con los medios y fondos necesarios para su planificación.* Madrid, 1779. First published 1762.

Warren, Harris Gaylord. *Rebirth of the Paraguayan Republic: The First Colorado Era, 1878–1904.* Pittsburgh: University of Pittsburgh Press, 1985.

Whigham, Thomas, and Barbara Potthast. "The Paraguayan Rosetta Stone: New Evidence on the Demographics of the Paraguayan War, 1864-1870." *Latin American Research Review* 34, no. 1 (1999): 174–86.

White, Richard. *The Middle Ground: Indians, Empires, and Republics in the Great Lakes Region, 1650–1815.* Cambridge: Cambridge University Press, 2010.

White, Richard Alan. *Paraguay's Autonomous Revolution, 1810–1840.* Albuquerque: University of New Mexico Press, 1978.

Wilde, Guillermo. "The Political Dimension of Space-Time. Categories in the Jesuits Missions of Paraguay (Seventeenth and Eighteenth Centuries)." In *Space and Conversion in Global Perspective,* edited by Giuseppe Marcocci, Aliocha Maldavsky, Wietse de Boer, and Ilaria Pavan, 175–213. Leiden: Brill, 2014.

———. *Religión y poder en las misiones de guaraníes.* Buenos Aires: Editorial SB, 2009.

Wilding, Michael. *The Paraguayan Experiment.* New York: Penguin Books, 1985.

Wilson, Thomas. *Arte of Rhetorique.* Oxford: Clarendon, 1909. First published 1560.

Wright, Robin, and Manuela Carneiro de Cunha. "Destruction, Resistance, and Transformation—Southern Coastal, and Northern Brazil (1580–1890)." In vol 3, pt. 2 of *The Cambridge History of Native Peoples of the Americas,* edited by Frank Salomon and Stuart Schwartz, 287–381. Cambridge: Cambridge University Press, 1999.

Xerez, Francisco de. *Verdadera relación de la conquista del Perú.* Madrid, 1891. First published Sevilla, 1534.

Zavala, Silvio. *New Viewpoints on the Spanish Colonization of America.* Philadelphia: University of Pennsylvania Press, 1943.

———. *Orígenes de la colonización en el Río de la Plata.* México City: Editorial de El Colegio Nacional, 1977.

Zeballos, Jerónimo de. *Arte real para el buen gobierno de los reyes, y príncipes, y de sus vasallos.* Toledo, 1623.

Zelizer, Viviana A. *Economic Lives: How Culture Shapes the Economy.* Princeton, NJ: Princeton University Press, 2011.

Index

Page numbers in *italics* indicate figures and maps.

Made in the USA
Middletown, DE
24 October 2023

41337509R00239